Instant Vortex Air Fryer Oven Cookbook

The Complete Guide to Cooking Easier and Faster With 610+ Delicious Recipes That Your Whole Family Will Love

Written by:

Jeffrey Gordon

Table of Contents

Introduction

The Instant Vortex Air Fryer Oven is a new device on the market that makes it easier than ever to prepare delicious, healthy meals. It is a handheld device that can be used in the kitchen or when you are out and about. Made of high-quality materials, this item is durable as well as reliable. The Instant Vortex Air Fryer Oven uses air circulation to circulate hot air around food for a crispy, fried texture without adding any oil whatsoever.

This new product has many practical applications for today's families who value eating healthy and living green.

The technology of this Instant Vortex Air Fryer Oven is exceptionally straightforward. Fried foods get their crunchy feel because warm oil heats meals quickly and evenly onto their face. Oil is a superb heat conductor that aids with simultaneous and fast cooking across each ingredient. For decade's cooks have employed convection ovens to attempt and mimic the effects of cooking or frying the entire surface of the food.

However, the atmosphere never circulates quickly enough to precisely attain that yummy surface most of us enjoy in fried foods. With this mechanism, the atmosphere is spread high levels up to 400°F, into "air fry" any foods like poultry, fish or processors, etc. This technology has altered the entire cooking notion by decreasing the Fat: by around 80% compared to traditional fat skillet. There is also an exhaust fan directly over the cooking room, which offers the meals necessary airflow. This also contributes to precisely the identical heating reaching every region of the food that's being cooked. This is the only grill and exhaust fan that helps improve the air continuously to cook wholesome meals without fat. The inner pressure strengthens the temperature, which will be controlled by the exhaust system. Exhaust enthusiast releases filtered additional air to cook the meals in a far healthier way. The Instant Vortex Air Fryer Oven doesn't have any odor whatsoever, and it's benign, making it easy and environment-friendly.

Air fryers recreate the customary browning of foods by coursing hot air around food as opposed to submerging the food in oil. Similarly, as with searing, appropriately arranged foods are fresh, succulent, brilliant dark-colored, and delightful.

An air-fryer cooker or appliances is a convection oven in smaller than expected—a conservative round and hollow ledge convection oven, to be accurate (have a go at saying that multiple times quick).

The use of this kitchen appliance ensures that the making of some of your favorite snacks and meals will be carried out in a stress-free manner without hassling around, which invariably legitimizes its worth and gives you value for your money.

The air fryer truly is not a gadget that should stay on the shelf. Instead, take it out and give it a whirl when you are whipping up one of your tried-and-true recipes or if you are starting to get your feet wet with the air frying method.

Regardless of appliances, recipes, or dietary concerns, we hope you have fun in your kitchen. Between food preparation, cooking time, and then the cleanup, a lot of time is spent in this one room, so it should be as fun as possible.

This is just the start. There are a lot of choices to select from that it won't take long before you find a whole bunch of recipes to use, and before you start to wonder why you didn't get the air fryer so much sooner. There are so numerous things to admire about the air fryer, and it becomes an even better tool to use when you have the right recipes in place and can use them.

Remember, every person starts out being a beginner; we all have to learn what works best for us personally. Each time you make a new dish, you learn more, and your experience grows.

This is truly the healthiest way to prepare food that everyone in the family will enjoy and keep coming back for more without them even realizing that they are eating better.

Remember that healthy food doesn't mean that you need to slave away in the kitchen or pay big bucks for hand-delivered meals. All you need is to try new, delicious recipes that are sure to become family favorites in no time at all. Your air fryer will soon be the most used item in your kitchen!

Chapter 1: Breakfast Recipes

1. Mozzarella Tots

Preparation time: 12 minutes

Cooking time: 3 minutes

Servings: 5

Ingredients:

- 8 oz. mozzarella balls
- 1 egg
- 1/2 cup coconut flakes
- 1/2 cup almond flour
- 1 tsp. thyme
- 1 tsp. black pepper, ground
- 1 tsp. paprika

Directions:

1. Crack the egg in a bowl and whisk.
2. Combine the coconut flour with thyme, ground black pepper, and paprika. Stir carefully.
3. Sprinkle Mozzarella balls with coconut flakes.
4. Transfer the balls to the whisked egg mixture.
5. Coat in the almond flour mixture.
6. Put Mozzarella balls in the freezer for 5 minutes.
7. Meanwhile, preheat the air fryer to 400°F.
8. Put the frozen cheese balls in the preheated air fryer and cook them for 3 minutes.
9. Remove the cheese tots from the air fryer basket and chill them for 2 minutes.
10. Serve.

Nutrition:

- Calories: 166
- Fat: 12.8 g.
- Carbs: 2.8 g.
- Protein: 9.5 g.

2. Chicken Balls

Preparation time: 10 minutes

Cooking time: 8 minutes

Servings: 5

Ingredients:

- 8 oz. chicken, ground
- 1 egg white
- 1 tbsp. parsley, dried
- 1/2 tsp. salt
- 1/2 tsp. black pepper, ground
- 2 tbsp. almond flour
- 1 tbsp. olive oil
- 1 tsp. paprika

Directions:

1. Whisk the egg white and combine it with the ground chicken.
2. Sprinkle the chicken mixture with the dried parsley and salt.
3. Add ground black pepper and paprika.
4. Stir carefully using a spoon.
5. Using wet hands, make small balls from the ground chicken mixture.
6. Sprinkle each chicken ball with almond flour.
7. Preheat the air fryer to 380°F.
8. Grease the air fryer basket tray with olive oil and place the chicken balls inside.
9. Cook for 8 minutes.
10. Turn halfway to crisp each side.
11. Serve hot.

Nutrition:

- Calories: 180
- Fat: 11.8 g.
- Fiber: 1.5 g.
- Carbs: 2.9 g.
- Protein: 16.3 g.

3. Tofu Egg Scramble

Preparation time: 15 minutes

Cooking time: 20 minutes

Servings: 5

Ingredients:

- 10 oz. tofu cheese
- 2 eggs
- 1 tsp. chives
- 1 tbsp. apple cider vinegar
- 1/2 tsp. salt
- 1 tsp. white pepper, ground
- 1/4 tsp. coriander, ground

Directions:

1. Shred the tofu and sprinkle it with the apple cider vinegar, salt, ground white pepper, and ground coriander.
2. Mix and leave for 10 minutes to

marinade.

3. Meanwhile, preheat the air fryer to 370°F.

4. Transfer the marinated tofu to the air fryer basket tray and cook for 13 minutes.

5. Meanwhile, crack the eggs in a bowl and whisk them.

6. When the tofu has cooked, pour the egg mixture in the shredded tofu cheese and stir with a spatula.

7. When the eggs start to firm place the air fryer basket tray in the air fryer and cook the dish for 7 minutes more.

8. Remove the cooked meal from the air fryer basket tray and serve.

Nutrition:

- Calories: 109

- Fat: 6.7 g.
- Fiber: 1.4 g.
- Carbs: 2.9 g.
- Protein: 11.2 g.

4. Flax & Hemp Porridge

Preparation time: 10 minutes

Cooking time: 15 minutes

Servings: 3

Ingredients:

- 2 tbsp. flax seeds
- 4 tbsp. hemp seeds
- 1 tbsp. butter
- 1/4 tsp. salt
- 1 tsp. stevia
- 7 tbsp. almond milk
- 1/2 tsp. ginger, ground

Directions:

1. Place the flax seeds and hemp seeds in the air fryer basket.

2. Sprinkle the seeds with salt and ground ginger.

3. Combine the almond milk and stevia. Stir the liquid and pour it into the

seed mixture.

4. Add butter.

5. Preheat the air fryer to 370°F and cook the hemp seed porridge for 15 minutes.

6. Stir carefully after 10 minutes of cooking.

7. Remove the hem porridge from the air fryer basket tray and chill it for 3 minutes.

8. Transfer the porridge into serving bowls.

Nutrition:

- Calories: 196
- Fat: 18.2 g.
- Fiber: 2.4 g.
- Carbs: 4.2 g.
- Protein: 5.1 g.

5. Creamy Bacon Eggs

Preparation time: 10 minutes

Cooking time: 10 minutes

Servings: 4

Ingredients:

- 6 oz. bacon
- 4 eggs
- 5 tbsp. heavy cream
- 1 tbsp. butter
- 1 tsp. paprika
- 1/2 tsp. nutmeg
- 1 tsp. salt
- 1 tsp. black pepper, ground

Directions:

1. Chop the bacon into small pieces and sprinkle it with salt.

2. Mix to combine and put in the air fryer basket.

3. Preheat the air fryer to 360°F and cook the bacon for 5 minutes.

4. Meanwhile, crack the eggs in a bowl and whisk them using a hand whisker.

5. Sprinkle the egg mixture with paprika, nutmeg, and ground black pepper.

6. Whisk egg mixture gently.

7. Toss the butter into the bacon and pour the egg mixture.

8. Add the heavy cream and cook for 2 minutes.

9. Stir the mixture with a spatula until you get scrambled eggs and cook for 3 minutes more.

10. Transfer onto serving plates.

Nutrition:

- Calories: 387
- Fat: 32.1 g.

- Fiber: 0.4 g.
- Carbs: 2.3 g.
- Protein: 21.9 g.

6. Cheddar Bacon Hash

Preparation time: 8 minutes

Cooking time: 8 minutes

Servings: 4

Ingredients:

- 1 zucchini
- 7 oz. bacon, cooked
- 4 oz. cheddar cheese
- 2 tbsp. butter
- 1 tsp. salt
- 1 tsp. black pepper, ground
- 1 tsp. paprika
- 1 tsp. cilantro
- 1 tsp. thyme, ground

Directions:

1. Chop the zucchini into small cubes and sprinkle it with salt, ground black pepper, paprika, cilantro, and ground thyme.

2. Preheat the air fryer to 400°F and toss the butter into the air fryer basket tray.

3. Melt it and add the zucchini cubes.

4. Cook the zucchini for 5 minutes.

5. Meanwhile, shred cheddar cheese.

6. Shake the zucchini cubes carefully and add the cooked bacon.

7. Sprinkle the zucchini mixture with the shredded cheese and cook it for 3 minutes more.

8. Transfer the breakfast hash to the serving bowls and stir.

Nutrition:

- Calories: 445
- Fat: 36.1 g.
- Fiber: 1 g.
- Carbs: 3.5 g.
- Protein: 26.3 g.

7. Cheddar Soufflé With Herbs

Preparation time: 10 minutes

Cooking time: 8 minutes

Servings: 4

Ingredients:

- 5 oz. cheddar cheese, shredded
- 3 eggs
- 4 tbsp. heavy cream
- 1 tbsp. chives
- 1 tbsp. dill
- 1 tsp. parsley
- 1/2 tsp. thyme, ground

Directions:

1. Crack the eggs into a bowl and whisk them carefully.
2. Add the heavy cream and whisk it for 10 seconds more.

8. Bacon Butter Biscuits

Preparation time: 15 minutes

Cooking time: 10 minutes

Servings: 6

Ingredients:

- 1 egg
- 4 oz. bacon, cooked
- 1 cup almond flour
- 1/2 tsp. baking soda
- 1 tbsp. apple cider vinegar
- 3 tbsp. butter
- 4 tbsp. heavy cream
- 1 tsp. oregano, dried

Directions:

1. Crack the egg in a bowl and whisk it.
2. Chop the cooked bacon and add it to the whisked egg.
3. Sprinkle the mixture with baking soda

9. Keto Parmesan Frittata

Preparation time: 10 minutes

Cooking time: 15 minutes

Servings: 6

Ingredients:

- 6 eggs
- 1/3 cup heavy cream
- 1 tomato
- 5 oz. chive stems
- 1 tbsp. butter
- 1 tsp. salt
- 1 tbsp. oregano, dried

- 6 oz. Parmesan cheese
- 1 tsp. chili pepper

Directions:

- Crack the eggs into the air fryer basket tray and whisk them with a hand whisker.
- Chop the tomato and dice the chives.
- Add the vegetables to the egg mixture.
- Pour the heavy cream.
- Sprinkle the liquid mixture with butter, salt, dried oregano, and chili pepper.
- Shred Parmesan cheese and add it to the mixture too.
- Sprinkle the mixture with a silicone spatula.
- Preheat the air fryer to 375°F and cook the frittata for 15 minutes.

Nutrition:

- Calories: 202
- Fat: 15 g.
- Fiber: 0.7 g.
- Carbs: 3.4 g.
- Protein: 15.1 g.

10. Chicken Liver Pate

Preparation time: 10 minutes

Cooking time: 10 minutes

Servings: 7

Ingredients:

- 1 lb. chicken liver
- 1 tsp. salt
- 4 tbsp. butter
- 1 cup water
- 1 tsp. black pepper, ground
- 5 oz. chive stems
- 1/2 tsp. cilantro, dried

Directions:

1. Chop the chicken liver roughly and place it in the air fryer basket tray.
2. Dice the chives.
3. Pour the water into the air fryer basket tray and add the diced chives.

4. Preheat the air fryer to 360°F and cook the chicken liver for 10 minutes.

5. Once cooked, strain the chicken liver mixture to discard the liquid.

6. Transfer the chicken liver into a blender.

7. Add the butter, ground black pepper, and dried cilantro.

8. Blend the mixture till you get the pate texture.

9. Transfer the liver pate to a bowl and serve it immediately or keep it in the fridge.

Nutrition:

- Calories: 173
- Fat: 10.8 g.
- Fiber: 0.4 g.
- Carbs: 2.2 g.
- Protein: 16.1 g.

3. thyme.

4. Sprinkle the egg mixture with the shredded cheese and stir it.

5. Transfer the egg mixture into 4 ramekins and place the ramekins in the air fryer basket.

6. Preheat the air fryer to 390°F and cook the soufflé for 8 minutes.

7. Once cooked, chill well.

Nutrition:

- Calories: 244
- Fat: 20.6 g.
- Fiber: 0.2 g.
- Carbs: 1.7 g.
- Protein: 13.5 g.

11. Coconut Pancake Hash

Preparation time: 7 minutes

Cooking time: 9 minutes

Servings: 9

Ingredients:

- 1 tsp. baking soda
- 1 tbsp. apple cider vinegar
- 1 tsp. salt
- 1 tsp. ginger, ground
- 1 cup coconut flour
- 5 tbsp. butter
- 1 egg
- 1/4 cup heavy cream

Directions:

1. Combine the baking soda, salt, ground ginger, apple cider vinegar and coconut flour in a bowl.
2. Take a separate bowl and crack in the egg.
3. Add butter and heavy cream.
4. Use a hand mixer and mix well.
5. Combine the dry and liquid mixture and stir it until smooth.
6. Preheat the air fryer to 400°F.
7. Pour the pancake mixture into the air fryer basket tray.
8. Cook the pancake hash for 4 minutes.
9. Scramble the pancake hash well and keep cooking for 5 minutes more.
10. Transfer to serving plates and serve hot.

Nutrition:

- Calories: 148
- Fat: 11.3 g.
- Fiber: 5.3 g.
- Carbs: 8.7 g.
- Protein: 3.7 g.

12. Beef Slices

Preparation time: 10 minutes

Cooking time: 20 minutes

Servings: 6

Ingredients:

- 8 oz. pork, ground
- 7 oz. beef, ground
- 6 oz. chive stems
- 1 egg
- 1 tbsp. almond flour
- 1 tbsp. chives
- 1 tsp. salt
- 1 tsp. cayenne pepper
- 1 tbsp. oregano, dried
- 1 tsp. butter
- 1 tsp. olive oil

Directions:

1. Crack the egg into a large bowl.
2. Add the ground beef and ground pork.
3. Dice the chives.

4. Put the diced chives in the ground meat mixture.

5. Add the almond flour, salt, cayenne pepper, dried oregano, and butter.

6. Use your hands to combine the mixture.

7. Preheat the air fryer to 350°F.

8. Make the meatloaf form from the ground meat mixture.

9. Grease the air fryer basket with olive oil and place the meatloaf inside.

10. Cook the meatloaf for 20 minutes.

11. Allow the meatloaf to rest for a few minutes.

12. Slice and serve.

Nutrition:

- Calories: 176
- Fat: 2.2 g.
- Fiber: 1.3 g.
- Carbs: 3.4 g.
- Protein: 22.2 g.

13. Flax & Chia Porridge

Preparation time: 5 minutes

Cooking time: 8 minutes

Servings: 7

Ingredients:

- 2 tbsp. sesame seeds
- 4 tbsp. chia seeds
- 1 cup almond milk
- 3 tbsp. flax meal
- 1 tsp. stevia
- 1 tbsp. butter
- 1/2 tsp. vanilla extract

Directions:

1. Preheat the air fryer to 375°F.

2. Put the sesame seeds, chia seeds, almond milk, flax meal, stevia, and butter in the air fryer basket tray.

3. Add the vanilla extract and cook the porridge for 8 minutes.

4. Stir the porridge carefully and leave it for 5 minutes to rest.

5. Transfer to serving bowls or ramekins.

Nutrition:

- Calories: 198
- Fat: 21.7 g.
- Fiber: 6.4 g.
- Carbs: 8.3 g.
- Protein: 4.8 g.

14. Paprika Eggs With Bacon

Preparation time: 10 minutes

Cooking time: 15 minutes

Servings: 4

Ingredients:

- 4 eggs
- 6 oz. bacon
- 1/4 tsp. salt
- 1/2 tsp. dill, dried
- 1/2 tsp. paprika
- 1 tbsp. butter

Directions:

1. Crack the eggs in a mixer bowl.

2. Add salt, dried dill, and paprika. Mix the egg mixture carefully with a hand mixer.

3. Grease 4 ramekins with butter.

4. Slice the bacon and put it in the prepared ramekins in the shape of cups.

5. Pour the egg mixture in the middle of each bacon cup.

6. Set the air fryer to 360°F.

7. Put the ramekins in the air fryer and close it.

8. Cook the dish for 15 minutes.

9. Remove the egg cups from the air fryer and serve them.

Nutrition:

- Calories: 319
- Fat: 25.1 g.
- Fiber: 0.1 g.
- Carbs: 1.2 g.
- Protein: 21.4 g.

15. Eggs in Avocado

Preparation time: 8 minutes

Cooking time: 15 minutes

Servings: 2

Ingredients:

- 1 avocado, pitted
- 1/4 tsp. turmeric
- 1/4 tsp. black pepper, ground
- 1/4 tsp. salt
- 2 eggs
- 1 tsp. butter
- 1/4 tsp. flax seeds

Directions:

1. Take a shallow bowl and add the turmeric, butter, ground black pepper, salt, and flax seeds together. Shake gently to combine.
2. Cut the avocado into 2 halves.
3. Crack the eggs in a separate bowl.
4. Sprinkle the eggs with the spice mixture.
5. Place the eggs in the avocado halves.
6. Put the avocado boats in the air fryer.
7. Set the air fryer to 355°F and close it.
8. Cook the dish for 15 minutes or until the eggs are cooked to preference.
9. Serve immediately.

Nutrition:

- Calories: 288
- Fat: 26 g.
- Fiber: 6.9 g.
- Carbs: 9.4 g.
- Protein: 7.6 g.

16. Easy Scotch Eggs

Preparation time: 10 minutes

Cooking time: 20 minutes

Servings: 4

Ingredients:

- 1 lb. breakfast sausage, ground
- 3 tbsp. flour
- 4 hard-boiled eggs, peeled
- 1 egg
- 1 tbsp. water
- 3/4 cup panko bread crumbs

Directions:

1. In a bowl, mix the sausage and 1 tbsp. flour.
2. Divide the sausage mixture into 4 equal parts. Lay one hard-boiled egg in the center, then wrap the sausage around

the egg, sealing completely. Repeat with remaining sausage parts and hard-boiled eggs.

3. In a small bowl, whisk the egg and water until smooth.

4. Place the remaining flour and bread crumbs into separate bowls large enough to dredge the sausage-wrapped eggs.

5. Dredge the sausage-wrapped eggs in the flour, then in the whisked egg, and finally coat in the bread crumbs.

6. Arrange them in the basket. Put the air fryer lid on and cook in the preheated instant vortex at 375°F for 20 minutes. Flip them over when the lid screen indicates "TURN FOOD" halfway through, or

until the sausage is cooked to desired doneness.

7. Remove from the basket and serve on a plate.

Nutrition:

- Calories: 509
- Total fat: 16 g.
- Saturated fat: 5 g.
- Total carbs: 8 g.
- Net carbs: 2 g.
- Fiber: 7 g.
- Protein: 24 g.
- Sugar: 16 g.
- Sodium: 785 mg.
- Potassium: 459 mg.
- Phosphorus: 265 mg.
- Cholesterol: 543 mg.

17. Strawberry Toast

Preparation time: 10 minutes

Cooking time: 8 minutes

Servings: 4

Ingredients:

- 4 slices bread, 1/2-inch thick
- 1 cup sliced strawberries
- 1 tsp. sugar
- Cooking spray

Directions:

1. On a plate, place the bread slices. Spray one side of each bread slice with cooking spray.

2. Arrange the bread slices (sprayed side down) in the air fryer basket. Evenly spread the strawberries onto them and sprinkle

them with sugar.

3. Put the air fryer lid on and cook in the preheated instant vortex at 375°F for 8 minutes, or until the tops are covered with a beautiful glaze.

4. Remove from the basket and serve on a plate.

Nutrition:

- Calories: 375
- Total fat: 22 g.
- Saturated fat: 5 g.
- Total carbs: 2g.
- Net carbs: 2 g.
- Fiber: 4 g.
- Protein: 14 g.
- Sugar: 5 g.
- Sodium: 600 mg.
- Potassium: 429 mg.
- Phosphorus: 587 mg.
- Cholesterol: 182 mg.

18. Cinnamon Sweet-Potato Chips

Preparation time: 5 minutes **Cooking time:** 8 minutes **Servings:** 7

Ingredients:

- 1 small sweet potato, cut into 3/8-inch slices
- 2 tbsp. olive oil
- 2 tbsp. Cinnamon, ground

Directions:

1. In a bowl, toss the potato slices in olive oil. Sprinkle with the cinnamon and mix well.

2. Lay the potato slices in the air fryer basket. You may need to work in batches to avoid overcrowding.

3. Put the air fryer lid on and cook in the preheated instant vortex at 375°F for 4 minutes. Shake the basket when the lid screen indicates 'TURN FOOD' Cook for an additional 4 minutes or until fork-tender.

4. Remove from the basket and serve on a large dish lined with paper towels.

Nutrition:

- Calories: 385
- Total fat: 18 g.
- Saturated fat: 2 g.
- Total carbs: 5 g.
- Net carbs: 3 g.
- Fiber: 8 g.
- Protein: 20 g.
- Sugar: 3 g.
- Sodium: 518 mg.
- Potassium: 432 mg.
- Phosphorus: 357 mg.
- Cholesterol: 658 mg.

19. Quiche Muffin Cups

Preparation time: 8 minutes

Cooking time: 14 minutes

Servings: 10

Ingredients:

- 1/4 lb. all-natural pork sausage, ground
- 3 eggs
- 3/4 cup milk
- 4 oz. sharp cheddar cheese, grated
- 1 muffin pan
- Cooking spray

Directions:

1. On a clean work surface, slice the pork sausage into 2 oz. portions. Shape each portion into a ball and gently flatten it with your palm.
2. Lay the patties in the air fryer basket and cook in the preheated instant vortex at 375°F for 6 minutes. Flip the patties over when the lid screen indicates "TURN FOOD" during cooking time.
3. Meanwhile, whisk the eggs, cheddar cheese and milk in a bowl, and stir until creamy. Set aside.
4. Remove the patties from the basket to a large dish lined with paper towels. Crumble them into small pieces with a fork. Set aside.
5. Line a muffin pan with 10 paper liners. Lightly spray the muffin cups with cooking spray.
6. Divide crumbled sausage equally among the 10 muffin cups and sprinkle the tops with the cheese.
7. Arrange the muffin pan in the air fryer basket. Pour the egg mixture into the muffin cups, filling each about 3/4 full.
8. Put the air fryer lid on and cook in the preheated instant vortex at 375°F for 8 minutes, until the tops are golden and a toothpick inserted in the middle comes out clean.
9. Remove from the basket and let cool for 5 minutes before serving.

Nutrition:

- Calories: 497
- Total fat: 25 g.
- Saturated fat: 2 g.
- Total carbs: 1 g.
- Net carbs: 1 g.
- Fiber: 4 g.
- Protein: 28 g.
- Sugar: 5 g.
- Sodium: 742 mg.

- Potassium: 289 mg.
- Phosphorus: 573 mg.
- Cholesterol: 823 mg.

20. Vegetable and Ham Omelet

Preparation time: 5 minutes

Cooking time: 20 minutes

Servings: 6

Ingredients:

- 1/4 cup ham, diced
- 1/4 cup green or red bell pepper, cored and chopped
- 1/4 cup onion, chopped
- 1 tsp. butter
- 4 large eggs
- 2 tbsp. milk
- 1/8 tsp. salt
- 3/4 cup sharp

cheddar cheese, grated

Directions:

1. Add the ham, bell pepper, onion, and butter into a 6×6×2-inch baking pan. Place the pan inside the air fryer basket.
2. Put the air fryer lid on and cook in the preheated instant vortex at 375°F for 6 minutes. Stir once halfway through the cooking time, or until the vegetables are soft.
3. In a bowl, whisk the eggs, milk, and salt until smooth and creamy. Gently pour over the ham and vegetables in the pan.
4. Put the air fryer lid on and cook at 375°F for about 13 minutes, or until the

top begins to turn brown.

5. Top with the cheese and cook for 1 minute more, or until the cheese is bubbly and melted.

6. Remove from the basket and cool for 5 minutes before serving.

Nutrition:

- Calories: 367
- Total fat: 14 g.
- Saturated fat: 5 g.
- Total carbs: 13 g.
- Net carbs: 7 g.
- Fiber: 6 g.
- Protein: 18 g.
- Sugar: 2 g.
- Sodium: 423 mg.
- Potassium: 778 mg.
- Phosphorus: 396 mg.
- Cholesterol: 363 mg.

21. Cheesy Canadian Bacon English Muffin

Preparation time: 7 minutes

Cooking time: 8 minutes

Servings: 4

Ingredients:

- 4 English muffins
- 8 slices Canadian bacon
- 4 slices cheese
- Cooking spray

Directions:

1. On a clean work surface, cut each English muffin in half.
2. To assemble a sandwich, layer 2 slices of bacon and 1 cheese slice on the bottom of each

muffin and put the other half of the muffin on top. Repeat with remaining muffins, bacon, and cheese slices.

3. Arrange the sandwiches in the air fryer basket and spritz with cooking spray. You may need to work in batches to avoid overcrowding.

4. Put the air fryer lid on and cook in the preheated instant vortex at 375°F for 8 minutes. Flip the sandwiches when it shows 'TURN FOOD' on the air fryer lid screen during cooking time.

5. Transfer to a plate and repeat with remaining sandwiches.

6. Let them cool for 3 minutes before

serving.

Nutrition:

- Calories: 322
- Total fat: 15 g.
- Saturated fat: 8 g.
- Cholesterol: 58 mg.
- Sodium: 119 mg.
- Carbohydrates: 27 g.
- Fiber: 4 g.

Protein: 24 g.

22. Asparagus, Cheese and Egg Strata

Preparation time: 6 minutes **Cooking time:** 19 minutes **Servings:** 4

Ingredients:

- 6 asparagus spears, cut into 2-inch pieces
- 1/2 cup grated Havarti or Swiss cheese
- 4 eggs
- 2 slices whole-wheat bread, cut into 1/2-inch cubes
- 3 tbsp. whole milk
- 2 tbsp. flat-leaf parsley, chopped
- 1 tbsp. water
- Freshly ground black pepper and salt to taste
- Cooking spray

Directions:

1. Place a 6×6×2-inch baking pan into the air fryer basket. Add 1 tbsp. water and asparagus spears into the pan.

2. Put the air fryer lid on and cook in the preheated instant vortex at 325°F for 3–5 minutes, or until the asparagus spears are tender.

3. Remove the asparagus spears from the baking pan. Drain and dry them thoroughly. Place the asparagus spears and bread cubes in the pan, then spray with cooking spray. Set aside.

4. In a bowl, whisk the eggs and milk together. Add the cheese, parsley, salt, and pepper. Stir to combine. Pour the mixture into the pan and place the pan into the air fryer

basket.

5. Put the air fryer lid on and bake at 350°F for 11–14 minutes, or until a knife inserted in the center comes out clean.

6. Remove the strata from the pan. Let cool for 5 minutes before serving.

Nutrition:

- Calories: 1214
- Total fat: 90.11 g.
- Saturated fat: 29.721 g.
- Total carbs: 6.16 g.
- Fiber: 0.4 g.
- Protein: 32.73 g.
- Sugar: 2.68 g.
- Sodium: 973.1 mg.
- Potassium: 1279.2 mg.
- Phosphorus: 1448 mg.
- Cholesterol: 1052 mg.

23. Shrimp, Spinach and Rice Frittata

Preparation time: 12 minutes

Cooking time: 18 minutes

Servings: 4

Ingredients:

- 1/2 cup shrimp, cooked, chopped
- 1/2 cup baby spinach
- 1/2 cup rice, cooked
- 4 eggs
- 1/2 cup Monterey Jack cheese, grated
- 1/2 tsp. basil, dried
- Pinch salt
- Cooking spray

Directions:

1. In a bowl, whisk together the eggs, basil, and salt.

2. Spritz a 6×6×2-inch baking pan with cooking spray. Place the cooked shrimp, rice, and spinach into the pan, and stir to combine well. Pour in the egg mixture and sprinkle the cheese on top. Put the pan into the air fryer basket.

3. Put the air fryer lid on and bake in the preheated instant vortex at 325°F for 14–18 minutes, or until puffy and golden brown.

4. Remove from the pan and cool for 3 minutes before cutting into wedges to serve.

Nutrition:

- Calories: 1358
- Total fat: 81.86 g.
- Saturated fat: 29.089 g.
- Total carbs: 8.86 g.
- Fiber: 3.1 g.

- Protein: 35.54 g.
- Sugar: 0.98 g.
- Sodium: 831 mg.
- Potassium: 1731 mg.
- Phosphorus: 1744 mg.
- Cholesterol: 1579 mg.

24. Tender Monkey Bread With Cinnamon

Preparation time: 6 minutes

Cooking time: 9 minutes

Servings: 4

Ingredients:

- 1 can (8-oz.) refrigerated biscuits
- 3 tbsp. brown sugar
- 1/4 cup white sugar
- 1/2 tsp. cinnamon
- 1/8 tsp. nutmeg
- 3 tbsp. unsalted butter, melted

Directions:

1. On your cutting board, divide each biscuit into quarters.
2. In a mixing bowl, add the brown and white sugar, nutmeg, and cinnamon. Stir well.
3. Pour the melted butter into a medium bowl. Dip each biscuit in the melted butter, then in the sugar mixture to coat well.
4. Arrange the coated biscuits in a 6×6×2-inch baking pan and place the pan into the air fryer basket.
5. Put the air fryer lid on and bake in batches in the preheated instant vortex at 350°F for 6–9 minutes until set.
6. Transfer to a serving dish and cool for 5 minutes before serving.

Nutrition:

- Calories: 1228
- Total fat: 42.64 g.
- Saturated fat: 15.178 g.
- Total carbs: 31.53 g.

- Fiber: 1.2 g.
- Protein: 49.97 g.
- Sugar: 8.74 g.
- Sodium: 628 mg.
- Potassium: 1665 mg.
- Phosphorus: 1244 mg.
- Cholesterol: 433 mg.

25. Grilled Ham and Cheese Sandwiches

Preparation time: 7 minutes

Cooking time: 8 minutes

Servings: 2

Ingredients:

- 4 slices country ham, smoked
- 4 slices cheddar cheese
- 4 slices bread
- 4 tomato slices, thick
- 1 tsp. butter

Directions:

1. Spread one side of 2 slices of bread with 1/2 tsp. of butter.
2. To assemble a sandwich, layer 2 slices of ham, 2 slices of cheese, and 2 slices of tomato onto the unbuttered sides of bread slices. Then arrange the other bread slices (buttered side up) on top.
3. Place the sandwiches (buttered side down) in the air fryer basket.
4. Put the air fryer lid on and cook in the preheated instant vortex at 375°F for 8 minutes. Flip the sandwiches when it shows "TURN FOOD" on the air fryer lid screen during cooking time.
5. Transfer to a serving dish and enjoy.

Nutrition:

- Calories: 246
- Total fat: 11 g.
- Saturated fat: 14 g.
- Cholesterol: 88 mg.
- Sodium: 1618 mg.

- Carbohydrates: 22 g.
- Fiber: 3 g.

Protein: 17 g.

26. Pesto Cheese Gnocchi

Preparation time: 11 minutes

Cooking time: 16 minutes

Servings: 4

Ingredients:

- 1 jar pesto (8-oz.)
- 1/3 cup Parmesan cheese, grated
- 1 package shelf-stable gnocchi (16-oz.)
- 1 onion, finely chopped
- 3 cloves garlic, sliced
- 1 tbsp. olive oil

Directions:

1. Mix the oil, onion, garlic, and gnocchi in a 6×6×2-inch baking pan. Place the pan into the air fryer basket.
2. Put the air fryer lid on and bake in the preheated instant vortex at 400°F for 16 minutes, or until the gnocchi starts to brown. Stir once halfway through cooking time.
3. Transfer the gnocchi to a serving dish. Sprinkle with Parmesan cheese and pesto. Stir well and serve warm.

Nutrition:

- Calories: 1382
- Total fat: 48.35 g.
- Saturated fat: 15.423 g.

Total carbs: 83.21 g.

27. Red Bell Peppers Salad

Preparation time: 5 minutes

Cooking time: 20 minutes

Servings: 4

Ingredients:

- 1/2 cup cheddar cheese, shredded
- 1/4 cup coconut cream
- 1 cup red bell peppers, chopped.
- 2 tbsp. chives; chopped.
- Cooking spray
- A pinch of salt and black pepper

Directions:

1. Take a bowl and mix all the ingredients except the cooking spray and whisk well.
2. Pour the mix in a baking pan that fits the air fryer greased with cooking spray and place the pan in the machine
3. Cook at 360°F for 20 minutes, divide between plates and serve for breakfast.

Nutrition:

- Calories: 220
- Fat: 14 g.
- Fiber: 2 g.
- Carbs: 5 g.
- Protein: 11 g.

28. Cauliflower Rice Bowls

Preparation time: 5 minutes

Cooking time: 15 minutes

Servings: 4

Ingredients:

- 12 oz. cauliflower rice
- 1 lb. fresh spinach; torn
- 1 red bell pepper; chopped.
- 2 tbsp. olive oil
- 2 tbsp. lime juice
- 3 tbsp. stevia

Directions:

1. In your air fryer, mix all the ingredients toss, cook at 370°F for 15 minutes, shaking halfway, divide between plates and serve for breakfast

Nutrition:

- Calories: 219
- Fat: 14 g.
- Fiber: 3 g.
- Carbs: 5 g.
- Protein: 7 g.

29. Avocado and Coconut Cream Bake

Preparation time: 5 minutes

Cooking time: 20 minutes

Servings: 4

Ingredients:

- 1 avocado, pitted, peeled, and cubed
- 2 spring onions, chopped.
- 1 oz. Parmesan cheese, grated
- 1/2 cup coconut cream
- 2 eggs, whisked
- 1 tbsp. olive oil
- Salt and black pepper to taste

Directions:

1. Take a bowl and mix the eggs with the rest of the ingredients except the oil and whisk well.
2. Grease a baking pan that fits the air fryer with the oil, pour the avocado mix, spread, put the pan in the machine, and cook at 360°F for 20 minutes. Divide between plates and serve for breakfast

Nutrition:

- Calories: 271
- Fat: 14 g.
- Fiber: 3 g.
- Carbs: 5 g.

Protein: 11 g.

30. Cheesy Spinach Muffins

Preparation time: 5 minutes

Cooking time: 15 minutes

Servings: 4

Ingredients:

- 2 eggs, whisked
- 1 1/2 cups coconut milk
- 4 oz. baby spinach, chopped.
- 2 oz. Parmesan cheese, grated
- 3 oz. almond flour
- 1 tbsp. baking powder
- Cooking spray

Directions:

1. Take a bowl and mix all the ingredients except the cooking spray and whisk well.
2. Grease a muffin pan that fits your air fryer with the cooking spray, divide the muffins mix
3. Introduce the pan in the air fryer, cook at 380°F for 15 minutes, divide between plates and serve.

Nutrition:

- Calories: 210
- Fat: 12 g.
- Fiber: 3 g.
- Carbs: 5 g.

Protein: 8 g.

31. Celery and Bell Peppers

Preparation time: 5 minutes

Cooking time: 15 minutes

Servings: 4

Ingredients:

- 1/2 cup mozzarella cheese, shredded
- 1 celery stalk, chopped.
- 2 green onions, sliced
- 6 eggs; whisked
- 1 red bell pepper, roughly chopped.
- 2 tbsp. butter, melted
- A pinch of salt and black pepper

Directions:

1. Take a bowl and mix all the ingredients except the butter and whisk well.

2. Preheat the air fryer at 360°F, add the butter, heat it, add the celery and bell peppers mix and cook for 15 minutes, shaking the fryer once. Divide the mix between plates and serve for breakfast.

Nutrition:

- Calories: 222;
- Fat: 12 g.
- Fiber: 4 g.
- Carbs: 5 g.
- Protein: 7 g.

32. Spinach and Eggs

Preparation time: 5 minutes

Cooking time: 20 minutes

Servings: 4

Ingredients:

- 3 cups baby spinach
- 12 eggs, whisked
- 1 tbsp. olive oil
- 1/2 tsp. smoked paprika
- Salt and black pepper to taste.

Directions:

1. Take a bowl and mix all the dry ingredients and mix them well.
2. Heat your air fryer at 360°F, add the oil, heat it, add the eggs and spinach mix, cover, cook for 20 minutes, divide between plates and serve

Nutrition:

- Calories: 220
- Fat: 11 g.
- Fiber: 3 g.
- Carbs: 4 g.
- Protein: 6 g.

33. Red Cabbage Bowls

Preparation time: 5 minutes

Cooking time: 15 minutes

Servings: 4

Ingredients:

- 2 cups red cabbage, shredded
- 1 red bell pepper, sliced
- 1 small avocado, peeled, pitted, and sliced
- A drizzle of olive oil
- Salt and black pepper to taste.

Directions:

1. Grease your air fryer with the oil, add all the ingredients, toss, cover, and cook at 400°F for 15 minutes.

2. Divide into bowls and serve cold for breakfast

Nutrition:

- Calories: 209
- Fat: 8 g.
- Fiber: 2 g.
- Carbs: 4 g.
- Protein: 9 g.

34. Nuts Pudding

Preparation time: 5 minutes

Cooking time: 20 minutes

Servings: 4

Ingredients:

- 1 cup coconut flakes, unsweetened and shredded
- 1 cup almonds, chopped
- 1/2 cup walnuts, chopped
- 1/2 cup maple syrup
- 2 cups almond milk
- 1/2 cup heavy cream

Directions:

1. In your air fryer's pan, combine the coconut flakes with the nuts and the other ingredients, toss and cook at 360°F for 20 minutes.
2. Divide into bowls and serve for breakfast.

Nutrition:

- Calories: 201
- Fat: 6 g.
- Fiber: 8 g.
- Carbs: 19 g.
- Protein: 6 g.

35. Rice and Berries Pudding

Preparation time: 10 minutes

Cooking time: 20 minutes

Servings: 4

Ingredients:

- 1 cup white rice
- 3 cups almond milk
- 1 cup blackberries
- 2 tbsp. sugar
- 2 tbsp. butter, soft
- 1 tsp. vanilla extract

Directions:

1. In your air fryer's pan, combine the rice with the almond milk and the other ingredients, toss and cook at 370°F for 20 minutes.
2. Divide the rice pudding into bowls and serve.

Nutrition:

- Calories: 202
- Fat: 12 g.
- Fiber: 4 g.
- Carbs: 7 g.
- Protein: 2 g.

36. Chicken Bowls

Preparation time: 6 minutes

Cooking time: 20 minutes

Servings: 4

Ingredients:

- 8 eggs, whisked
- 1 lb. chicken breast, skinless, boneless and cut into strips
- 1 tbsp. olive oil
- 1 yellow onion, chopped
- 1 tsp. chili powder
- 1 cup baby spinach
- 1 tbsp. parsley, chopped
- 2 tbsp. chives, chopped
- Salt and black pepper to the taste

Directions:

1. Heat your air fryer with the oil at 360°F, add the meat

and onion and cook for 5 minutes.

2. Add the eggs mixed with the other ingredients, toss gently, cook for 15 minutes more, divide everything into bowls and serve for breakfast.

Nutrition:

- Calories: 251
- Fat: 8 g.
- Fiber: 4 g.
- Carbs: 15 g.

Protein: 4 g.

37. Fennel and Eggs Mix

Preparation time: 5 minutes

Cooking time: 20 minutes

Servings: 4

Ingredients:

- 1 tbsp. avocado oil
- 1 yellow onion, chopped
- 1/2 tsp. cumin, ground
- 1 tsp. Rosemary, dried
- 8 eggs, whisked
- 1 fennel bulb, shredded
- 1 tbsp. chives, chopped
- Salt and black pepper to the taste

Directions:

1. In a bowl, combine the onion with the eggs, fennel, and the other ingredients except for the oil and whisk.

2. Heat your air fryer with the oil at 360°F, add the oil, add the fennel mix, cover, cook for 20 minutes, divide between plates and serve for breakfast.

Nutrition:

- Calories: 220
- Fat: 11 g.
- Fiber: 3 g.
- Carbs: 4 g.

Protein: 6 g.

38. Chives Salmon and Shrimp Bowls

Preparation time: 5 minutes

Cooking time: 12 minutes

Servings: 4

Ingredients:

- 1 lb. shrimp, peeled and deveined
- 1/2 lb. salmon fillets, boneless and cubed
- 2 spring onions, chopped
- 2 tsp. olive oil
- 1 cup baby kale
- Salt and black pepper to the taste
- 1 tbsp. chives, chopped

Directions:

1. Preheat the air fryer with the oil at 330°F, add the shrimp, salmon, and the other ingredients, toss gently and cook for 12 minutes.
2. Divide everything into bowls and serve.

Nutrition:

- Calories: 244
- Fat: 11 g.
- Fiber: 4 g.
- Carbs: 5 g.
- Protein: 7 g.

39. Mozzarella Endives and Tomato Salad

Preparation time: 5 minutes

Cooking time: 20 minutes

Servings: 4

Ingredients:

- 2 endives, shredded
- 1/2 lb. cherry tomatoes, halved
- 1 tbsp. olive oil
- 4 eggs, whisked
- Salt and black pepper to the taste
- 1 tsp. sweet paprika
- 1/2 cup mozzarella cheese, shredded

Directions:

1. Preheat the air fryer with the oil at 350°F, add the tomatoes, endives, and the other ingredients except

for the mozzarella cheese, and toss.

2. Sprinkle the mozzarella on top, cook for 20 minutes, divide into bowls and serve for breakfast.

Nutrition:

- Calories: 229
- Fat: 13 g.
- Fiber: 3 g.
- Carbs: 4 g.
- Protein: 7 g.

40. Mixed Veggie Bake

Preparation time: 5 minutes

Cooking time: 20 minutes

Servings: 4

Ingredients:

- 2 garlic cloves, minced
- 7 oz. mozzarella, shredded
- 2 celery stalks, chopped
- 1/2 cup white mushrooms, chopped
- 1/2 cup red bell pepper, chopped
- 1 tbsp. lemon juice
- 1 tsp. olive oil
- 1 tsp. oregano, dried
- Salt and black pepper to taste

Directions:

Preheat the air fryer at 350°F, add the oil and heat it.

Add garlic, celery, mushrooms, bell pepper, salt, pepper, oregano, mozzarella, and lemon juice, toss and cook for 20 minutes. Divide between plates and serve for breakfast

Nutrition:

- Calories: 230
- Fat: 11 g.
- Fiber: 2 g.
- Carbs: 4 g.

Protein: 6 g.

41. Dates & Millet Pudding

Preparation time: 20 minutes

Cooking time: 10 minutes

Servings: 2

Ingredients:

- 1 cup cracked or whole millet
- 3 1/2 cups water
- A pinch of salt
- 1/2 cup whole milk (50–50) or evaporated milk
- 1/4–1/2 cup dates, pitted, chopped
- 1 tbsp Vegetable oil
- 1 tbsp honey

Directions:

1. Lightly grease the slow cooker's ceramic liner with vegetable oil. In a slow-cooker combine millet, water, and salt.
2. Cover and cook on low for some hours, or overnight. Stir with a whisk several times during cooking, if possible.
3. Turn the cooker to high and stir in the milk and dates; cover and cook until hot, 5–10 minutes. Stir well, scoop into bowls and serve with additional milk and honey.

Nutrition:

- Calories: 283
- Fat: 9 g.
- Fiber: 12 g.
- Carbs: 13 g.
- Protein: 17 g.

42. Rice, Almond & Raisins Pudding

Preparation time: 10 minutes

Cooking time: 20 Minutes

Servings: 2

Ingredients:

- 1 tbsp. butter
- 1/3 cup finely chopped onion
- 1 cup white rice, uncooked
- 2 tbsp. raisins
- 1/2 cups chicken broth
- Salt and pepper to taste
- 1/4 cup almonds, sliced

Directions:

1. Melt butter in a medium saucepan over medium heat.

2. Sauté onion, stirring, until tender. Stir in the rice, raisins, broth, salt, and pepper. Bring to a boil.

3. Reduce heat to low, cover, and simmer 15–20 minutes, or until rice is cooked and liquid is absorbed. Stir in almonds before serving.

Nutrition:

- Calories: 343
- Fat: 5 g
- Fiber: 1 g.
- Carbs: 4 g.
- Protein: 8 g.

43. Cherries Risotto

Preparation time: 10 minutes

Cooking time: 20 minutes

Servings: 3

Ingredients:

- 3–4 cups chicken stock,
- 1 cup cherries, chopped (about 20)
- 1 cup onion, chopped
- 1 tbsp. olive oil
- 1/2 tsp. salt
- 1/2 cup Parmesan cheese, shredded

Directions:

1. Heat stock in a small pot. Heat the olive oil over medium heat in a medium saucepan and add the cherries, onion, and salt.

2. Cook until the onions are soft and the cherries have released some of their juices. Now add the rice and cook with the cherries and onions for about a minute. Ladle in about 1/2 cup of the hot stock.

3. Stir the rice occasionally until the stock is absorbed and add another 1/2 cup. Continue this until the rice is creamy and soft, about 20 minutes. Stir in the Parmesan cheese and take it off the heat. Top with more Parmesan cheese before serving and enjoy!

Nutrition:

- Calories: 400
- Fat: 5 g.
- Fiber: 21 g.
- Carbs: 9 g.
- Protein: 27 g.

44. Cinnamon & Cream Oats

Preparation time: 15 minutes

Cooking time: 15 minutes

Servings: 2

Ingredients:

- 2 cups water
- 1 cup rolled oats
- 1/4 cup coconut cream concentrate
- 1 tsp. cinnamon, ground
- 1 tbsp. honey
- 1 tbsp. chia seeds (optional)

Directions:

1. Bring water to boil in a medium saucepan. Add oats and cook for 5 minutes, stirring occasionally.

2. After 5 minutes add honey, cinnamon, coconut cream

concentrate, and seeds (if desired). Let simmer for 5 more minutes.

3. Serve with extra honey and cinnamon to add to the taste.

Nutrition:

- Calories: 298
- Fat: 14 g.
- Fiber: 34 g.
- Carbs: 23 g.

Protein: 12 g.

45. Walnuts & Pear Oatmeal

Preparation time: 10 minutes

Cooking time: 25 minutes

Servings: 3

Ingredients:

- 1 cup rolled oats (sometimes called porridge oats)
- 2 cups milk
- 2 tbsp. maple syrup
- 2 pears, peeled, cored, and cut in chunks or 4 canned pear halves
- 1/2 tsp. ginger, ground
- 10 walnut halves (approx.), chopped

Directions:

1. Mix the oats and milk in a small saucepan with a spoon. Bring to a boil over medium heat, stirring regularly. Stir in the pear, maple syrup, and ginger. Turn the heat back a bit and set a timer for 5 minutes.

2. Cook, stirring almost constantly until the timer goes off. Divide the oatmeal between 2 bowls, top with the chopped walnuts, and serve. Serve with extra maple syrup, if you like. And be careful as the pears may be quite hot.

Nutrition:

- Calories: 321
- Fat: 11 g.
- Fiber: 22 g.
- Carbs: 4 g.

Protein: 12 g.

46. Mushroom Oatmeal

Preparation time: 15 minutes

Cooking time: 20 minutes

Servings: 2

Ingredients:

- 1 cup steel cut oats,
- 3 cups water
- 1 cup vegetable stock
- 1 tbsp. butter
- 8 oz. cremini mushrooms
- 1-inch fresh ginger, peeled and minced
- A dash of soy sauce
- A pinch of red pepper flakes
- 2 Scallions, garnish
- 2 soft-boiled eggs

Directions:

1. To cook the oats, bring the liquid to a simmer. I like to use mostly water, but add in some stock to enhance the savory flavors.

2. Then stir in the oats! Simmer the oats on low heat, covered, for about 25–30 minutes until they are tender. Stir them regularly and don't be afraid to add more liquid if they seem dry.

3. Meanwhile, it's mushroom time! Mushrooms have a great savory flavor and are easy to make for a breakfast dish like this. I sliced my mushrooms and added them to a skillet with some butter.

4. Cook them over medium heat until they cook down a bit and then add the minced ginger, soy sauce, and a small pinch of red pepper flakes. When the mushrooms are finished, remove about half of them, chop them up, and stir them into the oatmeal. Save the rest for topping each bowl. The rest is pretty straightforward.

5. Spoon some oatmeal into bowls, top with mushrooms and chives, and add your egg to the center.

Nutrition:

- Calories: 381
- Fat: 8.7 g.
- Fiber: 2.6 g.
- Carbs: 17 g.
- Protein: 27 g.

47. Potato & Pear Frittata

Preparation time: 15 minutes

Cooking time: 25 minutes

Servings: 2

Ingredients:

- 8 eggs
- 1/2 cup low-fat milk
- 1 cup sweet potato, peeled and diced
- 1 onion, diced
- 80 g. bacon eye, diced
- Pepper to taste
- Spray oil

Rocket and Pear Salad Ingredients:

- 1 bag rocket leaves
- 1 pear, thinly sliced or shaved with a vegetable peeler
- 1/2 cup walnuts, crumbled
- 1 tsp. balsamic vinegar
- 3 tsp. extra virgin olive oil
- Pepper to taste

Directions:

1. Preheat oven to 180°C. Crack the eggs into a bowl, add milk, and whisk. Spray an ovenproof pan or dish with oil, place it onto the stove, and heat it. Add sweet potato, onion, bacon, and sauté lightly.

2. Add the egg mixture. Stir and place into the oven for 25 minutes or until cooked. In the meantime, place rocket leaves onto a plate, sprinkle with pear and walnuts, drizzle with oil and vinegar, season with pepper.

3. Remove frittata from oven, leave to cool for 5 minutes, remove from pan and cut into portion size triangles. Serve with rocket salad on the side.

Nutrition:

- Calories: 583
- Fat: 18 g.
- Fiber: 20 g.
- Carbs: 15 g.
- Protein: 8 g.

48. Raspberry Rolls

Preparation time: 15 minutes

Cooking time: 39 Minutes

Servings: 5

Ingredients:

- 1/2 cup whole milk
- 1 1/4-oz. package active dry yeast
- 2 tbsp. granulated sugar
- 3 cups. all-purpose flour
- 4 tbsp. unsalted butter, melted
- 1 tsp. kosher salt,
- 2 tbsp. Oil
- 1/3 cup raspberry jam
- 2 tsp. lemon zest
- 2 tbsp. lemon juice, fresh
- 2 cup raspberries, frozen (do not thaw)
- 2 tbsp. heavy cream, for brushing
- 1/2 cup sour cream,
- 1/4 cup confectioner's sugar, sifted
- 1/2 tsp. pure vanilla extract

Directions:

1. In a small saucepan, heat milk and 1/2 cup water on medium-low until warm but not hot to the touch.
2. Meanwhile, in a large bowl, whisk together yeast, granulated sugar, and 1 cup flour. Stir in warm milk. Cover and set aside until thick and foamy, about 15 minutes.
3. Mix in melted butter and salt. Gradually mix in the remaining 2 cups flour. Cover and let rise until doubled in size, about 1 hour.
4. Meanwhile, lightly coat the 11x8-inch casserole dish with oil. Line pan with parchment paper, leaving a 3-inch overhang on 2 long sides; oil parchment. In a small bowl, combine jam, lemon zest, and 1 tbsp. lemon juice.
5. Turn dough out onto the floured surface. Roll into a 12x9-inch rectangle. Spread with jam mixture and top with raspberries. Starting from the long side, roll dough into a tight log, pinching seam to seal. Slide long piece of unflavored dental floss under log of dough about 1 inch from the end. Holding floss taut, lift ends, and cross to cut off the 1-piece dough. Repeat

to cut 12 1-inch-thick rolls. Transfer rolls, cut sides up, to prepared pan, spacing equally. Cover and let rise until rolls have doubled in size and are touching, 50–60 minutes.

6. Meanwhile, heat the oven to 375°F. Brush rolls with heavy cream and bakes until puffed and light golden brown, 25–27 minutes. Let cool on the wire rack for 10 minutes. Make the frosting: In a medium bowl, combine sour cream, confectioner's sugar, vanilla, and remaining 1 tbsp. lemon juice. Spread over warm rolls.

Nutrition:

- Calories: 183
- Fat: 12 g.
- Fiber: 15 g.
- Carbs: 8 g.
- Protein: 25 g.

49. Pea Tortilla

Preparation time: 5 minutes

Cooking time: 10 minutes

Servings: 5

Ingredients:

- 1 cup peas (yellow or green), dried split, rinsed 1and drained
- 2 2/3 cups water
- 1/4 tsp. salt

Directions:

1. Combine the rinsed split peas and water in a medium bowl or another container; loosely cover. Let stand, at room temperature, for at least 6 hours or up to 12 hours. Do not drain split peas.
2. Add the entire contents of the

bowl (soaked peas and remaining water) and salt to a blender. Blend on HIGH speed until completely smooth (no tiny bumps) stopping multiple times to scrape down the sides of the container (it will take 2–3 minutes). The batter should be very smooth. Scrape into a bowl or measuring cup.

3. Heat a nonstick skillet (well-seasoned cast-iron skillet is ideal), or a nonstick griddle, to medium heat (no hotter). Once warm, add 1/3 cup of batter to the center of the pan. Using a metal spoon, spread the batter into a 6-inch circle. Cook 2–3 minutes until the surface of the tortilla appears dry.

Slide a spatula underneath and flip. Cook about 1 minute longer to brown the other side.

4. Transfer to a cooling rack and cool completely. Repeat with the remaining batter.

Nutrition:

- Calories: 456
- Fat: 13 g.
- Fiber: 32 g.
- Carbs: 9 g.
- Protein: 27 g.

50. Shrimp Sandwiches

Preparation time: 10 minutes

Cooking time: 10 minutes

Servings: 5

Ingredients:

- 6 bread rolls, soft and fresh
- 1 small head of green lettuce
- 2 medium tomatoes, thickly sliced
- 2 avocados, pitted, peeled, and sliced (optional)
- 8–10 fresh basil leaves for garnish (optional)
- 1 lb. large shrimp, cooked, shelled, and coarsely chopped
- 1/4 cup real mayonnaise
- 2 tbsp. sour cream
- 2 tsp. Dijon mustard (Grey

Poupon®)

- 1 tsp. lemon juice
- 1 tbsp. dill, fresh, finely chopped
- 2 tbsp. green onion, fresh, finely chopped,
- 1 small cucumber, diced.

Directions:

1. Chop and pat dry your cooked shrimp. In a medium bowl, combine shrimp, 1/4 cup mayo, 2 tbsp. sour cream, 2 tsp. Dijon mustard, 1 tsp. lemon juice, 1 tbsp. chopped dill, 2 tbsp. chopped green onion. Mix well to combine then gently stir in chopped cucumbers. Cover and refrigerate until ready to serve.
2. Line your prepared vegetables up on a large serving platter.

Garnish the tomato slices with basil.

3. Brush your bread lightly on one side with butter and toast on a hot skillet until golden brown. Toasting makes all the difference with these sandwiches.

Nutrition:

- Calories: 283
- Fat: 7,8 g.
- Fiber: 12 g.
- Carbs: 26g.
- Protein: 22 g.

51. Tuna Sandwich

Preparation time: 5 minutes

Cooking time: 10 minutes

Servings: 4

Ingredients:

- 2 cans (6 oz. each) tuna in water, drained
- 1/2 cup celery, chopped
- 1/4 cup onion, chopped
- 1/2 cup mayonnaise or salad dressing
- 1 tsp. lemon juice
- 1/4 tsp. salt
- 1/4 tsp. pepper
- 8 slices bread.

Directions:

1. In a medium bowl, mix the tuna, celery, onion, mayonnaise, lemon juice, salt, and pepper.

2. Spread tuna mixture on 4 bread slices. Top with remaining bread slices.

Nutrition:

- Calories: 391
- Fat: 2 g.
- Fiber: 27 g.
- Carbs: 30 g.
- Protein: 43 g.

52. Cherry Risotto

Preparation time: 10 minutes

Cooking time: 10 minutes

Servings: 4

Ingredients:

- 1 1/2 cups Arborio rice
- 1/2 cup cherries, dried
- 3 cups milk
- 1 cup apple juice
- 1/3 cup brown sugar
- 1 1/2 tsp. cinnamon
- 2 apples, cored and diced
- 2 tbsp. butter
- 1/4 tsp. salt

Directions:

1. Add butter into the instant vortex and set the pot on sauté mode.
2. Add rice and cook for 3–4 minutes.
3. Add brown sugar, spices, apples, milk, and apple juice and stir well.
4. Seal pot with lid and cook on manual high pressure for 6 minutes.
5. Once done then release pressure using the quick-release method then open the lid.
6. Stir in dried cherries and serve.

Nutrition:

- Calories: 544
- Fat: 10.2 g.
- Carbs: 103.2 g.
- Sugar 37.6 g.
- Protein: 11.2 g.
- Cholesterol: 30 mg.

53. Almond Coconut Risotto

Preparation time: 10 minutes

Cooking time: 5 minutes

Servings: 4

Ingredients:

- 1 cup Arborio rice
- 1 cup coconut milk
- 3 tbsp. almonds, sliced and toasted
- 2 tbsp. coconut, shredded
- 2 cups almond milk
- 1/2 tsp. vanilla
- 1/3 cup coconut sugar

Directions:

1. Add coconut and almond milk in the instant vortex and set the pot on sauté mode.
2. Once the milk begins to boil then add rice and stir well.
3. Seal pot with lid and cook on manual high pressure for 5 minutes.
4. Once done then allow to release pressure naturally then open the lid.
5. Add remaining ingredients and stir well.
6. Serve and enjoy.

Nutrition:

- Calories: 425
- Fat: 20.6 g.
- Carbs: 53.7 g.
- Sugar 9.6 g.
- Protein: 6.8 g.
- Cholesterol: 0 mg.

54. Creamy Polenta

Preparation time: 10 minutes

Cooking time: 5 minutes

Servings: 3

Ingredients:

- 1/2 cup polenta
- 1 cup of coconut milk
- 1 cup of water
- 1/2 tbsp. butter
- 1/4 tsp. salt

Directions:

1. Set instant vortex on sauté mode.
2. Add milk, water, and salt to a pot and stir well.
3. Once the milk mixture begins to boil then add polenta and stir to combine.
4. Seal pot with lid and cook on high

pressure for 5 minutes.

5. Once done then allow to release pressure naturally then open the lid.

6. Stir and serve.

Nutrition:

- Calories: 293
- Fat: 21.2 g.
- Carbs: 24.7 g.
- Sugar 2.9 g.
- Protein: 3.8 g.

Cholesterol: 5 mg.

55. Sweet Cherry Chocolate Oat

Preparation time: 10 minutes

Cooking time: 15 minutes

Servings: 4

Ingredients:

- 2 cups steel cuts oats
- 3 tbsp. honey
- 2 cups water
- 2 cups milk
- 3 tbsp. chocolate chips
- 1 1/2 cups cherries
- 1/4 tsp. cinnamon
- A pinch of salt
- Cooking spray

Directions:

1. Spray instant vortex from inside with cooking spray.

2. Add all ingredients into the pot and stir everything well.

3. Seal pot with lid and cook on high pressure for 15 minutes.

4. Once done then allow to release pressure naturally then open the lid.

5. Stir well and serve.

Nutrition:

- Calories: 503
- Fat: 10.9 g.
- Carbs: 85.5 g.
- Sugar 22.5 g.
- Protein: 16.8 g.
- Cholesterol: 12 mg.

56. Coconut Lime Breakfast Quinoa

Preparation time: 10 minutes

Cooking time: 1 minute

Servings: 5

Ingredients:

- 1 cup quinoa, rinsed
- 1/2 tsp. coconut extract
- 1 lime juice
- 1 lime zest
- 2 cups coconut milk
- 1 cup of water

Directions:

1. Add all ingredients into the instant vortex and stir well.
2. Seal pot with lid and cook on manual high pressure for 1 minute.
3. Once done then allow to release pressure naturally for 10 minutes then release using the quick-release method. Open the lid.
4. Stir well and serve.

Nutrition:

- Calories: 350
- Fat: 25 g.
- Carbs: 28.1 g.
- Sugar 3.5 g.
- Protein: 7.1 g.
- Cholesterol: 0 mg.

57. Quick & Easy Farro

Preparation time: 5 minutes

Cooking time: 10 minutes

Servings: 4

Ingredients:

- 1 cup pearled farro
- 1 tsp. olive oil
- 2 cups vegetable broth
- 1/4 tsp. salt

Directions:

1. Add all ingredients into the instant vortex and stir well.
2. Seal pot with lid and cook on manual mode for 10 minutes.
3. Once done then allow to release pressure naturally for 5 minutes then release using the quick-release

method. Open the lid.

4. Stir well and serve.

Nutrition:

- Calories: 169
- Fat: 1.9 g.
- Carbs: 30.5 g.
- Sugar: 0.4 g.
- Protein: 8.4 g.
- Cholesterol: 0 mg.

58. Farro Breakfast Risotto

Preparation time: 10 minutes

Cooking time: 12 minutes

Servings: 4

Ingredients:

- 1 cup farro
- 1 tsp. Italian seasoning
- 1/2 cup Parmesan cheese, grated
- 1/2 cup mozzarella cheese, grated
- 2 tbsp. heavy whipping cream
- 2 cups vegetable stock
- 1 tbsp. butter

Directions:

1. Add butter into the instant vortex and set the pot on sauté mode.

2. Add farro and cook for 2 minutes. Add stock and stir everything well.

3. Seal pot with lid and cook on manual high pressure for 10 minutes.

4. Once done then allow to release pressure naturally for 10 minutes then release using the quick-release method. Open the lid.

5. Add remaining ingredients and stir well.

6. Serve and enjoy.

Nutrition:

- Calories: 206
- Fat: 13.7 g.
- Carbs: 13.4 g.
- Sugar: 1.8 g.
- Protein: 9.9 g.
- Cholesterol: 37 mg.

59. Tapioca Pudding

Preparation time: 10 minutes

Cooking time: 7 minutes

Servings: 4

Ingredients:

- 1/2 cup tapioca
- 2 cups water
- 2 egg yolks
- 1/2 tsp. vanilla
- 1/2 cup sugar
- 1/2 cup milk

Directions:

1. Add water and tapioca into the instant vortex and stir well.
2. Seal pot with lid and cook on high pressure for 5 minutes.
3. Once done then release pressure using the quick-release method then open the lid.
4. Set pot on sauté mode. In a small bowl, whisk together milk and egg yolks
5. Slowly pour egg mixture into the pot and stir constantly.
6. Add vanilla and sugar and stir until sugar is dissolved.
7. Transfer pudding to a bowl and let it cool completely.
8. Place in refrigerator until pudding thickens.
9. Serve and enjoy.

Nutrition:

- Calories: 206
- Fat: 2.9 g.
- Carbs: 43.7 g.
- Sugar: 27.1 g.
- Protein: 2.4 g.
- Cholesterol: 107 mg.

60. Sweetened Breakfast Oats

Preparation time: 10 minutes

Cooking time: 7 minutes

Servings: 4

Ingredients:

- 1 cup steel-cut oats
- 3/4 cup coconut, shredded
- 1/4 tsp. ginger, ground
- 1/4 tsp. nutmeg, ground
- 1/2 tsp. cinnamon, ground
- 1/4 cup. raisins
- 1 large apple, chopped
- 2 large carrots, grated
- 1 cup coconut milk
- 3 cups water

Directions:

1. Add oats, nutmeg, ginger, cinnamon, raisins, apple, carrots, milk, and water into the instant vortex and stir to combine.
2. Seal pot with lid and cook on manual mode for 4 minutes.
3. Once done then allow to release pressure naturally for 20 minutes then release using the quick-release method. Open the lid.
4. Top with coconut and serve.

Nutrition:

- Calories: 341
- Fat: 20.8 g.
- Carbs: 38.2 g.
- Sugar: 16.1 g.
- Protein: 5.3 g.
- Cholesterol: 0 mg.

61. Cauliflower Mash

Preparation time: 10 minutes

Cooking time: 3 minutes

Servings: 6

Ingredients:

- 1 large cauliflower head, cut into florets
- 1/2 cup Parmesan cheese, shredded
- 1/2 tsp. garlic powder
- 2 tbsp. butter
- 2 cups vegetable stock
- 1/4 tsp. salt

Directions:

1. Pour the stock into the instant vortex then place a steamer basket into the pot.
2. Add cauliflower florets into the steamer basket.
3. Seal pot with lid and cook on high pressure for 3 minutes.
4. Once done then release pressure using the quick-release method then open the lid.
5. Transfer cauliflower into the food processor along with remaining ingredients and blend until smooth.
6. Serve and enjoy.

Nutrition:

- Calories: 102
- Fat: 6 g.

- Carbs: 8.2 g.
- Sugar: 3.7 g.
- Protein: 6 g.
- Cholesterol: 17 mg.

62. Chia Oatmeal

Preparation time: 10 minutes

Cooking time: 15 minutes

Servings: 6

Ingredients:

- 1 cup steel-cut oatmeal
- 1/2 tsp. vanilla
- 2 tbsp. chia seeds
- 1 1/2 cups coconut milk
- 1 1/2 cup water
- 1/4 tsp. sea salt
- Cooking spray

Directions:

1. Spray instant vortex from inside with cooking spray.
2. Add all ingredients into the instant vortex and stir well.
3. Seal pot with lid and cook on porridge mode for 15 minutes.
4. Once done then allow to release pressure naturally for 10 minutes then release using the quick-release method. Open the lid.
5. Stir well and serve.

Nutrition:

- **Calories:** 210
- **Fat:** 17.7 g.
- **Carbs:** 11.8 g.
- **Sugar:** 2 g.
- **Protein:** 3.8 g.
- **Cholesterol:** 0 mg.

63. Blueberry Lemon Oatmeal

Preparation time: 10 minutes

Cooking time: 10 minutes

Servings: 6

Ingredients:

- 1 cup steel-cut oats
- 1/4 cup chia seeds
- 1 cup blueberries
- 1/2 tbsp. lemon zest
- 2 tbsp. sugar
- 1/2 cup half and half
- 3 cups water
- 1 tbsp. butter
- Salt at taste

Directions:

1. Add butter into the instant vortex and set the pot on sauté mode.
2. Add oats into the pot and stir well.
3. Add remaining ingredients and stir everything well.
4. Seal pot with lid and cook on manual high pressure for 10 minutes.
5. Once done then allow to release pressure naturally then open the lid.
6. Stir well and serve.

Nutrition:

- Calories: 130
- Fat: 5.6 g.
- Carbs: 18.2 g.
- Sugar: 6.6 g.
- Protein: 2.8 g.
- Cholesterol: 13 mg.

64. Breakfast Cobbler

Preparation time: 10 minutes

Cooking time: 15 minutes

Servings: 2

Ingredients:

- 2 tbsp. sunflower seeds
- 1/4 cup pecan
- 1/4 cup coconut, shredded
- 1/2 tsp. cinnamon
- 2 1/2 tbsp. coconut oil
- 2 tbsp. honey
- 1 plum, diced
- 1 apple, diced
- 1 pear, diced

Directions:

1. Add fruits, cinnamon, coconut oil, and honey into the instant vortex and stir well.
2. Seal pot with a lid

and select steam mode and set timer for 10 minutes.

3. Once done, release pressure using the quick-release method, then open the lid.
4. Transfer fruit mixture into the serving bowl.
5. Add sunflower seeds, pecans, and coconut into the pot and cook on sauté mode for 5 minutes.
6. Pour sunflower seed, pecans, and coconut mixture on top of fruit mixture.
7. Serve and enjoy.

Nutrition:

- Calories: 426
- Fat: 27.2 g.
- Carbs: 50.9 g.
- Sugar: 40.1 g.
- Protein: 2.6 g.
- Cholesterol: 0 mg.

65. Tomato Corn Risotto

Preparation time: 10 minutes

Cooking time: 13 minutes

Servings: 4

Ingredients:

- 1 1/2 cups Arborio rice
- 1 cup cherry tomatoes, halved
- 1/4 cup basil, chopped
- 1/4 cup Parmesan cheese, grated
- 1/4 cup half and half
- 32 oz. vegetable broth
- 1 cup sweet corn
- 3 garlic cloves, minced
- 1/2 cup onion, chopped
- 2 tbsp. olive oil
- 4 tbsp. butter
- 1 tsp. salt
- 1 tsp Pepper

Directions:

1. Add butter into the instant vortex and set the pot on sauté mode.
2. Add garlic and onion and sauté for 5 minutes.
3. Add rice and cook for 2–3 minutes.
4. Add broth, corn, pepper, and salt and stir well.
5. Seal pot with lid and cook on high pressure for 6 minutes.
6. Once done, release pressure using the quick-release method, then open the lid.
7. Stir in cherry tomatoes, basil, parmesan, and a half and half.
8. Serve and enjoy.

Nutrition:

1. Calories: 548
2. Fat: 24 g.
3. Carbs: 69.6 g.
4. Sugar: 3.8 g.
5. Protein: 14.1 g.
6. Cholesterol: 41 mg.

66. Pancetta & Spinach Frittata

Preparation time: 15 minutes

Cooking time: 16 minutes

Servings: 2

Ingredients:

- 1/4 cup pancetta
- 1/2 of tomato, cubed
- 1/4 cup fresh baby spinach
- 3 eggs
- Salt and ground black pepper, as required
- 1/4 cup Parmesan cheese, grated

Directions:

1. Heat a nonstick skillet over medium heat and cook the pancetta for about 5 minutes.
2. Add the tomato and spinach cook for about 2–3 minutes.
3. Remove from the heat and drain the grease from the skillet.
4. Set aside to cool slightly.
5. Meanwhile, in a small bowl, add the eggs, salt, and black pepper and beat well.
6. In the bottom of a greased baking pan, place the pancetta mixture and top with the eggs, followed by the cheese.
7. Press the "power button" of the air fry oven and turn the dial to select the "air fry" mode.
8. Press the time button and again turn the dial to set the cooking time to 8 minutes.
9. Now push the temp

button and rotate the dial to set the temperature at 355°F.

10. Press the "start/pause" button to start.

11. When the unit beeps to show that it is preheated, open the lid.

12. Arrange pan over the "wire rack" and insert in the oven.

13. Cut into equal-sized wedges and serve.

Nutrition:

- Calories: 287
- Total fat: 20.8 g.
- Saturated fat: 7.2 g.
- Cholesterol: 285 mg.
- Sodium 915 mg.
- Total carbs: 1.7 g.
- Fiber: 0.3 g.
- Sugar: 0.9 g.
- Protein: 23.1 g.

67. Cheddar Tortilla Chips

Preparation time: 9 minutes

Cooking time: 10 minutes

Servings: 4

Ingredients:

- 1 cup flour
- Salt and black pepper to taste
- 1 tbsp. golden flaxseed meal
- 2 cups cheddar cheese, shredded

Directions:

1. Melt cheddar cheese in the microwave for 1 minute. Once melted, add the flour, salt, flaxseed meal, and pepper. Mix well with a fork.

2. On a board, place the dough and knead it with your hands while warm until the ingredients are well combined. Divide the dough into 2 and with a rolling pin, roll them out flat into 2 rectangles.

3. Use a pastry cutter to cut out triangle-shaped pieces and line them in a single layer on a baking dish without touching or overlapping; spray with cooking spray.

4. Select the "Air Fry" function, adjust the temperature to 380°F, and press "Start". Cook for 10 minutes. Serve with tomato sauce.

Nutrition:

- Calories: 429
- Fat: 12 g.
- Protein:10.6 g.

68. Mustard Cheddar Twists

Preparation time: 25 minutes

Cooking time: 20 minutes

Servings: 4

Ingredients:

- 2 cups cauliflower florets, steamed
- 1 egg
- 3 1/2 oz. oats
- 1 red onion, diced
- 1 tsp. mustard
- 5 oz. cheddar cheese
- Salt and black pepper to taste

Directions:

1. Place the oats in a food processor and pulse until they resemble breadcrumbs. Place the steamed florets in a cheesecloth and squeeze out the excess liquid.
2. Transfer to a large bowl. Add in the rest of the ingredients. Mix well. Take a little bit of the mixture and twist it into a straw.
3. Place on a lined baking tray and repeat with the rest of the mixture. Select the "Air Fry" function, adjust the temperature to 360°F, and press "Start." Cook for 10 minutes, turn over and cook for an additional 10 minutes.

Nutrition:

- Calories: 139
- Fat: 13 g.
- Protein:15.3 g.

69. Garlicky Mushroom Spaghetti

Preparation time: 8 minutes

Cooking time: 12 minutes

Servings: 4

Ingredients:

- 1/2 lb. white button mushrooms, sliced
- 1 tsp. butter, softened
- 2 garlic cloves, chopped
- 12 oz. spaghetti, cooked
- 14 oz. mushroom sauce
- Salt and black pepper to taste

Directions:

1. Preheat Instant vortex on "Air Fry" function to 400°F.
2. In a round baking

dish, mix the mushrooms, butter, garlic, salt, and pepper. Press "Start" and cook for 10–12 minutes.

3. Heat the mushroom sauce in a pan over medium heat and stir in the mushrooms Pour over cooked spaghetti and serve.

Nutrition:

- Calories: 400
- Fat: 18 g.
- Protein: 14.6 g.

70. Pancetta & Goat Cheese Bombs With Almonds

Preparation time: 15 minutes

Cooking time: 10 minutes

Servings: 4

Ingredients:

- 16 oz. goat cheese, soft
- 2 tbsp. fresh Rosemary, finely chopped
- 1 cup almonds, chopped into small pieces
- Salt and black pepper
- 15 dried plums, chopped
- 15 pancetta slices

Directions:

1. Line the frying basket with baking paper. In a bowl, add cheese, Rosemary, almonds, salt, pepper, and plums and stir well.

2. Roll into balls and wrap with pancetta slices. Arrange the bombs on the frying basket. Select the "Air Fry" function, adjust the temperature to 400°F, and press "Start." Cook for 10 minutes. Check at the 5-minute mark to avoid overcooking.

3. Serve with toothpicks.

Nutrition:

- Calories: 254
- Fat: 14 g.
- Protein: 23 g.

71. Ham & Mozzarella Eggplant Boats

Preparation time: 8 minutes

Cooking time: 1 2 minutes

Servings: 2

Ingredients:

- 1 eggplant
- 4 ham slices, chopped
- 1 cup shredded mozzarella cheese, divided
- 1 tsp. dried parsley
- Salt and black pepper to taste

Directions:

1. Preheat Instant vortex on "Air Fry" function to 330°F.
2. Peel the eggplant and cut it in half, lengthwise; scoop some of the flesh out. Season with salt and pepper.
3. Divide half of the mozzarella cheese between the eggplant halves and top with the ham. Sprinkle with the remaining mozzarella cheese and cook for 12 minutes until nice and golden on top.
4. Serve topped with parsley.

Nutrition:

- Calories: 198
- Fat: 5 g.
- Protein: 35 g.

72. Paprika Pickle Chips

Preparation time: 5 minutes

Cooking time: 15 minutes

Servings: 3

Ingredients:

- 36 sweet pickle chips
- 1 cup buttermilk
- 3 tbsp. smoked paprika
- 2 cups flour
- 1/4 cup cornmeal
- Salt and black pepper to taste

Directions:

1. Preheat Instant vortex on air fryer function to 400°F.
2. In a bowl, mix flour, paprika, pepper, salt, and cornmeal. Place pickles in buttermilk and let sit for 5 minutes.

Drain and dip in the spice mixture.

3. Place them in the cooking basket. Cook for 10 minutes until brown and crispy.

Nutrition:

- Calories: 376
- Fat: 2 g.
- Protein:6 g.

73. Mini Salmon & Cheese Quiches

Preparation time: 10 minutes

Cooking time: 10 minutes

Servings: 15

Ingredients:

- 15 mini tart cases
- 4 eggs, lightly beaten
- 1/2 cup heavy cream
- Salt and black pepper
- 3 oz. smoked salmon
- 6 oz. cream cheese, divided into 15 pieces
- 6 fresh dill

Directions:

1. Mix eggs and heavy cream in a pourable measuring container.

2. Arrange the tarts on the basket. Fill them with the mixture, halfway up the side, and top with salmon and cream cheese. Bake for 10 minutes at 340°F on the "Bake" function, regularly checking to avoid overcooking.

3. Sprinkle with dill and serve chilled.

Nutrition:

- Calories: 209
- Fat: 3 g.
- Protein:19 g.

74. Pineapple Spareribs

Preparation time: 10 minutes

Cooking time: 25 minutes

Servings: 4

Ingredients:

- 2 lb. cut spareribs
- 7 oz. salad dressing
- 1 (5-oz) can pineapple juice
- 2 cups water
- 1 tsp. garlic powder
- Salt and black pepper

Directions:

1. Sprinkle the ribs with garlic powder, salt, and pepper. Arrange them on the frying basket. sprinkle with garlic salt.
2. Select the "Air Fry" function, adjust the temperature to 400°F, and add water press "Start." Cook for 20–25 minutes until golden brown.
3. Prepare the sauce by combining the salad dressing and the pineapple juice.
4. Serve the ribs drizzled with the sauce.

Nutrition:

- Calories: 465
- Fat: 15 g.
- Protein: 14.3 g.

75. Cinnamon Mixed Nuts

Preparation time: minutes

Cooking time: 25 minutes

Servings: 4

Ingredients:

- 1/2 cup pecans
- 1/2 cup walnuts
- 1/2 cup almonds
- A pinch of cayenne pepper
- 2 tbsp. sugar
- 2 tbsp. egg whites
- 2 tsp. cinnamon

Directions:

1. In a bowl, mix the cayenne pepper, sugar, and cinnamon; set aside. In another bowl, beat the egg whites and mix in the pecans, walnuts, and almonds. Add in the spice mixture and Mustard Chicken

Wings

Preparation time: 5 minutes

Cooking time: 25 minutes

Servings: 4

Ingredients:

- 1/2 tsp. celery salt
- 1/2 tsp. bay leaf powder
- 1/2 tsp. black pepper, ground
- 1/2 tsp. paprika
- 1/4 tsp. dry mustard
- 1/4 tsp. cayenne pepper
- 1/4 tsp. allspice
- 2 lb. chicken wings

Directions:

1. Preheat the Instant vortex to 400°F on the "Air Fry" function. In a bowl, mix celery salt, bay leaf powder, black pepper, paprika, dry mustard, cayenne pepper, and allspice. Add in the wings and toss to coat.

2. Arrange the wings in an even layer on the basket. Press "Start" and Air Fry the chicken until it's no longer pink around the bone, about 20–25 minutes until crispy on the outside. Serve.

Nutrition:

- Calories: 254
- Fat: 4g
- Protein: 40g

76. Mustard Chicken Wings

Preparation time: 5 minutes

Cooking time: 25 minutes

Servings: 4

Ingredients:

- 1/2 tsp. celery salt
- 1/2 tsp. bay leaf powder
- 1/2 tsp. black pepper, ground
- 1/2 tsp. paprika
- 1/4 tsp. dry mustard
- 1/4 tsp. cayenne pepper
- 1/4 tsp. allspice
- 2 lb. chicken wings

Directions:

3. Preheat the Instant vortex to 400°F on the "Air Fry" function. In a bowl, mix celery salt, bay

leaf powder, black pepper, paprika, dry mustard, cayenne pepper, and allspice. Add in the wings and toss to coat.

4. Arrange the wings in an even layer on the basket. Press "Start" and Air Fry the chicken until it's no longer pink around the bone, about 20–25 minutes until crispy on the outside. Serve.

Nutrition:

- Calories: 254
- Fat: 4g
- Protein: 40g

77. Apple & Cinnamon Chips

Preparation time: 15 minutes

Cooking time: 10 minutes

Servings: 2

Ingredients:

- 1 tsp. sugar
- 1 tsp. salt
- 1 whole apple, sliced
- 1/2 tsp. cinnamon
- Confectioner's sugar for serving

Directions:

1. Preheat your Instant Vortex Oven to 400°F on the "Bake" function.
2. In a bowl, mix cinnamon, salt, and sugar. Add in the apple slices and toss to coat.
3. Transfer to a greased baking tray.

Press "Start" and set the time to 10 minutes. When ready, dust with sugar and serve chilled.

Nutrition:

- Calories: 504
- Fat: 12 g.
- Protein: 11 g.

78. Sesame Cabbage & Prawn Egg Roll Wraps

Preparation time: 5 minutes

Cooking time: 20 minutes

Servings: 4

Ingredients:

- 2 tbsp. vegetable oil
- 1-inch piece fresh ginger, grated
- 1 tbsp. garlic, minced
- 1 carrot, cut into strips
- 1/4 cup chicken broth
- 2 tbsp. soy sauce
- 1 tbsp. sugar
- 1 cup Napa cabbage, shredded
- 1 tbsp. sesame oil
- 8 prawns, cooked, minced
- 1 egg
- 8 egg roll wrappers

Directions:

1. Warm vegetable oil in a skillet over high heat and sauté ginger and garlic for 40 seconds until fragrant. Stir in carrot and cook for another 2 minutes. Pour in chicken broth, soy sauce, and sugar and bring to a boil. Add cabbage and let simmer until softened, for 4 minutes.

Remove the skillet from the heat and stir in sesame oil. Strain cabbage mixture and fold in minced prawns. Whisk an egg in a small bowl. Fill each egg roll wrapper with prawn mixture,

2. arranging the mixture just below the center of the wrapper.

3. Fold the bottom part over the filling and tuck under. Fold in both sides and tightly roll-up. Use the whisked egg to seal the wrapper. Place the rolls into the frying basket and spray with oil. Select the "Air Fry" function, adjust the temperature to 380°F, and press "Start." Cook for 12 minutes.

Nutrition:

- Calories: 234
- Fat: 14 g.
- Protein: 7 g.

79. Rosemary Potatoes

Preparation time: minutes

Cooking time: 35 minutes

Servings: 4

Ingredients:

- 1 1/2 lb. potatoes, halved
- 2 tbsp. olive oil
- 3 garlic cloves, minced
- 1 tbsp. minced fresh Rosemary
- Salt and black pepper to taste

Directions:

1. In a bowl, mix potatoes, olive oil, garlic, Rosemary, salt, and pepper.

2. Arrange the potatoes on the basket. Select the "Air Fry" function, adjust the temperature to 380°F, and press "Start."

3. Cook for 20–25 minutes until crispy on the outside and tender on the inside. Serve warm.

Nutrition:

- Calories: 498
- Fat: 15 g.
- Protein: 37 g.

80. Crunchy Mozzarella Sticks With Sweet Thai Sauce

Preparation time: 10 minutes

Cooking time: 8 minutes

Servings: 4

Ingredients:

- 12 mozzarella string cheese
- 2 cups breadcrumbs
- 3 eggs
- 1 cup sweet Thai sauce
- 4 tbsp. skimmed milk

Directions:

1. Pour the crumbs into a bowl. Crack the eggs into another bowl and beat with the milk. One after the other, dip cheese sticks in the egg mixture, in the crumbs, then egg mixture again, and then in the crumbs again. Place the coated cheese sticks on a cookie sheet and freeze for 1 hour.
2. Preheat Instant Vortex on the "Air Fry" function to 380°F.
3. Arrange the sticks in the frying basket without overcrowding. Press "Start" and cook for 8 minutes until brown. Serve with sweet Thai sauce.

Nutrition:

- Calories: 478
- Fat: 18 g.
- Protein: 36 g.

81. Bacon Bombs

Preparation time: 10 minutes

Cooking time: 16 minutes

Servings: 4

Ingredients:

- 3 center-cut bacon slices
- 3 large eggs, lightly beaten
- 1 oz. 1/3-less-fat cream cheese, softened
- 1 tbsp. fresh chives, chopped
- 4 oz. fresh whole-wheat pizza dough
- Cooking spray

Directions:

1. Sear the bacon slices in a skillet until brown and crispy then chop into fine crumbles. Add eggs to the same pan and cook for 1 minute then stir in cream cheese, chives, and bacon. Mix well, then allow this egg filling to cool down.

2. Spread the pizza dough and slice into 4–5 inches circles. Divide the egg filling on top of each circle and seal its edge to make dumplings. Place the bacon bombs in the air fryer basket and spray them with cooking oil. Set the air fryer basket inside the air fryer toaster oven and close the lid. Select the "Air Fry" mode at 350°F temperature for 6 minutes. Serve warm.

Nutrition:

- Calories: 278
- Protein: 7.9 g.
- Carbs: 23 g.
- Fat: 3.9 g.

82. Morning Potatoes

Preparation time: 10 minutes

Cooking time: 23 minutes

Servings: 4

Ingredients:

- 2 russet potatoes, washed and diced
- 1/2 tsp. salt
- 1 tbsp. olive oil
- 1/4 tsp. garlic powder
- Parsley, chopped for garnish

Directions:

1. Soak the potatoes in cold water for 45 minutes, then drain and dry them.
2. Toss potato cubes with garlic powder, salt, and olive oil in the air fryer basket. Set the air fryer basket inside the air fryer toaster oven and close the lid. Select the "Air Fry" mode at 400°F temperature for 23 minutes. Toss them well when cooked halfway through then continue cooking.
3. Garnish with chopped parsley to serve.

Nutrition:

- Calories: 146
- Protein: 6.2 g.
- Carbs: 41.2 g.
- Fat: 5 g.

83. Breakfast Pockets

Preparation time: 10 minutes

Cooking time: 10 minutes

Servings: 6

Ingredients:

- 1 box puff pastry sheet
- 5 eggs
- 1/2 cup loose sausage, cooked
- 1/2 cup bacon, cooked
- 1/2 cup cheddar cheese, shredded

Directions:

1. Stir cook egg in a skillet for 1 minute then mix with sausages, cheddar cheese, and bacon.
2. Spread the pastry sheet and cut it into 4 rectangles of equal size. Divide the egg

mixture over each rectangle. Fold the edges around the filling and seal them.

3. Place the pockets in the air fryer basket. Set the air fryer basket inside the air fryer toaster oven and close the lid. Select the "Air Fry" mode at 370°F temperature for 10 minutes. Serve warm.

Nutrition:

- Calories: 387
- Protein: 14.6 g.
- Carbs: 37.4 g.
- Fat: 6 g.

84. Avocado Flautas

Preparation time: 10 minutes

Cooking time: 24 minutes

Servings: 8

Ingredients:

- 1 tbsp. butter
- 8 eggs, beaten
- 1/2 tsp. salt
- 1/4 tsp. pepper
- 1 1/2 tsp. cumin
- 1 tsp. chili powder
- 8 fajita-size tortillas
- 4 oz. cream cheese, softened
- 8 slices bacon, cooked

Avocado Crème:

- 2 small avocados
- 1/2 cup sour cream
- 1 lime, juiced
- 1/2 tsp. salt
- 1/4 tsp. pepper

Directions:

1. In a skillet, melt butter and stir in eggs, salt, cumin, pepper, and chili powder, then stir cook for 4 minutes.

2. Spread all the tortillas and top them with cream cheese and bacon. Then divide the egg scramble on top and finally add cheese. Roll the tortillas to seal the filling inside.

3. Place 4 rolls in the air fryer basket. Set the air fryer basket inside the air fryer toaster oven and close the lid. Select the "Air Fry" mode at 400°F temperature for 12 minutes. Cook the remaining tortilla rolls in the same manner.

4. Meanwhile, blend

avocado crème ingredients in a blender then serve with warm *flautas*.

Nutrition:

- Calories: 212
- Protein: 17.3 g.
- Carbs: 14.6 g.
- Fat: 11.8 g.

85. Cheese Sandwiches

Preparation time: 10 minutes

Cooking time: 10 minutes

Servings: 2

Ingredients:

- 1 egg
- 3 tbsp. half and half cream
- 1/4 tsp. vanilla extract
- 2 slices sourdough, white or multigrain bread
- 21/2 oz. Swiss cheese, sliced
- 2 oz. deli ham, sliced
- 2 oz. deli turkey, sliced
- 1 tsp. butter, melted
- Powdered sugar
- Raspberry jam, for serving

Directions:

1. Beat egg with half and half cream, sugar and vanilla extract in a bowl.
2. Place 1 bread slice on the working surface and top it with ham and turkey slices and Swiss cheese. Place the other bread slice on top, then dip the sandwich in the egg mixture, then place it in a suitable baking tray lined with butter.
3. Set the baking tray inside the air fryer toaster oven and close the lid. Select the "Air Fry" mode at 350°F temperature for 10 minutes. Flip the sandwich and continue cooking for 8 minutes.
4. Slice and serve with Raspberry jam.

Nutrition:

- Calories: 412
- Protein: 18.9 g.
- Carbs: 43.8 g.
- Fat: 24.8 g.

86. Sausage Cheese Wraps

Preparation time: 10 minutes

Cooking time: 3 minutes

Servings: 8

Ingredients:

- 8 sausages
- 2 piece's American cheese, shredded
- 8-count refrigerated crescent roll dough
- 1 tsp cooking oil

Directions:

1. Roll out each crescent roll and top it with cheese and 1 sausage. Fold both the top and bottom edges of the crescent sheet to cover the sausage and roll it around the sausage.
2. Place 4 rolls in the air fryer basket and spray them with cooking oil. Set the air fryer basket inside the air fryer toaster oven and close the lid. Select the "Air Fry" mode at 380°F temperature for 3 minutes.
3. Cook the remaining rolls in the same manner. Serve fresh.

Nutrition:

- Calories: 296
- Protein: 34.2 g.
- Carbs: 17 g.
- Fat: 22.1 g.

87. Chicken Omelet

Preparation time: 10 minutes

Cooking time: 18 minutes

Servings: 4

Ingredients:

- 2 eggs
- 1/2 cup chicken breast, cooked and diced
- 2 tbsp. cheese, shredded, divided
- 1/2 tsp. salt, divided
- 1/4 tsp. pepper, divided
- 1/4 tsp. granulated garlic, divided
- 1/4 tsp. onion powder, divided
- 1 tsp cooking oil

Directions:

1. Spray 2 ramekins with cooking oil and keep them aside.
2. Crack 2 large eggs into each ramekin then add cheese and seasoning.
3. Whisk well, then add 1/4 cup chicken. Place the ramekins in a baking tray.
4. Set the baking tray inside the air fryer toaster oven and close the lid. Select the "Bake" mode at 330°F temperature for 18 minutes. Serve warm.

Nutrition:

- Calories: 322
- Protein: 17.3 g.
- Carbs: 4.6 g.
- Fat: 21.8 g.

88. Sausage Burritos

Preparation time: 10 minutes

Cooking time: 10 minutes

Servings: 6

Ingredients:

- 6 medium flour tortillas
- 6 scrambled eggs
- 1/2 lb. ground sausage, browned
- 1/2 bell pepper, minced
- 1/3 cup bacon bits
- 1/2 cup cheese, shredded
- Cooking oil

Directions:

1. Mix eggs with cheese, bell pepper, bacon, and sausage in a bowl.
2. Spread each tortilla on the working surface and top it with 1/2 cup egg filling.
3. Roll the tortilla like a burrito then place 3 burritos in the air fryer basket. Spray them with cooking oil.
4. Set the air fryer basket inside the air fryer toaster oven and close the lid. Select the "Air Fry" mode at 330°F for 5 minutes. Cook the remaining burritos in the same manner. Serve fresh.

Nutrition:

- Calories: 197
- Protein: 7.9 g.
- Carbs: 58.5 g.
- Fat: 15.4 g.

89. Sausage Patties

Preparation time: 10 minutes

Cooking time: 20 minutes

Servings: 4

Ingredients:

- 1.5 lbs. sausage, ground
- 1 tsp. chili flakes
- 1 tsp. thyme, dried
- 1 tsp. onion powder
- 1/2 tsp. each paprika and cayenne
- Sea salt and black pepper, to taste
- 2 tsp. brown sugar
- 3 tsp. garlic, minced
- 2 tsp. Tabasco®
- Herbs for garnish

Directions:

1. Toss sausage ground with all the spices, herbs, sugar, garlic, and tabasco

sauce in a bowl. Make 1.5-inch-thick and 3-inch round patties out of this mixture.

2. Place the sausage patties in the air fryer basket. Set the air fryer basket inside the air fryer toaster oven and close the lid. Select the Air Fry mode at 370°F for 20 minutes. Flip the patties when cooked halfway through then continue cooking.

Nutrition:

- Calories: 208
- Protein: 24.3 g.
- Carbs: 9.5 g.
- Fat: 10.7 g.

90. Spicy Sweet Potato Hash

Preparation time: 10 minutes

Cooking time: 16 minutes

Servings: 4

Ingredients:

- 2 large sweet potatoes, diced
- 2 slices bacon, cooked and diced
- 2 tbsp. olive oil
- 1 tbsp. smoked paprika
- 1 tsp. sea salt
- 1 tsp. black pepper, ground
- 1 tsp. dried dill weed

Directions:

1. Toss sweet potato with all the spices and olive oil in the Air Fry basket. Set the air fryer basket inside the air fryer

toaster oven and close the lid. Select the "Air Fry" mode at 400°F for 16 minutes. Toss the potatoes after every 5 minutes. Once done, toss in bacon and serve warm.

Nutrition:

- Calories: 134
- Protein: 6.6 g.
- Carbs: 36.5 g.
- Fat: 6 g.

91. Cinnamon Cream Doughnuts

Preparation time: 10 minutes

Cooking time: 8 minutes

Servings: 4

Ingredients:

- 1/2 cup sugar
- 2 1/2 tbsp. butter
- 2 large egg yolks
- 2 1/4 cups all-purpose flour
- 1 1/2 tsp. baking powder
- 1 tsp. salt
- 1/2 cup sour cream

To garnish:

- 1/3 cup white sugar
- 1 tsp. cinnamon
- 2 tbsp. butter, melted

Directions:

1. Beat egg with sugar and butter in a mixer until creamy, then whisk in flour, salt, baking powder, and sour cream. Mix well until smooth then refrigerate the dough for 1 hour.
2. Spread this dough into a 1/2-inch thick circle then cut 9 large circles out of it. Make the hole at the center of each circle.
3. Place the doughnuts in the air fryer basket. Set the air fryer basket inside the air fryer toaster oven and close the lid. Select the "Air Fry" mode at 350°F for 8 minutes. Cook the doughnuts in 2 batches to avoid overcrowding.
4. Mix sugar, cinnamon, and butter and glaze the doughnuts with this mixture. Serve.

Nutrition:

- Calories: 387
- Protein: 10.6 g.
- Carbs: 26.4 g.
- Fat: 13 g.

92. Sausage Frittata

Preparation time: 15 minutes

Cooking time: 20 minutes

Servings: 4

Ingredients:

- 1/4-lb. sausage, cooked and crumbled
- 4 eggs, beaten
- 1/2 cup cheddar cheese blend, shredded
- 2 tbsp. red bell pepper, diced
- 1 green onion, chopped
- 1 pinch cayenne pepper
- Cooking spray

Directions:

1. Beat eggs with cheese, sausage, cayenne, onion, and bell pepper in a bowl.
2. Spread the egg mixture in a 6x2-inch baking tray, greased with cooking spray. Set the baking tray inside the air fryer toaster oven and close the lid. Select the "Bake" mode at 360°F for 20 minutes. Slice and serve.

Nutrition:

- Calories: 212
- Protein: 17.3 g.
- Carbs: 14.6 g.
- Fat: 11.8 g.

93. Potato Jalapeño Hash

Preparation time: 15 minutes

Cooking time: 24 minutes

Servings: 4

Ingredients:

- 1 1/2 lbs. potatoes, peeled and diced
- 1 tbsp. olive oil
- 1 red bell pepper, seeded and diced
- 1 small onion, chopped
- 1 jalapeño, seeded and diced
- 1/2 tsp. olive oil
- 1/2 tsp. taco seasoning mix
- 1/2 tsp. cumin, ground
- Salt and black pepper to taste

Directions:

1. Soak the potato in cold water for 20 minutes then drain them.
2. Toss the potatoes with 1 tbsp. olive oil. Spread them in the air fryer basket. Set the air fryer basket inside the air fryer toaster oven and close the lid. Select the "Air Fry" mode at 370°F for 18 minutes.
3. Meanwhile, toss onion, pepper, olive oil, taco seasoning, and all other ingredients in a salad bowl. Add this vegetable mixture to the air fryer basket, and return it to the oven. Continue cooking at 356°F for 6 minutes. Serve warm.

Nutrition:

- Calories: 242
- Protein: 8.9 g.
- Carbs: 36.8 g.
- Fat: 14.4 g.

94. Bread Rolls

Preparation time: 10 minutes

Cooking time: 39 minutes

Servings: 8

Ingredients:

- 8 bread slices
- 2 potatoes boiled and mashed
- 1 tsp. ginger, grated
- 1 tbsp. coriander powder
- 1 tsp. cumin powder
- 1/2 tsp. chili powder
- 1/2 tsp. Garam Masala
- 1/2 tsp. dry mango powder
- 1 1/2 tsp. salt
- 1 large bowl of water
- Cooking oil

Directions:

1. Mix mashed potatoes with ginger

and all the spices. Divide this mixture into 16 balls and keep them aside.

2. Slice the bread slices into half to get 16 rectangles. Dip each in water for 1 second, then place 1 potato ball at the center and wrap the slice around it.

3. Place half of these wrapped balls in the air fryer basket and spray them with cooking oil. Set the air fryer basket inside the air fryer toaster oven and close the lid. Select the "Air Fry" mode at 390°F for 18 minutes. Flip the balls after 10 minutes of cooking then continue cooking.

4. Cook the remaining balls in the same manner. Serve fresh.

Nutrition:

- Calories: 331
- Protein: 14.8 g.
- Carbs: 46 g.
- Fat: 2.5 g.

Chapter 2: Mains Recipes

95. Air-Fried Chicken Recipe

Preparation time: 15 minutes

Cooking time: 51 minutes

Servings: 10

Ingredients:

For the Chicken:

- 4 lb. chicken, cut into 10 parts (2 halved breasts, 2 legs, 2 wings, 2 thighs)
- 1 tsp. kosher salt
- 1 tsp. black pepper
- 2 cups buttermilk

For Chicken Coating:

- 2 cups all-purpose flour
- 1 tbsp. seasoned salt
- 1 tsp. kosher salt
- 1 tsp. black pepper, ground
- 1 tbsp. garlic powder
- 1 tbsp. paprika
- Olive oil spray to cook

Directions:

1. **Marinating the chicken:** Use salt and pepper to season the chicken. Take a bowl and add buttermilk and well-seasoned chicken in it. The bits of chicken should be brushed with buttermilk. Rest aside for an hour or until overnight.

2. **Bread the chicken:** Stir together flour, seasoned salt, salt, pepper, garlic powder, and paprika to prepare the breading mixture.

3. Remove pieces of chicken from buttermilk, shake off any excess, and then dip in the flour mixture and cover well. Put pieces of breaded chicken onto a clean plate or wire rack to rest.

4. **Air-frying the chicken:** If you're doing a full chicken, you'll need to work in 2 lots. Spray nonstick spray into your air fryer bowl.

5. Place half the pieces in your air fryer bowl. Try to make sure that there is enough space between the pieces. Air must be circulating them.

6. Sprinkle gently the spray oil on the chicken pieces. Place the basket in

the air fryer and change to 350°F for the air fryer.

7. Cook for 15 minutes, then flip the fried chicken with tongs, sprinkle lightly on the chicken's bottom side with oil a second time, and cook for another 8–10 minutes.

8. On the low end of the time scale, the half-breast pieces and the wings will be cooked, and the dark meat pieces will require a full 24–26 minutes to cook through. The pieces of dark meat will hit 175°F.

9. Spray those spots lightly with oil if you pull the chicken out and notice any dry flour spots on the chicken during the air frying process.

10. If it has no tiny bit of oil to hydrate it, the breading will never crisp up. It just is going to burn.

11. **Servings:** Let the fried chicken rest on a plate a few minutes before serving. Serve with salad, coleslaw, mashed potatoes, or your favorite side of fried chicken right away!

Nutrition:

- Calories: 332
- Fat: 9 g.
- Protein: 18 g.
- Carbs: 25 g.

96. Air Fried Chinese Pineapple Pork

Preparation time: 20 minutes

Cooking time: 20 minutes

Servings: 4

Ingredients:

- 450 g. pork loin, cut into cubes
- 1/2 tsp. salt
- 1/2 tsp. pepper
- 1/2 pineapple, cut into cubes
- 1 green pepper, cut into cubes
- 1 garlic clove, chopped
- 1 tsp. fresh ginger, chopped
- 2 tbsp. soy sauce
- 1 tbsp. brown sugar
- 1 tbsp. vegetable oil
- 1 small bunch of fresh coriander leaves, chopped
- Sesame seeds, toasted

Directions:

1. Use salt and pepper for seasoning the pork.
2. Add into the Air Fry basket the seasoned pork, pineapple, green pepper, garlic, and ginger.
3. In a cup, add the soy sauce and brown sugar. Pour the ingredients over the pork—drizzle ingredients over vegetable oil.
4. Turn on your Air Fry and set a 17-minute cooking timer. After you have completed the cooking process, test to ensure that all ingredients are cooked to your specifications.
5. Garnish with sesame seeds and chopped coriander. Serve with rice and enjoy!

Nutrition:

- Calories: 372
- Fat: 18.3 g.
- Cholesterol: 71 mg.
- Sodium 806 mg.
- Carbs: 28.6 g.
- Protein: 24.4 g.

97. Tandoori Paneer Naan Pizza

Preparation time: 10 minutes

Cooking time: 10 minutes

Servings: 2

Ingredients:

- 2 garlic naan
- 1/4 cup marinara or pizza sauce
- 1/4 cup grape tomatoes, cut in half
- 1/4 cup red onions, sliced
- 1/4 cup bell pepper, sliced
- 3/4 cup grated mozzarella
- 2 tbsp. feta cheese (optional)
- 2 tbsp. cilantro, chopped

For Paneer:

- 1/2 cup paneer, cut into small cubes
- 1 tbsp. greek yogurt
- 1/2 tsp. Garam masala
- 1/2 tsp. garlic powder
- 1/4 tsp. turmeric, ground
- 1/2 tsp. Kashmiri red chili powder or paprika powder, suitable for taste
- 1/4 tsp. salt, adjust to taste

Directions:

1. Mix all of the mentioned ingredients into a bowl for Tandoori Paneer.

2. Line a parchment-papered baking tray. Take a baking tray and place naans on it. Apply sauce and spread evenly on each naan. Spread a bit of mozzarella over the 2 naans.

3. Place the cubes of the paneer (mixed with yogurt and spices) over the 2 naans. Next, the red onions, bell peppers, and grape tomatoes start spreading.

4. Next, spread a straight coat of mozzarella over the veggies. Sprinkle some feta cheese on top, as an alternative. Finally, add some chopped cilantro.

5. air fryer: Cook 8–10 minutes on a 350°F. After 7 minutes, check and crisp to your preference.

6. Sprinkle chili flakes and serve

Nutrition:

- Calories: 738
- Carbs: 67 g.
- Protein: 30 g.
- Fat: 37 g.

98. Cauliflower and Chickpea Tacos

Preparation time: 15 minutes

Cooking time: 25 minutes

Servings: 6

Ingredients:

- 1 tbsp. olive oil
- 1 tbsp. lime juice
- 1 tsp. chili powder
- 1 tsp. cumin, ground
- 1 tsp. sea salt
- 1/4 tsp. garlic powder
- 1 can (15 oz.) canned chickpeas
- 1 small head of cauliflower, cut into pieces of bite-size

For the Sauce:

- 1 cup sour cream
- 1/4 cup coriander, fresh, chopped
- 1/8 cup lime juice
- 1 tbsp. Sriracha
- Salt to taste
- 6 (6 inches) corn tortillas

Directions:

1. Preheat an air fryer to 370°F (190 °C).
2. In a large bowl, whisk together olive oil, lime juice, chili powder, cumin, salt, and garlic powder. Add the chickpeas and cauliflower and mix until coated evenly.
3. Stir sour cream, coriander, lime juice, and Sriracha together in a bowl until mixed evenly. Season it with salt.
4. Place cauliflower mixture in the air fryer basket. Cook and shake after 10 minutes, then cook for another 10 minutes. Remove again and cook for about 5 minutes, until desired crispness.
5. Use a spoon to put the mixture over the corn tortillas and drizzle sauce on the top.

Nutrition:

- Calories: 232
- Fat: 11.8 g.
- Carbs: 27.6 g.
- Protein: 6.1 g.

99. Air Fryer Buffalo Cauliflower

Preparation time: 5 minutes

Cooking time: 15 minutes

Servings: 2

Ingredients:

- 1/2 head cauliflower
- 1/2 cup Red Hot Buffalo Wing Sauce (120 ml.)
- 2 tbsp. olive oil
- 1 tsp. garlic powder
- 1/2 tsp. salt

To servings:

- Creamy dip, like ranch or bleu cheese
- Celery stalks

Directions:

1. Cut the cauliflower into florets of bite-size. Gently stir the cauliflower and all remaining ingredients together in a large bowl.
2. Fill your air fryer basket or rack with light grease. Arrange cauliflower in one layer (working in batches if not all of them suit in one layer). Cook for 12–15 minutes at 375°F (190°C) or until tender and slightly brown.
3. Serve warm with your favorite celery sticks and dipping sauce.

Nutrition:

- Calories: 141
- Carbs: 4.5 g.
- Protein: 1.6 g.
- Fat: 14.1 g.

100. Air Fryer Mexican-Style Stuffed Chicken Breast

Preparation time: 20 minutes

Cooking time: 10 minutes

Servings: 2

Ingredients:

- 4 inches extra-long toothpicks
- 4 tsp. chili powder, divided
- 4 tsp. cumin, ground, divided
- 1 chicken breast, skinless and boneless
- 2 tsp. chipotle flakes
- 2 tsp. Mexican oregano
- Salt and ground pepper to taste
- 1/2 red pepper, cut into thin strips
- 1/2 Onion, cut in thin stripes
- 1 jalapeño pepper, fresh, cut in thin stripes
- 2 tsp. olive oil
- 1/2 lime juice

Directions:

1. Place the toothpicks in a small bowl and cover with water; let them soak for a while so they won't burn during cooking.
2. In a shallow dish, mix 2 tsp. of chili powder and 2 tsp. of cumin.
3. Preheat the air fryer to 400°F (200°C).
4. Place the breast on a flat working surface. Horizontally cut through the middle. Pound up to around 1/4-inch thickness per half using a kitchen mallet or rolling pin.
5. Sprinkle with remaining chili powder, remaining cumin, chipotle flakes, oregano, salt, and pepper evenly on each breast portion. Fill up the center of 1 half of the breast with 1/2 of the bell pepper, onion, and jalapeño. Roll the chicken upwards from the tapered end and use 2 toothpicks to secure it. Repeat with other breasts, spices, and vegetables, and use the remaining toothpicks to secure it. In the shallow bowl, roll each roll-up into the chili-

cumin mixture while drizzling with olive oil until coated evenly.

6. Place roll-ups with the toothpick side facing up, in the air-fryer basket. Set a 6-minute timer.

7. Turn over roll-ups. Continue cooking in the air fryer until the juices run clear, and an instant-read thermometer reads at least 165°F (74°C) when inserted into the center, about 5 minutes more.

8. Drizzle the lime juice evenly before serving onto roll-ups.

Nutrition:

- Calories: 185.3
- Protein: 14.8 g.
- Carbs: 15.2 g.
- Cholesterol: 32.3 mg.
- Sodium 170.8 mg.

101. Lemon Pepper Shrimp

Preparation time: 5 minutes

Cooking time: 10 minutes

Servings: 2

Ingredients:

- 1 tbsp. olive oil
- 1 lemon's juice
- Lemon pepper
- 1/4 tsp. paprika
- 1/4 tsp. garlic powder
- 12 oz. medium shrimp, uncooked, washed and deveined
- 1 lemon, sliced

Directions:

1. Preheat an air fryer to 400°F (200°C).
2. In a cup, mix olive oil with lemon juice, lemon pepper, paprika, and garlic powder. Add the shrimps and then toss in the mixture until fully coated.
3. Open the air fryer and put the shrimp on the air fryer basket and cook for 6–8 minutes, until pink and strong. Serve with sliced lemon.

Nutrition:

- Calories: 214.9
- Protein: 28.9 g.
- Carbs: 12.6 g.
- Cholesterol: 255.4 mg.
- Sodium 528 mg.

102. Air Fried Crumbed Fish

Preparation time: 10 Minutes

Cooking time: 12 Minutes

Servings: 4

Ingredients:

- 1 cup bread crumbs
- 1/4 cup vegetable oil
- 4 flounder fillets
- 1 egg, beaten
- 1 lemon, sliced

Directions:

- Preheat an air fryer to 350°F (180°C).
- In a cup, add the bread crumbs and the oil. Stir until the mixture becomes crumbly and loose.
- Dip the fish fillets in the egg mixture; shake off any excesses. Dip the fillets into a mixture of bread crumbs; until evenly and thoroughly coated.
- Gently lay coated fillets in the preheated air fryer. Cook, about 12 minutes, with a fork, until fish flakes easily. Garnish with sliced lemon.

Nutrition:

- Calories: 354
- Fat: 17.7 g.
- Carbs: 22.5 g.
- Protein: 26.9 g.

103. Air Fryer Meatloaf

Preparation time: 10 minutes

Cooking time: 25 minutes

Servings: 4

Ingredients:

- 1-lb. lean beef
- 1 egg, lightly beaten
- 3 tbsp. bread crumbs
- 1 small onion, finely chopped
- 1 tbsp. thyme, fresh, chopped
- 1 tsp. salt
- 1 pinch ground black pepper to taste
- 2 mushrooms, thickly sliced
- 1 tbsp. olive oil

Directions:

1. Preheat an air fryer up to 200°C (392°F).

2. In a bowl, combine ground beef, egg, bread crumbs, ointment, thyme, salt, and pepper. Knead and mix well.
3. Move the mixture of beef into a baking pan and smooth the rim— press chestnuts into the top and coat with olive oil. Place the saucepan in the basket of the air fryer and slide it into the air fryer.
4. Set 25-minute air fryer timer and roast meatloaf until well browned.
5. Set aside the meatloaf for at least 10 minutes before slicing and serving into wedges.

Nutrition:

- Calories: 296.8
- Protein: 24.8 g.
- Carbs: 5.9 g.

- Cholesterol: 125.5 mg.

104. Air Fryer Shrimp a la Bang Bang

Preparation time: 10 minutes

Cooking time: 12 minutes

Servings: 4

Ingredients:

- 1/2 cup mayonnaise
- 1/4 cup sweet chili sauce
- 1 tbsp. Sriracha sauce
- 1/4 cup all-purpose flour
- 1 cup Panko bread crumbs
- 1 lb. shrimp, raw, peeled, and deveined
- 1 leaf lettuce
- 2 green onions, chopped to taste (optional)

Directions:

1. Set temperature of air fryer to 400°F (200°C).
2. In a bowl, stir in mayonnaise, chili sauce, and sriracha sauce until smooth. Put some of this bang bang sauce, if desired, in a separate bowl for dipping.
3. Take a plate and place flour on it. Use a separate plate and place panko bread crumbs on it.
4. First coat the shrimp with flour, then mayonnaise mixture, then panko. Place shrimp covered on a baking sheet.
5. Place shrimp, without overcrowding, in the air fryer basket.
6. Cook for approximately 12 minutes. Repeat with shrimp leftover.
7. Use lettuce wraps for serving, garnished with green onion.

Nutrition:

- Calories: 415
- Fat: 23.9 g.
- Carbs: 32.7 g.
- Protein: 23.9 g.

105. Crumbed Chicken Tenderloins

Preparation time: 15 minutes

Cooking time: 12 minutes

Servings: 8

Ingredients:

- 1 egg
- 1/2 cup dry bread crumbs
- 2 tbsp. vegetable oil
- 8 chicken tenderloins

Directions:

1. Preheat an air fryer to 350°F (175°C).
2. Whisk the egg in a bowl.
3. In a second bowl, mix the bread crumbs and oil until the mixture becomes loose and crumbled.
4. Dip every

tenderloin of chicken into the egg bowl; shake off any remaining egg.

5. Dip the chicken into the crumb mixture, ensuring it is evenly and thoroughly coated. Place the chicken tenderloins into the air fryer basked. Cook, about 12 minutes, until the center, is no longer pink. A center-inserted instant-read thermometer should read at least 165°F (74°C).

Nutrition:

- Calories: 252.7
- Protein: 26.2 g.
- Carbs: 9.8 g.

106. Caribbean Spiced Chicken

Preparation time: 10 minutes

Cooking time: 10 minutes

Servings: 8

Ingredients:

- 3 lbs. chicken thigh fillets, boneless and skinless
- Black pepper, ground
- 1 tbsp. coriander seed, ground
- Salt
- 1 tbsp. cinnamon, ground
- 1 tbsp. cayenne pepper
- 1 1/2 tsp. ginger, ground
- 1 1/2 tsp. nutmeg, ground
- 3 tbsp. coconut oil

Directions:

1. Take chicken off the packaging and pat dry. To soak up any residual liquid, place it on a large baking sheet covered with paper towels. Chicken is salted and peppered on both sides. Let the chicken sit for 30 minutes, so when you go into the air fryer, it isn't that cold.

2. Combine coriander, cinnamon, cayenne, ginger, and nutmeg in a small bowl. Coat the spice mixture on each piece of chicken and brush both sides with coconut oil.

3. Place four pieces of chicken in your air fryer basket (they shouldn't overlap). Air fry for 10 minutes at 390°F.

Remove the chicken from the basket and place it in a safe stove dish, tightly covered with foil.

4. Keep the chicken in the oven to keep it warm until the remaining chicken is done—repeat the directions for air frying with the rest of the chicken.

Nutrition:

- Calories: 202
- Fat: 13.4 g.
- Carbs: 1.7 g.
- Protein: 24.9 g.

107. Air Fryer Jalapeño Popper Hasselback Chicken

Preparation time: 10 minutes

Cooking time: 15 minutes

Servings: 2

Ingredients:

- 4 slices sugar:-free bacon, cooked and crumbled
- 2 oz. cream cheese, softened
- 1/4 cup pickled jalapeños, chopped
- 1/2 cup cheddar cheese, split, shredded, and sharp
- 2 breasts chicken, boneless and skinless

Directions:

1. Stir bacon, cream cheese, jalapeños, and 1/4-cup shredded cheddar cheese together in a medium bowl.

2. Use a knife and cut about 6 slits across the top of the chicken, and be careful not to cut through all the way.

3. Stuff the mixture with cream cheese into the slits.

4. Place the chicken in the air-fryer basket and set for 15 minutes to "Air Fry" at 350°F. Open the air fryer with a 1-minute left, and sprinkle the remaining cheese on top. Last-minute Air Fry.

Nutrition:

- Calories: 530
- Fat: 30 g.
- Saturated fat: 12 g.
- Carbs: 2 g.

Protein: 41 g.

108. Air Fryer Steak & Asparagus

Preparation time: 10 minutes

Cooking time: 5 minutes

Servings: 2

Ingredients:

- 1 bunch asparagus
- 1 tbsp. olive oil
- 1 tsp. sea salt
- 2 Sirloin steaks with a boneless chuck eye
- Steak marinade of your choice

Directions:

1. Marinate the steak in your favorite steak marinade for 1–8 hours.
2. Trim asparagus and place in the air fryer's bottom.
3. Drizzle with coarse sea salt and olive oil.
4. Remove steak from marinade and top with asparagus
5. Set the air fryer temperature to 350°F, fry for 5 minutes.
6. Remove and serve the asparagus warm
7. You can cook the steak for another 3–8 minutes, depending on your taste.

Nutrition:

- Calories: 245
- Protein: 3.9 g.
- Carbs: 46.8 g.
- Fat: 12.4 g.

109. Lettuce Salad With Beef Strips

Preparation time: 10 minutes

Cooking time: 12 minutes

Servings: 5

Ingredients:

- 2 cup lettuce
- 10 oz. beef brisket
- 2 tbsp. sesame oil
- 1 tbsp. sunflower seeds
- 1 cucumber
- 1 tsp. black pepper, ground
- 1 tsp. paprika
- 1 tsp. Italian spices
- 2 tsp. butter
- 1 tsp. dried dill
- 2 tbsp. coconut milk

Directions:

1. Cut the beef brisket into strips.
2. Sprinkle the beef strips with the ground black pepper, paprika, and dried dill.
3. Preheat the air fryer to 365°F.
4. Put the butter in the air fryer basket tray and melt it.
5. Then add the beef strips and cook them for 6 minutes on each side.
6. Meanwhile, tear the lettuce and toss it in a big salad bowl.
7. Crush the sunflower seeds and sprinkle them over the lettuce.
8. Chop the cucumber into the small cubes and add to the salad bowl.
9. Then combine the sesame oil and Italian spices. Stir the oil.
10. Combine the lettuce mixture with the coconut milk and stir it using 2

wooden spatulas.

11. When the meat is cooked—let it chill to room temperature.

12. Add the beef strips to the salad bowl.

13. Stir it gently and sprinkle the salad with the sesame oil dressing.

14. Serve the dish immediately.

Nutrition:

- Calories: 199
- Fat: 12.4 g.
- Carbs: 3.9 g.
- Protein: 18.1 g.

110. Cayenne Rib Eye Steak

Preparation time: 10 minutes

Cooking time: 13 minutes

Servings: 2

Ingredients:

- 1-lb. rib eye steak
- 1 tsp. salt
- 1 tsp. cayenne pepper
- 1/2 tsp. chili flakes
- 3 tbsp. cream
- 1 tsp. olive oil
- 1 tsp. lemongrass
- 1 tbsp. butter
- 1 tsp. garlic powder

Directions:

1. Preheat the air fryer to 360°F.

2. Take a shallow bowl and combine the cayenne pepper, salt, chili flakes, lemongrass, and garlic powder.

3. Mix the spices gently.

4. Sprinkle the rib eye steak with the spice mixture.

5. Melt the butter and combine it with cream and olive oil.

6. Churn the mixture.

7. Pour the churned mixture into the air fryer basket tray.

8. Add the rib eye steak.

9. Cook the steak for 13 minutes. Do not stir the steak during the cooking.

10. When the steak is cooked transfer it to a paper towel to soak all the excess fat.

11. Serve the steak. You can slice the steak if desired.

Nutrition:

- Calories: 708
- Fat: 59 g.
- Carbs: 2.3 g.

- Protein: 40.4 g.

111. Beef-Chicken Meatball Casserole

Preparation time: 15 minutes

Cooking time: 21 minutes

Servings: 7

Ingredients:

- 1 eggplant
- 10 oz. chicken, ground
- 8 oz. beef, ground
- 1 tsp. garlic, minced
- 1 tsp. white pepper, ground
- 1 tomato
- 1 egg
- 1 tbsp. coconut flour
- 8 oz. Parmesan cheese, shredded
- 2 tbsp. butter
- 1/3 cup cream

Directions:

1. Combine the ground chicken and ground beef in a large bowl.
2. Add the minced garlic and ground white pepper.
3. Crack the egg into the bowl with the ground meat mixture and stir it carefully until well combined.
4. Then add the coconut flour and mix.
5. Make small meatballs from the ground meat.
6. Preheat the air fryer to 360°F.
7. Sprinkle the air fryer basket tray with the butter and pour the cream.
8. Peel the eggplant and chop it.
9. Put the meatballs over the cream and sprinkle them with

the chopped eggplant.

10. Slice the tomato and place it over the eggplant.

11. Make a layer of shredded cheese over the sliced tomato.

12. Put the casserole in the air fryer and cook it for 21 minutes.

13. Let the casserole cool to room temperature before serving.

Nutrition:

- Calories: 314
- Fat: 16.8 g.
- Carbs: 7.5 g.
- Protein: 33.9 g.

112. Chicken Goulash

Preparation time: 10 minutes

Cooking time: 17 minutes

Servings: 6

Ingredients:

- 4 oz. chive stems
- 2 green peppers, chopped
- 1 tsp. olive oil
- 14 oz. chicken, ground
- 2 tomatoes
- 1/2 cup chicken stock
- 2 garlic cloves, sliced
- 1 tsp. salt
- 1 tsp. black pepper, ground
- 1 tsp. mustard

Directions:

1. Chop chives roughly.

2. Spray the air fryer basket tray with olive oil.

3. Preheat the air fryer to 365°F.

4. Put the chopped chives in the air fryer basket tray.

5. Add the chopped green pepper and cook the vegetables for 5 minutes.

6. Add the ground chicken.

7. Chop the tomatoes into small cubes and add them to the air fryer mixture too.

8. Cook the mixture for 6 minutes more.

9. Add the chicken stock, sliced garlic cloves, salt, ground black pepper, and mustard.

10. Mix well to combine.

11. Cook the goulash for 6 minutes more.

Nutrition:

- Calories: 161
- Fat: 6.1 g.
- Carbs: 6 g.
- Protein: 20.3 g.

113. Chicken & Turkey Meatloaf

Preparation time: 15 minutes

Cooking time: 25 minutes

Servings: 12

Ingredients:

- 3 tbsp. butter
- 10 oz. ground turkey
- 7 oz. ground chicken
- 1 tsp. dried dill
- 1/2 tsp. coriander, ground
- 2 tbsp. almond flour
- 1 tbsp. garlic, minced
- 3 oz. fresh spinach
- 1 tsp. salt
- 1 egg
- 1/2 tbsp. paprika
- 1 tsp. sesame oil

Directions:

1. Put the ground turkey and ground chicken in a large bowl.
2. Sprinkle the meat with dried dill, ground coriander, almond flour, minced garlic, salt, and paprika.
3. Then chop the fresh spinach and add it to the ground poultry mixture.
4. Crack the egg into the meat mixture and mix well until you get a smooth texture.
5. Great the air fryer basket tray with the olive oil.
6. Preheat the air fryer to 350°F.
7. Roll the ground meat mixture gently to make the flat layer.
8. Put the butter in the center of the meat

layer.

9. Make the shape of the meatloaf from the ground meat mixture. Use your fingertips for this step.

10. Place the meatloaf in the air fryer basket tray.

11. Cook for 25 minutes.

12. When the meatloaf is cooked allow it to rest before serving.

Nutrition:

- Calories: 142
- Fat: 9.8 g.
- Carbs: 1.7 g.
- Protein: 13 g.

114. Turkey Meatballs With Dried Dill

Preparation time: 15 minutes

Cooking time: 11 minutes

Servings: 9

Ingredients:

- 1 lb. turkey, ground
- 1 tsp. chili flakes
- 1/4 cup chicken stock
- 2 tbsp. dried dill
- 1 egg
- 1 tsp. salt
- 1 tsp. paprika
- 1 tbsp. coconut flour
- 2 tbsp. heavy cream
- 1 tsp. olive oil

Directions:

1. Crack the egg in a bowl and whisk it with a fork.

2. Add the ground turkey and chili flakes.

3. Sprinkle the mixture with dried dill, salt, paprika, coconut flour, and mix it up.

4. Make the meatballs from the ground turkey mixture.

5. Preheat the air fryer to 360°F.

6. Grease the air fryer basket tray with olive oil.

7. Then put the meatballs inside.

8. Cook the meatballs for 6 minutes—for 3 minutes on each side.

9. Sprinkle the meatballs with heavy cream.

10. Cook the meatballs for 5 minutes more.

11. When the turkey meatballs are cooked—let them rest for 2–3 minutes.

Nutrition:

- Calories: 124
- Fat: 7.9 g.
- Carbs: 1.2 g.
- Protein: 14.8 g.

115. Chicken Coconut Poppers

Preparation time: 10 minutes

Cooking time: 10 minutes

Servings: 6

Ingredients:

- 1/2 cup coconut flour
- 1 tsp. chili flakes
- 1 tsp. black pepper, ground
- 1 tsp. garlic powder
- 11 oz. chicken breast, boneless, skinless
- 1 tbsp. olive oil

Directions:

1. Cut the chicken breast into medium cubes and put them in a large bowl.
2. Sprinkle the chicken cubes with chili flakes, ground black pepper, garlic powder, and stir them well using your hands.
3. After this, sprinkle the chicken cubes with coconut flour.
4. Shake the bowl with the chicken cubes gently to coat the meat.
5. Preheat the air fryer to 365°F.
6. Grease the air fryer basket tray with olive oil.
7. Place the chicken cubes inside.
8. Cook the chicken poppers for 10 minutes.
9. Turn the chicken poppers over after 5 minutes of cooking.
10. Allow the cooked chicken poppers to cool before serving.

Nutrition:

- Calories: 123

- Fat: 4.6 g.
- Carbs: 6.9 g.
- Protein: 13.2 g.

116. Parmesan Beef Slices

Preparation time: 14 minutes

Cooking time: 25 minutes

Servings: 4

Ingredients:

- 12 oz. beef brisket
- 1 tsp. kosher salt
- 7 oz. Parmesan cheese, sliced
- 5 oz. chive stems
- 1 tsp. turmeric
- 1 tsp. dried oregano
- 2 tsp. butter

Directions:

1. Slice the beef brisket into 4 slices.
2. Sprinkle every beef slice with turmeric and dried oregano.
3. Grease the air fryer basket tray with butter.
4. Put the beef slices inside.
5. Dice the chives.
6. Make a layer using the diced chives over the beef slices.
7. Then make a layer using the Parmesan cheese.
8. Preheat the air fryer to 365°F.
9. Cook the beef slices for 25 minutes.

Nutrition:

- Calories: 348
- Fat: 18 g.
- Carbs: 5 g.
- Protein: 42.1 g.

117. Chili Beef Jerky

Preparation time: 25 minutes

Cooking time: 2.5 hours

Servings: 6

Ingredients:

- 14 oz. beef flank steak
- 1 tsp. chili pepper
- 3 tbsp. apple cider vinegar
- 1 tsp. black pepper, ground
- 1 tsp. onion powder
- 1 tsp. garlic powder
- 1/4 tsp. liquid smoke

Directions:

1. Slice the beefsteak into the medium strips and then tenderize each piece.
2. Take a bowl and combine the apple cider vinegar, ground black pepper, onion powder, garlic powder, and liquid smoke.
3. Whisk gently with a fork.
4. Then transfer the beef pieces to the mixture and stir well.
5. Leave the meat to marinate for up to 8 hours.
6. Put the marinated beef pieces in the air fryer rack.
7. Cook the beef jerky for 2.5 hours at 150°F.

Nutrition:

- Calories: 129
- Fat: 4.1 g.
- Carbs: 1.1 g.
- Protein: 20.2 g.

118. Spinach Beef Heart

Preparation time: 15 minutes

Cooking time: 20 minutes

Servings: 4

Ingredients:

- 1 lb. beef heart
- 5 oz. chive stems
- 1/2 cup fresh spinach
- 1 tsp. salt
- 1 tsp. black pepper, ground
- 3 cups chicken stock
- 1 tsp. butter

Directions:

1. Remove all the fat from the beef heart.
2. Dice the chives.
3. Chop the fresh spinach.
4. Combine the diced chives, fresh spinach, and butter.

Stir it.

5. Cut the beef heart and fill it with the spinach-chives mixture.

6. Preheat the air fryer to 400°F.

7. Pour the chicken stock into the air fryer basket tray.

8. Sprinkle the Prepared stuffed beef heart with salt and ground black pepper.

9. Put the beef heart in the air fryer and cook it for 20 minutes.

10. Remove the cooked heart from the air fryer and slice it.

11. Sprinkle the slices with the remaining liquid from the air fryer.

Nutrition:

- Calories: 216
- Fat: 6.8 g.
- Fiber: 0.8 g.
- Carbs: 3.8 g.
- Protein: 33.3

119. Paprika Pulled Pork

Preparation time: 15 minutes

Cooking time: 20 minutes

Servings: 4

Ingredients:

- 1 tbsp. chili flakes
- 1 tsp. black pepper, ground
- 1/2 tsp. paprika
- 1 tsp. cayenne pepper
- 1/3 cup cream
- 1 tsp. kosher salt
- 1 lb. pork tenderloin
- 1 tsp. thyme, ground
- 4 cup chicken stock
- 1 tsp. butter

Directions:

1. Pour the chicken stock into the air fryer basket tray.

2. Add the pork steak

and sprinkle the mixture with chili flakes, ground black pepper, paprika, cayenne pepper, thyme, and kosher salt.

3. Preheat the air fryer to 370°F and cook the meat for 20 minutes.

4. Strain the liquid and shred the meat with 2 forks.

5. Then add the butter and cream and mix it.

6. Cook the pulled pork for 4 minutes more at 360°F.

7. When the pulled pork is cooked allow to rest briefly.

Nutrition:

- Calories: 198
- Fat: 6.8 g.
- Carbs: 2.3 g.
- Protein: 30.7 g.

120. Paprika Whole Chicken

Preparation time: 15 minutes

Cooking time: 75 minutes

Servings: 12

Ingredients:

- 6 lb. whole chicken
- 1 tsp. kosher salt
- 1 tsp. black pepper, ground
- 1 tsp. paprika, ground
- 1 tbsp. garlic, minced
- 3 tbsp. butter
- 1 tsp. olive oil
- 1/4 cup water
- 3 oz. chive stems

Directions:

1. Rub the whole chicken with kosher salt and ground black pepper inside and outside.

2. Sprinkle it with the ground paprika and minced garlic.

3. Dice the chives.

4. Put the diced chives inside the whole chicken.

5. Then add the butter.

6. Rub the chicken with olive oil.

7. Preheat the air fryer to 360°F and pour water into the air fryer basket.

8. Place the chicken on the rack inside the air fryer.

9. Cook the chicken for 75 minutes.

10. When the chicken is cooked it should have slightly crunchy skin.

11. Cut the cooked chicken into the servings.

Nutrition:

- Calories: 464
- Fat: 20.1 g.
- Carbs: 0.9 g.
- Protein: 65.8 g.

121. Pork Almond Bites

Preparation time: 10 minutes

Cooking time: 14 minutes

Servings: 6

Ingredients:

- 1 lb. pork tenderloin
- 2 eggs
- 1 tsp. butter
- 1/4 cup almond flour
- 1 tsp. kosher salt
- 1 tsp. paprika
- 1 tsp. coriander, ground
- 1/2 tsp. lemon zest

Directions:

1. Chop the pork tenderloin into large cubes.
2. Sprinkle the pork cubes with kosher salt, paprika, ground coriander, and lemon zest.
3. Mix the meat gently.
4. Crack the egg into a bowl and whisk it.
5. Coat the meat cubes with the egg mixture and then the almond flour.
6. Preheat the air fryer to 365°F.
7. Put the butter in the air fryer basket tray and then place the pork bites inside.
8. Cook the pork bites for 14 minutes.
9. Turn the pork bites over after 7 minutes of cooking.
10. When the pork bites are cooked—serve them hot.

Nutrition:

- Calories: 142
- Fat: 5.4 g.
- Carbs: 0.6 g.
- Protein: 21.9 g.

122. Pandan Coconut Chicken

Preparation time: 20 minutes

Cooking time: 10 minutes

Servings: 4

Ingredients:

- 15 oz. chicken
- 1 pandan leaf
- 3 oz. chive stems, diced
- 1 tsp. garlic, minced
- 1 tsp. chili flakes
- 1 tsp. stevia
- 1 tsp. black pepper, ground
- 1 tsp. turmeric
- 1 tbsp. butter
- 1/4 cup coconut milk
- 1 tbsp. chives powder

Directions:

1. Cut the chicken into 4 big cubes.
2. Put the chicken cubes in a large bowl.
3. Sprinkle the chicken with minced garlic, butter diced chives, chili flakes, stevia, ground black pepper, chives powder, and turmeric.
4. Mix the meat up using your hands.
5. Cut the pandan leaf into 4 parts.
6. Wrap the chicken cubes into the pandan leaf.
7. Pour the coconut milk into a bowl with the wrapped chicken and leave it for 10 minutes.
8. Preheat the air fryer to 380°F.
9. Put the pandan chicken in the air fryer basket and cook for 10 minutes.
10. When the chicken is cooked—transfer to serving plates and let it chill for at least 2–3 minutes.

Nutrition:

- Calories: 250
- Fat: 12.6 g,
- Carbs: 3.1 g.
- Protein: 29.9 g.

123. Air Fryer Raspberry Balsamic Smoked Pork Chops

Preparation time: 15 minutes

Cooking time: 15 minutes

Servings: 4

Ingredients:

- 4 (71/2 oz. each) bone-in pork chops, smoked
- 2 large egg
- 1 cup bread crumbs
- 1/4 cup milk, low-fat
- 1 cup pecans, chopped
- 1/3 cup balsamic vinegar
- 2 tbsp. brown sugar
- 2 tbsp. raspberry jam
- 1/4 cup all-purpose flour
- 1 tbsp. orange juice concentrate
- Cooking spray as required

Directions:

1. Set the air fryer at 200°C and preheat.
2. Slightly coat the air fryer basket with non-stick cooking spray.
3. Combine milk and eggs in a medium bowl.
4. Toss bread crumbs and pecans in another medium bowl and keep ready.
5. Lightly coat the pork chops with flour, shrug off excess flour.
6. Dip the pork chop in the egg mixture and dredge in the bread crumbs.
7. Place the dredged chops in the frying basket.
8. Spray non-stick cooking oil over it.
9. Set the timer for 15 minutes and cook until it becomes golden brown.
10. Flip the chops after 8 minutes or intermittently.
11. Spray non-stick oil while flipping.
12. After cooking, remove the food for serving.
13. If you have many pieces to cook, you can do the cooking in batches. Do not place the chops layer above the layer.
14. In a saucepan pour raspberry jam, brown sugar, balsamic vinegar, milk, and orange juice to make the glaze.
15. Heat on medium temperature and bring to boil.
16. Stir continuously

and cook for about 8 minutes until it transforms into a thick consistency.

17. Serve hot along with chops.

Nutrition:

- Calories: 579
- Carbs: 36 g.
- Fat: 36 g.
- Protein: 32 g.

124. American Air Fried Cheese Sandwich

Preparation time: 2 minutes

Cooking time: 8 minutes

Servings: 1

Ingredients:

- 2 slices sandwich bread
- 2 tsp. butter
- 3 slices cheddar cheese

Directions:

1. Keep the cheese between the sandwich bread slices.
2. Butter the bread outside.
3. Put in the air fryer basket.
4. Set the temperature at 190°C and timer to 8 minutes.
5. After 4 minutes, pull out the fryer basket and flip the sandwich and continue cooking further 4 minutes.
6. Serve hot.

Nutrition:

- Calories: 546
- Carbohydrate: 29.1 g.
- Fat: 37.5 g.
- Protein: 25 g.

125. Midnight Nutella Banana Sandwich

Preparation time: 4 minutes

Cooking time: 8 minutes

Servings: 2

Ingredients:

- 4 slices white bread
- 1/4 cup Nutella® chocolate hazelnut spread
- 1 banana
- 2 tbsp. Soft butter for spreading
- Cooking Spray

Directions:

1. Set your air fryer at 190°C.
2. Spread the butter on one side of the bread slice and keep the buttered side down on a flat surface.
3. Now, spread the chocolate hazelnut on the non-buttered side of the bread slice.
4. Cut the banana in half and slice it lengthwise into 3 portions.
5. For making 2 sandwiches, place the bananas on 2 bread slices and put the remaining bananas on top of the bread slice.
6. Cut the sliced bread into a triangle shape.
7. Put the sliced bread sandwiches into the air fryer basket.
8. Set the timer for 5 minutes and temperature at 190°C.
9. Flip the sandwiches halfway.
10. When both sides become brown, it is ready to serve.

Nutrition:

- Calories: 341
- Carbohydrate: 42.6 g.
- Fat: 18.4 g.
- Protein: 4.1 g.

126. Air Fried Pork Chops With Brussels Sprouts

Preparation time: 10 minutes

Cooking time: 25 minutes

Servings: 1

Ingredients:

- 8 oz. pork chop with bone
- 6 oz. Brussels sprouts quartered
- 1 tsp. olive oil
- 1/2 tsp. black pepper, crushed
- 1 tsp. mustard
- 1 tsp. maple syrup
- 1/8 tsp. kosher salt
- Cooking Spray

Directions:

1. Clean pork chops in running water and pat dry.
2. Oil coat pork lightly with cooking spray.
3. Sprinkle 1/4 tsp. pepper over it and also sprinkle salt and keep it aside.
4. Now in a medium bowl pour olive oil.
5. Add the remaining pepper, mustard, maple syrup, and combine.
6. Put the quartered Brussels sprouts and toss them gently, to coat the mix.
7. Now place the coated pork chop and Brussel sprouts in the air fryer basket.
8. Set the temperature at 200°C and timer to 10 minutes.
9. If you wish to have well-done pork, you can increase the cooking time to the required level.

Nutrition:

- Calories: 955
- Carbohydrate: 21.8 g.
- Fat: 71.9 g.
- Protein: 57.7 g.

127. Air Fryer Fish and Fries

Preparation time: 15 minutes

Cooking time: 25 minutes

Servings: 4

Ingredients:

For fish fry:

- 1/3 cup all-purpose flour
- 1 egg, large
- 2/3 cup cornflakes, crushed
- 1 lb. cod fillets
- 1/4 tsp. pepper, ground
- 1 tbsp. Parmesan cheese, shredded
- 1/8 tsp. cayenne pepper
- 2 tbsp. tartar sauce
- 2 tbsp. water
- 1/4 tsp. salt

For potato fry:

- 1 lb. potatoes
- 2 tbsp. olive oil
- 1/4 tsp. pepper

Directions:

1. Peel, wash, and cut the potatoes in lengthwise 1/2-inch size and again cut into half.
2. Set the air fryer to 200°C and pre-heat.
3. Toss the cut size potatoes with pepper, salt, and oil in a large bowl.
4. Place the potatoes in the frying basket by not overlapping one another.
5. Fry for 10 minutes or until the potatoes become tender.
6. After 10 minutes toss the potatoes in the air fryer basket and again fry for another 10 minutes.
7. While the frying is in progress, let us prepare for fish frying.
8. Whisk egg and water in a small bowl.
9. In another medium bowl, combine pepper and flour.
10. Take yet another bowl and toss cheese and cayenne with cornflakes.
11. Dust salt on the fish.
12. Dredge the fish in the flour mixture and let it have an even coating. If any excess coating is there, shake it to remove.
13. Now dip the fish into the egg mixture and after that dredge in the cornflake mixture.
14. By the time the potatoes frying will be over. Remove it and keep warm.
15. Now place the coated fish in the air fryer basket for

frying.

16. Set cooking for 8–10 minutes.
17. When the fish turns light brown, flip it carefully.
18. Once done, transfer the fried potatoes over to fish fillet, so that the potatoes can absorb some heat from fish.
19. Serve along with tartar sauce.

Nutrition:

- Calories: 312
- Carbs: 35 g.
- Fat: 9 g.
- Protein: 23 g.

128. Air Fried Broccoli With Cheese Sauce

Preparation time: 15 minutes

Cooking time: 20 minutes

Servings: 4

Ingredients:

- 6 cups broccoli florets
- 10 tbsp. evaporated milk, low-fat
- 4 tsp. *Ají Amarillo* paste
- 1 1/2 oz. fresh Mexican cheese, grated
- Cooking spray as required
- 6 saltine crackers, low-sodium

Directions:

1. Slightly coat cooking spray on the broccoli florets.
2. Place the broccoli in the air fryer basket.
3. Set the temperature at 190°C and cook for about 8 minutes.
4. Put Mexican cheese, milk, *Ají Amarillo* paste, and saltine crackers in a blender and process it until it becomes smooth.
5. Transfer the cheese sauce into a microwave oven-safe bowl and microwave it for 30 seconds.
6. Serve the fried broccoli florets with cheese sauce.

Nutrition:

- Calories: 108
- Carbs: 15 g.
- Fat: 2 g.
- Protein: 8 g.

129. Air Fryer Chicken Sandwich

Preparation time: 10 minutes

Cooking time: 16 minutes

Servings: 6

Ingredients:

- 2 chicken breast, boneless skinless
- 1/2 cup dill pickle juice
- 1/2 cup milk
- 2 eggs
- 2 tbsp. potato starch
- 1 cup all-purpose flour
- 2 tbsp. sugar powdered
- 1 tsp. paprika
- 1/2 tsp. black pepper, ground
- 1/2 tsp. garlic powder
- 1/4 tsp. celery seed, ground
- 1 tbsp. extra virgin olive oil
- 1/2 tsp. salt
- 1/2 cups dill pickle chips
- 6 hamburger buns
- Cooking spray as required
- 1/4 cup mayonnaise

Directions:

1. Pound the chicken put in a zip lock bag so that the chicken thickness become even in all side. The ideal thickness is 1/2-inch.
2. Cut the chicken into 2–3 pieces.
3. Now put back the chicken pieces into the zip lock bag and pour pickle juice and shake.
4. Keep it in the refrigerator for about 30 minutes to get a better marinade effect.
5. Blend egg and milk in a medium bowl.
6. Combine all spices, starch, and flour in another bowl.
7. Using a tong, dip the chicken in the egg mixture and then dredge in the flour mixture.
8. Remove any excess flour if stuck with the chicken by shaking.
9. Grease the air fryer basket with cooking spray.
10. Place the coated chicken into the air fryer tray and drizzle some cooking spray over it.
11. Set the temperature at 170°C and cook for 6 minutes.
12. After 6 minutes, flip the chicken and spray some cooking oil and continue cooking for 6 more minutes.
13. Now increase the temperature to

200°C and cook for 2 more minutes.

14. Flip the chicken and cook the other side also for 2 minutes at 200°C.

15. Toast the bun and cut open.

16. Place the chicken between the opened buns along with 2 pickle chips and mayonnaise.

Nutrition:

- Calories: 281
- Carbs: 38 g.
- Protein: 15 g.
- Fat: 6 g.

130. Air Fryer Orange Turkey Burgers

Preparation time: 15 minutes

Cooking time: 11 minutes

Servings: 4

Ingredients:

- 1 lb. turkey, ground
- 1 tsp. mustard seed, ground
- 1 tbsp. grape nuts nuggets
- 1/4 tsp. Chinese 5 spice
- 1 scallion, diced

Orange basting sauce:

- 1/2 cup orange marmalade
- 1 tbsp. soy sauce
- 1 tsp. fish sauce
- 2 tsp. oyster sauce

Orange aioli:

- 1 tbsp. orange juice
- 1 tsp. orange zest
- 1/2 cup mayonnaise
- 1 tsp. ground chili paste

Directions:

1. In a small bowl, whisk orange aioli ingredients and refrigerate.

2. In another bowl combine basting sauce and keep aside.

3. Set the air fryer at 200°C and preheat for about 10 minutes.

4. In a medium bowl combine the burger ingredients and add 1 tbsp. of basting sauce.

5. Shape the mix into 6 patties and create an indentation at the center of the patties.

6. Now lightly grease the surface of the air fryer basket with

cooking oil and place the patties in the frying basket.

7. Set the temperature at 180ºC and cook for 9 minutes.
8. Flip the burgers intermittently every 4 minutes.
9. Baste burger after every 2 minutes.
10. After 9 minutes of cooking, baste the burger and cook a further 3 minutes.
11. Serve hot along with orange aioli.

Nutrition:

- Calories: 443
- Carbs: 34.9 g.
- Fat: 22.5 g.
- Protein: 32 g.

131. Cheesy Ravioli Lunch

Preparation time: 5 minutes

Cooking time: 15 minutes

Servings: 6

Ingredients:

- 1 package cheese ravioli
- 2 cup Italian breadcrumbs
- 1/4 cup Parmesan cheese, grated
- 1 cup buttermilk
- 1 tsp. olive oil
- 1/4 tsp. garlic powder

Directions:

1. Preheat Instant Vortex on "Air Fry" function to 390ºF. In a bowl, combine breadcrumbs, Parmesan cheese, garlic, and olive oil. Dip the ravioli in the buttermilk and coat with the breadcrumb mixture.
2. Line a baking sheet with parchment paper and arrange the ravioli on it. Press "Start" and cook for 5 minutes. Serve with marinara jar sauce.

Nutrition:

- Calories: 381
- Carbs: 18 g.
- Protein: 25 g.

Fat: 5 g.

132. Carrots & Shallots With Yogurt

Preparation time: 10 minutes

Cooking time: 25 minutes

Servings: 4

Ingredients:

- 2 tsp. olive oil
- 2 shallots, chopped
- 3 carrots, sliced
- Salt to taste
- 1/4 cup yogurt
- 2 garlic cloves, minced
- 3 tbsp. parsley, chopped
- 2 tsp Basil and garlic mayo

Directions:

1. In a bowl, mix sliced carrots, salt, garlic, shallots, parsley, and yogurt. Sprinkle with oil.

Place the veggies in the basket and press "Start."

2. Cook for 15 minutes on the "Air Fry" function at 370°F. Serve with basil and garlic mayo.

Nutrition:

- Calories: 251
- Carbs: 30 g.
- Protein: 16 g.
- Fat: 2 g.

133. Grandma's Ratatouille

Preparation time: 15 minutes

Cooking time: 30 minutes

Servings: 2

Ingredients:

- 1 tbsp. olive oil
- 3 Roma tomatoes, thinly sliced
- 2 garlic cloves, minced
- 1 zucchini, thinly sliced
- 2 yellow bell peppers, sliced
- 1 tbsp. vinegar
- 2 tbsp. herbs de Provence
- Salt and black pepper to taste

Directions:

1. Preheat Instant Vortex on the "Air Fry" function to 390°F. Place all

ingredients in a bowl. Season with salt and pepper and stir to coat.

2. Arrange the vegetable on a baking dish and place it in the Instant vortex oven. Cook for 15 minutes, shaking occasionally. Let sit for 5 more minutes after the timer goes off.

Nutrition:

- Calories: 181
- Carbs: 39 g.
- Protein: 18 g.

Fat: 8 g.

134. Amazing Macadamia Delight

Preparation time: 10 minutes

Cooking time: 20 minutes

Servings: 6

Ingredients:

- 3 cups macadamia nuts
- 3 tbsp. liquid smoke
- Salt to taste
- 2 tbsp. molasses

Directions:

1. Preheat Instant Vortex on the "Bake" function to 360°F. In a bowl, add salt, liquid, molasses, and macadamia nuts and toss to coat. Place the macadamia nuts in the baking tray and press "Start." Cook for 10 minutes, shaking the basket every 5 minutes. Serve.

Nutrition:

- Calories: 191
- Carbs: 18 g.
- Protein: 35 g.
- Fat: 3 g.

135. Veggie Mix Fried Chips

Preparation time: 25 minutes

Cooking time: 45 minutes

Servings: 4

Ingredients:

- 1 large eggplant, cut into strips
- 5 potatoes, peeled and cut into strips
- 3 zucchinis, cut into strips
- 1/2 cup cornstarch
- 1/2 cup olive oil
- Salt to taste
- 1 cup water

Directions:

1. Preheat Instant vortex on the "Air Fry" function to 390°F.
2. In a bowl, stir cornstarch, 1/2 cup of water, salt, pepper, olive oil, eggplants, zucchini, and potatoes.
3. Place the veggie mixture in the basket and press "Start." Cook for 12 minutes. Serve warm.

Nutrition:

- Calories: 276
- Carbs: 38 g.
- Protein: 19 g.
- Fat: 13 g.

136. Cheese Stuffed Green Peppers With Tomato Sauce

Preparation time: 15 minutes

Cooking time: 35 minutes

Servings: 4

Ingredients:

- 2 cans green chili peppers
- 1 cup Cheddar cheese, shredded
- 1 cup Monterey Jack cheese, shredded
- 2 tbsp. all-purpose flour
- 2 large eggs, beaten
- 1/2 cup milk
- 1 can tomato sauce

Directions:

1. Preheat Instant Vortex on the "Air Fry" function to

380°F.

2. Spray a baking dish with cooking spray. Take half of the chilies and arrange them in the baking dish. Top with half of the cheese and cover with the remaining chilies. In a medium bowl, combine eggs, milk, and flour and pour over the chilies.

3. Press "Start" and cook for 20 minutes. Remove the chilies and pour the tomato sauce over them; cook for 15 more minutes. Top with the remaining cheese and serve.

Nutrition:

- Calories: 309
- Carbs: 33 g.
- Protein: 22 g.

Fat: 12 g.

137. Basil White Fish

Preparation time: 10 minutes

Cooking time: 20 minutes

Servings: 4

Ingredients:

- 2 tbsp. fresh basil, chopped
- 2 garlic cloves, minced
- 1 tbsp. Parmesan cheese, grated
- Salt and black pepper to taste
- 2 tbsp. pine nuts
- 4 white fish fillets
- 2 tbsp. olive oil

Directions:

1. Preheat Instant Vortex on the "Air Fry" function to 350°F. Season the fillets with salt and pepper and place them in the basket.

Drizzle with some olive oil and press "Start." Cook for 12–14 minutes.

2. In a bowl, mix basil, remaining olive oil, pine nuts, garlic, and Parmesan cheese and spread on the fish. Serve.

Nutrition:

- Calories: 298
- Carbs: 31 g.
- Protein: 34 g.

Fat: 8 g.

138. Cajun Salmon With Lemon

Preparation time: 5 minutes

Cooking time: 10 minutes

Servings: 1

Ingredients:

- 1 salmon fillet
- 1/4 tsp. brown sugar
- Juice of 1/2 lemon
- 1 tbsp. Cajun seasoning
- 2 lemon wedges
- 1 tbsp. fresh parsley, chopped

Directions:

1. Preheat Instant Vortex on the "Bake" function to 350°F.
2. Combine sugar and lemon and coat in the salmon. Sprinkle with the Cajun seasoning as well. Place parchment paper on a baking tray and press "Start." Cook for 14–16 minutes.
3. Serve with lemon wedges and chopped parsley.

Nutrition:

- Calories: 221
- Carbs: 11 g.
- Protein: 12g.
- Fat: 7 g.

139. Lemon Salmon

Preparation time: 10 minutes

Cooking time: 20 minutes

Servings: 2

Ingredients:

- 2 salmon fillets
- Salt to taste
- Zest of 1 lemon

Directions:

1. Preheat the Instant Vortex oven for 14 minutes at 360°F.
2. Rub the fillets with salt and lemon zest. Place them in the frying basket and spray with cooking spray. Press "Start" and cook the salmon for 14 minutes at 360°F on the "Air Fry" function.
3. Serve with steamed

asparagus and a drizzle of lemon juice.

Nutrition:

- Calories: 332
- Carbs: 41 g.
- Protein: 14 g.
- Fat: 10 g.

140. Saucy Cod With Green Onions

Preparation time: 10 minutes

Cooking time: 20 minutes

Servings: 4

Ingredients:

- 4 cod fillets
- 2 tbsp. fresh coriander, chopped
- Salt to taste
- 4 green onions, chopped
- 5 slices of ginger, chopped
- 5 tbsp. soy sauce
- 3 tbsp. olive oil
- 5 rock sugar cubes
- 1 cup water

Directions:

1. Preheat Instant Vortex on the "Air Fry" function to 390°F. Season the cod with salt and coriander and drizzle with some olive oil. Place the fish fillet in the basket and press "Start." Cook for 15 minutes.
2. Heat the remaining olive oil in a skillet over medium heat and sauté green onions and ginger for 3 minutes. Add in soy sauce and the remaining ingredients and 1 cup of water. Bring to a boil and cook for 5 minutes until the sauce thickens. Pour the sauce over the fish and serve.

Nutrition:

- Calories: 266
- Carbs: 28 g.
- Protein: 18 g.
- Fat: 9 g.

141. Parmesan Tilapia Fillets

Preparation time: 5 minutes

Cooking time: 15 minutes

Servings: 4

Ingredients:

- 3/4 cup Parmesan cheese, grated
- 1 tbsp. olive oil
- 1 tsp. paprika
- 1 tbsp. fresh parsley, chopped
- 1/4 tsp. garlic powder
- 1/4 tsp. salt
- 4 tilapia fillets

Directions:

1. Preheat Instant vortex on the "Air Fry" function to 350°F.
2. In a bowl, mix parsley, Parmesan cheese, garlic, salt, and paprika. Coat in the tilapia fillets and place them in a lined baking sheet. Drizzle with the olive oil press "Start." Cook for 8–10 minutes until golden. Serve warm.

Nutrition:

- Calories: 145
- Carbs: 43 g.
- Protein: 21 g.
- Fat: 17 g.

142. Party Cod Nuggets

Preparation time: 15 minutes

Cooking time: 25 minutes

Servings: 4

Ingredients:

- 1 1/4 lb. cod fillets, cut into 4 chunks each
- 1/2 cup flour
- 1 egg
- 1 cup cornflakes
- 1 tbsp. olive oil
- Salt and black pepper to taste
- 1 cup water

Directions:

1. Place the oil and

cornflakes in a food processor and process until crumbed. Season the fish chunks with salt and pepper. In a bowl, beat the egg with 1 tbsp. of water.

2. Dredge the chunks in flour first, then dip in the egg, and finally coat with cornflakes. Arrange on a lined sheet and press "Start." Cook on the "Air Fry" function at 350°F for 15 minutes until crispy. Serve.

Nutrition:

- Calories: 391
- Carbs: 56 g.
- Protein: 11 g.
- Fat: 2 g.

143. Lemon Pepper

Tilapia Fillets

Preparation time: 8 minutes

Cooking time: 15 minutes

Servings: 4

Ingredients:

- 1 lb. tilapia fillets
- 1 tbsp. Italian seasoning
- 2 tbsp. canola oil
- 2 tbsp. lemon pepper
- Salt to taste
- 2–3 butter buds

Directions:

1. Preheat your Instant Vortex oven to 400°F on the "Bake" function.
2. Drizzle tilapia fillets with canola oil. In a bowl, mix salt, lemon pepper, butter buds, and Italian seasoning; spread on the fish.

Place the fillet on a baking tray and press "Start." Cook for 10 minutes until tender and crispy. Serve warm.

Nutrition:

- Calories: 201
- Carbs: 28 g.
- Protein: 17 g.
- Fat: 13 g.

144. Citrus Cilantro Catfish

Preparation time: 10 minutes

Cooking time: 20 minutes

Servings: 2

Ingredients:

- 2 catfish fillets
- 2 tsp. blackening seasoning
- Juice of 1 lime
- 2 tbsp. butter, melted
- 1 garlic clove, mashed
- 2 tbsp. fresh cilantro, chopped

Directions:

1. In a bowl, blend garlic, lime juice, cilantro, and butter. Pour half of the mixture over the fillets and sprinkle with blackening seasoning.
2. Place the fillets in the basket and press "Start." Cook for 15 minutes at 360°F on the "Air Fry" function. Serve the fish topped with the remaining sauce.

Nutrition:

- Calories: 141
- Carbs: 32 g.
- Protein: 10 g.
- Fat: 7 g.

145. Salmon & Caper Cakes

Preparation time: 10 minutes

Cooking time: 15 minutes

Servings: 2

Ingredients:

- 8 oz. salmon, cooked
- 1 1/2 oz. potatoes, mashed
- A handful of capers
- 1 tbsp. fresh parsley, chopped
- Zest of 1 lemon
- 1 3/4 oz. plain flour

Directions:

1. Carefully flake the salmon. In a bowl, mix the salmon, zest, capers, dill, and mashed potatoes. Form small cakes from the mixture and dust them with flour; refrigerate for

60 minutes.

2. Preheat Instant Vortex to 350°F. Press "Start" and cook the cakes for 10 minutes on the "Air Fry" function. Serve chilled.

Nutrition:

- Calories: 132
- Carbs: 28 g.
- Protein: 25 g.
- Fat: 15 g.

146. Lunch Egg Rolls

Preparation time: 25 minutes

Cooking time: 20 minutes

Servings: 4

Ingredients:

- 1/2 cup mushrooms
- 1/2 cup carrots
- 1/2 cup zucchini
- 2 green onions
- 2 tbsp. soy sauce
- 8 egg roll
- 1 egg
- 1 tbsp. cornstarch

Directions:

1. Mix carrots with soy sauce, zucchini, green onions, and mushrooms in a bowl. Stir.
2. Organize egg roll wrappers on a surface. Divide veggie mix on each. Roll well.
3. Mix cornstarch plus egg in a bowl. Whisk well. Brush egg rolls with this mix.
4. Seal edges. Place all rolls in a preheated air fryer. Cook for 15 minutes at 370°F.
5. Arrange them on a platter. Serve.

Nutrition:

- Calories: 581
- Carbs: 12 g.
- Protein: 16 g.

Fat: 22 g.

147. Veggie Toast

Preparation time: 25 minutes

Cooking time: 15 minutes

Servings: 4

Ingredients:

- 1 red bell pepper
- 1 cup cremini mushrooms
- 2 green onions
- 1 tbsp. olive oil
- 4 bread slices
- 2 tbsp. butter
- 1/2 cup goat cheese

Directions:

1. Mix mushrooms and red bell pepper in a bowl. Add oil and green onions. Toss. Transfer to the air fryer. Cook them for 10 minutes at 350°F. Transfer to a bowl.
2. On bread slices, spread butter. Place them in the air fryer. Cook for 5 minutes at 350°F.
3. Divide the veggie mix into the bread slices. Top using crumbled cheese. Serve.

Nutrition:

- Calories: 432
- Carbs: 32 g.
- Protein: 13 g.
- Fat:12 g.

148. Stuffed Mushrooms

Preparation time: 30 minutes

Cooking time: 20 minutes

Servings: 4

Ingredients:

- 4 big Portobello mushroom caps
- 1 tbsp. olive oil
- 1/4 cup ricotta cheese
- 5 tbsp. Parmesan cheese
- 1 cup spinach
- 1/3 cup bread crumbs
- 1/4 tsp. Rosemary

Directions:

1. Rub mushrooms caps with the oil. Place them in your air fryer's basket. Cook for 2 minutes at 350°F.
2. Mix half of the

parmesan with bread crumbs, Rosemary, spinach, and ricotta in a bowl. Stir.

3. Stuff mushrooms with this mix. Drizzle with Parmesan cheese. Place in your air fryer's basket. Cook for 10 minutes at 350°F.

4. Divide among plates and serve.

Nutrition:

- Calories: 231
- Carbs: 33 g.
- Protein: 13 g.

Fat: 3 g.

149. Quick Lunch Pizzas

Preparation time: 17 minutes

Cooking time: 15 minutes

Servings: 4

Ingredients:

- 4 pitas
- 1 tbsp. olive oil
- 3/4 cup pizza sauce
- 4 oz. jarred mushrooms
- 1/2 tsp. basil
- 2 green onions
- 2 cup mozzarella
- 1 cup grape tomatoes

Directions:

1. On each pita bread, spread pizza sauce. Drizzle basil and green onions.
2. Divide mushrooms top with cheese.
3. Assemble pita pizzas in the air

fryer. Cook for 7 minutes at 400°F.

4. Top pizza with tomato slices. Divide among plates. Serve.

Nutrition:

- Calories: 235
- Carbs: 32 g.
- Protein: 12 g.

Fat: 9 g.

150. Lunch Gnocchi

Preparation time: 10 Minutes

Cooking time: 5 minutes

Servings: 4

Ingredients:

- 1 yellow onion
- 1 tbsp. olive oil
- 3 garlic cloves
- 16 oz. gnocchi
- 1/4 cup parmesan
- 8 oz. spinach pesto

Directions:

1. Lubricate the air fryer's pan with olive oil. Add garlic, onion, and gnocchi. Toss. Place pan in the air fryer. Cook for 10 minutes at 400°F.
2. Add the pesto. Toss. Cook for 7 minutes at 350°F.
3. Divide among plates. Serve.

Nutrition:

- Calories: 280
- Carbs: 12 g.
- Protein: 11 g.
- Fat: 15 g.

151. Tuna and Zucchini Tortillas

Preparation time: 10 minutes

Cooking time: 6 minutes

Servings: 4

Ingredients:

- 4 corn tortillas
- 4 tbsp. butter
- 6 oz. canned tuna
- 1 cup zucchini
- 1/3 cup mayonnaise
- 2 tbsp. mustard
- 1 cup cheddar cheese

Directions:

1. Spread butter on tortillas. Put in an air fryer's basket. Cook for 3 minutes at 400°F.
2. Mix mustard with mayo, zucchini, and tuna in a bowl. Stir.

3. Mix on each tortilla. Garnish with cheese. Position in your air fryer's basket. Cook for 4 minutes at 400°F.

4. Serve.

Nutrition:

- Calories: 381
- Carbs: 28 g.
- Protein: 19 g.
- Fat: 18 g.

152. Squash Fritters

Preparation time: 10 minutes

Cooking time: 6 minutes

Servings: 4

Ingredients:

- 3 oz. cream cheese
- 1 egg
- 1/2 tsp. oregano
- Black pepper and a pinch of salt
- 1 yellow summer squash
- 1/3 cup carrot
- 2/3 cup bread crumbs
- 2 tbsp. olive oil

Directions:

1. Mix cream cheese with pepper, salt, egg, oregano, carrot, bread crumbs, and squash in a bowl. Stir.

2. Make medium patties from this mix. Brush them with oil.

3. Arrange squash patties in the air fryer. Cook for 7 minutes at 400°F.

4. Serve.

Nutrition:

- Calories: 151
- Carbs: 25 g.
- Protein: 13 g.

Fat: 11 g.

153. Lunch Shrimp Croquettes

Preparation time: 18 minutes

Cooking time: 10 minutes

Servings: 4

Ingredients:

- 2/3 lb. shrimp
- 1 1/2 cups bread crumbs
- 1 egg
- 2 tbsp. lemon juice
- 3 green onions
- 1/2 tsp. basil
- Salt and black pepper to taste
- 2 tbsp. olive oil

Directions:

1. Mix egg and half of the bread crumbs with lemon juice in a bowl. Stir.
2. Add basil, green onions, pepper, shrimp, and salt. Stir.
3. Mix the rest of the bread crumbs with the oil in a separate bowl. Toss well.
4. Make round balls from the shrimp mix. Dredge in bread crumbs. Put them in a heated air fryer and cook for 8 minutes at 400°F.
5. Serve.

Nutrition:

- Calories: 431
- Carbs: 20 g.
- Protein: 18 g.
- Fat: 6 g.

154. Lunch Special Pancake

Preparation time: 10 minutes

Cooking time: 8 minutes

Servings: 2

Ingredients:

- 1 tbsp. butter
- 3 eggs
- 1/2 cup flour
- 1/2 cup milk
- 1 cup salsa
- 1 cup small shrimp

Directions:

1. Heat air fryer at 400°F. Include 1 tbsp. butter. Melt it.
2. Mix eggs with milk and in a bowl. Whisk. Pour into the air fryer's pan. Cook for 12 minutes at 350°F. Transfer to a plate.

3. Mix salsa with shrimp in a bowl. Stir.
4. Serve.

Nutrition:

- Calories: 97
- Carbs: 8 g.
- Protein: 6 g.

Fat: 3 g.

155. Scallops and Dill

Preparation time: 15 minutes

Cooking time: 10 minutes

Servings: 4

Ingredients:

- 1 lb. sea scallops
- 1 tbsp. lemon juice
- 1 tsp. dill
- 2 tsp. olive oil
- Black pepper and salt

Directions:

1. Mix scallops with oil, dill, pepper, lemon juice, and salt in the air fryer. Close. Cook for 5 minutes at 360°F.
2. Dispose of uncovered ones. Divide dill sauce and scallops on plates.
3. Serve.

Nutrition:

- Calories: 254
- Carbs: 5 g.
- Protein: 11 g.
- Fat: 2 g.

156. Chicken Sandwiches

Preparation time: 20 minutes

Cooking time: 10 minutes

Servings: 4

Ingredients:

- 2 chicken breasts, boneless, skinless
- 1 red onion
- 1 red bell pepper
- 1/2 cup Italian seasoning
- 1/2 tsp. thyme
- 2 cups butter lettuce
- 4 pita pockets
- 1 cup cherry tomatoes
- 1 tbsp. olive oil

Directions:

1. Mix chicken with bell pepper, onion, oil, and Italian seasoning. Toss. Cook for 10 minutes at 380°F.

2. Place chicken mixture into a bowl. Include butter lettuce, cherry tomatoes, and thyme. Toss. Stuff pita pockets with this mix. Serve.

Nutrition:

- Calories: 167
- Carbs: 16 g.
- Protein: 16 g.
- Fat: 1 g.

157. Hot Bacon Sandwiches

Preparation time: 10 minutes

Cooking time: 8 minutes

Servings: 4

Ingredients:

- 1/3 cup BBQ sauce
- 2 tbsp. honey
- 8 bacon slices
- 1 red bell pepper
- 1 yellow bell pepper
- 3 pita pockets
- 1 1/4 cup butter lettuce leaves
- 2 tomatoes

Directions:

1. Mix BBQ with honey with sauce in a bowl. Whisk.
2. Brush all bell peppers and bacon with this mix. Put them in the air fryer. Cook at 350°F for 4 minutes.

3. Stuff pita pockets with lettuce, bacon mix, and tomatoes. Spread the rest of the BBQ sauce and serve for lunch.

Nutrition:

- Calories: 354
- Carbs: 27 g.
- Protein: 25 g.

Fat: 20 g.

158. Tasty Air Fried Cod

Preparation time: 22 minutes

Cooking time: 15 minutes

Servings: 4

Ingredients:

- 2 codfish (7 oz.)
- Sesame oil
- Salt and black pepper
- 1 cup water
- 1 tsp. dark soy sauce
- 4 tbsp. light soy sauce
- 1 tbsp. sugar
- 3 tbsp. olive oil
- 4 ginger slices
- 3 green onions
- 2 tbsp. coriander

Directions:

1. Season fish with pepper, salt, sprinkle sesame oil, rub well and allow for 10 minutes.
2. Add fish to the air fryer. Cook at 356°F for 12 minutes.
3. Heat a pot with the water over medium heat. Add sugar, light and dark soy sauce. Allow simmering. Take off heat.
4. Heat pan with olive oil over medium heat. Add onions and ginger. Cook for a few minutes. Take off heat.
5. Divide fish on plates. Top with ginger and green onions. Drizzle soy sauce mix. Sprinkle coriander and serve.

Nutrition:

- Calories: 182
- Carbs: 23 g.
- Protein: 22 g.
- Fat: 21 g.

159. Delicious Catfish

Preparation time: 10 minutes

Cooking time: 20 minutes

Servings: 4

Ingredients:

- 4 catfish fillets
- Black pepper and salt
- A pinch of sweet paprika
- 1 tbsp. parsley
- 1 tbsp. lemon juice
- 1 tbsp. olive oil

Directions:

1. Season catfish fillets with salt, paprika, pepper, drizzle oil, rub well. Then put in the air fryer basket and cook at 400°F for 20 minutes. Flip the fish after 10 minutes.

2. Share fish on plates. Sprinkle parsley and drizzle some lemon juice over it, serve.

Nutrition:

- Calories: 225
- Carbs: 10 g.
- Protein: 13 g.
- Fat: 18 g.

160. Cod Fillets With Fennel and Grapes Salad

Preparation time: 5 minutes

Cooking time: 20 minutes

Servings: 2

Ingredients:

- 2 black cod fillets
- 1 tbsp. olive oil
- Black pepper and salt
- 1 fennel bulb
- 1 cup grapes
- 1/2 cup pecans

Directions:

1. Sprinkle half of the oil over fish fillets, season with pepper and salt, rub well, place fillets in the air fryer basket. Then cook for 10 minutes at 400°F and put on

the plate.

2. Mix pecans with grapes, fennel, the rest of the oil, salt, and pepper, toss to coat, in a bowl. Add to pan that fits air fryer. Cook at 400°F for 5 minutes.

3. Share cod on plates, add grapes and fennel mix on the side then serve.

Nutrition:

- Calories: 185
- Carbs: 20 g.
- Protein: 13 g.
- Fat: 9 g.

Chapter 3: Sides

161. Cabbage and Radishes Mix

Preparation time: 20 minutes

Cooking time: 15 minutes

Servings: 4

Ingredients:

- 6 cups green cabbage, shredded
- 1/2 cup celery leaves, chopped.
- 1/4 cup green onions, chopped.
- 6 radishes, sliced
- 3 tbsp. olive oil
- 2 tbsp. balsamic vinegar
- 1/2 tsp. hot paprika
- 1 tsp. lemon juice

Directions:

1. In your air fryer's pan, combine all the ingredients and toss well.
2. Introduce the pan in the fryer and cook at 380°F for 15 minutes. Divide between plates and serve as a side dish.

Nutrition:

- Calories: 130
- Fat: 4 g.
- Carbs: 4 g.
- Protein: 7 g.

162. Kale Chips

Preparation time: 10 minutes

Cooking time: 5 minutes

Servings: 4

Ingredients:

- 4 cups kale, stemmed
- 1/2 tsp. salt
- 2 tsp. avocado oil

Directions:

1. Take a large bowl, toss the kale in avocado oil and sprinkle with salt. Place into the air fryer basket.
2. Adjust the temperature to 400°F and set the timer for 5 minutes. Kale will be crispy when done. Serve immediately.

Nutrition:

- Calories: 25
- Protein: 0.5 g.
- Fat: 2.2 g.
- Carbs: 1.1 g.

163. Spinach and Artichokes Sauté

Preparation time: 20 minutes

Cooking time: 15 minutes

Servings: 4

Ingredients:

- 10 oz. artichoke hearts, halved
- 2 cups baby spinach
- 3 garlic cloves
- 1/4 cup veggie stock
- 2 tsp. lime juice
- Salt and black pepper to taste

Directions:

1. In a pan that fits your air fryer, mix all the ingredients, toss, introduce in the fryer and cook at 370°F for 15 minutes
2. Divide between plates and serve as a side dish.

Nutrition:

- Calories: 209
- Fat: 6 g.
- Carbs: 4 g.
- Protein: 8 g.

164. Balsamic Cabbage

Preparation time: 10 minutes

Cooking time: 15 minutes

Servings: 4

Ingredients:

- 6 cups red cabbage, shredded
- 4 garlic cloves, minced
- 1 tbsp. olive oil
- 1 tbsp. balsamic vinegar
- Salt and black pepper to taste.

Directions:

1. In a pan that fits the air fryer, combine all the ingredients, toss, introduce the pan in the air fryer and cook at 380°F for 15 minutes
2. Divide between plates and serve as a side dish.

Nutrition:

- Calories: 151
- Fat: 2 g.
- Carbs: 5 g.
- Protein: 5 g.

165. Roasted Tomatoes

Preparation time: 5 minutes

Cooking time: 15 minutes

Servings: 4

Ingredients:

- 4 tomatoes, halved
- 1/2 cup Parmesan cheese, grated
- 1 tbsp. basil, chopped.
- 1/2 tsp. onion powder
- 1/2 tsp. oregano, dried
- 1/2 tsp. smoked paprika
- 1/2 tsp. garlic powder
- Cooking spray

Directions:

1. Take a bowl and mix all the ingredients except the cooking spray

and the parmesan.

2. Arrange the tomatoes in your air fryer's pan, sprinkle the Parmesan cheese on top, and grease with cooking spray

3. Cook at 370°F for 15 minutes, divide between plates and serve.

Nutrition:

- Calories: 200
- Fat: 7 g.
- Carbs: 4 g.

Protein: 6 g.

166. Broccoli Gratin

Preparation time: 10 minutes

Cooking time: 30 minutes

Smart Points: 1

Servings: 6

Ingredients:

- 2 cups broccoli florets
- 1 tsp. salt
- 1 tsp. chili flakes
- 3 eggs, whisked
- 2 oz. Swiss cheese, grated
- 1 onion, diced
- 1 cup heavy cream

Directions:

1. Whisk together chili flakes, salt, eggs, and heavy cream.
2. Add the diced onion to the mixture and stir gently.
3. After this, place broccoli florets into the non-sticky gratin mold.

4. Sprinkle the vegetables with Swiss cheese and heavy cream mixture.

5. Cover the gratin with foil and secure the edges.

6. Cook gratin for 30 minutes in the preheated to 360°F oven.

7. When the time is over, discard the foil and check if the broccoli is tender.

8. Chill the gratin little and transfer on the serving plates.

Nutrition:

- Calories: 154
- Fat: 12.3 g.
- Carbs: 5 g.
- Protein: 6.8 g.

167. Coleslaw

Preparation time: 10 minutes

Cooking time: 2 minutes

Servings: 2

Ingredients:

- 1 cup white cabbage
- 1 tbsp. mayonnaise
- 1/2 tsp. ground black pepper
- 1/2 tsp. salt

Directions:

1. Shred the white cabbage and place it in the big salad bowl.
2. Sprinkle it with ground black pepper and salt.
3. Add mayonnaise and mix up the coleslaw very carefully.

Nutrition:

- **Calories:** 39
- Fat: 2.5 g.
- Carbs: 4.1 g.
- Protein: 0.6 g.

168. Roasted Zucchini and Pumpkin Cubes

Preparation time: 10 minutes

Cooking time: 20 minutes

Servings: 3

Ingredients:

- 1 cup zucchini, chopped
- 1/4 cup pumpkin, chopped
- 1/4 tsp. thyme
- 1/2 tsp. coriander, ground
- 1/2 tsp. cloves, ground
- 1 tbsp. olive oil
- 1/2 tsp. butter
- 1 tsp. dried dill

Directions:

1. Toss butter in the skillet and melt it.
2. Add olive oil,

zucchini, and pumpkin.

3. Start to roast vegetables over medium heat for 5 minutes.

4. Then sprinkle them with thyme, ground coriander, ground cloves, and dried dill.

5. Mix up well and close the lid.

6. Cook the vegetables on low heat for 15 minutes.

Nutrition:

- Calories: 66
- Fat: 5.5 g.
- Carbs: 3.4 g.
- Protein: 0.8 g.

169. Chile Casserole

Preparation time: 15 minutes

Cooking time: 15 minutes

Servings: 4

Ingredients:

- 1 cup chili peppers, green, raw
- 1 tsp. olive oil
- 3 oz. cheddar cheese, shredded
- 1 tsp. butter
- 2 eggs, whisked
- 1/4 cup heavy cream
- 1/2 tsp. salt

Directions:

1. Preheat the grill well and place chili peppers on it.

2. Grill the chili peppers for 5 minutes. Stir them from time to time.

3. Then chill the peppers a little and peel them. Remove the seeds.

4. Place the peppers in the casserole tray.

5. Add butter and sprinkle with salt.

6. In the separated bowl, mix up together heavy cream, whisked eggs, and cheese.

7. Pour the liquid over the chili peppers and transfer casserole in the reheated to the 365°F oven.

8. Cook casserole for 10 minutes.

Nutrition:

- Calories: 169
- Fat: 14.2 g.
- Carbs: 2.4 g.
- Protein: 8.6 g.

170. Pickled Jalapeño

Preparation time: 10 minutes

Cooking time: 10 minutes

Servings: 6

Ingredients:

- 6 jalapeño peppers
- 1/4 cup apple cider vinegar
- 1/3 cup water
- 1/4 tsp. peppercorns
- 1 garlic clove, peeled
- 1/2 tsp. coriander, ground
- 1 tsp cinnamon

Directions:

1. Pour apple cider vinegar into the saucepan.
2. Add water, peppercorns, and bring the liquid to boil.
3. Wash the jalapeño peppers and slice them.
4. Put the sliced jalapeños in the glass jar.
5. Add ground cinnamon and garlic clove.
6. After this, add boiled apple cider vinegar liquid and close the lid.
7. Marinate the jalapeños as a minimum for 1 hour.

Nutrition:

- Calories: 9
- Fat: 0.2 g.
- Carbs: 1.4 g.
- Protein: 0.2 g.

171. Naan

Preparation time: 10 minutes

Cooking time: 4 minutes

Servings: 2

Ingredients:

- 1 tbsp. butter
- 1 tbsp. almond flour
- 3/4 tsp. baking powder
- 1/4 tsp. lemon juice
- 1 tsp. coconut oil, softened
- 1 tsp. psyllium husk powder

Directions:

1. In the mixing bowl, mix up together almond flour, baking powder, lemon juice, coconut oil, and psyllium husk powder.
2. Knead the dough and cut it into 2

pieces.

3. Roll up the dough pieces to get a naan bread shape.

4. Toss butter in the skillet and bring it to boil.

5. Place naan bread in the preheated butter and roast for 1 minute from each side.

6. The time of cooking depends on the naan size.

7. It is recommended to serve naan bread warm.

Nutrition:

- Calories: 157
- Fat: 15.1 g.
- Fiber: 2.7 g.
- Carbs: 5.2 g.
- Protein: 3.1 g.

172. Sautéed Tomato Cabbage

Preparation time: 10 minutes

Cooking time: 35 minutes

Servings: 4

Ingredients:

- 1 tbsp. tomato paste
- 1 bell pepper, chopped
- 1/2 oz. celery, grated
- 2 cups white cabbage, shredded
- 1 tbsp. butter
- 1 tbsp. dried oregano
- 1/3 cup water
- 1/4 cup coconut cream
- 1 tsp. salt

Directions:

1. Mix up together tomato paste, coconut cream, and water.

2. Pour the liquid into the saucepan.

3. Add bell pepper, grated celery, white cabbage, butter, and dried oregano.

4. Sprinkle the mixture with salt and mix up gently.

5. Close the lid and sauté cabbage for 35 minutes over medium-low heat.

Nutrition:

- Calories: 86
- Fat: 6.7 g.
- Fiber: 2.3 g.
- Carbs: 6.7 g.
- Protein: 1.4 g.

173. Tender Radicchio

Preparation time: 10 minutes

Cooking time: 8 minutes

Servings: 4

Ingredients:

- 8 oz. radicchio
- 1 tsp. canola oil
- 1/2 tsp. apple cider vinegar
- 1/4 cup heavy cream
- 1 tsp. garlic, minced
- 1 tsp. dried dill

Directions:

1. Slice the radicchio into 4 slices.
2. Line the baking dish with parchment and put sliced radicchio on it.
3. Sprinkle the vegetables with canola oil, apple cider vinegar, and dried dill.
4. Bake radicchio in the preheated oven to 360°F for 8 minutes.
5. Meanwhile, whisk together heavy cream with minced garlic.
6. Transfer the cooked radicchio to the serving plates and sprinkle with minced heavy cream mixture.

Nutrition:

- Calories: 43
- Fat: 4 g.
- Fiber: 0.2 g.
- Carbs: 1.5 g.
- Protein: 0.5 g.

174. Green Salad With Walnuts

Preparation time: 10 minutes

Cooking time: 0 minutes

Servings: 2

Ingredients:

- 1 cup arugula
- 2 tbsp. walnuts, chopped
- 1 tbsp. avocado oil
- 1/2 tsp. sesame seeds
- 1 tsp. lemon juice
- 1/2 tsp. lemon zest, grated
- 1 tomato, chopped

Directions:

1. Chop arugula roughly and put it in the salad bowl.
2. Add walnuts, sesame seeds, and chopped tomato.
3. Make the dressing: mix up together

avocado oil, sesame seeds, lemon juice, and grated lemon zest.

4. Pour the dressing over salad and shake it gently.

Nutrition:

- Calories: 71
- Fat: 6 g.
- Carbs: 3.1 g.

Protein: 2.7 g.

175. Jicama Slaw

Preparation time: 10 minutes

Cooking time: 0 minutes

Servings: 4

Ingredients:

- 1 cup jicama, julienned
- 1 bell pepper, julienned
- 1 onion, sliced
- 1 tbsp. fresh cilantro, chopped
- 1/2 carrot, julienned
- 2 tbsp. olive oil
- 1 tsp. apple cider vinegar
- 1/2 tsp. cayenne pepper
- 1/2 tsp. salt
- 1/3 cup red cabbage, shredded
- 1/4 tsp. liquid stevia

Directions:

1. In the mixing bowl, combine jicama, bell pepper, sliced onion, fresh cilantro, carrot, olive oil, apple cider vinegar, and liquid stevia. Mix up the salad mixture.

2. Then sprinkle slaw with cayenne pepper, salt, and red cabbage.

3. Mix up the cooked slaw one more time and transfer on the serving plates.

Nutrition:

- Calories: 98
- Fat: 7.2 g.
- Fiber: 2.9 g.
- Carbs: 8.7 g.
- Protein: 1 g.

176. Peanut Slaw

Preparation time: 10 minutes

Cooking time: 2 minutes

Servings: 4

Ingredients:

- 1 cup white cabbage
- 1 tsp. peanut butter
- 1 tsp. lemon juice
- 1 tbsp. peanuts, chopped
- 1/2 tsp. black pepper, ground
- 1 tbsp. canola oil
- 1 oz. scallions, chopped
- 1 tsp. sriracha
- 1/4 cup fresh parsley, chopped

Directions:

1. Shred the white cabbage and transfer it to the mixing bowl.
2. Add peanuts, chopped fresh parsley, and scallions.
3. Then make the slaw dressing: whisk together peanut butter, lemon juice, ground black pepper, and canola oil.
4. Pour the dressing over the white cabbage mixture.
5. Add sriracha and chopped parsley.
6. Shake the slaw gently and transfer it to the serving plates.

Nutrition:

- Calories: 62
- Fat: 5.4 g.
- Fiber: 1.1 g.
- Carbs: 2.9 g.
- Protein: 1.4 g.

177. White Mushroom Sauté

Preparation time: 15 minutes

Cooking time: 25 minutes

Servings: 6

Ingredients:

- 10 oz. white mushrooms, chopped
- 1 carrot, chopped
- 1 onion, chopped
- 1/2 cup of water
- 3 tbsp. coconut cream
- 1 tsp. salt
- 1/2 tsp. turmeric
- 1 tsp. chili flakes
- 1 tsp. coconut oil
- 1/2 tsp. Italian seasoning

Directions:

1. In the saucepan, combine white

mushrooms, chopped carrot, onion, and mix up gently.

2. Sprinkle the vegetables with coconut cream, salt, turmeric, chili flakes, and coconut oil.

3. Add Italian seasoning and mix up well.

4. Cook the mixture over high heat for 5 minutes.

5. Stir the vegetables constantly.

6. Then add water and close the lid.

7. Sauté the meal for 20 minutes over medium heat.

8. Then let sauté rest for 10 minutes before serving.

Nutrition:

- Calories: 47
- Fat: 2.9 g.
- Fiber: 1.3 g.
- Carbs: 4.9 g.
- Protein: 1.9 g.

178. Caesar Salad

Preparation time: 15 minutes

Cooking time: 0 minutes

Servings: 5

Ingredients:

- 1 tbsp. capers
- 2 cups lettuce, chopped
- 1 tsp. walnuts, chopped
- 1 tsp. mustard
- 2 tbsp. canola oil
- 1 tsp. lime juice
- 1/2 tsp. white pepper
- 1 avocado, peeled, chopped

Directions:

1. Place walnuts, mustard, canola oil, lime juice, white pepper, and avocado in the blender.

2. Blend the mixture until smooth.
3. After this, transfer the avocado smooth mixture into the salad bowl.
4. Add chopped lettuce.
5. Sprinkle the salad with capers. Don't stir the salad before serving.

Nutrition:

- Calories: 142
- Fat: 14 g.
- Fiber: 3.1 g.
- Carbs: 4.6 g.
- Protein: 1.2 g.

179. Cranberry Relish

Preparation time: 5 minutes

Cooking time: 2 minutes

Servings: 6

Ingredients:

- 1 cup cranberries
- 1 orange, peeled, chopped
- 1 tbsp. erythritol
- 3 tbsp. lemon juice

Directions:

1. Place cranberries and chopped orange in the blender.
2. Add erythritol and lemon juice.
3. Pulse the ingredients for 1 minute.
4. Transfer the relish to the serving plate.
5. The side dish tastes the best with meat meals.

Nutrition:

- Calories: 26
- Fat: 0.1 g.
- Fiber: 1.4 g.
- Carbs: 5.4 g.
- Protein: 0.4 g.

180. Vegetable Tots

Preparation time: 15 minutes

Cooking time: 12 minutes

Servings: 8

Ingredients:

- 2 cups cauliflower
- 1 cup broccoli
- 4 eggs
- 1/3 cup almond flour
- 3 oz. Parmesan, grated
- 1 tsp. coriander, ground
- 1/2 tsp. thyme, ground
- 1 tsp. olive oil

Directions:

1. Grate the broccoli and cauliflower.
2. Transfer the grated vegetables to the cheesecloth and squeeze the liquid.
3. Then put vegetables in the mixing bowl.
4. Beat the eggs in the mixture and add grated cheese.
5. Then add almond flour, ground coriander, ground thyme, and mix it up.
6. Line the baking tray with baking paper and brush with 1 tsp. of olive oil.
7. Make the medium size tots from the vegetable mixture and put them in the baking tray.
8. Bake the vegetable tots for 12 minutes at 365°F.
9. Chill the meal to room temperature before serving.

Nutrition:

- Calories: 88
- Fat: 5.7 g.
- Fiber: 1.1 g.
- Carbs: 2.9 g.
- Protein: 7.3 g.

181. Air Fried Pickles

Preparation time: 15 minutes

Cooking time: 5 minutes

Servings: 4

Ingredients:

- 1/3 cup almond flour, blanched finely ground
- 1 cup pickles, sliced
- 1 egg, large
- 1 tbsp. coconut flour.
- 1/4 tsp. garlic powder.
- 1 tsp. chili powder

Directions:

1. Whisk coconut flour, almond flour, chili powder, and garlic powder together in a medium bowl. Whisk egg in a small bowl.

2. Pat each pickle with a paper towel and dip it into the egg. Then dredge in the flour mixture. Place pickles into the air fryer basket.

3. Adjust the temperature to 400°F and set the timer for 5 minutes. Flip the pickles halfway through the cooking time.

Nutrition:

- Calories: 85
- Protein: 3 g.
- Fiber: 3 g.
- Fat: 1 g.
- Carbs: 6 g.

182. Air Fried Green Tomatoes

Preparation time: 17 minutes

Cooking time: 7 minutes

Servings: 4

Ingredients:

- 2 medium green tomatoes
- 1/3 cup Parmesan cheese, grated
- 1/4 cup almond flour, blanched, finely ground
- 1 egg, large

Directions:

1. Slice tomatoes into 1/2-inch-thick slices. Take a medium bowl, whisk the egg. Take a large bowl, mix the almond flour and Parmesan cheese.

2. Dip each tomato slice into the egg, then dredge in the almond flour mixture. Place the slices into the air fryer basket.

3. Adjust the temperature to 400°F and set the timer for 7 minutes. Flip the slices halfway through the cooking time. Serve immediately.

Nutrition:

- Calories: 106
- Protein: 2 g.
- Fiber: 4 g.
- Fat: 7 g.
- Carbs: 9 g.

183. Green Beans

Preparation time: 25 minutes

Cooking time: 20 minutes

Servings: 4

Ingredients:

- 6 cups green beans, trimmed
- 1 tbsp. hot paprika
- 2 tbsp. olive oil
- A pinch of salt and black pepper

Directions:

1. Take a bowl and mix the green beans with the other ingredients, toss, put them in the air fryer's basket and cook at 370°F for 20 minutes.

2. Divide between plates and serve as a side dish.

Nutrition:

- Calories: 120
- Fat: 5 g.
- Fiber: 1 g.
- Carbs: 4 g.
- Protein: 2 g.

184. Chives Radishes

Preparation time: 20 minutes

Cooking time: 15 minutes

Servings: 4

Ingredients:

- 20 radishes, halved
- 2 tbsp. olive oil
- 1 tbsp. garlic, minced
- 1 tsp. chives, chopped.
- Salt and black pepper to taste.

Directions:

1. In your air fryer's pan, combine all the ingredients and toss.
2. Introduce the pan in the machine and cook at 370°F for 15 minutes.
3. Divide between plates and serve as a side dish.

Nutrition:

- Calories: 160
- Fat: 2 g.
- Fiber: 3 g.
- Carbs: 4 g.
- Protein: 6 g.

185. Kale and Pine Nuts

Preparation time: 20 minutes

Cooking time: 15 minutes

Servings: 4

Ingredients:

- 10 cups kale, torn
- 1/3 cup pine nuts
- 2 tbsp. lemon zest, grated
- 1 tbsp. lemon juice
- 2 tbsp. olive oil
- Salt and black pepper to taste.

Directions:

1. In a pan that fits the air fryer, combine all the ingredients, toss, introduce the pan in the machine and cook at 380°F for 15 minutes.
2. Divide between plates and serve as a side dish.

Nutrition:

- Calories: 121
- Fat: 9 g.
- Fiber: 2 g.
- Carbs: 4 g.
- Protein: 5 g.

186. Turmeric Mushroom

Preparation time: 20 minutes

Cooking time: 15 minutes

Servings: 4

Ingredients:

- 1 lb. brown mushrooms
- 4 garlic cloves, minced
- 1/4 tsp. cinnamon powder
- 1 tsp. olive oil
- 1/2 tsp. turmeric powder
- Salt and black pepper to taste.

Directions:

1. In a bowl, combine all the ingredients and toss.
2. Put the mushrooms in your air fryer's basket and cook at 370°F for 15 minutes.
3. Divide the mix between plates and serve as a side dish.

Nutrition:

- Calories: 208
- Fat: 7 g.
- Fiber: 3 g.
- Carbs: 5 g.
- Protein: 7 g.

187. Cheesy Garlic Biscuits

Preparation time: 17 minutes

Cooking time: 12 minutes

Servings: 4

Ingredients:

- 1 large egg
- 1 scallion, sliced
- 1/4 cup unsalted butter, melted and divided
- 1/2 cup cheddar cheese, shredded, sharp
- 1/3cup coconut flour
- 1/2 tsp. baking powder
- 1/2 tsp. garlic powder

Directions:

1. Take a large bowl, mix coconut flour, baking powder, and garlic powder.
2. Stir in egg, half of the melted butter, cheddar cheese, and scallions. Pour the mixture into a 6-inch round baking pan. Place into the air fryer basket.
3. Adjust the temperature to 320°F and set the timer for 12 minutes.
4. To serve, remove from pan and allow to fully cool. Slice into four pieces and pour the remaining melted butter over each.

Nutrition:

- Calories: 218
- Protein: 2 g.
- Fiber: 4 g.
- Fat: 19 g.
- Carbs: 8 g.

188. Jicama Fries

Preparation time: 10 minutes

Cooking time: 20 minutes

Servings: 4

Ingredients:

- 1 small jicama, peeled
- 1/4 tsp. onion powder
- 3/4tsp. chili powder
- 1/4 tsp. black pepper, ground
- 1/4 tsp. garlic powder

Directions:

1. Cut jicama into matchstick-sized pieces.
2. Place pieces into a small bowl and sprinkle with remaining ingredients. Place the fries into the air

fryer basket.

3. Adjust the temperature to 350°F and set the timer for 20 minutes. Toss the basket 2 or 3 times during cooking. Serve warm.

Nutrition:

- Calories: 37
- Protein: 8 g.
- Fiber: 7 g.
- Fat: 1 g.
- Carbs: 7 g.

189. Bok Choy and Butter Sauce

Preparation time: 20 minutes

Cooking time: 15 minutes

Servings: 4

Ingredients:

- 2 bok choy heads, trimmed and cut into strips
- 1 tbsp. butter, melted
- 2 tbsp. chicken stock
- 1 tsp. lemon juice
- 1 tbsp. olive oil
- A pinch of salt and black pepper

Directions:

1. In a pan that fits your air fryer, mix all the ingredients, toss, introduce the pan in the air fryer and cook at 380°F for 15 minutes.
2. Divide between plates and serve as a side dish.

Nutrition:

- Calories: 141
- Fat: 3 g.
- Fiber: 2 g.
- Carbs: 4 g.
- Protein: 3 g.

190. Roasted Garlic

Preparation time: 25 minutes

Cooking time: 20 minutes

Servings: 12

Ingredients:

- 1 medium head garlic
- 2 tsp. avocado oil

Directions:

1. Remove any hanging excess peel from the garlic but leave the cloves covered. Cut off 1/4 of the head of garlic, exposing the tips of the cloves.
2. Drizzle with avocado oil. Place the garlic head into a small sheet of aluminum foil, completely enclosing it. Place it into the air fryer basket. Adjust the temperature to 400°F and set the timer for 20 minutes. If your garlic head is a bit smaller, check it after 15 minutes.
3. When done, garlic should be golden brown and very soft.
4. To serve, cloves should pop out and easily be spread or sliced. Store in an airtight container in the refrigerator for up to 5 days.
5. You may also freeze individual cloves on a baking sheet, then store them together in a freezer-safe storage bag once frozen.

Nutrition:

- Calories: 11
- Protein: 2 g.
- Fiber: 1 g.
- Fat: 7 g.
- Carbs: 0 g.

191. Coriander Artichokes

Preparation time: 20 minutes

Cooking time: 15 minutes

Servings: 4

Ingredients:

- 12 oz. artichoke hearts
- 1 tbsp. lemon juice
- 1 tsp. coriander, ground
- 1/2 tsp. cumin seeds
- 1/2 tsp. olive oil
- Salt and black pepper to taste.

Directions:

1. In a pan that fits your air fryer, mix all the ingredients, toss, introduce the pan in the fryer and cook at 370°F for 15 minutes.
2. Divide the mix between plates and serve as a side dish.

Nutrition:

- Calories: 200
- Fat: 7 g.
- Fiber: 2 g.
- Carbs: 5 g.
- Protein: 8 g.

192. Herbed Radish Sauté

Preparation time: 20 minutes

Cooking time: 15 minutes

Servings: 4

Ingredients:

- 2 bunches red radishes; halved
- 2 tbsp. parsley; chopped.
- 2 tbsp. balsamic vinegar
- 1 tbsp. olive oil
- Salt and black pepper to taste.

Directions:

1. Take a bowl and mix the radishes with the remaining ingredients except for the parsley, toss and put them in your air fryer's basket.
2. Cook at 400°F for

15 minutes, divide between plates, sprinkle the parsley on top, and serve as a side dish.

Nutrition:

- Calories: 180
- Fat: 4 g.
- Fiber: 2 g.
- Carbs: 3 g.
- Protein: 5 g.

193. Mexican Style Cauliflower Bake

Preparation time: 25 minutes

Cooking time: 20–30 minutes

Servings: 4

Ingredients:

- 2 cups cauliflower florets, roughly chopped
- 1 red chili pepper, chopped
- 2 tomatoes, cubed
- 1 avocado, peeled, pitted, and sliced
- 4 garlic cloves, minced
- 1 tbsp. coriander, chopped
- 1 tbsp. lime juice
- 1 tbsp. olive oil
- 1 tsp. cumin powder
- 1/2 tsp. chili powder
- Salt and black pepper to taste.

Directions:

1. In a pan that fits the air fryer, combine the cauliflower with the other ingredients except for the coriander, avocado, and lime juice, toss, introduce the pan in the machine and cook at 380°F for 20 minutes.
2. Divide between plates, top each serving with coriander, avocado, and lime juice. Serve as a side dish.

Nutrition:

- Calories: 187
- Fat: 8 g.
- Fiber: 2 g.
- Carbs: 5 g.

- Protein: 7 g.

194. Curry Cabbage

Preparation time: 25 minutes

Cooking time: 20-30 minutes

Servings: 4

Ingredients:

- 30 oz. green cabbage, shredded
- 3 tbsp. coconut oil, melted
- 1 tbsp. red curry paste
- A pinch of salt and black pepper

Directions:

1. In a pan that fits the air fryer, combine the cabbage with the rest of the ingredients, toss, introduce the pan in the machine and cook at 380°F for 20 minutes.

2. Divide between plates and serve as a side dish.

Nutrition:

- Calories: 180
- Fat: 14 g.
- Fiber: 4 g.
- Carbs: 6 g.
- Protein: 8 g.

195. Brussels Sprouts

Preparation time: 15 minutes

Cooking time: 20–30 minutes

Servings: 4

Ingredients:

- 1 lb. Brussels sprouts
- 1 tbsp. unsalted butter, melted.
- 1 tbsp. coconut oil

Directions:

1. Remove all loose leaves from Brussels sprouts and cut each in half.
2. Drizzle sprouts with coconut oil and place them into the air fryer basket.
3. Adjust the temperature to 400°F and set the timer for 10 minutes.
4. You may want to gently stir halfway through the cooking time, depending on how they are beginning to brown.
5. When completely cooked, they should be tender with darker caramelized spots.
6. Remove from fryer basket and drizzle with melted butter.
7. Serve immediately.

Nutrition:

- Calories: 90
- Protein: 2.9 g.
- Fiber: 3.2 g.
- Fat: 6.1 g.
- Carbs: 7.5 g.

196. Kale and Walnuts

Preparation time: 20 Minutes

Cooking time: 20–30 minutes

Servings: 4

Ingredients:

- 3 garlic cloves
- 10 cups kale, roughly chopped
- 1/3 cup parmesan, grated
- 1/2 cup almond milk
- 1/4 cup walnuts, chopped
- 1 tbsp. butter, melted
- 1/4 tsp. nutmeg, ground
- Salt and black pepper to taste

Directions:

1. In a pan that fits the air fryer, combine all

the ingredients, toss, introduce the pan in the machine and cook at 360°F for 15 minutes.

2. Divide between plates and serve.

Nutrition:

- Calories: 160
- Fat: 7 g.
- Fiber: 2 g.
- Carbs: 4 g.

Protein: 5 g.

197. Pesto Zucchini Pasta

Preparation time: 20 minutes

Cooking time: 20–30 minutes

Servings: 4

Ingredients:

- 4 oz. Mozzarella, shredded
- 2 cups zucchinis, cut with a spiralizer
- 1/2 cup coconut cream
- 1/4 cup basil pesto
- 1 tbsp. olive oil
- Salt and black pepper to taste

Directions:

1. In a pan that fits your air fryer, mix the zucchini noodles with the pesto and the rest of the ingredients, toss, introduce the pan in the fryer and cook at 370°F for 15 minutes.

2. Divide between plates and serve as a side dish.

Nutrition:

- Calories: 200
- Fat: 8 g.
- Fiber: 2 g.
- Carbs: 4 g.
- Protein: 10 g.

198. Kale and Cauliflower Mash

Preparation time: 25 minutes

Cooking time: 20–30 minutes

Servings: 4

Ingredients:

- 1 cauliflower head, florets separated
- 4 garlic cloves, minced
- 3 cups kale, chopped
- 2 scallions, chopped
- 1/3 cup coconut cream
- 1 tbsp. parsley, chopped
- 4 tsp. butter; melted
- A pinch of salt and black pepper

Directions:

1. In a pan that fits the air fryer, combine the cauliflower with the butter, garlic, scallions, salt, pepper, and the cream, toss, introduce the pan in the machine and cook at 380°F for 20 minutes.
2. Mash the mix well, add the remaining ingredients, whisk, divide between plates and serve.

Nutrition:

- Calories: 198
- Fat: 9 g.
- Fiber: 2 g.
- Carbs: 6 g.
- Protein: 8 g.

199. Zucchini Gratin

Preparation time: 30 minutes

Cooking time: 20–30 minutes

Servings: 4

Ingredients:

- 4 cups zucchinis, sliced
- 1 1/2 cups mozzarella, shredded
- 1/2 cup coconut cream
- 1/2 tbsp. parsley, chopped.
- 2 tbsp. butter, melted
- 1/2 tsp. garlic powder

Directions:

1. In a baking pan that fits the air fryer, mix all the ingredients except for the

mozzarella and the parsley and toss.

2. Sprinkle the mozzarella and parsley, introduce in the air fryer and cook at 370°F for 25 minutes.

3. Divide between plates and serve as a side dish.

Nutrition:

- Calories: 220
- Fat: 14 g.
- Fiber: 2 g.
- Carbs: 5 g.

Protein: 9 g.

200. Spiced Cauliflower

Preparation time: 20 minutes

Cooking time: 20-30 minutes

Servings: 4

Ingredients:

- 1 cauliflower head, florets separated
- 1 tbsp. olive oil
- 1 tbsp. butter, melted
- 1/4 tsp. cinnamon powder
- 1/4 tsp. cloves, ground
- 1/4 tsp. turmeric powder
- 1/2 tsp. cumin, ground
- A pinch of salt and black pepper

Directions:

1. Take a bowl and mix cauliflower florets with the rest of the ingredients and toss.

2. Put the cauliflower in your air fryer's basket and cook at 390°F for 15 minutes.

3. Divide between plates and serve as a side dish.

Nutrition:

- Calories: 182
- Fat: 8 g.
- Fiber: 2 g.
- Carbs: 4 g.

Protein: 8 g.

201. Cauliflower and Artichokes

Preparation time: 25 minutes

Cooking time: 20–30 minutes

Servings: 4

Ingredients:

- 2 garlic cloves, minced
- 1/2 cup chicken stock
- 1 cup cauliflower florets
- 15 oz. canned artichoke hearts, chopped.
- 1 1/2 tbsp. parsley, chopped.
- 1 tbsp. olive oil
- 1 tbsp. Parmesan cheese, grated
- Salt and black pepper to taste

Directions:

1. In a pan that fits your air fryer, mix all the ingredients except for the Parmesan cheese and toss.
2. Sprinkle the parmesan on top, introduce the pan in the air fryer and cook at 380°F for 20 minutes.
3. Divide between plates and serve as a side dish.

Nutrition:

- Calories: 195
- Fat: 6 g.
- Fiber: 2 g.
- Carbs: 4 g.
- Protein: 8 g.

202. Zucchini Noodles and Sauce

Preparation time: 20 minutes

Cooking time: 20–30 minutes

Servings: 4

Ingredients:

- 4 zucchinis, cut with a spiralizer
- 1 1/2 cups tomatoes, crushed
- 4 garlic cloves, minced
- 1/4 cup green onions, chopped.
- 1 tbsp. olive oil
- 1 tbsp. basil,

chopped.
- Salt and black pepper to taste.

Directions:

1. In a pan that fits your air fryer, mix zucchini noodles with the other ingredients, toss, introduce in the fryer and cook at 380°F for 15 minutes.
2. Divide between plates and serve as a side dish.

Nutrition:

- Calories: 194
- Fat: 7 g.
- Fiber: 2 g.
- Carbs: 4 g.
- Protein: 9 g.

203. Broccoli Mash

Preparation time: 25 minutes

Cooking time: 20–30 minutes

Servings: 4

Ingredients:

- 20 oz. broccoli florets
- 3 oz. butter; melted
- 1 garlic clove, minced
- 4 tbsp. basil, chopped.
- A drizzle of olive oil
- A pinch of salt and black pepper

Directions:

1. Take a bowl and mix the broccoli with the oil, salt, and pepper, toss and transfer to your air fryer's basket.
2. Cook at 380°F for 20 minutes, cool the broccoli down and put it in a blender.
3. Add the rest of the ingredients, pulse, divide the mash between plates and serve as a side dish.

Nutrition:

- Calories: 200
- Fat: 14 g.
- Fiber: 3 g.
- Carbs: 6 g.

Protein: 7 g.

204. Cream Cheese Zucchini

Preparation time: 20 minutes

Cooking time: 20-30 minutes

Servings: 4

Ingredients:

- 1 lb. zucchinis, cut into wedges
- 1 green onion, sliced
- 1 cup cream cheese, soft
- 1 tbsp. butter, melted
- 2 tbsp. basil, chopped.
- 1 tsp. garlic powder
- A pinch of salt and black pepper

Directions:

1. In a pan that fits your air fryer, mix the zucchinis with all the other ingredients, toss, introduce in the air fryer and cook at 370°F for 15 minutes.
2. Divide between plates and serve as a side dish.

Nutrition:

- Calories: 129
- Fat: 6 g.
- Fiber: 2 g.
- Carbs: 5 g.
- Protein: 8 g.

205. Parmesan Zucchini Rounds

Preparation time: 25 minutes

Cooking time: 20–30 minutes

Servings: 4

Ingredients:

- 4 zucchinis, sliced
- 1 1/2 cups Parmesan cheese, grated
- 1/4 cup parsley; chopped.
- 1 egg, whisked
- 1 egg white, whisked
- 1/2 tsp. garlic powder
- Cooking spray

Directions:

1. Take a bowl and mix the egg with egg whites, Parmesan

cheese, parsley, garlic powder, and whisk.

2. Dredge each zucchini slice in this mix, place them all in your air fryer's basket, grease them with cooking spray and cook at 370°F for 20 minutes.

3. Divide between plates and serve as a side dish.

Nutrition:

- Calories: 183
- Fat: 6 g.
- Fiber: 2 g.
- Carbs: 3 g.

Protein: 8 g.

206. Zucchini Spaghetti

Preparation time: 20 minutes

Cooking time: 20–30 minutes

Servings: 4

Ingredients:

- 1 lb. Zucchinis, cut with a spiralizer
- 1 cup parmesan, grated
- 1/4 cup parsley, chopped
- 1/4 cup olive oil
- 6 garlic cloves, minced
- 1/2 tsp. red pepper flakes
- Salt and black pepper to taste

Directions:

1. In a pan that fits your air fryer, mix all the ingredients, toss, introduce in the fryer and cook at 370°F for 15 minutes.

2. Divide between plates and serve as a side dish.

Nutrition:

- Calories: 200
- Fat: 6 g.
- Fiber: 3 g.
- Carbs: 4 g.
- Protein: 5 g.

207. Parmesan Sweet Potato Casserole

Preparation time: 15 minutes

Cooking time: 35 minutes

Servings: 2

Ingredients:

- 2 sweet potatoes, peeled
- 1/2 yellow onion, sliced
- 1/2 cup cream
- 1/4 cup spinach
- 2 oz. Parmesan cheese, shredded
- 1/2 tsp. salt
- 1 tomato
- 1 tsp. olive oil

Directions:

1. Chop the sweet potatoes, the tomato, and the spinach.
2. Spray the air fryer tray with olive oil.
3. Then place on the layer of the chopped sweet potato.
4. Add the layer of the sliced onion.
5. After this, sprinkle the sliced onion with the chopped spinach and tomatoes.
6. Sprinkle the casserole with salt and shredded cheese. Pour the cream.
7. Preheat the air fryer to 390°F. Cover the air fryer tray with foil. Cook the casserole for 35 minutes.
8. When the casserole is cooked—serve it. Enjoy!

Nutrition:

- Calories: 93
- Fat: 1.8 g.
- Fiber: 3.4 g.
- Carbs: 20.3 g.
- Protein: 1.8 g.

208. Spicy Zucchini Slices

Preparation time: 10 minutes

Cooking time: 6 minutes

Servings: 2

Ingredients:

- 1 tsp. cornstarch
- 1 zucchini
- 1/2 tsp. chili flakes
- 1 tbsp. flour
- 1 egg
- 1/4 tsp. salt

Directions:

1. Slice the zucchini and sprinkle with chili flakes and salt.
2. Crack the egg into the bowl and whisk it.
3. Dip the zucchini slices into the whisked egg.
4. Combine cornstarch with the flour. Stir it.
5. Coat the zucchini slices with the cornstarch mixture.
6. Preheat the air fryer to 400°F.
7. Place the zucchini slices in the air fryer tray.
8. Cook the zucchini slices for 4 minutes.
9. After this, flip the slices to another side and cook for 2 minutes more.
10. Serve the zucchini slices hot. Enjoy!

Nutrition:

- Calories: 67
- Fat: 2.4 g.
- Fiber: 1.2 g.
- Carbs: 7.7 g.
- Protein: 4.4 g.

209. Cheddar Potato Gratin

Preparation time: 15 minutes

Cooking time: 20 minutes

Servings: 2

Ingredients:

- 2 potatoes
- 1/3 cup half and half
- 1 tbsp. oatmeal flour
- 1/4 tsp. black pepper, ground
- 1 egg
- 2 oz. cheddar cheese

Directions:

1. Wash the potatoes and slice them into thin pieces.
2. Preheat the air fryer to 365°F.
3. Put the potato slices in the air fryer and cook them for 10 minutes.

4. Meanwhile, combine the half and half, oatmeal flour, and ground black pepper.
5. Crack the egg into the liquid and whisk it carefully.
6. Shred cheddar cheese.
7. When the potato is cooked take 2 ramekins and place the potatoes on them.
8. Pour the half and half mixture.
9. Sprinkle the gratin with shredded cheddar cheese.
10. Cook the gratin for 10 minutes at 360°F.
11. Serve the meal immediately. Enjoy!

Nutrition:

- Calories: 353
- Fat: 16.6 g.
- Fiber: 5.4 g.
- Carbs: 37.2 g.
- Protein: 15 g.

210. Salty Lemon Artichokes

Preparation time: 15 minutes

Cooking time: 45 minutes

Servings: 2

Ingredients:

- 1 lemon
- 2 artichokes
- 1 tsp. kosher salt
- 1 garlic head
- 2 tsp. olive oil

Directions:

1. Cut off the edges of the artichokes.
2. Cut the lemon into the halves.
3. Peel the garlic head and chop the garlic cloves roughly.
4. Then place the chopped garlic in the artichokes.
5. Sprinkle the artichokes with olive

oil and kosher salt.

6. Then squeeze the lemon juice into the artichokes.

7. Wrap the artichokes in the foil.

8. Preheat the air fryer to 330°F.

9. Place the wrapped artichokes in the air fryer and cook for 45 minutes.

10. When the artichokes are cooked discard the foil and serve. Enjoy!

Nutrition:

- Calories: 133
- Fat: 5 g.
- Fiber: 9.7 g.
- Carbs: 21.7 g.
- Protein: 6 g.

211. Asparagus & Parmesan

Preparation time: 10 minutes

Cooking time: 6 minutes

Servings: 2

Ingredients:

- 1 tsp. sesame oil
- 11 oz. asparagus
- 1 tsp. chicken stock
- 1/2 tsp. white pepper, ground
- 3 oz. Parmesan cheese

Directions:

1. Wash the asparagus and chop it roughly.

2. Sprinkle the chopped asparagus with the chicken stock and ground white pepper.

3. Then sprinkle the vegetables with the sesame oil and shake them.

4. Place the asparagus in the air fryer basket.

5. Cook the vegetables for 4 minutes at 400°F.

6. Meanwhile, shred Parmesan cheese.

7. When the time is over shake the asparagus gently and sprinkle with the shredded cheese.

8. Cook the asparagus for 2 minutes more at 400°F.

9. After this, transfer the cooked asparagus to the serving plates.

10. Serve and taste it!

Nutrition:

- Calories: 189
- Fat: 11.6 g.
- Fiber: 3.4 g.
- Carbs: 7.9 g.
- Protein: 17.2 g.

Carrot Lentil Burgers

Preparation time: 10 minutes

Cooking time: 12 minutes

Servings: 2

Ingredients:

- 6 oz. lentils, cooked
- 1 egg
- 2 oz. carrot, grated
- 1 tsp. semolina
- 1/2 tsp. salt
- 1 tsp. turmeric
- 1 tbsp. butter

Directions:

1. Crack the egg into the bowl and whisk it.
2. Add the cooked lentils and mash the mixture with the help of the fork.
3. Then sprinkle the mixture with the grated carrot, semolina, salt, and turmeric.
4. Mix it up and make the medium burgers.
5. Put the butter into the lentil burgers. It will make them juicy.
6. Preheat the air fryer to 360°F.
7. Put the lentil burgers in the air fryer and cook for 12 minutes.
8. Flip the burgers into another side after 6 minutes of cooking.
9. Then chill the cooked lentil burgers and serve them. Enjoy!

Nutrition:

- Calories: 404
- Fat: 9 g.
- Fiber: 26.9 g.
- Carbs: 56 g.
- Protein: 25.3 g.

212. Corn on Cobs

Preparation time: 10 minutes

Cooking time: 10 minutes

Servings: 2

Ingredients:

- 2 fresh corn on cobs
- 2 tsp. butter
- 1 tsp. salt
- 1 tsp. paprika
- 1/4 tsp. olive oil

Directions:

1. Preheat the air fryer to 400°F.
2. Rub the corn on cobs with salt and paprika.
3. Then sprinkle the corn on cobs with olive oil.
4. Place the corn on cobs in the air fryer basket.
5. Cook the corn on

cobs for 10 minutes.

6. When the time is over transfer the corn on cobs in the serving plates and rub with the butter gently.

7. Serve the meal immediately. Enjoy!

Nutrition:

- Calories: 122
- Fat: 5.5 g.
- Fiber: 2.4 g.
- Carbs: 17.6 g.
- Protein: 3.2 g.

213. Sugary Carrot Strips

Preparation time: 10 minutes

Cooking time: 10 minutes

Servings: 2

Ingredients:

- 2 carrots
- 1 tsp. brown sugar
- 1 tsp. olive oil
- 1 tbsp. soy sauce
- 1 tsp. honey
- 1/2 tsp. ground black pepper

Directions:

1. Peel the carrot and cut it into strips.
2. Then put the carrot strips in the bowl.
3. Sprinkle the carrot strips with olive oil, brown sugar, soy sauce, honey, and ground black pepper.
4. Shake the mixture

gently.

5. Preheat the air fryer to 360°F.
6. Cook the carrot for 10 minutes.
7. After this, shake the carrot strips well. Enjoy!

Nutrition:

- Calories: 67
- Fat: 2.4 g.
- Fiber: 1.7 g.
- Carbs: 11.3 g.
- Protein: 1.1 g.

214. Mozzarella Radish Salad

Preparation time: 10 minutes

Cooking time: 20 minutes

Servings: 2

Ingredients:

- 8 oz. radish
- 4 oz. Mozzarella cheese
- 1 tsp. balsamic vinegar
- 1/2 tsp. salt
- 1 tbsp. olive oil
- 1 tsp. dried oregano

Directions:

1. Wash the radish carefully and cut it into the halves.
2. Preheat the air fryer to 360°F.
3. Put the radish halves in the air fryer basket.
4. Sprinkle the radish with salt and olive oil.
5. Cook the radish for 20 minutes.
6. Shake the radish after 10 minutes of cooking.
7. When the time is over transfer the radish to the serving plate.
8. Chop Mozzarella cheese roughly.
9. Sprinkle the radish with Mozzarella, balsamic vinegar, and dried oregano.
10. Stir it gently with the help of 2 forks.
11. Serve it immediately.

Nutrition:

- Calories: 241
- Fat: 17.2 g.
- Fiber: 2.1 g.
- Carbs: 6.4 g.
- Protein: 16.9 g.

215. Cremini Mushroom Satay

Preparation time: 10 minutes

Cooking time: 6 minutes

Servings: 2

Ingredients:

- 7 oz. cremini mushrooms
- 2 tbsp. coconut milk
- 1 tbsp. butter
- 1 tsp. chili flakes
- 1/2 tsp. balsamic vinegar
- 1/2 tsp. curry powder
- 1/2 tsp. white pepper

Directions:

1. Wash the mushrooms carefully.
2. Then sprinkle the mushrooms with

chili flakes, curry powder, and white pepper.

3. Preheat the air fryer to 400°F.
4. Toss the butter in the air fryer basket and melt it.
5. Put the mushrooms in the air fryer and cook for 2 minutes.
6. Shake the mushrooms well and sprinkle with coconut milk and balsamic vinegar.
7. Cook the mushrooms for 4 minutes more at 400°F.
8. Then skewer the mushrooms on the wooden sticks and serve. Enjoy!

Nutrition:

- Calories: 116
- Fat: 9.5 g.
- Fiber: 1.3 g.
- Carbs: 5.6 g.
- Protein: 3 g.

216. Eggplant Ratatouille

Preparation time: 15 minutes

Cooking time: 15 minutes

Servings: 2

Ingredients:

- 1 eggplant
- 1 sweet yellow pepper
- 3 cherry tomatoes
- 1/3 white onion, chopped
- 1/2 tsp. garlic clove, sliced
- 1 tsp. olive oil
- 1/2 tsp. ground black pepper
- 1/2 tsp. Italian seasoning

Directions:

1. Preheat the air fryer to 360°F.
2. Peel the eggplants and chop them.
3. Put the chopped eggplants in the air fryer basket.
4. Chop the cherry tomatoes and add them to the air fryer basket.
5. Then add chopped onion, sliced garlic clove, olive oil, ground black pepper, and Italian seasoning.
6. Chop the sweet yellow pepper roughly and add it to the air fryer basket.
7. Shake the vegetables gently and cook for 15 minutes.
8. Stir the meal after 8 minutes of cooking.
9. Transfer the cooked ratatouille to the serving plates. Enjoy!

Nutrition:

- Calories: 149
- Fat: 3.7 g.
- Fiber: 11.7 g.

- Carbs: 28.9 g.
- Protein: 5.1 g.

217. Cheddar Portobello Mushrooms

Preparation time: 15 minutes

Cooking time: 6 minutes

Servings: 2

Ingredients:

- 2 Portobello mushroom hats
- 2 slices cheddar cheese
- 1/4 cup panko breadcrumbs
- 1/2 tsp. salt
- 1/2 tsp. black pepper, ground
- 1 egg
- 1 tsp. oatmeal
- 2 oz. bacon, chopped cooked

Directions:

1. Crack the egg into the bowl and whisk it.
2. Combine the ground black pepper, oatmeal, salt, and breadcrumbs in a separate bowl.
3. Dip the mushroom hats in the whisked egg.
4. After this, coat the mushroom hats in the breadcrumb mixture.
5. Preheat the air fryer to 400°F.
6. Place the mushrooms in the air fryer basket tray and cook for 3 minutes.
7. After this, put the chopped bacon and sliced cheese over the mushroom hats and cook the meal for 3 minutes.
8. When the meal is cooked—let it chill gently. Enjoy!

Nutrition:

- Calories: 376
- Fat: 24.1 g.
- Fiber: 1.8 g.
- Carbs: 14.6 g.
- Protein: 25.2 g.

218. Air Fried French Fries

Preparation time: 5 minutes

Cooking time: 29 minutes

Servings: 3

Ingredients:

- 3 Potatoes
- 3 tsp. olive oil
- 1/2 tsp. salt

Directions:

1. Peel and wash the potatoes.
2. Cut the potatoes into 1/2-inch sticks.
3. Boil a bowl of salted water.
4. Blanch the potato cuts for 4 minutes in boiling saltwater.
5. Drain the potato cuts and pat dry.
6. Set the air fryer temperature to 200°C and preheat for 2 minutes.
7. Pour olive oil into the potato cuts and toss.
8. Place the oil-coated potatoes in the air fryer basket.
9. Air fry it for 25 minutes.
10. Shake the air fryer basket intermittently after every 5 minutes.
11. Drizzle salt in the middle of the frying for seasoning.
12. Serve it along with ketchup, shredded Parmesan cheese, or mayonnaise, and lemon zest.

Nutrition:

- Calories: 187
- Carbs: 33.5 g.
- Cholesterol:: 0 mg.
- Dietary Fiber: 5.1 g.
- Fat: 4.9 g.
- Sodium: 400 mg.
- Sugar:s: 2.5 g.
- Potassium: 867 mg.

219. Air Fried Brussels Sprouts

Preparation time: 5 minutes

Cooking time: 10 minutes

Servings: 2

Ingredients:

- 2 cups Brussels sprouts, cut into halves
- 1 tbsp. balsamic vinegar
- 1 tbsp. olive oil
- 1/4 tsp. salt

Directions:

1. In a medium bowl, add vinegar, olive oil, salt and combine.
2. Add the halved Brussels sprouts into the bowl mix and toss to coat evenly.
3. Place the coated Brussels sprouts in the air fryer basket.
4. Set the temperature at 200°C for 10 minutes.
5. Shake the air fryer basket every 3–4 minutes so that you can have even cooking.
6. Once done, serve hot.

Nutrition:

- Calories: 100
- Carbs: 8.1 g.
- Cholesterol: 0 mg.
- Fat: 7.3 g.
- Sodium: 73 mg.

- Dietary Fiber: 3.3 g.
- Potassium: 347 mg.
- Sugar:s: 1.9 g.

220. Air Fried Breaded Mushrooms

Preparation time: 10 minutes

Cooking time: 7 minutes

Servings: 4–6

Ingredients:

- 1/2 lb. button mushrooms
- 1 large egg
- 3 oz. cheese, grated
- Breadcrumb, as required to coat
- Flour, as necessary to coat
- 1/4 tsp. pepper, ground
- 1/8 tsp. salt

Directions:

1. In a medium bowl combine bread crumbs with grated cheese and keep it aside.
2. Now beat the egg in another medium bowl and keep it aside.
3. Wash the mushrooms and dry pat.
4. Put the flour on a flat plate and roll the mushroom in the flour.
5. Dip the flour-rolled mushroom in the beaten egg.
6. Now dip the mushroom again in the cheese and bread crumb mixture.
7. Place the coated mushroom in the air

fryer cooking basket.

8. Set the temperature at 180°C and timer for 7 minutes.

9. Shake the air fryer basket between 3–4 times so that it can have an even frying.

10. Serve hot along with any dipping sauce.

Nutrition:

- Calories: 169
- Carbs: 13 g.
- Cholesterol: 63 mg.
- Fat: 8.7 g.
- Sodium: 204 mg.
- Dietary Fiber: 1.1 g.
- Protein: 10.2 g.
- Potassium: 238 mg.
- Sugar: 1.6 g.

221. Air Fried Zucchini, Carrots & Yellow Squash

Preparation time: 10 minutes

Cooking time: 35 minutes

Servings: 4

Ingredients:

- 1/2 lb. carrot
- 1 lb. zucchini
- 1 lb. yellow squash
- 6 tsp. olive oil
- 1/2 tsp. white pepper, ground
- 1 tbsp. tarragon leaves, coarsely chopped
- 1 tsp. kosher salt

Directions:

1. Peel and wash carrots in running water, cut into 1-inch cubes and keep aside.

2. Remove end and stem of zucchini and cut into 3/4-inch half-moon size. Keep it aside.

3. Clean yellow squash, remove root end, stem, and cut into 3/4-inch half-moon size. Keep it aside.

4. In a medium bowl, pour 2 tsp. of olive oil and combine the cubed carrots.

5. Place the carrots in

the air fryer basket and set the temperature at 200°C.

6. Adjust the timer for 5 minutes.

7. While the cooking continues, take another medium bowl and pour the remaining olive oil.

8. Now put the chopped zucchini and yellow squash along with salt and pepper in the new bowl.

9. Toss it gently so that it will have an even coating.

10. When the cooking timer elapses, put the combined mix of yellow squash and zucchini into the fryer basket without removing the fried carrots already there.

11. Keeping the same temperature, set the timer for 30 minutes

and start cooking.

12. Toss the vegetables in between occasionally, so that it can have an even frying.

13. Browning is the right tone of well-done cooking.

14. Once the cooking is over toss it with tarragon and serve hot.

Nutrition:

- Calories: 112
- Carbs: 11.4 g.
- Cholesterol: 0 mg.
- Sodium: 623 mg.
- Fat: 7.3 g.
- Dietary Fiber: 3.3 g.
- Protein: 2.7 g.
- Potassium: 429 mg.

Sugar: 8.9 g.

222. Air Fried Cauliflower Tater Tots

Preparation time: 10 minutes

Cooking time: 10 minutes

Servings: 6

Ingredients:

- 1 head cauliflower
- 1/4 cup all-purpose flour
- 2 eggs
- 1/2 cup Parmesan cheese, grated
- 1/2 tsp. black pepper, ground
- Cooking spray as required
- 1/2 tsp. salt

- Parchment sheet

Directions:

1. Coarsely chop the cauliflower head.
2. Put in a clean kitchen towel and slightly twist the towel to squeeze out water from the cauliflower.
3. Now put the squeezed cauliflower in a medium bowl.
4. Add flour, Parmesan cheese, eggs, ground black pepper, and salt.
5. Combine the mix thoroughly.
6. Make tater tots by using 1 tbsp. of mixture.
7. Place the tater tots on the parchment paper.
8. Spritz cooking oil over the tater tots.
9. Set the air fryer at 200°C for about 2 minutes.
10. Place the tater tots in the air fryer basket in one layer, without overlapping.
11. Air fry it for 10 minutes at 200°C.
12. Flip the tater totes intermittently, but gently.
13. During the end process of cooking, season it with salt and pepper.
14. Serve hot with dipping.

Nutrition:

- Calories: 45
- Carbs: 5.1 g.
- Cholesterol: 55 mg.
- Fat: 1.6 g.
- Dietary Fiber: 0.6 g.
- Sugar: 0.5 g.
- Protein: 2.8 g.
- Potassium: 78 mg.
- Sodium: 222 mg.

223. Roasted Vegetable Pasta Salad

Preparation time: 5 minutes:

Cooking time: 15 minutes

Servings: 8

Ingredients:

- 4 oz. brown mushrooms, halved
- 1 cup grape tomatoes, halved
- 1 cup Kalamata olives, halved
- 1 orange pepper, large cut pieces
- 1 red pepper, large cut pieces
- 1 green pepper, large cut pieces
- 1 yellow squash, sliced
- 1 onion, sliced
- 1 zucchini, halved
- 1 tsp. Italian seasoning
- 1 lb. penne rigatoni, cooked
- 1/4 cup olive oil
- 3 tbsp. balsamic vinegar
- 2 tbsp. fresh basil, chopped
- 1/2 tsp. black pepper, ground
- 1/2 tsp. salt

Directions:

1. Preheat the air fryer at 190ºC.
2. Combine yellow squash, peppers, mushrooms, zucchini, and onion.
3. Spritz some olive oil and toss gently.
4. Add salt, Italian seasoning, pepper, and toss gently.
5. Air fry it for 15 minutes until the vegetable becomes soft.
6. Shake the air fryer basket intermittently during the cooking.
7. In a large bowl put roasted vegetables, cooked pasta, olives, and tomatoes.
8. Combine the mix gently.
9. Add balsamic vinegar and toss thoroughly.
10. Season it with ground pepper and salt.
11. Refrigerate the salad, and serve when required.
12. Add the fresh basil before serving.

Nutrition:

- Calories: 118
- Carbs: 9.8 g.
- Cholesterol: 0 mg.
- Dietary Fiber: 2.1 g.
- Fat: 8.6 g.
- Sugar: 3.1 g.

- Sodium: 324 mg.
- Protein: 2 g.
- Potassium: 267 mg.

224. Air Fryer Zucchini Chips

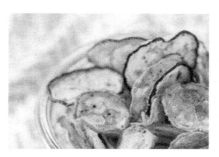

Preparation time: 10 minutes

Cooking time: 24 minutes

Servings: 4

Ingredients:

- 1 cup bread crumbs
- 1 medium zucchini, thinly sliced
- 1 egg
- 3/4 cup Parmesan cheese, grated
- Cooking spray as required

Directions:

1. Mix bread crumbs, grated Parmesan cheese in a medium bowl.
2. Beat egg in a medium bowl.
3. Set the air fryer temperature to 175°C and preheat the air fryer.
4. Dip one zucchini slice at a time in the beaten egg and dredge in the bread crumb mixture.
5. Press to coat and place in the air fryer basket.
6. Repeat the process, place all zucchini slices and put them in the air fryer basked side by side. Do not overlap it.
7. Spray cooking oil slightly over the coated zucchini.
8. Now start cooking for 10 minutes.
9. After 10 minutes, flip using a tong and cook again for 2 minutes.
10. You may have to

complete the cooking in batches.

Nutrition:

- Calories: 159
- Carbs: 21.2 g.
- Cholesterol: 60 mg
- Sodium: 384 mg.
- Potassium: 164 mg.
- Dietary Fiber: 0.5 g.
- Protein: 10.8 g.
- Sugar: 1 g.

225. Air Fried Ratatouille

Preparation time: 25 minutes

Cooking time: 25 minutes

Servings: 4

Ingredients:

- 1 zucchini, diced
- 1/2 eggplant, small diced
- 1 medium tomato, chopped into cubes
- 1/2 large red bell pepper, chopped
- 1/2 onion, cut into cubes
- 1 cayenne pepper, fresh, chopped
- 1 tsp. vinegar

- 1 garlic clove, grated
- 5 springs basil, fresh, stemmed and chopped
- 2 springs oregano, fresh, stemmed, and cut into pieces
- 1 tbsp. olive oil
- 1 tbsp. white wine
- Salt to taste
- 1/2 tsp. pepper

Directions:

1. Put zucchini, eggplant, bell pepper, tomato, onion in a bowl and mix.
2. After that, you can add basil, garlic, cayenne pepper, oregano, pepper, and salt. Mix all the ingredients.
3. Now pour vinegar, oil, and wine into the mix and let it coat evenly on the vegetables.
4. Preheat the air fryer at 200°C before you

start the cooking.

5. Now transfer the vegetable mix into a baking dish and put it in the air fryer basket.

6. Start cooking for 8 minutes and stir it.

7. Again, cook for another 8 minutes and stir. It would be better if you can stir it every 5 minutes and cook for a total of 25–30 minutes.

8. After cooking keep the dish in the air fryer for some time.

9. Serve hot.

Nutrition:

- Calories: 79
- Carbs: 10.2 g.
- Cholesterol: 0 mg.
- Dietary Fiber: 3.3 g.
- Potassium: 425 mg.
- Sodium: 48 mg.
- Protein: 2.1 g.
- Sugar: 5 g.

226. Air Fryer Rosemary Potato Wedges

Preparation time: 10 minutes

Cooking time: 20 minutes

Servings: 4

Ingredients:

- 2 potatoes
- 1 tbsp. fresh Rosemary, chopped
- 1 tbsp. olive oil
- 2 tbsp. salt

Directions:

1. Wash, clean, and slice the potatoes in 12 wedges with skin.

2. Put the potatoes in a large vessel.

3. Drizzle olive oil over it and toss.

4. Sprinkle chopped Rosemary, salt and toss it to mix the ingredients.

5. Preheat the air fryer at 190°C before you start cooking.

6. When the air fryer is hot, layer the potato wedges in the air fryer basked without crowding or overlapping.

7. Air fry it for 10 minutes and flip the wedges by using a tong and continue cooking for another 10 minutes.

8. If your air fryer basket is too small, you need to cook it in batches.

9. Serve hot.

Nutrition:

- Calories: 115
- Carbs: 19.2 g.
- Cholesterol: 0 mg.
- Dietary Fiber: 2.5 g.
- Protein: 2.2 g.
- Sugar: 1 g.
- Potassium: 461 mg.
- Sodium: 465 mg.
- Fat: 1.0 g.

227. Air Fried Asparagus

Preparation time: 5 minutes

Cooking time: 10 minutes

Servings: 4

Ingredients:

- 1/2 bunch asparagus
- 1/4 tsp. salt
- 1/2 tsp. black pepper
- Olive oil spray as required

Directions:

1. Cut and remove 2-inch from the bottom portion of the asparagus.
2. Place the asparagus sticks in the air fryer basket.
3. Spray coat olive oil on it.
4. Sprinkle the black pepper powder and salt.
5. Set the temperature to 200°C and timer for 10 minutes.
6. Serve hot.

Nutrition:

- Calories: 11
- Carbs: 0.2 g.
- Cholesterol: 0 mg.
- Sodium: 147 mg.
- Dietary Fiber: 0.1 g.
- Sugar: 0 g.
- Potassium: 4 mg.

228. Quinoa Pilaf

Preparation time: 2 minutes

Cooking time: 10 minutes

Servings: 4

Ingredients:

- 2 cups quinoa
- 2 garlic cloves, minced.
- 3 cups water
- 2 tsp. turmeric
- 1 handful parsley, chopped.
- 2 tsp. cumin, ground.
- 2 tbsp. extra virgin olive oil
- Salt to taste

Directions:

1. Set your air fryer on "Sauté" mode; add oil and heat it.
2. Add garlic, stir and cook for 30 seconds.
3. Add water, quinoa, cumin, turmeric, and salt; then stir well. close the lid and cook at "High" for 1 minute
4. Release the pressure naturally for 10 minutes, then release the remaining pressure by turning the valve to "Venting", fluff quinoa with a fork, transfer to plates, season with more salt if needed, sprinkle parsley on top, and serve as a side dish.

Nutrition:

- Calories: 110
- Protein: 13 g.
- Carbs: 15 g.
- Fat: 5 g.

229. Mashed Squash

Preparation time: 10 minutes

Cooking time: 20 minutes

Servings: 4

Ingredients:

- 2 Acorn squash, cut into halves and seeded
- 1/4 tsp. baking soda
- 2 tbsp. butter
- 1/2 cup water
- 1/2 tsp. nutmeg, grated
- 2 tbsp. brown sugar
- Salt and black pepper to the taste

Directions:

1. Sprinkle squash halves with salt, pepper, and baking soda and place them in the steamer basket of your

instant vortex.

2. Add 1/2 cup water to the pot, close the lid and cook at "High" for 20 minutes.

3. Quick release the pressure, take squash and leave aside on a plate to cool down.

4. Scrape flesh from the squash and put it in a bowl.

5. Add salt, pepper to the taste, butter, sugar, and nutmeg, and mash everything with potato mashes. Stir well and serve.

Nutrition:

- Calories: 250
- Protein: 14 g.
- Carbs: 12 g.
- Fat: 10 g.

230. Apple and Butternut Mash

Preparation time: 17 minutes

Cooking time: 8 minutes

Servings: 4

Ingredients:

- 1 butternut squash, peeled and cut into medium chunks
- 1/2 tsp. apple pie spice
- 2 tbsp. brown butter
- 2 apples, sliced
- 1 cup water
- 1 yellow onion, thinly sliced
- Salt to the taste

Directions:

1. Put squash, onion, and apple pieces in the steamer basket of your instant vortex, put the water in the pot, close the lid and cook at "High" for 8 minutes.

2. Quick release the pressure and transfer squash, onion, and apple pieces to a bowl.

3. Mash using a potato masher, add salt, apple pie spice, and brown butter, stir well and serve warm.

Nutrition:

- Calories: 321
- Protein: 33 g.
- Carbs: 28 g.

Fat: 10 g.

231. Sweet Carrot Puree

Preparation time: 6 minutes

Cooking time: 4 minutes

Servings: 4

Ingredients:

- 1 1/2 lb. carrots, peeled and chopped.
- 1 tsp. brown sugar
- 1 tbsp. soft butter
- 1 tbsp. honey
- 1 cup water
- Salt to the taste

Directions:

1. Put carrots in your instant vortex, add the water, close the lid and cook at "High" for 4 minutes.
2. Release the pressure naturally, drain carrots and place them in a bowl.
3. Mash them using a hand blender, add butter, salt, and honey.
4. Blend again well, add sugar on top, and serve right away.

Nutrition:

- Calories: 421
- Protein: 43 g.
- Carbs: 30 g.
- Fat: 15 g.

232. Pumpkin Risotto

Preparation time: 3 minutes

Cooking time: 12 minutes

Servings: 4

Ingredients:

- 6 oz. pumpkin puree
- 2 oz. extra virgin olive oil
- 1 small yellow onion, chopped.
- 1/2 tsp. nutmeg
- 1 tsp. thyme, chopped.
- 1/2 tsp. ginger, grated
- 4 oz. heavy cream
- 1/2 tsp. cinnamon
- 1/2 tsp. allspice
- 2 garlic cloves, minced.
- 12 oz. risotto rice
- 4 cups chicken stock

Directions:

1. Set your instant vortex on "Sauté" mode; add oil and heat it.
2. Add onion and garlic, stir and cook for 1–2 minutes.
3. Also add risotto, chicken stock, pumpkin puree, thyme, nutmeg, cinnamon, ginger, and allspice and stir.
4. Close the instant vortex lid and cook at "High" for 10 minutes.
5. Quick release the pressure, add cream, stir very well and serve as a side dish.

Nutrition:

- Calories: 243
- Protein: 25 g.
- Carbs: 16 g.
- Fat: 9 g.

233. Flavored Mashed Sweet Potatoes

Preparation time: 10 minutes

Cooking time: 10 minutes

Servings: 8

Ingredients:

- 3 lb. sweet potatoes, peeled and chopped.
- 2 garlic cloves
- 1/4 cup milk
- 1/4 tsp. sage, dried
- 1/2 tsp. Rosemary, dried
- 1/2 tsp. thyme dried
- 1/2 cup Parmesan cheese, grated
- 2 tbsp. butter
- Salt and black pepper to the taste
- 1/2 tsp. parsley, dried
- 1 1/2 cups water

Directions:

1. Put potatoes and garlic in the steamer basket of your instant vortex, add 1 1/2 cups water in the pot, close the lid and cook at "High" for 10 minutes.
2. Quick release the pressure, drain water, transfer the potatoes and garlic to a bowl and mash them using your kitchen mixer.
3. Add butter, Parmesan cheese, milk, salt, pepper, parsley, sage, Rosemary, and thyme and blend everything well.
4. Divide among plates and serve.

Nutrition:

- Calories: 244
- Protein: 29 g.
- Carbs: 21 g.

- Fat: 3 g.

234. Israeli Couscous Dish

Preparation time: 10 minutes

Cooking time: 5 minutes

Servings: 10

Ingredients:

- 16 oz. harvest grains blend
- 2 1/2 cups chicken stock
- 2 tbsp. butter
- Parsley leaves, chopped for serving
- Salt and black pepper to the taste

Directions:

1. Set your instant vortex on "Sauté" mode; add butter and melt it.
2. Add grains and stock and stir.
3. Close the instant vortex lid and cook at "High" for 5 minutes.
4. Quick release the pressure, fluff couscous with a fork, season with salt and pepper to the taste, divide among plates, sprinkle parsley on top, and serve.

Nutrition:

- Calories: 390
- Protein: 32 g.
- Carbs: 25.4 g.
- Fat: 14 g.

235. Cauliflower Mash Dish

Preparation time: 7 minutes

Cooking time: 8 minutes

Servings: 4

Ingredients:

- 1 cauliflower, florets separated
- 1 tbsp. butter
- 1 1/2 cups water
- 1/2 tsp. turmeric
- 3 chives, finely chopped
- Salt and black pepper to the taste

Directions:

1. Pour the water in your instant vortex, place cauliflower in the steamer basket, seal the instant vortex lid and cook at "High" for 6 minutes.
2. Release the pressure naturally for 2 minutes and then release the rest quickly.
3. Transfer cauliflower to a bowl and mash it with a potato masher.
4. Add salt, pepper, butter, and turmeric; then stir well. transfer to a blender and pulse well.
5. Serve with chives sprinkled on top.

Nutrition:

- Calories: 278
- Protein: 22 g
- Carbs: 29 g.
- Fat: 19 g.

236. Mashed Turnips Dish

Preparation time: 10 minutes

Cooking time: 5 minutes

Servings: 4

Ingredients:

- 4 turnips, peeled and chopped.
- 1 yellow onion; chopped.
- 1/4 cup sour cream
- 1/2 cup chicken stock
- Salt and black pepper to the taste

Directions:

1. In your instant vortex, mix turnips with stock and onion.
2. Stir, close the lid and cook at "High" for 5 minutes.
3. Release the pressure naturally, drain turnips and transfer them to a bowl.
4. Puree them using your mixer and add salt, pepper to the taste, and sour cream.
5. Blend again and serve right away.

Nutrition:

- Calories: 260
- Protein: 40 g.
- Carbs: 31 g.
- Fat: 16 g.

237. Refried Beans

Preparation time: 10 minutes

Cooking time: 20 minutes

Servings: 4

Ingredients:

- 3 cups pinto beans, soaked for 4 hours and drained
- 1 jalapeño, chopped
- 2 tbsp. garlic, minced.
- 9 cups vegetable stock
- 1/8 tsp. cumin, ground.
- 1 yellow onion, cut into halves
- Salt and black pepper to the taste

Directions:

1. In your instant vortex, mix beans with salt, pepper,

stock, onion, jalapeño, garlic, and cumin.

2. Stir, close the lid and cook at "High" for 20 minutes.
3. Release the pressure naturally, discard onion halves, strain beans, transfer them to your blender and reserve cooking liquid.
4. Blend very well adding some of the liquid, transfer to a bowl and serve them as a side dish.

Nutrition:

- Calories: 247
- Protein: 26.6 g.
- Carbs: 22.4 g.

Fat: 3 g.

238. Potatoes Side Dish

Preparation time: 11 minutes

Cooking time: 5 minutes

Servings: 4

Ingredients:

- 1 lb. new potatoes, peeled and thinly sliced
- 2 garlic cloves, minced.
- 1 cup water
- 1/4 tsp. Rosemary, dried
- 1 tbsp. extra-virgin olive oil
- Salt and black pepper to the taste

Directions:

1. Put the potatoes and the water in the steamer basket of your instant vortex, close the lid and cook at "High" for 4 minutes.
2. In a heatproof dish, mix Rosemary with oil and garlic, cover and microwave for 1 minute.
3. Quick release the pressure, drain potatoes and spread them on a lined baking sheet.
4. Add heated oil mix, salt and pepper to the taste, toss to coat, divide among plates and serve as a side dish.

Nutrition:

- Calories: 320
- Protein: 43 g.
- Carbs: 35 g.
- Fat: 18 g.

239. Special Side Dish

Preparation time: 9 minutes

Cooking time: 21 minutes

Servings: 4

Ingredients:

- 1 bread loaf, cubed and toasted
- 1 cup celery, chopped
- 1/2 cup butter
- 1 1/4 cup turkey stock
- 1 yellow onion, chopped
- 1 tsp. sage
- 1 tsp. poultry seasoning
- 1 1/2 cups water
- Salt and black pepper to the taste

Directions:

1. Set your instant vortex on "Sauté" mode, add butter and melt it.
2. Add stock, onion, celery, salt, pepper, sage and poultry seasoning and stir well
3. Add bread cubes, stir and cook for 1 minute
4. Transfer this to a bundt pan and close the lid with tin foil
5. Clean your instant vortex, add the water and place the pan in the steamer basket, seal the instant vortex lid and cook at "High" for 15 minutes.
6. Quick release the pressure, take out the pan, introduce it in the oven at 350°F and bake for 5 minutes. Serve hot.

Nutrition:

- Calories: 165
- Protein: 14 g.
- Carbs: 17 g.
- Fat: 5 .g

240. Onions & Parsnips

Preparation time: 12 minutes

Cooking time: 28 minutes

Servings: 4

Ingredients:

- 1 yellow onion, thinly sliced.
- 1 1/2 cups beef stock
- 2 1/2 lb. parsnips, chopped.
- 1 thyme spring
- 4 tbsp. pastured lard
- Salt and black pepper to the taste

Directions:

1. Set your instant vortex on "Sauté" mode, add 3 tbsp. lard and heat it up
2. Add parsnips, stir and cook for 15 minutes
3. Add stock and thyme; then stir well. close the lid and cook at "High" for 3 minutes
4. Quick release the pressure, transfer the parsnips mix to your blender, add salt and pepper to the taste, and pulse very well.
5. Set the pot on "Sauté" mode again, add the rest of the lard, and heat it.
6. Add onion, stir and cook for 10 minutes
7. Transfer blended parsnips to plates, top with sautéed onions, and serve.

Nutrition:

- Calories: 142
- Protein: 253 g.
- Carbs: 13 g.
- Fat: 12 g.

241. Potato Casserole

Preparation time: 15 minutes

Cooking time: 30 minutes

Servings: 4

Ingredients:

- 3 lb. sweet potatoes, scrubbed
- 2 tbsp. coconut flour
- 1 tsp. cinnamon
- 1/4 tsp. allspice
- 1/3 cup palm sugar
- 1/2 tsp. nutmeg, ground
- 1 cup water
- 1/4 cup coconut milk
- Salt to the taste

For the topping:

- 1/2 cup almond flour
- 1/4 cup pecans, soaked, drained, and

ground

- 1/4 cup coconut, shredded
- 1 tbsp. chia seeds
- 1/2 cup walnuts, soaked, drained, and ground
- 1/4 cup palm sugar
- 1 tsp. cinnamon, ground
- 5 tbsp. salted butter
- A pinch of salt

Directions:

1. Prick potatoes with a fork, place them in the steamer basket of your instant vortex, add 1 cup of water to the pot, close the lid and cook at "High" for 20 minutes.
2. Meanwhile, in a bowl, mix almond flour with pecans, walnuts, 1/4 cup coconut, 1/4 cup palm sugar, chia seeds, 1 tsp. cinnamon, a pinch of salt, and the butter and stir everything.
3. Release the pressure naturally from the pot, take potatoes and peel them and add 1/2 cup water to the pot.
4. Chop potatoes and place them in a baking dish
5. Add Coconut flour, cinnamon, allspice, sugar, nutmeg, coconut milk, salt
6. Add crumble mix you've made, stir everything, spread evenly in the dish, place in the steamer basket, seal the instant vortex lid again and cook at "High" for 10 minutes.
7. Quick release the pressure, take the dish out of the pot, leave it to cool down, cut, and serve as a side dish.

Nutrition:

- Calories: 311
- Protein: 21 g.
- Carbs: 25 g.
- Fat: 8 g.

242. Spicy Chickpeas

Preparation time: 5 minutes

Cooking time: 10 minutes

Servings: 4

Ingredients:

- 1 (15-oz.) can chickpeas, rinsed and drained
- 1 tbsp. olive oil
- 1/2 tsp. cumin, ground
- 1/2 tsp. cayenne pepper
- 1/2 tsp. smoked paprika
- Salt, as required

Directions:

1. In a bowl, add all the ingredients and toss to coat well.
2. Press "Power Button" of Air Fry Oven and turn the dial to select the "Air Fry" mode.
3. Press the "Time" button and again turn the dial to set the cooking time to 10 minutes.
4. Now push the "Temp" button and rotate the dial to set the temperature at 390°F.
5. Press the "Start/Pause" button to start.
6. When the unit beeps to show that it is preheated, open the lid.
7. Arrange the chickpeas in "Air Fry Basket" and insert them in the oven.
8. Serve warm.

Nutrition:

- Calories: 146
- Total fat: 4.5 g.
- Saturated fat: 0.5 g.
- Cholesterol: 0 mg.
- Sodium 66 mg.
- Total carbs: 18.8 g.
- Fiber: 4.6 g.
- Sugar: 0.1 g.
- Protein: 6.3 g.

243. Roasted Peanuts

Preparation time: 5 minutes

Cooking time: 14 minutes

Servings: 6

Ingredients:

- 1 1/2 cups raw peanuts
- Nonstick cooking spray

Directions:

1. Press "Power Button" of Air Fry Oven and turn the dial to select the "Air Fry" mode.
2. Press the "Time" button and again turn the dial to set the cooking time to 14 minutes.
3. Now push the "Temp" button and rotate the dial to set the temperature at 320°F.
4. Press the "Start/Pause" button to start.
5. When the unit beeps to show that it is preheated, open the lid.
6. Arrange the peanuts in "Air Fry Basket" and insert them in the oven.
7. Toss the peanuts twice.
8. After 9 minutes of cooking, spray the peanuts with cooking spray.
9. Serve warm.

Nutrition:

- Calories: 207
- Total fat: 18 g.
- Saturated fat: 2.5 g.
- Cholesterol: 0 mg.
- Sodium 7 mg.
- Total carbs: 5.9 g.
- Fiber: 3.1 g.
- Sugar: 1.5 g.
- Protein: 9.4 g.

244. Roasted Cashews

Preparation time: 5 minutes

Cooking time: 5 minutes

Servings: 6

Ingredients:

- 1 1/2 cups raw cashew nuts
- 1 tsp. butter, melted
- Salt and freshly ground black pepper, as needed

Directions:

1. In a bowl, mix all the ingredients.
2. Press the "Power Button" of Air Fry Oven and turn the dial to select the "Air Fry" mode.
3. Press the Time button and again turn the dial to set the cooking time to 5 minutes.

4. Now push the Temp button and rotate the dial to set the temperature at 355°F.
5. Press the "Start/Pause" button to start.
6. When the unit beeps to show that it is preheated, open the lid.
7. Arrange the cashews in "Air Fry Basket" and insert them in the oven.
8. Shake the cashews once halfway through.

Nutrition:

- Calories: 202
- Total fat: 16.5 g
- Saturated fat: 3.5 g
- Cholesterol: 2 mg
- Sodium 37 mg
- Total carbs: 11.2 g
- Fiber: 1 g
- Sugar: 1.7 g
- Protein: 5.3 g

245. French Fries

Preparation time: 15 minutes

Cooking time: 30 minutes

Servings: 4

Ingredients:

- 1 lb. potatoes, peeled and cut into strips
- 3 tbsp. olive oil
- 1/2 tsp. onion powder
- 1/2 tsp. garlic powder
- 1 tsp. paprika

Directions:

1. In a large bowl of water, soak the potato strips for about 1 hour.
2. Drain the potato strips well and pat them dry with paper towels.
3. In a large bowl, add the potato strips and the remaining ingredients and toss to coat well.
4. Press the "Power Button" of Air Fry Oven and turn the dial to select the "Air Fry" mode.
5. Press the "Time" button and again turn the dial to set the cooking time to 30 minutes.
6. Now push the "Temp" button and rotate the dial to set the temperature at 375°F.
7. Press the "Start/Pause" button to start.
8. When the unit beeps to show that it is preheated, open the lid.
9. Arrange the potato fries in "Air Fry Basket" and insert them in the oven.
10. Serve warm.

Nutrition:

- Calories: 172
- Total fat: 10.7 g.
- Saturated fat: 1.5 g.
- Cholesterol: 0 mg.
- Sodium 7 mg.
- Total carbs: 18.6 g.
- Fiber: 3 g.
- Sugar: 1.6 g.
- Protein: 2.1 g.

246. Zucchini Fries

Preparation time: 10 minutes

Cooking time: 20 minutes

Servings: 4

Ingredients:

- 1 lb. zucchini, sliced into 2 1/2-inch sticks
- Salt, as required
- 2 tbsp. olive oil
- 3/4 cup Panko breadcrumbs

Directions:

1. In a colander, add the zucchini and sprinkle with salt. Set aside for about 10 minutes.
2. Gently pat dry the zucchini sticks with the paper towels and coat with oil.
3. In a shallow dish, add the breadcrumbs.
4. Coat the zucchini sticks with breadcrumbs evenly.
5. Press the "Power Button" of Air Fry Oven and turn the dial to select the "Air Fry" mode.
6. Press the "Time" button and again turn the dial to set the cooking time to 12 minutes.
7. Now push the "Temp" button and rotate the dial to set the temperature at 400°F.
8. Press the "Start/Pause" button to start.
9. When the unit beeps to show that it is preheated, open the lid.
10. Arrange the zucchini fries in "Air Fry Basket" and insert them in the oven.
11. Serve warm.

Nutrition:

- Calories: 151
- Total fat: 8.6 g.
- Saturated fat: 1.6 g.
- Cholesterol: 0 mg.
- Sodium 50 mg.
- Total carbs: 6.9 g.
- Fiber: 1.3 g.
- Sugar: 2 g.
- Protein: 1.9 g.

247. Spicy Carrot Fries

Preparation time: 10 minutes

Cooking time: 12 minutes

Servings: 2

Ingredients:

- 1 large carrot, peeled and cut into sticks
- 1 tbsp. fresh Rosemary, chopped finely
- 1 tbsp. olive oil
- 1/4 tsp. cayenne pepper
- Salt and ground black pepper, as required

Directions:

1. In a bowl, add all the ingredients and mix well.
2. Press the "Power Button" of Air Fry Oven and turn the dial to select the "Air Fry" mode.
3. Press the Time button and again turn the dial to set the cooking time to 12 minutes.
4. Now push the "Temp" button and rotate the dial to set the temperature at 390°F.
5. Press the "Start/Pause" button to start.
6. When the unit beeps to show that it is preheated, open the lid.
7. Arrange the carrot fries in "Air Fry Basket" and insert them in the oven.
8. Serve warm.

Nutrition:

- Calories: 81
- Total fat: 8.3 g.
- Saturated fat: 1.1 g.
- Cholesterol: 0 mg.
- Sodium 36 mg.

- Total carbs: 4.7 g.
- Fiber: 1.7 g.
- Sugar: 1.8 g.
- Protein: 0.4 g.

248. Maple Carrot Fries

Preparation time: 10 minutes

Cooking time: 12 minutes

Servings: 6

Ingredients:

- 1 lb. carrots, peeled and cut into sticks
- 1 tsp. maple syrup
- 1 tsp. olive oil
- 1/2 tsp. cinnamon, ground
- Salt, to taste

Directions:

1. In a bowl, add all the ingredients and mix well.
2. Press the "Power Button" of the Air Fry Oven and turn the dial to select the "Air Fry" mode.
3. Press the Time button and again turn the dial to set the cooking time to 12 minutes.
4. Now push the Temp button and rotate the dial to set the temperature at 400°F.
5. Press the "Start/Pause" button to start.
6. When the unit beeps to show that it is preheated, open the lid.
7. Arrange the carrot fries in "Air Fry Basket" and insert them in the oven.
8. Serve warm.

Nutrition:

- Calories: 41
- Total fat: 0.8 g.
- Saturated fat: 0.1 g.
- Cholesterol: 0 mg.
- Sodium 79 mg.
- Total carbs: 8.3 g.
- Fiber: 2 g.
- Sugar: 4.4 g.
- Protein: 0.6 g.

249. Squash Fries

Preparation time: 10 minutes

Cooking time: 35 minutes

Servings: 2

Ingredients:

- 14 oz. butternut squash, peeled, seeded, and cut into strips
- 2 tsp. olive oil
- 1/2 tsp. cinnamon, ground
- 1/2 tsp. red chili powder
- 1/4 tsp. garlic salt
- Salt and freshly ground black pepper, as needed

Directions:

1. In a bowl, add all the ingredients and toss to coat well.
2. Press the "Power Button" of the Air Fry Oven and turn the dial to select the "Air Fry" mode.
3. Press the Time button and again turn the dial to set the cooking time to 30 minutes.
4. Now push the Temp button and rotate the dial to set the temperature at 400 F.
5. Press the "Start/Pause" button to start.
6. When the unit beeps to show that it is preheated, open the lid.
7. Arrange the squash fries in "Air Fry Basket" and insert them in the oven.
8. Serve warm.

Nutrition:

- Calories: 134
- Total fat: 5 g.
- Saturated fat: 0.7 g.
- Cholesterol: 0 mg.
- Sodium 92 mg.
- Total carbs: 24.3 g.
- Fiber: 4.5 g.
- Sugar: 4.5 g.
- Protein: 2.1 g.

250. Avocado Fries

Preparation time: 15 minutes

Cooking time: 7 minutes

Servings: 2

Ingredients:

- 1/4 cup all-purpose flour
- Salt and freshly ground black pepper, as needed
- 1 egg
- 1 tsp. water
- 1/2 cup Panko breadcrumbs
- 1 avocado, peeled, pitted, and sliced into 8 pieces
- Non-stick cooking spray

Directions:

1. In a shallow bowl, mix the flour, salt, and black pepper.
2. In a second bowl, mix well egg and water.
3. In a third bowl, put the breadcrumbs.
4. Coat the avocado slices with flour mixture, then dip into the egg mixture, and finally, coat evenly with the breadcrumbs.
5. Now, spray the avocado slices evenly with cooking spray.
6. Press the "Power Button" of Air Fry Oven and turn the dial to select the "Air Fry" mode.
7. Press the "Time" button and again turn the dial to set the cooking time to 7 minutes.
8. Now push the "Temp" button and rotate the dial to set the temperature at 400°F.
9. Press the "Start/Pause" button to start.
10. When the unit beeps to show that it is preheated, open the lid.
11. Arrange the avocado fries in "Air Fry Basket" and insert them in the oven.
12. Serve warm.

Nutrition:

- Calories: 391
- Total fat: 23.8 g.
- Saturated fat: 5.6 g.
- Cholesterol: 82 mg.
- Sodium 115 mg.
- Total carbs: 24.8 g.
- Fiber: 7.3 g.
- Sugar: 0.8 g.
- Protein: 7 g.

251. Dill Pickle Fries

Preparation time: 15 minutes

Cooking time: 15 minutes

Servings: 8

Ingredients:

- 1 (16-oz.) jar spicy dill pickle spears, drained and pat dried
- 3/4 cup all-purpose flour
- 1/2 tsp. paprika
- 1 egg, beaten
- 1/4 cup milk
- 1 cup panko breadcrumbs
- Nonstick cooking spray

Directions:

1. In a shallow dish, mix the flour, and paprika.
2. In a second dish, place the milk and egg and mix well.
3. In a third dish, put the breadcrumbs.
4. Coat the pickle spears with flour mixture, then dip into the egg mixture, and finally, coat evenly with the breadcrumbs.
5. Now, spray the pickle spears evenly with cooking spray.
6. Press the "Power Button" of the Air Fry Oven and turn the dial to select the "Air Fry" mode.
7. Press the "Time" button and again turn the dial to set the cooking time to 15 minutes.
8. Now push the "Temp" button and rotate the dial to set the temperature at 400 F.
9. Press the "Start/Pause" button to start.
10. When the unit beeps to show that it is preheated, open the lid.
11. Arrange the squash fries in "Air Fry Basket" and insert them in the oven.
12. Flip the fries once halfway through.
13. Serve warm.

Nutrition:

- Calories: 110
- Total fat: 1.9 g.
- Saturated fat: 0.7 g.
- Cholesterol: 21 mg.
- Sodium 697 mg.
- Total carbs: 12.8 g.
- Fiber: 1.1 g.
- Sugar: 1.1 g.
- Protein: 2.7 g.

Chapter 4: Vegetables

252. Low-Carb Carrot Cake

Preparation time: 20 minutes

Cooking time: 40 minutes

Servings: 12

Ingredients:

- 350 g. carrots
- 250 g. almond flour
- 200 g. almonds, ground
- 2 tsp. tartar baking powder
- 150 g. Xucker
- 2 tsp. cinnamon
- 100 g. powdered sugar
- 250 ml. vegetable oil
- 4 eggs
- 1 dash of lemon, fresh
- 1 vanilla pod
- 1 pinch of salt

Directions:

1. Preheat the air fryer to 180°C.
2. Put the almond flour, tartar powder, cinnamon, almonds, Xucker, and a pinch of salt in a bowl and mix
3. Add eggs, oil, and the mark of vanilla bean
4. Finally, the grated carrots and fold in a squeeze of lemon.
5. Put the dough in a greasy spring from the air fryer and bake for about 40 minutes at 180°C. Let the cake cool down and then sprinkle with powdered sugar.

Nutrition:

- Calories: 415
- Protein: 3.7 g.
- Carbs: 14.9 g.
- Fat: 32.5 g.

253. Low-Carb Strawberry Cake

Preparation time: 10 minutes

Cooking time: 15 minutes

Servings: 6

Ingredients:

- 100 g. almonds
- 200 g. walnuts
- 200 g. strawberries
- 1 tbsp. coconut flakes
- 1 vanilla pod
- 1 orange
- 6 dates without stone

Directions:

1. Chop almonds and walnuts with a *moulinette* until they are ground.
2. Squeeze orange and pour the juice into a measuring cup. Cut the vanilla pod and scrape out the pith with a knife.
3. Put the vanilla pod and four pitted dates in the measuring cup and mix with a mixer until one creamy mixture is formed.
4. Pour the juice-date mixture into a bowl, add the ground nuts and coconut flakes, stir and form the dough into a ball.
5. Place the dough ball on a cake plate and roll out to a 1 cm. thick bottom.
6. Wash strawberries, dry, remove green halve and halve.
7. Place 2 dates and half of the strawberries in a measuring cup and finely puree with a blender.
8. Spread fruit puree on the cake base.
9. Put the pieces of strawberry on it and the cake is ready.

Nutrition:

- Calories: 381
- Protein: 9 g.
- Carbs: 9 g.
- Fiber: 33 g.

254. Low-Carb Chocolate Brownies

Preparation time: 25 minutes

Cooking time: 20 minutes

Servings: 9

Ingredients:

- 150 g. dark chocolate (at least 75%)
- 220 g. butter
- 150 g. almond flour
- 4 eggs, medium size
- 200 g. Xucker
- 1 tbsp. powdered sugar
- 20 g. almonds
- 30 g. walnuts
- 3/4 rack baking soda
- Pinch of salt

Directions:

1. Preheat the air fryer to 175°C (circulating air). Grease the baking tin. Chop walnuts and almonds. Break the chocolate into pieces, dice the butter and melt both together in a hot water bath, then allow to cool.
2. Whisk eggs, add Xucker and salt, and beat until fluffy. Add flour, baking powder, and the chocolate-butter mixture and mix with a hand mixer.
3. Lifting nuts under the dough, put everything in the greased baking tin and bake for 15–20 minutes After 10 minutes, make a chopstick tasting, who likes it very juicy, will bring the cake out of the air fryer at the desired consistency
4. Let it cool down and sprinkle with powdered sugar.

Nutrition:

- Calories: 396
- Protein: 5.7 g.
- Carbs: 12.2 g.
- Fat: 34.6 g.

255. Salad With Tuna and Egg

Preparation time: 5 minutes

Cooking time: 10 minutes

Servings: 1

Ingredients:

- 2 eggs, medium size
- 60 g. tuna, in its juice (canned)
- 50 g. rocket
- 50 g. of cucumber
- 8 cherry tomatoes
- 1 spring onion
- 30 g. mozzarella cheese, grated
- 2 tbsp. olive oil
- Sea-salt
- Pepper

Directions:

1. Boil eggs in boiling water for 8–10 minutes. Quench eggs with cold water and peel, then slice.
2. First, open the tuna can one piece at a time and drain the tuna juice.
3. Open the can and then pluck the tuna into pieces with the fork.
4. Wash the rocket and remove long stalks, Wash and slice the tomatoes, Wash the cucumber and cut into pieces, clean the spring onion and cut into thin rings.
5. Arrange everything on a plate and drizzle with oil, season the salad with tuna and egg with salt and pepper and then sprinkle with mozzarella cheese.

Nutrition:

- Calories: 508
- Protein: 9 g.
- Carbs: 36 g.
- Fat: 35 g.

256. Sauerkraut With Pork Belly

Preparation time: 5 minutes

Cooking time: 10 minutes

Servings: 4

Ingredients:

- 500 g. sauerkraut, from the glass
- 600 g. pork belly, in whole
- 4 onions
- 2 tsp. Dijon mustard
- 1 Whole pimento
- 2 garllic Cloves
- 1 tsp. caraway
- 2 bay leaves
- 500 ml. of meat fond
- 1 tsp Sea-salt
- 1 tsp Pepper
- 2 tbsp. olive oil

Directions:

1. Rinse the pork belly and pat dry, then slice with a sharp knife.
2. Season the slices with salt and pepper and sprinkle with mustard.
3. Heat the oil in the air fryer and fry the slices from both sides.
4. Peel the onions and cut them into rings, Fry the onions golden yellow in the Air fryer
5. Put the sauerkraut in a sauce air fryer and distribute half of the onions, add caraway, bay leaves, pimento, cloves, and remaining ingredients and finally add the pork belly with the remaining onions.
6. Add the meat fond and simmer over low heat until the meat is tender and the bottom is almost overcooked.
7. Serve the slices of meat on the plates.
8. Season the sauerkraut with salt, sweeten something if necessary, and serve with the meat.

Nutrition:

- Calories: 599
- Protein: 13 g.
- Carbs: 26 g.
- Fat: 47 g.

257. Tomato Salad With Herbs and Basil

Preparation time: 5 minutes

Cooking time: 5 minutes

Servings: 1

Ingredients:

- 200 g. tomatoes
- 2 parsley stems
- 2 basil stems
- 1 tbsp. fig and date balsamic vinegar
- Sea salt
- Pepper

Directions:

1. Wash tomatoes and drain, then quarter, wash the parsley and basil and shake dry, then peel off leaves and chop.
2. Season the tomatoes with salt and pepper
3. Drizzle the balsamic vinager over the tomatoes and sprinkle with parsley and basil.

Nutrition:

- Calories: 68
- Protein: 13 g.
- Carbs: 2 g.
- Fat: 0 g.

258. Low-Carb Wraps With Vegetables

Preparation time: 10 minutes

Cooking time: 30 minutes

Servings: 4

Ingredients:

For the wraps:

- 2 eggs, medium size
- 50 g. butter
- 85 ml. soy drink or other milk
- 20 g. spelt flour, type 630
- 45 g. coconut flour

For the filling:

- 50 g. broccoli
- 1/2 red pepper
- 2 tbsp. corn (canned)
- 4 salad leaves
- 1 spring onion
- 4 tbsp. yogurt, natural
- Sea-salt
- Pepper
- Herbs at will

Directions:

1. Melt the butter in a sauce air fryer and allow to cool briefly.
2. Mix the eggs, butter, flour, and soy drink in a bowl to a smooth dough.
3. Wash vegetables and salad leaves and drain, Cut the broccoli florets from the stem, cut into small florets
4. Cut the peppers into small pieces, drain the corn in a sieve, small pluck the salad leaves
5. Clean the spring onion and cut it into fine rings.
6. Heat a small coated air fryer, then add about 1/4 of the dough and spread evenly in the air fryer by air fryer ning.
7. As soon as the rim is detached from the air fryer bottom, invert the wrap and bake briefly on the other side.
8. Prepare the other 3 wraps in the same procedure, stack finished wraps, and keep them warm and flexible.
9. Spread each wrap in the middle with 1 tbsp. yogurt, salt, and pepper, center the wraps with the prepared ingredients and fold them together.

Nutrition:

- Calories: 199
- Protein: 9 g.
- Carbs: 6 g.
- Fat: 14 g.

259. Fried Egg With Asparagus Bacon Rolls

Preparation time: 10 minutes

Cooking time: 15 minutes

Servings: 1

Ingredients:

- 1 egg, medium size
- 6 bars of green asparagus
- 100 g. bacon
- 2 tbsp. olive oil
- Sea-salt
- Pepper

Directions:

1. Peel the green asparagus in the lower third and cut off the dry ends
2. Wrap 2 asparagus spears in the middle with bacon slices.
3. Heat the oil in the air fryer and roast the asparagus with bacon.
4. Beat the egg and add to the air fryer.
5. Fry for several minutes, then season with salt, pepper, and serve.

Nutrition:

- Calories: 558
- Protein: 3 g.
- Carbs: 27g.
- Fat: 48 g.

260. Baking Paprika With Vegetables and Meat

Preparation time: 15 minutes

Cooking time: 30 minutes

Servings: 3

Ingredients:

- 3 peppers
- 200 g. chicken breast fillet
- 4 slices cheddar cheese or cave cheese
- 100 g. zucchini
- 100 g. mushrooms
- 2 shallots
- 2 tbsp. olive oil
- Sea salt
- Pepper

Directions:

1. Cut the peppers in half, corer them,

261. Roasted Bell Peppers

Servings: 6 cups

Preparation time: 15 min

Cooking time: 25 min

Ingredients:

- 1 tbsp. olive oil
- 1 tbsp. Maggi®
- 1 onion (sliced)
- 12 bell peppers (sliced

Directions:

1. Toss all the ingredients in an air fryer.
2. Cook in the air fryer for 25 minutes.

Nutrition:

- Cal: 61
- Total fat: 18 g.

2. and wash them. Wash the zucchini and cut into small pieces
3. Clean the mushrooms, remove the dry ends of the stems, and cut the mushrooms into pieces
4. Peel the shallots and finely chop.
5. Wash chicken breast and pat dry, then cut into small pieces.
6. Heat oil in the air fryer and sauté shallots and meat.
7. Add zucchini and mushrooms, fry everything, and season with salt and pepper.
8. Fill vegetables and meat mixture in the halves of the pepper and top with cheese.
9. Put the peppers in a refractory dish and gratinate in a preheated air fryer for 10–15 minutes at 175°C.
10. Serve with herbs as desired.

Nutrition:

- Calories: 308
- Protein: 7 g.
- Carbs: 27g.
- Fat: 18 g.

262. Chicken Breast Fillet With Shallots and Tomatoes in Red Wine Sauce

Preparation time: 15 minutes

Cooking time: 15 minutes

Servings: 2

Ingredients:

- 500 g. chicken breast fillet, 2 pieces
- 200 g. cherry tomatoes
- 200 ml. red wine
- 6 shallots
- 3 garlic cloves
- 2 sprigs of parsley
- 2 sprigs of Rosemary
- 2 tsp. honey
- 4 tbsp. olive oil
- Sea salt
- Pepper

Directions:

1. Wash chicken breasts and pat dry, peel the garlic and crush with the wide side of the knife
2. Wash herbs and shake dry, and peel the shallots.
3. Heat 2 tbsp. of oil in the air fryer and fry chicken fillets with thyme and 2 cloves of garlic. Cook the chicken in the air fryer for about 10 minutes in a preheated air fryer at 160°C.
4. In a second Air fryer, heat 2 tbsp. of oil and fry shallots, remaining garlic, and tomatoes. Deglaze everything with red wine and cook for a few minutes.
5. Season the sauce with honey, salt, and pepper.
6. Slicing the chicken breast, arrange the shallots, tomatoes, red wine sauce, and parsley leaves with the chicken and serve.

Nutrition:

- Calories: 534
- Protein: 9 g.
- Carbs: 71 g.
- Fat: 20 g.

263. Spice Stuffed Okra

Preparation time: 10 minutes

Cooking time: 7 minutes

Servings: 4

Ingredients:

- 8 3/4 oz. okra, split lengthwise
- A pinch of turmeric
- 2 tsp. chili powder
- 2 tsp. cumin powder
- 1 tsp. Chaat masala
- 2 tsp. coriander powder
- Salt to taste
- 1/2 cup chickpea flour
- 2 tsp. lime juice
- 1 tsp. oil

Directions:

1. Preheat the air fryer to 360°F.
2. Combine all the ingredients except the okra in a bowl and mix well to make a paste.
3. Stuff the okra with the spiced mixture.
4. Cook in the air fryer for 7 minutes.

Nutrition:

- Calories: 379
- Fat: 1 g.
- Carbs: 19 g.
- Protein: 7.7 g.
- Sugar: 17 g.

264. Chili Butternut Squash

Preparation time: 10 minutes

Cooking time: 20 minutes

Servings: 4

Ingredients:

- 1 butternut squash, seeds discarded, chunked
- 2 tsp. cumin seeds
- 1 pinch chili flakes
- 1 tbsp. olive oil
- 1 bunch fresh coriander, chopped
- 3/5 cup plain Greek yogurt
- 1 1/2 oz. pine nuts, toasted

Directions:

1. Toss the squash with the oil and seasonings.
2. Preheat the air fryer to 375°F.
3. Roast the squash in the air fryer for 20 minutes, tossing in between.
4. Serve topped with the yogurt, nuts, and coriander.

Nutrition:

- Calories: 139
- Fat: 12 g.
- Carbs: 13 g.
- Protein: 17 g.
- Sugar: 27 g.
-

265. Mediterranean Veggies

Preparation time: 5 minutes

Cooking time: 20 minutes

Servings: 4

Ingredients:

- 1 3/4 oz. cherry tomatoes
- 1 courgette, sliced
- 1 green pepper, sliced
- 1 parsnip, diced)
- 1 carrot, diced
- 1 tsp. mixed herbs
- 2 tbsp. honey
- 1 tsp. mustard
- 2 tsp. garlic puree
- 6 tbsp. olive oil
- Salt and pepper to taste

Directions:

1. Toss all the veggies together with oil and place them in the air fryer.
2. Cook in the air fryer for 15 minutes at 360°F.
3. Mix the rest of the ingredients in a bowl and then toss the veggies in it.
4. Cook for another 5 minutes at 392°F.

Nutrition:

- Calories: 300
- Fat: 3 g.
- Carbs: 12 g.
- Protein: 21 g.
- Sugar: 5 g.

266. Roasted Winter Veggies

Preparation time: 10 minutes

Cooking time: 20 minutes

Servings: 4

Ingredients:

- 1 1/3 cup parsnips, peeled, cubed
- 1 1/3 cup celery, cubed
- 2 red onions, peeled, wedged
- 1 1/3 cup butternut squash, seeds discarded, cubed
- 1 tbsp. fresh thyme needles
- 1 tbsp. olive oil
- Salt and pepper to taste

Directions:

1. Preheat the air fryer to 390°F.
2. Toss together all the ingredients and place them in the air fryer basket.
3. Cook for 20 minutes, stirring twice in between.

Nutrition:

- Calories: 406
- Fat: 5 g.
- Carbs: 20 g,
- Protein: 33 g,
- Sugar: 2 g,

267. Spaghetti Squash

Preparation time: 10 minutes

Cooking time: 50 minutes

Servings: 3

Ingredients:

- 1/2 spaghetti squash, seeds discarded
- 2 tsp. grape seed oil
- A pinch of salt
- A pinch of pepper
- 6 grape tomatoes, halved
- 1 chili Poblano, chop into strips

Directions:

1. Season the inside of the squash with salt, pepper, and oil.
2. Preheat the air fryer to 350°F.
3. Place the squash halves in the air fryer basket and

cook for 30–35 minutes.

4. Mix the tomatoes and pepper with salt and oil and place in the squash.
5. Cook for 15–20 minutes more.
6. Remove the squash skin using a fork.

Nutrition:

- Calories: 229
- Fat: 6 g.
- Carbs: 12 g.
- Protein: 30 g.

Sugar: 11 g.

268. Roasted Cauliflower

Preparation time: 5 minutes

Cooking time: 8 minutes

Servings: 1–2

Ingredients:

- 1 Cauliflower head, separated into florets
- A drizzle of olive oil
- Salt to taste

Directions:

1. Preheat the air fryer to 360°F.
2. Toss all the ingredients together and place them in the air fryer basket.
3. Cook for 8 minutes, tossing the cauliflower once midway.

Nutrition:

- Calories: 186
- Fat: 8 g.
- Carbs: 22 g.
- Protein: 37 g.
- Sugar: 14 g.

269. Zucchini Casserole

Preparation time: 10 minutes

Cooking time: 16 minutes

Servings: 4

Ingredients:

- 1 onion, chopped
- 4 zucchinis, chopped
- 1 1/2 tbsp. olive oil
- 1 garlic clove, chopped
- 3/4 tbsp. basil, chopped
- 3 cups semi-skimmed milk
- 1 1/2 tbsp. cornstarch
- 3 tbsp. cheese, grated
- Salt and pepper to taste
- Nutmeg to taste

Directions:

1. Combine the zucchini, onion, nutmeg, salt, and pepper in an air fryer.
2. Cook for 12 minutes.
3. Mix the milk and cornstarch, and add it to the air fryer pan along with the basil and garlic.
4. Cook for 4 minutes more.
5. Serve garnished with cheese.

Nutrition:

- Calories: 226
- Fat: 2 g.
- Carbs: 10 g.
- Protein: 29 g.
- Sugar: 9 g.

270. Vegetable Ratatouille

Preparation time: 10 minutes

Cooking time: 16 minutes

Servings: 4

Ingredients:

- 8 cherry tomatoes
- 2 garlic cloves, minced
- 1 red bell pepper, chopped
- 1 1/2 cups eggplant, cubed
- 1/2 cup zucchini, cubed
- 1/3 cup onion, chopped
- 2 tsp. olive oil
- 1/4 tsp. salt
- 1/8 tsp. black pepper
- 1/4 cup fresh basil, chopped
- 2 tbsp. Parmesan cheese, grated

Directions:

1. Toss together all the ingredients except the cheese and basil.
2. Place in an air fryer basket, cooking for 13–17 minutes, tossing every 5 minutes.
3. Serve garnished with basil and cheese.

Nutrition:

- Calories: 371
- Fat: 12 g.
- Carbs: 17 g.
- Protein: 21 g.
- Sugar: 1.8 g.

271. Garlic Mushrooms

Preparation time: 5 minutes

Cooking time: 8 minutes

Servings: 2

Ingredients:

- 5 1/4 oz. chestnut mushrooms, chopped
- 2 garlic cloves, chopped
- 1 tsp. paprika
- 1 tsp. chili powder
- 1 tsp. olive oil
- 1 tbsp. chives, chopped
- 2 tbsp. red wine

Directions:

1. Place the garlic and mushrooms in an air fryer tray and drizzle olive oil over.
2. Sprinkle the spices over and air fry for 4 minutes.
3. Drizzle the red wine over and air fry for another 4 minutes.
4. Serve garnished with the chives.

Nutrition:

- Calories: 237
- Fat: 8 g.
- Carbs: 13 g.
- Protein: 22.7 g.

Sugar: 17.3 g.

272. Curry Spiced Cauliflower

Preparation time: 10 minutes

Cooking time: 22 minutes

Servings: 2–3

Ingredients:

- 1 head organic cauliflower, separated into florets
- 1 tsp. curry powder
- 1/2 tbsp. olive oil
- Lemon juice of 1/2 lemon
- Sea salt and black pepper to taste

Directions:

1. Heat oil in the air fryer for 2 minutes, and then mix in the curry powder, and lemon juice.
2. Add the rest of the ingredients and toss.
3. Air fry for 20 minutes.

Nutrition:

- Calories: 170
- Fat: 15 g.
- Carbs: 18 g.
- Protein: 41 g.
- Sugar: 12 g.

273. Roasted Eggplant

Preparation time: 15 minutes

Cooking time: 25 minutes

Servings: 6

Ingredients:

- 1 1/2 lbs. eggplant, cubed
- 1 tbsp. + 1 tsp. olive oil
- 1 tbsp. Maggi® seasoning sauce
- 1 tsp. Onion powder
- 1 tsp. Garlic powder
- 1 tsp. sumac
- 2 bay leaves
- 3 tsp. Za'atar
- Lemon juice of 1/2 lemon

Directions:

1. Mix all the ingredients in an air fryer except the eggplant 1 tsp. olive

oil and lemon juice and cook for a minute.

2. Toss in the eggplant and cook for 25 minutes.

3. Mix the lemon juice and olive oil and toss sit in the eggplant.

Nutrition:

- Calories: 67
- Total fat: 3.4 g.
- Saturated fat: 0.9 g.
- Sodium: 2 mg.
- Cholesterol: 2 mg.
- Carbs: 9.5 g.
- Fiber: 5 g.
- Protein: 1.6 g.

274. Soya Manchurian

Preparation time: 15 minutes

Cooking time: 15 minutes

Servings: 5–6

Ingredients:

- 1 cup soya chunks, soaked, boiled
- 1 bell pepper, thinly sliced
- 2 tsp. gram flour
- 1 cup spring onions, chopped
- 1 tsp. ginger garlic paste
- 2 tsp. cornflour
- 1 tbsp. chili sauce
- 1 tbsp. tomato ketchup
- 1 tbsp. soy sauce
- Salt and black pepper to taste
- 3 tsp. olive oil

Directions:

1. Combine the soya, 2 tsp. oil and gram flour and toss.

2. Cook in an air fryer for 8 minutes at 180°F.

3. Heat the remaining oil in a pan and sauté the spring onions, bell pepper, and ginger garlic paste for 2 minutes.

4. Combine cornflour with some water and add to the pan, cooking for 15 minutes.

5. Add the sauces, salt, and pepper and cook for another 5 minutes.

6. Add water if required if the sauce is too thick and heat.

7. Serve garnished with some spring onions.

Nutrition:

- Calories: 372
- Fat: 2.4 g.
- Carbs: 13.4 g.
- Protein: 27.3 g.
- Sugar: 8.4 g.

275. Grilled Endives

Preparation time: 10 minutes

Cooking time: 10 minutes

Servings: 6

Ingredients:

- 6 heads Belgian endives, halved
- 1/2 cup yogurt, plain, fat-free
- 1 tsp. garlic powder
- 1/2 tsp. curry powder
- 1/2 tsp. salt
- 1/2 tsp. black pepper, ground
- 3 tbsp. lemon juice

Directions:

1. Combine all the ingredients except the endives and mix well.
2. Marinate the endives in the prepared marinade for 30 minutes.
3. Spray the air fryer basket and cook the endives in it for 10 minutes.

Nutrition:

- Calories: 106
- Total fat: 1.3 g.
- Saturated fat: 0.5 g.
- Sodium: 321 mg.
- Cholesterol: 1 mg.
- Carbs: 19.7 g.
- Fiber: 16.1 g.
- Protein: 7.7 g.

276. Tomato Bites With Creamy Parmesan Sauce

Preparation time: 7 minutes

Cooking time: 13 minutes

Servings: 4

Ingredients:

For the sauce:

- 1/2 cup Parmigiano-Reggiano cheese, grated
- 4 tbsp. pecans, chopped
- 1 tsp. garlic puree
- 1/2 tsp. fine sea salt
- 1/3 cup extra-virgin olive oil

For the tomato bites:

- 2 large-sized Roma tomatoes, cut into thin slices and pat them dry
- 8 oz. Halloumi cheese, cut into thin slices
- 1/3 cup onions, sliced
- 1 tsp. basil, dried
- 1/4 tsp. red pepper flakes, crushed
- 1/8 tsp. sea salt

Directions:

1. Start by preheating your air fryer to 385°F.
2. Make the sauce by mixing all ingredients, except the extra-virgin olive oil, in your food processor.
3. While the machine is running, slowly and gradually pour in the olive oil, puree until everything is well-blended.
4. Now, spread 1 tsp. of the sauce over the top of each tomato slice. Place a slice of Halloumi cheese on each tomato slice. Top with onion slices. Sprinkle with basil, red pepper, and sea salt.
5. Transfer the assembled bites to the air fryer cooking basket. Drizzle with a nonstick cooking spray and cook for approximately 13 minutes.
6. Arrange these bites on a nice serving platter, garnish with the remaining sauce and serve at room temperature. Bon appétit!

Nutrition:

- Calories: 428
- Fat: 38.4 g.
- Carbs: 4.5 g.
- Protein: 18.8 g.

- Sugar: 2.3 g.
- Fiber: 1.3 g.

277. Creamy Cauliflower and Broccoli

Preparation time: 4 minutes

Cooking time: 16 minutes

Servings: 6

Ingredients:

- 1 lb. cauliflower florets
- 1 lb. broccoli florets
- 2 1/2 tbsp. sesame oil
- 1/2 tsp. cayenne pepper, smoked
- 3/4 tsp. sea salt flakes
- 1 tbsp. lemon zest, grated
- 1/2 cup Colby cheese, shredded

Directions:

1. Prepare the cauliflower and broccoli using your favorite steaming method. Then, drain them well; add the sesame oil, cayenne pepper, and salt flakes.

2. Air fry at 390°F for approximately 16 minutes; make sure to check the vegetables halfway through the cooking time.

3. Afterward, stir in the lemon zest and Colby cheese; toss to coat well and serve immediately!

Nutrition:

- Calories: 133
- Fat: 9.0 g
- Carbs: 9.5 g
- Protein: 5.9 g
- Sugar: 3.2 g

- Fiber: 3.6 g

278. Mediterranean-Style Eggs With Spinach

Preparation time: 3 minutes

Cooking time: 12 minutes

Servings: 2

Ingredients:

- 2 tbsp. olive oil, melted
- 4 eggs, whisked
- 5 oz. fresh spinach, chopped
- 1 medium-sized tomato, chopped
- 1 tsp. fresh lemon juice
- 1/2 tsp. coarse salt
- 1/2 tsp. black pepper, ground
- 1/2 cup fresh basil, roughly chopped

Directions:

1. Add the olive oil to an air fryer baking pan. Make sure to tilt the pan to spread the oil evenly.
2. Simply combine the remaining ingredients, except for the basil leaves; whisk well until everything is well incorporated.
3. Cook in the preheated air fryer for 8–12 minutes at 280°F. Garnish with fresh basil leaves. Serve warm with a dollop of sour cream if desired.

Nutrition:

- Calories: 274
- Fat: 23.2 g.
- Carbs: 5.7 g.
- Protein: 13.7 g.
- Sugar: 2.6 g.
- Fiber: 2.6 g.

279. Spicy Zesty Broccoli With Tomato Sauce

Preparation time: 5 minutes

Cooking time: 15 minutes

Servings: 6

Ingredients:

For the broccoli bites:

- 1 medium-sized head broccoli, broken into florets
- 1/2 tsp. lemon zest, freshly grated
- 1/3 tsp. sea salt, fine
- 1/2 tsp. hot paprika
- 1 tsp. shallot powder
- 1 tsp. porcini powder
- 1/2 tsp. granulated garlic
- 1/3 tsp. celery seeds
- 1 1/2 tbsp. olive oil

For the Hot Sauce:

- 1/2 cup tomato sauce
- 1 tbsp. balsamic vinegar
- 1/2 tsp. ground allspice

Directions:

1. Toss all the ingredients for the broccoli bites in a mixing bowl, covering the broccoli florets on all sides.
2. Cook them in the preheated air fryer at 360°F for 13–15 minutes. In the meantime, mix all ingredients for the hot sauce.
3. Pause your air fryer, mix the broccoli with the prepared sauce and cook for a further 3 minutes. Bon appétit!

Nutrition:

- Calories:70
- Fat: 3.8 g.
- Carbs: 5.8 g.
- Protein: 2 g.
- Sugar: 6.6 g.
- Fiber: 1.5 g.

280. Cheese Stuffed Mushrooms With Horseradish Sauce

Preparation time: 3 minutes

Cooking time: 12 minutes

Servings: 5

Ingredients:

- 1/2 cup Parmesan cheese, grated
- 2 cloves garlic, pressed
- 2 tbsp. fresh coriander, chopped
- 1/3 tsp. kosher salt
- 1/2 tsp. crushed red pepper flakes
- 1 1/2 tbsp. olive oil
- 20 mushrooms, medium-sized, cut off the stems
- 1/2 cup Gorgonzola cheese, grated
- 1/4 cup mayonnaise, low-fat
- 1 tsp. prepared horseradish, well-drained
- 1 tbsp. fresh parsley, finely chopped

Directions:

1. Mix the Parmesan cheese with the garlic, coriander, salt, red pepper, and olive oil; mix to combine well.
2. Stuff the mushroom caps with the cheese filling. Top with grated Gorgonzola.
3. Place the mushrooms in the air fryer grill pan and slide them into the machine. Grill them at 380°F for 8–12 minutes or until the stuffing is warmed through.
4. Meanwhile, prepare the horseradish sauce by mixing the mayonnaise, horseradish, and parsley. Serve the horseradish sauce with the warm fried mushrooms. Enjoy!

Nutrition:

- Calories: 180
- Fat: 13.2 g.
- Carbs: 6.2 g.
- Protein: 8.6 g.
- Sugar: 2.1 g.
- Fiber: 1 g.

281. Broccoli With Herbs and Cheese

Preparation time: 8 minutes

Cooking time: 17 minutes

Servings: 4

Ingredients:

- 1/3 cup yellow cheese, grated
- 1 head broccoli, large-sized, stemmed and cut small florets
- 2 1/2 tbsp. canola oil
- 2 tsp. Rosemary, dried
- 2 tsp. basil, dried
- Salt and ground black pepper, to taste

Directions:

1. Bring a medium pan filled with a lightly salted water to a boil. Then, boil the broccoli florets for about 3 minutes.
2. Then, drain the broccoli florets well; toss them with the canola oil, Rosemary, basil, salt and black pepper.
3. Set your air fryer to 390°F; arrange the seasoned broccoli in the cooking basket; set the timer for 17 minutes. Toss the broccoli halfway through the cooking process.
4. Serve warm topped with grated cheese and enjoy!

Nutrition:

- Calories: 103
- Fat: 9.1 g.
- Carbs: 4.9 g.
- Protein: 1.9 g.
- Sugar: 1.2 g.
- Fiber: 0.4 g.

282. Family Favorite Stuffed Mushroom

Preparation time: 4 minutes

Cooking time: 12 minutes

Servings: 2

Ingredients:

- 2 tsp. cumin powder
- 4 garlic cloves, peeled and minced
- 1 small onion, peeled and chopped
- 18 medium-sized white mushrooms
- Fine sea salt and freshly ground black pepper, to your liking
- A pinch ground allspice
- 2 tbsp. olive oil

Directions:

1. First, clean the mushrooms; remove the middle stalks from the mushrooms to prepare the "shells".
2. Grab a mixing dish and thoroughly combine the remaining items. Fill the mushrooms with the prepared mixture.
3. Cook the mushrooms at 345°F heat for 12 minutes. Enjoy!

Nutrition:

- Calories: 179
- Fat: 14.7 g.
- Carbs: 8.5 g.
- Protein: 5.5 g.
- Sugar: 4.6 g.
- Fiber: 2.6 g.

283. Spanish-Style Eggs With Manchego Cheese

Preparation time: 10 minutes

Cooking time: 38 minutes

Servings: 4

Ingredients:

- 1/3 cup Manchego cheese, grated
- 5 eggs
- 1 small onion, finely chopped
- 2 green garlic stalks, peeled and finely minced
- 1 1/2 cups white mushrooms, chopped
- 1 tsp. basil, dried
- 1 1/2 tbsp. olive oil
- 3/4 tsp. oregano, dried
- 1/2 tsp. dried parsley flakes or 1 tbsp. fresh flat-leaf Italian parsley
- 1 tsp. porcini powder
- Table salt and freshly ground black pepper, to savor

Directions:

1. Start by preheating your air fryer to 350°F. Add the oil, mushrooms, onion, and green garlic to the air fryer baking dish. Bake this mixture for 6 minutes or until it is tender.

2. Meanwhile, crack the eggs into a mixing bowl; beat the eggs until they're well whisked. Next, add the seasonings and mix again. Pause your air fryer and take the baking dish out of the basket.

3. Pour the whisked egg mixture into the baking dish with sautéed mixture. Top with the grated Manchego cheese.

4. Bake for about 32 minutes at 320°F or until your frittata is set. Serve warm. Bon appétit!

Nutrition:

- Calories: 153
- Fat: 11.9 g.
- Carbs: 3.2 g.
- Protein: 9.3 g.
- Sugar: 1.7 g.
- Fiber: 0.9 g.

284. Famous Fried Pickles

Preparation time: 5 minutes

Cooking time: 15 minutes

Servings: 6

Ingredients:

- 1/3 cup milk
- 1 tsp. garlic powder
- 2 eggs, medium-sized
- 1 tsp. sea salt, fine
- 1/3 tsp. chili powder
- 1/3 cup all-purpose flour
- 1/2 tsp. shallot powder
- 2 jars sweet and sour pickle spears

Directions:

1. Pat the pickle spears dry with a kitchen towel. Then, take 2 mixing bowls.
2. Whisk the egg and milk in a bowl. In another bowl, combine all dry ingredients.
3. Firstly, dip the pickle spears into the dry mix; then coat each pickle with the egg/milk mixture; dredge them in the flour mixture again for additional coating.
4. Air fry battered pickles for 15 minutes at 385°F. Enjoy!

Nutrition:

- Calories: 58
- Fat: 2 g.
- Carbs: 6.8 g.
- Protein: 3.2 g.
- Sugar: 0.9 g.
- Fiber: 0.4 g.

285. Fried Squash Croquettes

Preparation time: 5 minutes

Cooking time: 17 minutes

Servings: 4

Ingredients:

- 1/3 cup all-purpose flour
- 1/3 tsp. black pepper, freshly ground, or more to taste
- 1/3 tsp. dried sage
- 4 cloves garlic, minced
- 1 1/2 tbsp. olive oil
- 1/3 butternut squash, peeled and grated
- 2 eggs, well whisked
- 1 tsp. sea salt, fine
- A pinch of ground allspice

Directions:

1. Thoroughly combine all ingredients in a mixing bowl.
2. Preheat your air fryer to 345°F and set the timer for 17 minutes; cook until your fritters are browned; serve right away.

Nutrition:

- Calories: 152
- Fat: 10.02 g.
- Carbs: 9.4 g.
- Protein: 5.8 g.
- Sugar: 0.3 g.
- Fiber: 0.4 g.

286. Tamarind Glazed Sweet Potatoes

Preparation time: 2 minutes

Cooking time: 22 minutes

Servings: 4

Ingredients:

- 1/3 tsp. white pepper
- 1 tbsp. butter, melted
- 1/2 tsp. turmeric powder
- 5 garnet sweet potatoes, peeled and diced
- A few drops of liquid Stevia
- 2 tsp. tamarind paste
- 1 1/2 tbsp. fresh lime juice
- 1 1/2 tsp. ground allspice

Directions:

1. In a mixing bowl, toss all ingredients until sweet potatoes are well coated.
2. Air-fry them at 335°F for 12 minutes.
3. Pause the air fryer and toss again. Increase the temperature to 390°F and cook for an additional 10 minutes. Eat warm.

Nutrition:

- Calories:103
- Fat: 9.1 g.
- Carbs: 4.9 g.
- Protein: 1.9 g.
- Sugar: 1.2 g.
- Fiber: 0.3 g.

287. Roasted Cauliflower With Pepper Jack Cheese

Preparation time: 4 minutes

Cooking time: 21 minutes

Servings: 2

Ingredients:

- 1/3 tsp. shallot powder
- 1 tsp. black pepper, ground
- 1 1/2 large-sized heads of cauliflower, broken into florets
- 1/4 tsp. cumin powder
- 1/2 tsp. garlic salt
- 1/4 cup Pepper Jack cheese, grated
- 1 1/2 tbsp. vegetable oil
- 1/3 tsp. paprika

Directions:

1. Boil cauliflower in a large pan of salted water for approximately 5 minutes. After that, drain the cauliflower florets; now, transfer them to a baking dish.
2. Toss the cauliflower florets with the rest of the above ingredients.
3. Roast at 395°F for 16 minutes, turn them halfway through the process. Enjoy!

Nutrition:

- Calories: 271
- Fat: 23 g.
- Carbs: 8.9 g.
- Protein: 9.8 g.
- Sugar: 2.8 g.
- Fiber: 4.5 g.

288. Ginger Chili Broccoli

Preparation time: 15 minutes

Cooking time: 25 minutes

Servings: 5

Ingredients:

- 8 cups broccoli florets
- 1/2 cup olive oil
- 2 fresh lime juice
- 2 tbsp. fresh ginger, grated
- 2 tsp. chili pepper, chopped

Directions:

1. Add broccoli florets into the steamer and steam for 8 minutes.
2. Meanwhile, for dressing in a small bowl, combine lime juice, oil, ginger, and chili pepper.
3. Add steamed broccoli in a large bowl then pour dressing over broccoli. Toss well.

Nutrition:

- Calories: 239
- Fat: 20.8 g,
- Carbs: 13.7 g,
- Sugar: 3 g,
- Protein: 4.5 g,
- Cholesterol: 0 mg

Chapter 5: Poultry Recipes

289. Asian Spicy Turkey

Preparation time: 10 minutes

Cooking time: 25 minutes

Servings: 6

Ingredients:

- 1 tbsp. sesame oil
- 2 lb. turkey thighs
- 1 tsp. Chinese 5-spice powder
- 1 tsp. pink Himalayan salt
- 1/4 tsp. Sichuan pepper
- 1 tbsp. Chinese rice vinegar
- 2 tbsp. soy sauce
- 1 tbsp. chili sauce
- 1 tbsp. mustard

Directions:

1. Preheat your air fryer to 360°F.
2. Brush the sesame oil all over the turkey thighs. Season them with spices.
3. Cook for 23 minutes, turning over once or twice. Make sure to work in batches to ensure even cooking
4. In the meantime, combine the remaining ingredients in a wok (or similar type pan) that is preheated over medium-high heat. Cook and stir until the sauce reduce by about a third.
5. Add the fried turkey thighs to the wok; gently stir to coat with the sauce.
6. Let the turkey rest for 10 minutes before slicing and serving. Enjoy!

Nutrition:

- Calories: 279
- Fat: 16.2 g.
- Carbs: 2.4 g.
- Protein: 29 g.
- Sugar: 1.4 g.
- Fiber: 2.2 g.

290. Spicy Chicken Drumsticks With Herbs

Preparation time: 10 minutes

Cooking time: 30 minutes

Servings: 6

Ingredients:

- 6 chicken drumsticks

Sauce:

- 6 oz. hot sauce
- 3 tbsp. olive oil
- 3 tbsp. tamari sauce
- 1 tsp. thyme, dried
- 1/2 tsp. oregano, dried

Directions:

1. Spritz the sides and bottom of the cooking basket with a nonstick cooking spray.

2. Cook the chicken drumsticks at 380°F for 35 minutes, flipping them over halfway through.

3. Meanwhile, heat the hot sauce, olive oil, tamari sauce, thyme, and oregano in a pan over medium-low heat; reserve.

4. Drizzle the sauce over the prepared chicken drumsticks; toss to coat well and serve. Bon appétit!

Nutrition:

- Calories: 280
- Fat: 18.7 g.
- Carbs: 2.6 g.
- Protein: 24.1 g.
- Sugar: 1.4 g.
- Fiber: 0.5 g.

291. Classic Chicken With Peanuts

Preparation time: 10 minutes

Cooking time: 15 minutes

Servings: 4

Ingredients:

- 1 1/2 lb. chicken tenderloins
- 2 tbsp. peanut oil
- 1/2 cup Parmesan cheese, grated
- Sea salt and ground black pepper, to taste
- 1/2 tsp. garlic powder
- 1 tsp. red pepper flakes
- 2 tbsp. peanuts, roasted and roughly chopped

Directions:

1. Start by preheating

your air fryer to 360°F.

2. Brush the chicken tenderloins with peanut oil on all sides.

3. In a mixing bowl, thoroughly combine grated Parmesan cheese, salt, black pepper, garlic powder, and red pepper flakes. Dredge the chicken in the breading, shaking off any residual coating.

4. Lay the chicken tenderloins into the cooking basket. Cook for 12–13 minutes or until it is no longer pink in the center. Work in batches; an instant-read thermometer should read at least 165°F.

5. Serve garnished with roasted peanuts. Bon appétit!

Nutrition:

- Calories: 354
- Fat: 17.4 g.
- Carbs: 6.3 g.
- Protein: 40 g.
- Sugar: 1.4 g.
- Fiber: 0.7 g.

292. Turkey With Paprika and Tarragon

Preparation time: 10 minutes

Cooking time: 30 minutes

Servings: 6

Ingredients:

- 2 lb. turkey tenderloins
- 2 tbsp. olive oil
- Salt and ground black pepper, to taste
- 1 tsp. smoked paprika
- 2 tbsp. dry white wine
- 1 tbsp. fresh tarragon leaves, chopped

Directions:

1. Brush the turkey tenderloins with olive oil. Season

with salt, black pepper, and paprika.

2. Afterward, add the white wine and tarragon.

3. Cook the turkey tenderloins at 350°F for 30 minutes, flipping them over halfway through. Let them rest for 5–9 minutes before slicing and serving. Enjoy!

Nutrition:

- Calories: 217
- Fat: 7.5 g.
- Carbs: 1.2 g.
- Protein: 34.7 g.
- Sugar: 0.5 g.

Fiber: 0.3 g.

293. Italian-Style Chicken With Roma Tomatoes

Preparation time: 15 minutes

Cooking time: 30 minutes

Servings: 8

Ingredients:

- 2 tsp. olive oil, melted
- 3 lb. chicken breasts, bone-in
- 1/2 tsp. black pepper, freshly ground
- 1/2 tsp. salt
- 1 tsp. cayenne pepper
- 2 tbsp. fresh parsley, minced
- 1 tsp. fresh basil, minced
- 1 tsp. fresh Rosemary, minced
- 4 Roma tomatoes, medium-sized, halved

Directions:

1. Start by preheating your air fryer to 370°F. Brush the cooking basket with 1 tsp. of olive oil.

2. Sprinkle the chicken breasts with all seasonings listed above.

3. Cook for 25 minutes or until chicken breasts are slightly browned. Work in batches.

4. Arrange the tomatoes in the cooking basket and brush them with the remaining tsp. of olive oil. Season with sea salt.

5. Cook the tomatoes at 350°F for 10 minutes, shaking halfway through the cooking time. Serve with chicken

breasts. Bon appétit!

Nutrition:

- Calories: 315
- Fat: 17.1 g.
- Carbs: 2.7 g.
- Protein: 36 g.
- Sugar: 1.7 g.
- Fiber: 0.9 g.

294. Duck Breasts With Candy Onion and Coriander

Preparation time: 10 minutes

Cooking time: 25 minutes

Servings: 4

Ingredients:

- 1 1/2 lb. duck breasts, skin removed
- 1 tsp. kosher salt
- 1/2 tsp. cayenne pepper
- 1/3 tsp. black pepper
- 1/2 tsp. smoked paprika
- 1 tbsp. Thai red curry paste
- 1 cup candy onions, halved
- 1/4 small pack coriander, chopped

Directions:

1. Place the duck breasts between 2 sheets of foil; then, use a rolling pin to bash the duck until they are 1-inch thick.
2. Preheat your air fryer to 395°F.
3. Rub the duck breasts with salt, cayenne pepper, black pepper, paprika, and red curry paste. Place the duck breast in the cooking basket.
4. Cook for 11–12 minutes. Top with candy onions and cook for another 10–11 minutes.
5. Serve garnished with coriander and enjoy!

Nutrition:

- Calories: 362
- Fat: 18.7 g.
- Carbs: 4 g.

258

- Protein: 42.3 g.
- Sugar: 1.3 g.
- Fiber: 2.5 g.

295. Turkey Burgers With Crispy Bacon

Preparation time: 10 minutes

Cooking time: 30 minutes

Servings: 4

Ingredients:

- 2 tbsp. vermouth
- 2 strips Canadian bacon, sliced
- 1-lb. ground turkey
- 1/2 shallot, minced
- 2 garlic cloves, minced
- 2 tbsp. fish sauce
- Sea salt and ground black pepper, to taste
- 1 tsp. red pepper flakes
- 4 tbsp. tomato ketchup
- 4 tbsp. mayonnaise
- 4 (1-oz.) slices cheddar cheese
- 4 lettuce leaves

Directions:

1. Start by preheating your air fryer to 400°F. Brush the Canadian bacon with the vermouth.
2. Cook for 3 minutes. Flip the bacon over and cook an additional 3 minutes.
3. Then, thoroughly combine the ground turkey, shallots, garlic, fish sauce, salt, black pepper, and red pepper. Form the meat mixture into 4 burger patties.
4. Bake in the preheated air fryer at 370°F for 10 minutes. Flip them over and cook for another 10 minutes.
5. Serve turkey burgers with ketchup, mayonnaise, bacon,

cheese, and lettuce; serve immediately.

Nutrition:

- Calories: 308
- Fat: 16.4 g.
- Carbs:7.4 g.
- Protein: 30.9 g.
- Sugar: 4.4 g.
- Fiber: 0.6 g.

296. Chicken Sausage Casserole

Preparation time: 10 minutes

Cooking time: 15 minutes

Servings: 4

Ingredients:

- 8 oz. zucchini, spiralizer
- 1 lb. smoked chicken sausage, sliced
- 1 tomato, pureed
- 1/2 cup Asiago cheese, shredded
- 1 tbsp. Italian seasoning mix
- 3 tbsp. Romano cheese, grated
- 1 tbsp. fresh basil leaves, chiffonade
- Cooking spray

Directions:

1. Salt the zucchini and let it stand for 30 minutes, pat it dry with kitchen towels.
2. Then, spritz a baking pan with cooking spray; add the zucchini to the pan. Stir in the chicken sausage, tomato puree, Asiago cheese, and Italian seasoning mix.
3. Bake in the preheated air fryer at 325°F for 11 minutes.
4. Top with the grated Romano cheese. Turn the temperature to 390°F and cook an additional 5 minutes or until everything is thoroughly heated and the cheese is melted.
5. Garnish with fresh basil leaves. Bon appétit!

Nutrition:

- Calories: 300
- Fat: 17.8 g.
- Carbs: 9.7 g.
- Protein: 25.3 g.
- Sugar: 4.7 g.
- Fiber: 2.3 g.

297. Turkey Tenderloins With Gravy

Preparation time: 10 minutes

Cooking time: 20 minutes

Servings: 4

Ingredients:

- 1 lb. turkey tenderloins
- 1 tbsp. Dijon-style mustard
- 1 tbsp. olive oil
- Sea salt and ground black pepper, to taste
- 1 tsp. Italian seasoning mix
- 1 cup turkey stock
- 1/2 tsp. xanthan gum
- 4 tbsp. tomato ketchup
- 4 tbsp. mayonnaise
- 4 pickles, sliced

Directions:

1. Rub the turkey tenderloins with mustard and olive oil. Season with salt, black pepper, and Italian seasoning mix.
2. Cook the turkey tenderloins at 350°F for 30 minutes, flipping them over halfway through. Let them rest for 5–7 minutes before slicing.
3. For the gravy, in a saucepan, place the drippings from the roasted turkey. Add in turkey stock and bring to a boil.
4. Stir in xanthan gum and whisk to combine. Let simmer another 5–10 minutes until starting to thicken. Gravy will thicken more as it cools.
5. Serve turkey

tenderloins with gravy, tomato ketchup, mayonnaise, and pickles. Serve and enjoy!

Nutrition:

- Calories: 276
- Fat: 16.4 g.
- Carbs: 5.2 g.
- Protein: 26.9 g.
- Sugar: 2.3 g.
- Fiber:1.9 g.

298. Old-Fashioned Turkey Chili

Preparation time: 10 minutes

Cooking time: 40 minutes

Servings: 4

Ingredients:

- 1/2 medium-sized leek, chopped
- 1/2 red onion, chopped
- 2 garlic cloves, minced
- 1 jalapeño pepper, seeded and minced
- 1 bell pepper, seeded and chopped
- 2 tbsp. olive oil
- 1 lb. ground turkey, 85% lean 15% fat
- 2 cups tomato puree
- 2 cups chicken stock
- 1/2 tsp. black peppercorns

- Salt, to taste
- 1 tsp. chili powder
- 1 tsp. mustard seeds
- 1 tsp. ground cumin

Directions:

1. Start by preheating your air fryer to 365°F.
2. Place the leeks, onion, garlic, and peppers in a baking pan; drizzle olive oil evenly over the top. Cook for 4–6 minutes.
3. Add the ground turkey. Cook for 6 minutes more or until the meat is no longer pink.
4. Now, add the tomato puree, 1 cup of chicken stock, black peppercorns, salt, chili powder, mustard seeds, and cumin to the baking pan. Cook for 24 minutes, stirring every 7–10 minutes.

5. Bon appétit!

Nutrition:

- Calories: 271
- Fat: 15.7 g.
- Carbs: 7.6 g.
- Protein: 25.7 g.
- Sugar: 3.6 g.
- Fiber: 1.4 g.

299. Korean Chicken Wings

Preparation time: 10 minutes

Cooking time: 25 minutes

Servings: 4

Ingredients:

Wings:

- 1 tsp. pepper
- 1 tsp. salt
- 2 lb. chicken wings

Sauce:

- 2 packets Splenda
- 1 tbsp. garlic, minced
- 1 tbsp. ginger, minced
- 1 tbsp. sesame oil
- 1 tsp. agave nectar
- 1 tbsp. mayo
- 2 tbsp. gochujang

Finishing:

- 1/4 cup green onions, chopped
- 2 tsp. sesame seeds

Directions:

1. Ensure the air fryer is preheated to 400°F.
2. Line a small pan with foil and place a rack onto the pan, then place into the air fryer.
3. Season wings with pepper and salt and place them onto the rack.
4. Air fry 20 minutes, turning at 10 minutes.
5. As chicken air fries, mix all the sauce components.
6. Once a

thermometer says that the chicken has reached 160°F, take out wings and place them into a bowl.

7. Pour half of the sauce mixture over wings, tossing well to coat.

8. Put coated wings back into air fryer for 5 minutes or till they reach 165°F.

9. Remove and sprinkle with green onions and sesame seeds. Dip into the extra sauce.

Nutrition:

- Calories: 356
- Fat: 26 g.
- Protein: 23 g.
- Sugar:: 2 g.

300. Buffalo Chicken Wings

Preparation time: 15 minutes

Cooking time: 30 minutes

Servings: 8

Ingredients:

- 1 tsp. salt
- 1–2 tbsp. brown sugar
- 1 tbsp. Worcestershire sauce
- 1/2 cup vegan butter
- 1/2 cup cayenne pepper sauce
- 4 lb. chicken wings
- 3 celery sticks

Directions:

1. Whisk salt, brown sugar, Worcestershire sauce, butter, and cayenne pepper sauce together and set to the side.

2. Dry wings and add to air fryer basket.

3. Cook 25 minutes at 380°F, tossing halfway through.

4. When the timer sounds, shake wings and bump up the temperature to 400°F and cook for another 5 minutes.

5. Take out wings and place them into a big bowl. Add sauce and toss well.

6. Serve alongside celery sticks!

Nutrition:

- Calories: 402
- Fat: 16 g.
- Protein: 17 g.

- Sugar: 4 g.

301. Chicken Fajita Rollups

Preparation time: 5 minutes

Cooking time: 12 minutes

Servings: 8

Ingredients:

- 1/2 tsp. oregano
- 1/2 tsp. cayenne pepper
- 1 tsp. cumin
- 1 tsp. garlic powder
- 2 tsp. paprika
- 1/2 sliced red onion
- 1/2 yellow bell pepper, sliced into strips
- 1/2 green bell pepper, sliced into strips
- 1/2 red bell pepper, sliced into strips
- 3 chicken breasts
- 1 tsp salt and pepper

Directions:

1. Mix oregano, cayenne pepper, garlic powder, cumin, and paprika along with 1–2 pinch of pepper and salt. Set to the side.
2. Slice chicken breasts lengthwise into 2 slices.
3. Between 2 pieces of parchment paper, add breast slices and pound till they are 1/4-inch thick. With seasoning, liberally season both sides of chicken slices.
4. Put 2 strips of each color of bell pepper and a few onion slices onto chicken pieces.

5. Roll up tightly and secure with toothpicks.

6. Repeat with remaining ingredients and sprinkle and rub the mixture that is left over the chicken rolls.

7. Lightly grease your air fryer basket and place 3 rollups into the fryer. Cook 12 minutes at 400 degrees.

8. Repeat with remaining rollups.

9. Serve with salad!

Nutrition:

- Calories: 189
- Fat: 14 g.
- Protein: 11 g.
- Sugar: 1 g.

302. Crispy Honey Garlic Chicken Wings

Preparation time: 15 minutes

Cooking time: 35 minutes

Servings: 8

Ingredients:

- 1/8 cup water
- 1/2 tsp. salt
- 4 tbsp. garlic, minced
- 1/4 cup vegan butter
- 1/4 cup raw honey
- 3/4 cup almond flour
- 16 chicken wings

Directions:

1. Rinse off and dry chicken wings well.

2. Spray the air fryer basket with olive oil.

3. Coat chicken wings with almond flour and add coated wings to the air fryer. Cook 25 minutes at 380°F, shaking every 5 minutes.

4. When the timer goes off, cook 5–10 minutes at 400°F till the skin becomes crispy and dry.

5. As chicken cooks, melt butter in a saucepan and add garlic. Sauté garlic 5 minutes. Add salt and honey, simmer for 20 minutes. Make sure to stir every so often, so the sauce does not burn. Add a bit of water after 15 minutes to ensure

the sauce does not harden.

6. Take out chicken wings from the air fryer and coat in sauce. Enjoy!

Nutrition:

- Calories: 435
- Fat: 19 g.
- Protein: 31 g.
- Sugar: 6 g.

303. Rosemary Turkey Breast With Maple Mustard Glaze

Preparation time: 20 minutes

Cooking time: 30 minutes

Servings: 7

Ingredients:

- 1 tbsp. vegan butter
- 1 tbsp. stone-ground brown mustard
- 1/4 cup pure maple syrup
- 1 tsp. pepper, crushed
- 2 tsp. salt
- 1/2 tsp. Rosemary, dried
- 2 garlic cloves, minced
- 1/4 cup. olive oil
- 2.5 lb. turkey breast loin

Directions:

1. Mix pepper, salt, Rosemary, garlic, and olive oil together. Spread herb mixture over turkey breast. Cover and chill 2 hours or overnight to marinade.

2. Make sure to remove from the fridge about 1/2 hour before cooking.

3. Ensure your air fryer is greased well and preheated to 400°F. Place loin into the fryer and cook for 20

minutes.

4. Open fryer and spoon on butter and mustard mixture over turkey. Cook another 10 minutes.

5. Remove turkey from the fryer and let rest 5–10 minutes before attempting to slice.

6. Slice against the grain and enjoy!

Nutrition:

- Calories: 278
- Fat: 15 g.
- Protein: 29 g.
- Sugar: 7 g.

304. Mexican Chicken Burgers

Preparation time: 5 minutes

Cooking time: 20 minutes

Servings: 8

Ingredients:

- 1 jalapeño pepper
- 1 tsp. cayenne pepper
- 1 tbsp. mustard powder
- 1 tbsp. oregano
- 1 tbsp. thyme
- 3 tbsp. smoked paprika
- 1 egg, beaten

- 1 small head of cauliflower
- 4 chicken breasts
- 1 tsp salt and pepper

Directions:

1. Ensure your air fryer is preheated to 350°F.

2. Add seasonings to a blender. Slice cauliflower into florets and add to blender.

3. Pulse till mixture resembles that of breadcrumbs.

4. Take out 3/4 of the cauliflower mixture and add to a bowl. Set to the side. In another bowl, beat your egg and set it to the side.

5. Remove skin and bones from chicken breasts and add to blender with remaining cauliflower mixture.

Season with pepper and salt.

6. Take out mixture and form into burger shapes. Roll each patty in cauliflower crumbs, then the egg, and back into crumbs again.

7. Place coated patties into the air fryer, cooking for 20 minutes.

8. Flip over at the 10-minute mark. They are done when crispy!

Nutrition:

- Calories: 234
- Fat: 18 g.
- Protein: 24 g.
- Sugar: 1 g.

305. Crispy Southern Fried Chicken

Preparation time: 10 minutes

Cooking time: 25 minutes

Servings: 4

Ingredients:

- 1 tsp. cayenne pepper
- 2 tbsp. mustard powder
- 2 tbsp. oregano
- 2 tbsp. thyme
- 3 tbsp. coconut milk
- 1 egg, beaten
- 1/4 cup cauliflower
- 1/4 cup gluten-free oats
- 8 chicken drumsticks
- 1 tsp salt and pepper

Directions:

1. Ensure the air fryer is preheated to 350°F.

2. Layout chicken and season with pepper and salt on all sides.

3. Add all other ingredients to a blender, blending till a smooth-like breadcrumb mixture is created. Place in a bowl and add a beaten egg to another bowl.

4. Dip chicken into breadcrumbs, then into the egg, and breadcrumbs once more.

5. Place coated drumsticks into the air fryer and cook 20 minutes. Bump up the temperature to 390 and cook for another 5 minutes till crispy.

Nutrition:

- Calories: 504
- Fat: 18 g.
- Protein: 35 g.
- Sugar: 5 g.

306. Air Fryer Turkey Breast

Preparation time: 5 minutes

Cooking time: 60 minutes

Servings: 8

Ingredients:

- Pepper and salt to taste
- 1 oven-ready turkey breast
- Turkey seasonings of choice

Directions:

1. Preheat the air fryer to 350°F.
2. Season turkey with pepper, salt, and other desired seasonings.
3. Place turkey in the air fryer basket.
4. Cook 60 minutes. The meat should be at 165°F when done.
5. Allow resting 10–15 minutes before slicing. Enjoy!

Nutrition:

- Calories: 212
- Fat: 12 g.
- Protein: 24 g.
- Sugar: 0 g.

307. Chicken Kabobs

Preparation time: 15 minutes

Cooking time: 20 minutes

Servings: 4

Ingredients:

- 2 chicken breasts, diced
- 3 bell peppers
- 6 mushrooms
- 6 Sesame seeds
- 1/3 cup low-sodium soy sauce
- 1/3 cup raw honey
- 1 tbsp. Olive oil
- 1 tsp salt and pepper

Directions:

1. Chop up chicken into cubes, seasoning with a few sprays of olive oil, pepper, and salt.
2. Dice up bell peppers and cut mushrooms in half.
3. Mix soy sauce and honey till well combined. Add sesame seeds and stir.
4. Skewer chicken, peppers, and mushrooms onto wooden skewers.
5. Ensure the air fryer is preheated to 388°F. Coat kabobs with honey-soy sauce.
6. Place coated kabobs in the air fryer basket and cook for 15–20 minutes.

Nutrition:

- Calories: 296
- Fat: 13 g.
- Protein: 17 g.
- Sugar: 1 g.

308. Mustard Chicken Tenders

Preparation time: 10 minutes

Cooking time: 15 minutes

Servings: 6

Ingredients:

- 1/2 cup coconut flour
- 1 tbsp. spicy brown mustard
- 2 eggs, beaten
- 1 lb. of chicken tenders
- 1 tsp salt and pepper

Directions:

1. Season tenders with pepper and salt.
2. Place a thin layer of mustard onto tenders and then dredge in flour and dip in egg.
3. Add to air fryer and cook 10–15 minutes at 390°F till crispy.

Nutrition:

- Calories: 403
- Fat: 20 g.
- Protein: 22 g.
- Sugar: 4 g.

309. Keto Fried "Mock KFC" Chicken

Preparation time: 15 minutes

Cooking time: 20 minutes

Servings: 6

Ingredients:

- 1 tsp. chili flakes
- 1 tsp. curcumin
- 1 tsp. white pepper
- 1 tsp. ginger powder
- 1 tsp. garlic powder
- 1 tsp. paprika
- 1 tsp. powdered mustard
- 1 tsp. pepper
- 1 tbsp. celery salt
- 1/3 tsp. oregano

- 1/2 tbsp. basil
- 1/2 tsp. thyme
- 2 garlic cloves
- 1 egg
- 6 boneless, skinless chicken thighs
- 2 tbsp. unsweetened almond milk
- 1/4 cup whey protein isolate powder

Directions:

1. Wash and pat dry chicken thighs. Slice into small chunks.
2. Mash cloves and add them along with all spices in a blender. Blend until smooth and pour over chicken, adding milk and egg. Mix thoroughly.
3. Cover chicken and chill for 1 hour.
4. Add whey protein to a bowl and dredge coated chicken pieces. Shake excess

powder.

Nutrition:

- Calories: 521
- Fat: 21 g.
- Protein: 36 g.
- Sugar: 6 g

.

310. Cheesy Chicken Fritters

Preparation time: 10 minutes

Cooking time: 20 minutes

Servings: 18

Ingredients:

Chicken fritters:

- 1/2 tsp. salt
- 1/8 tsp. pepper
- 1 1/2 tbsp. fresh dill
- 1 1/3 cup Mozzarella cheese, shredded
- 1/3 cup coconut flour
- 1/3 cup vegan mayo
- 2 eggs

- 1 1/2 lb. chicken breasts

Garlic dip:

- 1/8 tsp. pepper
- 1/4 tsp. salt
- 1/2 tbsp. lemon juice
- 1 pressed garlic cloves
- 1/3 cup vegan mayo

Directions:

1. Slice chicken breasts into 1/3-inch pieces and place in a bowl. Add all remaining fritter ingredients to the bowl and stir well. Cover and chill for 2 hours or overnight.
2. Ensure your air fryer is preheated to 350°F. Spray basket with a bit of olive oil.
3. To make the dipping sauce, combine all the dip ingredients until smooth.

Nutrition:

- Calories: 467
- Fat: 27 g.
- Protein: 21 g.
- Sugar: 3 g.

311. Air Fryer Chicken Parmesan

Preparation time: 15 minutes

Cooking time: 9 minutes

Servings: 4

Ingredients:

- 1/2 cup keto marinara
- 6 tbsp. Mozzarella cheese
- 1 tbsp. ghee, melted
- 2 tbsp. Parmesan cheese, grated
- 6 tbsp. gluten-free seasoned breadcrumbs
- 2 (8 oz.) chicken breasts

Directions:

1. Ensure the air fryer is preheated to 360°F. Spray the basket with olive oil.
2. Mix Parmesan cheese and breadcrumbs together. Melt ghee.
3. Brush melted ghee onto the chicken and dip into breadcrumb mixture.
4. Place coated chicken in the air fryer and top with olive oil.
5. Cook 2 breasts for 6 minutes and top each breast with 1 tbsp. of sauce and 1 1/2 tbsp. of Mozzarella cheese. Cook another 3 minutes to melt the cheese.
6. Keep cooked pieces warm as you repeat the process with the remaining breasts.

Nutrition:

- Calories: 251
- Fat: 10 g.
- Protein: 31 g.
- Sugar: 0 g.

312. Jerk Chicken Wings

Preparation time: 10 minutes

Cooking time: 16 minutes

Servings: 8

Ingredients:

- 1 tsp. salt
- 1/2 cup red wine vinegar
- 5 tbsp. lime juice
- 4 scallions, chopped
- 1 tbsp. ginger, grated
- 2 tbsp. brown sugar
- 1 tbsp. chopped thyme
- 1 tsp. white pepper
- 1 tsp. cayenne

pepper

- 1 tsp. cinnamon
- 1 tbsp. allspice
- 1 *Habanero* pepper (seeds/ribs removed and chopped finely)
- 6 garlic cloves, chopped
- 2 tbsp. low-sodium soy sauce
- 2 tbsp. olive oil
- 4 lb. of chicken wings

Directions:

1. Combine all ingredients except wings in a bowl. Pour into a gallon bag and add chicken wings. Chill 2–24 hours to marinate.
2. Ensure your air fryer is preheated to 390°F.
3. Place chicken wings into a strainer to drain excess liquids.
4. Pour half of the wings into your air fryer and cook for 14–16 minutes, making sure to shake halfway through the cooking process.
5. Remove and repeat the process with the remaining wings.

Nutrition:

- Calories: 374
- Fat: 14 g.
- Protein: 33 g.
- Sugar: 4 g.

313. Chicken Parmigiana With Fresh Rosemary

Preparation time: 5 minutes

Cooking time: 15 minutes

Servings: 4

Ingredients:

- 1 lb. chicken breasts, halved
- 1 cup seasoned breadcrumbs
- 1/2 cup Parmesan cheese, grated
- Salt and black pepper to taste
- 2 eggs
- 2 sprigs Rosemary, chopped
- Cooking spray

Directions:

1. Preheat the air fryer to 380°F. Spray the air fryer basket with

cooking spray.

2. Put the chicken halves on a clean flat surface and cover with clingfilm. Gently pound them to become thinner using a rolling pin. Beat the eggs in a bowl and season with salt and black pepper. In a separate bowl, mix breadcrumbs with Parmesan cheese.

3. Dip the chicken in the eggs, then in the breadcrumbs. Spray with cooking spray and air fry in the fryer for 6 minutes. Flip and cook for 6 more minutes. Sprinkle with Rosemary and serve.

Nutrition:

- Calories: 344
- Carbs: 30 g.
- Fiber: 4 g.
- Protein: 14 g.

314. Chicken *"Pinchos"* With Salsa Verde

Preparation time: 10 minutes

Cooking time: 25 minutes

Servings: 3

Ingredients:

- 2 chicken breasts, cut into large cubes
- Salt to taste
- 1 tbsp. chili powder
- 1/4 cup maple syrup
- 1/2 cup soy sauce
- 2 red peppers, cut into sticks
- 1 green pepper, cut into sticks
- 7 mushrooms, halved
- 2 tbsp. sesame seeds

Salsa verde:

- 1 garlic clove

- 2 tbsp. olive oil
- Zest and juice from 1 lime
- 1/4 cup fresh parsley, chopped
- A bunch of skewers
- Cooking spray

Directions:

1. In a bowl, mix chili powder, salt, maple syrup, soy sauce, sesame seeds, and toss in the chicken to coat. Start stacking up the ingredients, alternately, on skewers: red pepper, green pepper, a chicken cube, and a mushroom half, until the skewer is fully loaded. Repeat the process for all the ingredients.

2. Preheat the air fryer to 330°F. Brush the *pinchos* with soy sauce mixture and place them into the

frying basket. Grease with cooking spray and cook for 20 minutes, flipping once halfway through. Blend all salsa *verde* ingredients in a food processor until you obtain a chunky paste; season with salt. Serve *pinchos* with salsa *verde*.

Nutrition:

- Calories: 324
- Carbs: 20 g.
- Fiber: 8 g.
- Protein: 24 g.

315. Paprika Chicken Breasts

Preparation time: 5 minutes

Cooking time: 20 minutes

Servings: 4

Ingredients:

- 4 chicken breasts
- Salt and black pepper to taste
- 1/4 tsp. garlic powder
- 1 tbsp. paprika
- 2 tbsp. butter, melted
- 2 tbsp. fresh thyme, chopped
- Cooking spray

Directions:

1. Preheat air fryer to 360°F. Grease the frying basket with cooking spray.
2. Rub the chicken with salt, black pepper, garlic powder, and paprika. Brush with butter.
3. Place in the air fryer and air fry for 15 minutes, flipping once halfway through cooking.
4. Let cool slightly, then slice, and sprinkle with thyme to serve.

Nutrition:

- Calories: 244
- Carbs: 10 g.
- Fiber: 14 g.
- Protein: 19 g.

316. Spinach Loaded Chicken Breasts

Preparation time: 5 minutes

Cooking time: 10 minutes

Servings: 4

Ingredients:

- 1 cup spinach, chopped
- 4 tbsp. cottage cheese
- 2 chicken breasts
- Juice of 1/2 lime
- 2 tbsp. Italian seasoning
- 2 tbsp. olive oil
- Cooking spray

Directions:

1. Preheat the air fryer to 390°F and grease the basket with cooking spray. Mix spinach and cottage cheese in a bowl. Halve the breasts with a knife and flatten them with a meat mallet. Season with Italian seasoning. Divide the spinach/cheese mixture between the chicken pieces.

2. Roll up to form cylinders and use toothpicks to secure them. Brush with olive oil and place them in the frying basket. Bake for 7–8 minutes, flip, and cook for 6 minutes. Serve warm.

Nutrition:

- Calories: 144
- Carbs: 10 g.
- Fiber: 12 g.
- Protein: 34 g.

317. Texas BBQ Chicken Thighs

Preparation time: 5 minutes

Cooking time: 25 minutes

Servings: 4

Ingredients:

- 8 chicken thighs
- Salt and black pepper to taste
- 2 tsp. Texas BBQ Jerky seasoning
- 1 tbsp. olive oil
- 2 tbsp. fresh coriander, chopped
- Cooking spray

Directions:

1. Preheat the air fryer to 380°F. Grease the frying basket with cooking spray.
2. Drizzle the chicken with olive oil, season with salt and

black pepper, and sprinkle with BBQ seasoning. Place in the fryer and "Bake" for 15 minutes in total, flipping once. Top with fresh coriander to serve.

Nutrition:

- Calories: 234
- Carbs: 11 g.
- Fiber: 16 g.
- Protein: 17 g.

318. French-Style Chicken Thighs

Preparation time: 5 minutes

Cooking time: 15 minutes

Servings: 4

Ingredients:

- 1 tbsp. herbes de Provence
- 1 lb. bone-in, skinless chicken thighs
- Salt and black pepper to taste
- 2 garlic cloves, minced
- 1/2 cup honey
- 1/4 cup Dijon mustard
- 2 tbsp. butter
- 2 tbsp. dill, chopped

Directions:

1. Preheat the air fryer to 390°F. Spray the air fryer basket with cooking spray.
2. In a bowl, mix herbes de Provence, salt, and black pepper. Rub the chicken with this mixture. Transfer to the greased air fryer basket and "Bake" for 15 minutes, flipping once halfway through.
3. Melt butter in a saucepan over medium heat. Stir in honey, dill, mustard, and garlic; cook until reduced to a thick consistency, about 3 minutes. Serve the chicken drizzled with the honey-mustard sauce.

Nutrition:

- Calories: 200
- Carbs: 15 g.
- Fiber: 18 g.
- Protein: 12 g.

319. Sweet Chili & Ginger Chicken Wings

Preparation time: 5 minutes

Cooking time: 15 minutes

Servings: 4

Ingredients:

- 1 lb. chicken wings
- 1 tsp. ginger root powder
- 1 tbsp. tamarind powder
- 1/4 cup sweet chili sauce
- Cooking spray

Directions:

1. Preheat air fryer to 390°F. Rub the chicken wings with tamarind and ginger root powders. Spray with cooking spray and place in the air fryer basket. Cook for 6 minutes.
2. Slide-out the basket and cover with sweet chili sauce; cook for 8 more minutes. Serve warm.

Nutrition:

- Calories: 244
- Carbs: 22 g.
- Fiber: 33 g.
- Protein: 37 g.

320. Spice-Rubbed Jerk Chicken Wings

Preparation time: 5 minutes

Cooking time: 20 minutes

Servings: 4

Ingredients:

- 2 lb. chicken wings
- 2 tbsp. olive oil
- 3 cloves garlic, minced
- 1 tbsp. chili powder
- 1/2 tbsp. cinnamon powder
- 1/2 tsp. allspice
- 1 *Habanero* pepper, seeded
- 1 tbsp. soy sauce
- 1/2 tbsp. lemon pepper
- 1/4 cup red wine vinegar
- 3 tbsp. lime juice
- 1/2 tbsp. ginger,

- grated
- 1/2 tbsp. fresh thyme, chopped
- 1/3 tbsp. sugar
- 1/2 tbsp. salt
- blue cheese dip or ranch dressing for servings

Directions:

1. In a bowl, add olive oil, soy sauce, garlic, *habanero* pepper, allspice, cinnamon powder, chili powder, lemon pepper, salt, sugar, thyme, ginger, lime juice, and red wine vinegar; mix well. Add the chicken wings to the mixture and toss to coat. Cover and refrigerate for 1 hour.
2. Preheat the air fryer to 380°F. Remove the chicken from the fridge, drain all the liquid, and pat dry with paper towels. Working in batches, cook the wings in the air fryer for 16 minutes in total. Shake once halfway through. Remove to a serving platter and serve with a blue cheese dip or ranch dressing.

Nutrition:

- Calories: 320
- Carbs: 20 g.
- Fiber: 14 g.
- Protein: 34 g.

321. Juicy Chicken With Bell Peppers

Preparation time: 15 minutes

Cooking time: 25 minutes

Servings: 2

Ingredients:

- 2 chicken fillets, cubed
- Salt and black pepper to taste
- 1 cup flour
- 2 eggs
- 1/2 cup apple cider vinegar
- 1/2 tbsp. ginger paste
- 1/2 tbsp. garlic paste
- 1 tbsp. sugar
- 1 red chili, minced
- 2 tbsp. tomato puree
- 1 red bell pepper, seeded, cut into

strips

- 1 green bell pepper, seeded, cut into strips
- 1 tbsp. paprika
- 4 tbsp. water
- Cooking spray

Directions:

1. Preheat the air fryer to 350°F.
2. Pour the flour into a bowl, add in eggs, salt, and black pepper, and whisk.
3. Put chicken cubes in the flour mixture; mix to coat and place them in the frying basket. Spray with cooking spray and air fry for 8 minutes. Shake the basket, and cook for 7 more minutes until golden and crispy.
4. Remove the chicken to a plate. In a bowl, add water, apple cider vinegar, sugar,

ginger paste, garlic paste, red chili, tomato puree, and paprika; mix with a fork.

5. Place a skillet over medium heat and spray with cooking spray. Add the red and green pepper strips. Stir and cook until the peppers are sweaty but still crunchy. Pour the chili mixture over, stir, and bring to a simmer for 10 minutes. Serve the chicken in a bowl, drizzled with pepper-chili sauce.

Nutrition:

- Calories: 434
- Carbs: 19 g.
- Fiber: 9 g.
- Protein: 44 g.

322. Quinoa Chicken Nuggets

Preparation time: 5 minutes

Cooking time: 10 minutes

Servings: 2

Ingredients:

- 2 chicken breasts, cut into bite-size chunks
- 1/2 cup cooked quinoa, cooled
- 1/2 cup flour
- 1 egg
- 1/2 tsp. cayenne pepper
- Salt and black pepper to taste
- Cooking spray

Directions:

1. In a bowl, beat the egg with salt and black pepper.
2. Spread flour on a

plate and mix with cayenne pepper. Coat the chicken in flour, then in the egg, shake off and place in the quinoa. Press firmly so quinoa sticks on the chicken pieces.

3. Spray with cooking spray and air fry the nuggets in the greased frying basket for 14–16 minutes on 360°F, turning once halfway through. Serve hot.

Nutrition:

- Calories: 104
- Carbs: 22 g.
- Fiber: 23 g.
- Protein: 35 g.

323. Tarragon & Garlic Roasted Chicken

Preparation time: 15 minutes

Cooking time: 40 minutes

Servings: 4

Ingredients:

- 1 chicken (around 3 lb.), rinsed, pat-dried
- 1 sprig fresh tarragon
- 2 tbsp. butter, melted
- Salt and black pepper to taste
- 1 lemon, cut into wedges
- 1 garlic bulb
- Cooking spray

Directions:

1. Preheat the air fryer to 380°F. Grease the air fryer basket with cooking spray.

2. Brush the chicken with melted butter and season with salt and pepper. Put tarragon, garlic, and lemon into the cavity of the chicken and place in the air fryer basket. "Bake" for 40 minutes. Then, cover with foil and let rest for 10 minutes, then carve, slice, and serve with a fresh salad or baked potatoes.

Nutrition:

- Calories: 424
- Carbs: 27 g.
- Fiber: 28 g.
- Protein 20 g.

324. Comfort Chicken Drumsticks

Preparation time: 10 minutes

Cooking time: 10 minutes

Servings: 4

Ingredients:

- 1 lb. chicken drumsticks
- 1 tsp. garlic powder
- 1 tsp. cayenne pepper
- 1/2 cup flour
- 1/4 cup milk
- 1/4 tbsp. lemon juice
- Salt and black pepper to taste
- Cooking spray

Directions:

1. Preheat the air fryer to 390°F. Spray the air fryer basket with cooking spray.

2. In a small bowl, mix garlic powder, cayenne pepper, salt, and black pepper. Rub the chicken drumsticks with the mixture. In a separate bowl, combine milk with lemon juice. Pour the flour on a plate.

3. Dunk the chicken in the milk mixture, then roll in the flour to coat. Place the chicken in the frying basket and spray it with cooking spray. Air fry for 14 minutes, flipping once. Serve warm.

Nutrition:

- Calories: 214
- Carbs: 15 g.
- Fiber: 16 g.
- Protein: 28 g.

325. Greek-Style Chicken Tacos

Preparation time: 5 minutes

Cooking time: 20 minutes

Servings: 4

Ingredients:

- 2 chicken breasts, cut into strips
- 1 tbsp. taco seasoning
- Salt and black pepper to taste
- 1 cup flour
- 1 egg, beaten
- 1/2 cup breadcrumbs
- 4 taco shells
- 2 cups white cabbage. shredded
- 3 tbsp. Greek yogurt dressing
- Cooking spray

Directions:

1. Preheat the air fryer to 380°F. Spray the air fryer basket with cooking spray. Season the chicken with taco seasoning, salt, and black pepper.

2. In 3 separate bowls, add breadcrumbs to one bowl, flour to another, and beaten egg to a third bowl. Dredge chicken in flour, then in egg, and then in the breadcrumbs. Spray with cooking spray and transfer to the frying basket. Air fry for 12 minutes, flipping once halfway through. Fill the taco shells with chicken strips, cabbage, and yogurt dressing to serve.

Nutrition:

- Calories: 194
- Carbs: 10 g.
- Fiber: 32 g.
- Protein: 44 g.

326. Cheesy Chicken Thighs With Parmesan Crust

Preparation time: 15 minutes

Cooking time: 10 minutes

Servings: 4

Ingredients:

- 1/2 cup Italian breadcrumbs
- 2 tbsp. Parmesan cheese, grated
- 1 tbsp. butter, melted
- 4 chicken thighs
- 1/2 cup marinara sauce
- 1/2 cup Monterrey Jack cheese, shredded

Directions:

1. Preheat the air fryer to 380°F. In a bowl,

mix the crumbs with Parmesan cheese. Brush the thighs with butter. Dip each thigh into the crumb mixture. Arrange them on the greased air fryer basket.

2. Air fry for 6–7 minutes at 380°F, flip, top with marinara sauce and shredded Monterrey Jack cheese, and continue to cook for another 4–5 minutes. Serve immediately.

Nutrition:

- Calories: 287
- Carbs: 33 g.
- Fiber: 20 g.
- Protein: 39 g.

327. Pretzel Crusted Chicken With Spicy Mustard Sauce

Preparation time: 10 minutes

Cooking time: 14 minutes

Servings: 6

Ingredients:

- 2 eggs
- 1 1/2 lb. chicken breasts, boneless, skinless, cut into bite-sized chunks
- 1/2 cup pretzels, crushed
- 1 tsp. shallot powder
- 1 tsp. paprika
- Sea salt and ground black pepper, to taste
- 1/2 cup vegetable broth

- 1 tbsp. cornstarch
- 3 tbsp. Worcestershire sauce
- 3 tbsp. tomato paste
- 1 tbsp. apple cider vinegar
- 2 tbsp. olive oil
- 2 garlic cloves, chopped
- 1 jalapeño pepper, minced
- 1 tsp. yellow mustard

Directions:

1. Start by preheating your air fryer to 390°F.
2. In a mixing dish, whisk the eggs until frothy; toss the chicken chunks into the whisked eggs and coat well.
3. In another dish, combine the crushed pretzels with shallot powder, paprika, salt and

pepper. Then, lay the chicken chunks in the pretzel mixture; turn it over until well coated.

4. Place the chicken pieces in the air fryer basket. Cook the chicken for 12 minutes, shaking the basket halfway through.

5. Meanwhile, whisk the vegetable broth with cornstarch, Worcestershire sauce, tomato paste, and apple cider vinegar.

6. Preheat a cast-iron skillet over medium flame. Heat the olive oil and sauté the garlic with jalapeño pepper for 30–40 seconds, stirring frequently.

7. Add the cornstarch mixture and let it simmer until the sauce has thickened a little. Now, add the air-fried chicken and mustard; let it simmer for 2 minutes more or until heated through.

8. Serve immediately and enjoy!

Nutrition:

- Calories: 332
- Fat: 14.6 g.
- Carbs: 22.3 g.
- Protein: 21.1 g.
- Sugar: 2.3 g.

328. Chinese-Style Sticky Turkey Thighs

Preparation time: 10 minutes

Cooking time: 35 minutes

Servings: 6

Ingredients:

- 1 tbsp. sesame oil
- 2 lb. turkey thighs
- 1 tsp. Chinese 5-spice powder
- 1 tsp. pink Himalayan salt
- 1/4 tsp. Sichuan pepper
- 6 tbsp. honey
- 1 tbsp. Chinese rice vinegar
- 2 tbsp. soy sauce
- 1 tbsp. sweet chili sauce
- 1 tbsp. mustard

Directions:

1. Preheat your air fryer to 360°F.
2. Brush the sesame oil all over the turkey thighs. Season them with spices.
3. Cook for 23 minutes, turning over once or twice. Make sure to work in batches to ensure even cooking.
4. In the meantime, combine the remaining ingredients in a wok (or similar type pan) that is preheated over medium-high heat. Cook and stir until the sauce reduce by about a third.
5. Add the fried turkey thighs to the wok; gently stir to coat with the sauce.
6. Let the turkey rest for 10 minutes before slicing and serving. Enjoy!

Nutrition:

- Calories: 279
- Fat: 10.1 g.
- Carbs: 19 g.
- Protein: 27.7 g.
- Sugar: 17.9 g.

329. Easy Hot Chicken Drumsticks

Preparation time: 10 minutes

Cooking time: 30 minutes

Servings: 6

Ingredients:

- 6 chicken drumsticks

Sauce:

- 6 oz. hot sauce
- 3 tbsp. olive oil
- 3 tbsp. tamari sauce
- 1 tsp. thyme, dried
- 1/2 tsp. oregano, dried
- Cooking spray

Directions:

1. Spritz the sides and bottom of the cooking basket with a nonstick cooking spray.

2. Cook the chicken drumsticks at 380°F for 35 minutes, flipping them over halfway through.

3. Meanwhile, heat the hot sauce, olive oil, tamari sauce, thyme, and oregano in a pan over medium-low heat, reserve.

4. Drizzle the sauce over the prepared chicken drumsticks; toss to coat well and serve. Bon appétit!

Nutrition:

- Calories: 280
- Fat: 18.7 g.
- Carbs: 2.6 g.
- Protein: 24.1 g.
- Sugar: 1.4 g.

330. Crunchy Munchy Chicken Tenders With Peanuts

Preparation time: 10 minutes

Cooking time: 25 minutes

Servings: 4

Ingredients:

- 1 1/2 lb. chicken tenderloins
- 2 tbsp. peanut oil
- 1/2 cup tortilla chips, crushed
- Sea salt and ground black pepper, to taste
- 1/2 tsp. garlic powder
- 1 tsp. red pepper flakes
- 2 tbsp. peanuts, roasted and roughly chopped

Directions:

1. Start by preheating your air fryer to 360°F.

2. Brush the chicken tenderloins with peanut oil on all sides.

3. In a mixing bowl, thoroughly combine the crushed chips, salt, black pepper, garlic powder, and red pepper flakes. Dredge the chicken in the breading, shaking off any residual coating.

4. Lay the chicken tenderloins into the cooking basket. Cook for 12–13 minutes or until it is no longer pink in the center. Work in batches; an instant-read thermometer should read at least 165°F.

5. Serve garnished with roasted

peanuts. Bon appétit!

Nutrition:

- Calories: 343
- Fat: 16.4 g.
- Carbs: 10.6 g.
- Protein: 36.8 g.
- Sugar: 1 g.

331. Tarragon Turkey Tenderloins With Baby Potatoes

Preparation time: 10 minutes

Cooking time: 40 minutes

Servings: 6

Ingredients:

- 2 lb. turkey tenderloins
- 2 tsp. olive oil
- Salt and ground black pepper, to taste
- 1 tsp. smoked paprika
- 2 tbsp. dry white wine
- 1 tbsp. fresh tarragon leaves, chopped
- 1 lb. baby potatoes, rubbed

Directions:

1. Brush the turkey tenderloins with olive oil. Season with salt, black pepper, and paprika.
2. Afterward, add the white wine and tarragon.
3. Cook the turkey tenderloins at 350°F for 30 minutes, flipping them over halfway through. Let them rest for 5–9 minutes before slicing and serving.
4. After that, spritz the sides and bottom of the cooking basket with the remaining 1 tsp. of olive oil.
5. Then, preheat your air fryer to 400°F; cook the baby potatoes for 15 minutes. Serve with the turkey and enjoy!

Nutrition:

- Calories: 317
- Fat: 7.4 g.
- Carbs: 14.2 g.
- Protein: 45.7 g.
- Sugar: 1.1 g.

332. Mediterranean Chicken Breasts

Preparation time: 10 minutes

Cooking time: 1 hour

Servings: 8

Ingredients:

- 2 tsp. olive oil, melted
- 3 lb. chicken breasts, bone-in
- 1/2 tsp. black pepper, freshly ground
- 1/2 tsp. salt
- 1 tsp. cayenne pepper
- 2 tbsp. fresh parsley, minced
- 1 tsp. fresh basil, minced
- 1 tsp. fresh Rosemary, minced
- 4 Roma tomatoes, medium-sized, halved

Directions:

1. Start by preheating your air fryer to 370°F. Brush the cooking basket with 1 tsp. of olive oil.
2. Sprinkle the chicken breasts with all seasonings listed above.
3. Cook for 25 minutes or until chicken breasts are slightly browned. Work in batches.
4. Arrange the tomatoes in the cooking basket and brush them with the remaining tsp. of olive oil. Season with sea salt.
5. Cook the tomatoes at 350°F for 10 minutes, shaking halfway through the cooking time. Serve with chicken breasts. Bon appétit!

Nutrition:

- Calories: 315
- Fat: 17.1 g.
- Carbs: 2.7 g.
- Protein: 36 g.
- Sugar: 1.7 g.

333. Thai Red Duck With Candy Onion

Preparation time: 10 minutes

Cooking time: 25 minutes

Servings: 4

Ingredients:

- 1 1/2 lb. duck breasts, skin removed
- 1 tsp. kosher salt
- 1/2 tsp. cayenne pepper
- 1/3 tsp. black pepper
- 1/2 tsp. smoked paprika
- 1 tbsp. Thai red curry paste
- 1 cup candy onions, halved
- 1/4 small pack coriander, chopped

Directions:

1. Place the duck breasts between 2 sheets of foil, then, use a rolling pin to bash the duck until they are 1-inch thick.
2. Preheat your air fryer to 395°F.
3. Rub the duck breasts with salt, cayenne pepper, black pepper, paprika, and red curry paste. Place the duck breast in the cooking basket.
4. Cook for 11–12 minutes. Top with candy onions and cook for another 10–11 minutes.
5. Serve garnished with coriander and enjoy!

Nutrition:

- Calories: 362
- Fat: 18.7 g.
- Carbs: 4 g.

- Protein: 42.3 g.
- Sugar: 1.3 g.

334. Rustic Chicken Legs With Turnip Chips

Preparation time: 10 minutes

Cooking time: 20 minutes

Servings: 3

Ingredients:

- 1 lb. chicken legs
- 1 tsp. Himalayan salt
- 1 tsp. paprika
- 1/2 tsp. black pepper, ground
- 1 tsp. butter, melted
- 1 turnip, trimmed, and sliced
- Cooking spray

Directions:

1. Spritz the sides and bottom of the cooking basket with a nonstick cooking spray.
2. Season the chicken legs with salt, paprika, and ground black pepper.
3. Cook at 370°F for 10 minutes. Increase the temperature to 380°F.
4. Drizzle turnip slices with melted butter and transfer them to the cooking basket with the chicken. Cook the turnips and chicken for 15 minutes more, flipping them halfway through the cooking time.
5. As for the chicken, an instant-read thermometer should read at least 165°F.
6. Serve and enjoy!

Nutrition:

- Calories: 207
- Fat: 7.8 g.
- Carbs: 3.4 g.
- Protein: 29.5 g.
- Sugar: 1.6 g.

335. Old-Fashioned Chicken Drumettes

Preparation time: 10 minutes

Cooking time: 30 minutes

Servings: 3

Ingredients:

- 1/3 cup all-purpose flour
- 1/2 tsp. ground white pepper
- 1 tsp. seasoning salt
- 1 tsp. garlic paste
- 1 tsp. Rosemary
- 1 whole egg + 1 egg white
- 6 chicken drumettes
- 1 heaping tbsp. fresh chives, chopped

Directions:

1. Start by preheating your air fryer to 390°F.
2. Mix the flour with white pepper, salt, garlic paste, and Rosemary in a small-sized bowl.
3. In another bowl, beat the eggs until frothy.
4. Dip the chicken into the flour mixture, then into the beaten eggs; coat with the flour mixture one more time.
5. Cook the chicken drumettes for 22 minutes. Serve warm, garnished with chives.

Nutrition:

- Calories: 347
- Fat: 9.1 g.
- Carbs: 11.3 g.
- Protein: 41 g.
- Sugar: 0.1 g.

336. Easy Ritzy Chicken Nuggets

Preparation time: 10 minutes

Cooking time: 20 minutes

Servings: 4

Ingredients:

- 1 1/2 lb. chicken tenderloins, cut into small pieces
- 1/2 tsp. garlic salt
- 1/2 tsp. cayenne pepper
- 1/4 tsp. black pepper, freshly cracked
- 4 tbsp. olive oil
- 1/3 cup saltines (e.g. Ritz crackers), crushed
- 4 tbsp. Parmesan cheese, freshly grated

Directions:

1. Start by preheating your air fryer to 390°F.
2. Season each piece of the chicken with garlic salt, cayenne pepper, and black pepper.
3. In a mixing bowl, thoroughly combine the olive oil with crushed saltines. Dip each piece of chicken in the cracker mixture.
4. Finally, roll the chicken pieces over the Parmesan cheese. Cook for 8 minutes, working in batches.
5. Later, if you want to warm the chicken nuggets, add them to the basket and cook for 1 minute more. Serve with French fries, if desired.

Nutrition:

- Calories: 355
- Fat: 20.1 g.
- Carbs: 5.3 g.
- Protein: 36.6 g.
- Sugar: 0.2 g.

337. Asian Chicken Filets With Cheese

Preparation time: 10 minutes

Cooking time: 50 minutes

Servings: 2

Ingredients:

- 4 rashers smoked bacon
- 2 chicken fillets
- 1/2 tsp. coarse sea salt
- 1/4 tsp. black pepper, preferably freshly ground
- 1 tsp. garlic, minced
- 1 (2-inch) piece

ginger, peeled and minced
- 1 tsp. black mustard seeds
- 1 tsp. mild curry powder
- 1/2 cup coconut milk
- 1/3 cup tortilla chips, crushed
- 1/2 cup Pecorino Romano cheese, freshly grated

Directions:

1. Start by preheating your air fryer to 400°F. Add the smoked bacon and cook in the preheated air fryer for 5–7 minutes. Reserve.
2. In a mixing bowl, place the chicken fillets, salt, black pepper, garlic, ginger, mustard seeds, curry powder, and milk. Let it marinate in your refrigerator for about 30 minutes.
3. In another bowl, mix the crushed chips and grated *Pecorino Romano* cheese.
4. Dredge the chicken fillets through the chips mixture and transfer them to the cooking basket. Reduce the temperature to 380°F and cook the chicken for 6 minutes.
5. Turn them over and cook for a further 6 minutes. Repeat the process until you have run out of ingredients.
6. Serve with reserved bacon. Enjoy!

Nutrition:

- Calories: 376
- Fat: 19.6 g.
- Carbs: 12.1 g.
- Protein: 36.2 g.
- Sugar: 3.4 g.

338. Paprika Chicken Legs With Brussels Sprouts

Preparation time: 10 minutes

Cooking time: 30 minutes

Servings: 2

Ingredients:

- 2 chicken legs
- 1/2 tsp. paprika
- 1/2 tsp. kosher salt
- 1/2 tsp. black pepper
- 1 lb. Brussels sprouts
- 1 tsp. dill, fresh or dried

Directions:

1. Start by preheating your air fryer to 370°F.
2. Now, season your chicken with paprika, salt, and pepper. Transfer the chicken legs to the cooking basket. Cook for 10 minutes.
3. Flip the chicken legs and cook an additional 10 minutes. Reserve.
4. Add the Brussels sprouts to the cooking basket; sprinkle with dill. Cook at 380°F for 15 minutes, shaking the basket halfway through.
5. Serve with the reserved chicken legs. Bon appétit!

Nutrition:

- Calories: 355
- Fat: 20.1 g.
- Carbs: 5.3 g.
- Protein: 36.6 g.
- Sugar: 0.2 g.

339. Chicken Tears

Preparation time: 15 minutes

Cooking time: 25 minutes

Servings: 4

Ingredients:

- 2 chicken breasts
- 2 oz. Flour
- 1 tbspSalt
- 1 tsp Pepper, ground
- 1 tbsp Extra virgin olive oil
- 3 tbsp Lemon juice
- 1 tbsp Garlic powder

Directions:

1. Cut the chicken breasts into tears. Season and put some lemon juice and garlic powder. Let flirt well.
2. Go through the flour and shake.

3. Place the tears in the basket of the air fryer and paint with extra virgin olive oil.
4. Select 180°F, 20 minutes.
5. Move from time to time, so that the tears are made on all their faces.

Nutrition:

- Calories: 197
- Fat: 8 g.
- Carbs: 16 g.
- Protein: 14 g.
- Sugar: 0 mg.
- Cholesterol: 0 mg.

340. Breaded Chicken With Seed Chips

Preparation time: 10 minutes

Cooking time: 40 minutes

Servings: 4

Ingredients:

- 12 chicken breast fillets
- Salt
- 2 eggs
- 1 small bag of seed chips
- Breadcrumbs
- Extra virgin olive oil

Directions:

1. Put salt into chicken fillets.
2. Crush the seed chips and when we have them fine, bind with the breadcrumbs.
3. Beat the 2 eggs.
4. Pass the chicken breast fillets through the beaten egg and then through the seed chips that you have tied with the breadcrumbs.
5. When you have them all breaded, paint with a brush of extra virgin olive oil.
6. Place the fillets in the basket of the air fryer without being piled up.
7. Select 170°C, 20 minutes.
8. Take out and put another batch, repeat temperature and time. So, until you use up all the steaks.

Nutrition:

- Calories: 242
- Fat: 13 g.
- Carbs: 13.5 g.
- Protein: 18 g.
- Sugar: 0 g.

- Cholesterol: 42 mg.

341. Salted Biscuit Pie Turkey Chops

Preparation time: 5 minutes

Cooking time: 20 minutes

Servings: 4

Ingredients:

- 8 large turkey chops
- 300 g. crackers
- 2 eggs
- Extra virgin olive oil
- Salt
- Pepper, ground

Directions:

1. Put the turkey chops on the worktable, and salt and pepper.
2. Beat the eggs in a bowl.
3. Crush the cookies in the Thermos mix with a few turbo strokes until they are made grit, or you can crush them with the blender.
4. Put the cookies in a bowl.
5. Pass the chops through the beaten egg and then passed them through the crushed cookies. Press well so that the empanada is perfect.
6. Paint the empanada with a silicone brush and extra virgin olive oil.
7. Put the chops in the basket of the air fryer, not all will

enter. They will be done in batches.

8. Select 200°C, 15 minutes.

9. When you have all the chops made, serve.

Nutrition:

- Calories: 126
- Fat: 6 g.
- Carbs: 0 g.
- Protein: 18 g.
- Sugar: 0 g.

342. Lemon Chicken With Basil

Preparation time: 10 minutes

Cooking time: 1 hour

Servings: 4

Ingredients:

- 1 kg. chicken, chopped
- 2 lemons
- 1 tbsp Basil
- 1 tsp Salt
- 1 tsp Pepper, ground
- 1 tbsp Extra virgin olive oil

Directions:

1. Put the chicken in a bowl with a jet of extra virgin olive oil.
2. Put salt, pepper, and basil.
3. Bind well and let stand for at least 30

minutes stirring occasionally.

4. Put the pieces of chicken in the air fryer basket and take the air fryer.
5. Select 30 minutes.
6. Occasionally remove.
7. Take out and put another batch.
8. Do the same operation.

Nutrition:

- Calories: 126
- Fat: 6 g.
- Carbs: 0 g.
- Protein: 18 g.
- Sugar: 0 g.

43. Fried Chicken Tamari and Mustard

Preparation time: 15 minutes

Cooking time: 1 hour 20 minutes

Servings: 4

Ingredients:

- 1 kg. chicken, very small chopped
- Tamari sauce
- Original mustard
- Pepper, ground
- 1 lemon
- Flour
- Extra virgin olive oil

Directions:

1. Put the chicken in a bowl, you can put the chicken with or without the skin, to everyone's taste.
2. Add a generous stream of tamari, 1–2 tbsp. of mustard, a little ground pepper, and a splash of lemon juice.
3. Link everything very well and let macerate for 1 hour.
4. Pass the chicken pieces for flour and place them in the air fryer basket.
5. Put 20 minutes at 200°F. At halftime, move the chicken from the basket.
6. Do not crush the chicken, it is preferable to make 2–3 batches of chicken to pile up., or do not fry the pieces well.

Nutrition:

- Calories: 100
- Fat: 6 g.
- Carbs: 0 g.
- Protein: 18 g.
- Sugar: 0 g.

344. Breaded Chicken Fillets

Preparation time: 10 minutes

Cooking time: 25 minutes

Servings: 4

Ingredients:

- 3 small chicken breasts or 2 large chicken breasts
- Salt
- Pepper, ground
- 3 garlic cloves
- 1 lemon
- Eggs, beaten
- Breadcrumbs
- Extra virgin olive oil

Directions:

1. Cut the breasts into fillets.
2. Put in a bowl and add the lemon juice, chopped garlic cloves, and pepper.

3. Flirt well and leave 10 minutes.
4. Beat the eggs and put breadcrumbs on another plate.
5. Pass the chicken breast fillets through the beaten egg and the breadcrumbs.
6. When you have them all breaded, start to fry.
7. Paint the breaded breasts with a silicone brush and extra virgin olive oil.
8. Place a batch of fillets in the basket of the air fryer and select 10 minutes 180°C.
9. Turn around and leave another 5 minutes at 180°C.

Nutrition:

- Calories: 120
- Fat: 6 g.
- Carbs: 0 g.
- Protein: 18 g.
- Sugar: 0 g.

345. Dry Rub Chicken Wings

Preparation time: 5 minutes

Cooking time: 30 minutes

Servings: 4

Ingredients:

- 9 g. garlic powder
- 1 cube of chicken broth, reduced-sodium
- 5 g. salt
- 3 g. black pepper
- 1 g. smoked paprika
- 1 g. cayenne pepper
- 3 g. Old Bay® seasoning, sodium-free
- 3 g. onion powder
- 1 g. oregano, dried
- 453 g. chicken wings
- Nonstick spray oil
- Ranch sauce, to serve

Directions:

1. Preheat the air fryer. Set the temperature to 180°C.
2. Put ingredients in a bowl and mix well.
3. Season the chicken wings with half the seasoning mixture and sprinkle abundantly with oil spray.
4. Place the chicken wings in the preheated air fryer.
5. Select "Chicken," set the timer to 30 minutes.
6. Shake the baskets halfway through cooking.
7. Transfer the chicken wings to a bowl and sprinkle them with the other half of the seasonings until they are well covered. Serve with ranch sauce.

Nutrition:

- Calories: 120
- Fat: 6 g.
- Carbs: 0 g.
- Protein: 18 g.
- Sugar: 0 g.

346. Chicken Soup

Preparation time: 20 minutes

Cooking time: 1 hour 20 minutes

Servings: 6

Ingredients:

- 4 lbs. chicken, cut into pieces
- 5 carrots, sliced thick
- 8 cups water
- 2 celery stalks, sliced 1-inch thick
- 2 large onions, sliced

Directions:

1. In a large pot add chicken, water, and salt. Bring to boil.
2. Add celery and onion to the pot and stir well.
3. Turn heat to medium-low and simmer for 30 minutes.
4. Add carrots and cover pot with a lid and simmer for 40 minutes.
5. Remove chicken from the pot and remove bones and cut the chicken into bite-size pieces.
6. Return chicken into the pot and stir well.
7. Serve and enjoy.

Nutrition:

- Calories: 89
- Fat: 6.33 g.
- Carbs: 0 g.
- Protein: 7.56 g.
- Sugar: 0 g.
- Cholesterol: 0 mg.

347. Chicken Wings With Garlic Parmesan

Preparation time: 5 minutes

Cooking time: 25 minutes

Servings: 3

Ingredients:

- 25 g. cornstarch
- 20 g. Parmesan cheese, grated
- 9 g. garlic powder
- Salt and pepper to taste
- 680 g. chicken wings
- Nonstick spray oil

Directions:

1. Select "Preheat", set the temperature to 200°C, and press "Start/Pause."
2. Combine corn starch, Parmesan, garlic powder, salt, and pepper in a bowl.
3. Mix the chicken wings in the seasoning and dip until well coated.
4. Spray the baskets and the air fryer with oil spray and add the wings, sprinkling the tops of the wings as well.
5. Select Chicken and press "Start/Pause." Be sure to shake the baskets in the middle of cooking.
6. Sprinkle with what's left of the Parmesan mix and serve.

Nutrition:

- Calories: 204
- Fat: 15 g.
- Carbs: 1 g.
- Protein:s: 12 g.
- Sugar: 0 g.
- Cholesterol: 63 mg.

348. Jerk Style Chicken Wings

Preparation time: 5 minutes

Cooking time: 25 minutes

Servings: 3

Ingredients:

- 1 g. thyme, dried
- 1 g. Rosemary, dried
- 2 g. allspice
- 4 g. ginger, ground
- 3 g. garlic powder
- 2 g. onion powder
- 1 g. cinnamon
- 2 g. paprika
- 2 g. chili powder
- 1 g. nutmeg
- Salt to taste
- 30 ml. vegetable oil
- 0.5–1 kg. of chicken wings
- 1 lime juiced

Directions:

1. Select "Preheat," set

the temperature to 200°C, and press "Start/Pause."

2. Combine all spices and oil in a bowl to create a marinade.

3. Mix the chicken wings in the marinade until they are well covered.

4. Place the chicken wings in the preheated air fryer.

5. Select chicken and press "Start/Pause." Be sure to shake the baskets in the middle of cooking.

6. Remove the wings and place them on a serving plate.

7. Squeeze fresh lemon juice over the wings and serve.

Nutrition:

- Calories: 240
- Fat: 15 g.
- Carbs: 5 g.
- Protein: 19 g.
- Sugar: 4 g.
- Cholesterol: 60 mg.

349. Tasty Chicken Tenders

Preparation time: 10 minutes

Cooking time: 25 minutes

Servings: 4

Ingredients:

- 1 1/2 lbs. chicken tenders
- 1 tbsp. extra virgin olive oil
- 1 tsp. rotisserie chicken seasoning
- 2 tbsp. BBQ sauce

Directions:

1. Add all ingredients except oil in a zip-lock bag.
2. Seal bag and place in the refrigerator for 2–3 hours.
3. Heat oil in a large pan over medium heat.
4. Cook marinated chicken tenders in a pan until lightly brown and cooked.

Nutrition:

- Calories: 365
- Fat: 16.1 g.
- Carbs: 2.8 g.
- Sugar: 2 g.
- Protein: 49.2 g.
- Cholesterol: 151 mg.

350. Chicken Skewers With Yogurt

Preparation time: 4 hours 10 minutes

Cooking time: 10 minutes

Servings: 4

Ingredients:

- 123 g. Greek yogurt, plain whole milk
- 20 ml. olive oil
- 2 g. paprika
- 1 g. cumin
- 1 g. red pepper, crushed
- 1 lemon juice, and zest of the peel
- 5 g. salt
- 1g black pepper, freshly ground
- 4 cloves garlic, minced
- 454 g. chicken thighs, boneless, skinless, cut into 38 mm. pieces
- 2 wooden skewers, cut in half
- Nonstick spray oil

Directions:

1. Mix the yogurt, olive oil, paprika, cumin, red paprika, lemon juice, lemon zest, salt, pepper, and garlic in a large bowl.
2. Add the chicken to the marinade and marinate in the fridge for at least 4 hours.
3. Select "Preheat" and press "Start/Pause."
4. Cut the marinated chicken thighs into 38 mm pieces and spread them on skewers.
5. Place the skewers in the preheated air fryer.
6. Cook at 200°C for 10 minutes.
7. Remove from oven and serve.

Nutrition:

- Calories: 113
- Fat: 3.4 g.
- Carbs: 0 g.
- Protein: 20.6 g.

351. Fried Lemon Chicken

Preparation time: 5 minutes

Cooking time: 20 minutes

Servings: 6

Ingredients:

- 6 chicken thighs
- 2 tbsp. olive oil
- 2 tbsp. lemon juice
- 1 tbsp. Italian herbal seasoning mix
- 1 tsp. Celtic sea salt
- 1 tsp. ground fresh pepper
- 1 lemon, thinly sliced

Directions:

1. Add all ingredients, except sliced lemon, to bowl or bag, stir to cover chicken.
2. Let marinate for 30 minutes overnight.
3. Remove the chicken and let the excess oil drip (it does not need to dry out, just do not drip with tons of excess oil).
4. Arrange the chicken thighs and the lemon slices in the fryer basket, being careful not to push the chicken thighs too close to each other.
5. Set the fryer to 200 and cook for 10 minutes.
6. Remove the basket from the fryer and turn the chicken thighs to the other side.
7. Cook again at 200 for another 10 minutes.

Nutrition:

- Calories: 215
- Fat: 13g
- Carbs: 1g
- Protein: 2

- Sugar: 1g
- Cholesterol: 130mg

352. Chicken's Liver

Preparation time: 10 minutes

Cooking time: 30 minutes

Servings: 4

Ingredients:

- 500 g. chicken livers
- 2–3 carrots
- 1 green pepper
- 1 red pepper
- 1 onion
- 4 tomatoes
- Salt
- Pepper, ground
- 1 glass of white wine
- 1/2 glass of water
- Extra virgin olive oil

Directions:

1. Peel the carrots, cut them into slices, and add them to the bowl of the air fryer with 1 tbsp. of extra virgin olive oil for 5 minutes.
2. After 5 minutes, add the peppers and onion in julienne. Select 5 minutes.
3. After that time, add the tomatoes in wedges and select 5 more minutes.
4. Add now the chicken liver clean and chopped.
5. Season, add the wine and water.
6. Select 10 minutes.
7. Check that the liver is tender.

Nutrition:

- Calories: 76
- Fat: 13 g.
- Carbs: 1 g.
- Protein: 2 g.
- Sugar: 1 g.
- Cholesterol: 130 mg.

Chapter 6: Meat Recipes

353. Pork Taquitos

Preparation time: 10 minutes

Cooking time: 16 minutes

Servings: 8

Ingredients:

- 1 juiced lime
- 10 whole-wheat tortillas
- 2 1/2 cup Mozzarella cheese, shredded
- 30 oz. pork tenderloin, cooked and shredded

Directions:

1. Ensure your Instant vortex air fryer oven is preheated to 380°F.
2. Drizzle pork with lime juice and gently mix.
3. Heat the tortillas in the microwave with a dampened paper towel to soften.
4. Add about 3 oz. of pork and 1/4 cup of shredded cheese to each tortilla. Tightly roll them up.
5. Spray the air fryer basket with a bit of olive oil.
6. Set temperature to 380°F, and set time to 10 minutes. Air fry taquitos 7–10 minutes till tortillas turn a slight golden color, making sure to flip halfway through the cooking process.

Nutrition:

- Calories: 309
- Fat: 11 g.
- Protein:21 g.
- Sugar: 2 g.

354. Panko-Breaded Pork Chops

Preparation time: 5 minutes

Cooking time: 12 minutes

Servings: 6

Ingredients:

- 5 (3 1/2–5-oz.) pork chops, bone-in or boneless
- 1 tsp Seasoning salt to taste
- 1 tsp Pepper to taste
- 1/4 cup all-purpose flour
- 3 tbsp. panko bread crumbs
- 3 tbsp Cooking oil

Directions:

1. Season the pork chops with the seasoning salt and pepper to taste.
2. Sprinkle the flour on both sides of the pork chops, then coat both sides with panko bread crumbs.
3. Place the pork chops in the air fryer. Stacking them is okay.
4. Spray the pork chops with cooking oil. Pour into the oven rack/basket. Place the rack on the middle-shelf of the Instant vortex air fryer oven. Set temperature to 375°F, and set time to 6 minutes. Cook for 6 minutes.
5. Open the Instant vortex air fryer oven and flip the pork chops. Cook for an additional 6 minutes
6. Cool before serving.
7. Typically, bone-in pork chops are juicier than boneless. If you prefer juicy pork chops, use bone-in.

Nutrition:

- Calories: 246
- Fat: 13 g.
- Protein: 26 g.
- Fiber: 0 g.

355. Apricot Glazed Pork Tenderloins

Preparation time: 5 minutes

Cooking time: 30 minutes

Servings: 3

Ingredients:

- 1 tsp. salt
- 1/2 tsp. pepper
- 1 lb. pork tenderloin
- 2 tbsp. fresh Rosemary, minced or 1 tbsp. dried Rosemary, crushed
- 2 tbsp. olive oil, divided
- 2 garlic cloves, minced
- Cooking spray

For Apricot Glaze:

- 1 cup apricot preserves
- 3 garlic cloves, minced
- 1 tbsp. lemon juice

Directions:

1. Mix well pepper, salt, garlic, oil, and Rosemary. Brush all over pork. If needed cut pork crosswise in half to fit in the air fryer.
2. Lightly grease baking pan of the air fryer with cooking spray. Add pork.
3. For 3 minutes per side, brown pork in a preheated 390°F air fryer.
4. Meanwhile, mix well all glaze ingredients in a small bowl. Baste pork every 5 minutes.
5. Cook for 20 minutes at 330°F.
6. Serve and enjoy.

Nutrition:

- Calories: 281
- Fat: 9 g.
- Protein: 23 g.
- Fiber: 0 g.

356. Pork Tenders With Bell Peppers

Preparation time: 5 minutes

Cooking time: 15 minutes

Servings: 4

Ingredients:

- 11 oz. pork tenderloin
- 1 bell pepper, in thin strips
- 1 red onion, sliced
- tsp. Provencal Herbs
- Black pepper to taste
- 1 tbsp. olive oil
- 1/2 tbsp. mustard
- Round oven dish

Directions:

1. Preheat the Instant vortex air fryer oven to 390°F.
2. In the oven dish, mix the bell pepper strips with the onion, herbs, and some salt and pepper to taste.
3. Add half 1 tbsp. of olive oil to the mixture.
4. Cut the pork tenderloin into four pieces and rub it with salt, pepper, and mustard.
5. Thinly coat the pieces with remaining olive oil and place them upright in the oven dish on top of the pepper mixture.
6. Place the bowl into the Instant vortex air fryer oven. Set the timer to 15 minutes and roast the meat and the vegetables.
7. Turn the meat and mix the peppers halfway through.
8. Serve with a fresh salad.

Nutrition:

- Calories: 234
- Fat: 4 g.
- Carbs: 23 g.
- Protein: 24 .g

357. Barbecue Flavored Pork Ribs

Preparation time: 5 minutes

Cooking time: 15 minutes

Servings: 6

Ingredients:

- 1/4 cup honey, divided
- 3/4 cup BBQ sauce
- 2 tbsp. tomato ketchup
- 1 tbsp. Worcestershire sauce
- 1 tbsp. soy sauce
- 1/2 tsp. garlic powder
- White pepper, freshly ground to taste
- 1 3/4 lb. pork ribs

Directions:

1. In a large bowl, mix 3 tbsp. of honey and remaining ingredients except for pork ribs.
2. Refrigerate to marinate for about 20 minutes.
3. Preheat the Instant vortex air fryer oven to 355°F.
4. Place the ribs in the air fryer basket.
5. Cook for about 13 minutes.
6. Remove the ribs from the Instant vortex air fryer oven and coat with remaining honey.
7. Serve hot.

Nutrition:

- Calories: 574
- Fat: 6 g.
- Carbs: 20 g.
- Protein: 25 g.

358. Balsamic Glazed Pork Chops

Preparation time: 5 minutes

Cooking time: 50 minutes

Servings: 4

Ingredients:

- 3/4 cup balsamic vinegar
- 1 1/2 tbsp. sugar
- 1 tbsp. butter
- tbsp. olive oil
- 3 tbsp. salt
- 3 pork rib chops

Directions:

1. Place all ingredients in bowl and allow the meat to marinate in the fridge for at least 2 hours.
2. Preheat the Instant vortex air fryer oven to 390°F.

3. Place the grill pan accessory in the air fryer.
4. Grill the pork chops for 20 minutes making sure to flip the meat every 10 minutes for even grilling.
5. Meanwhile, pour the balsamic vinegar on a saucepan and allow to simmer for at least 10 minutes until the sauce thickens.
6. Brush the meat with the glaze before serving.

Nutrition:

- Calories: 274
- Fat: 18 g.

Protein:17 g.

359. Rustic Pork Ribs

Preparation time: 5 minutes

Cooking time: 15 minutes

Servings: 4

Ingredients:

- 1 rack of pork ribs
- tbsp. dry red wine
- 1 tbsp. soy sauce
- 1/2 tsp. thyme, dried
- 1/2 tsp. onion powder
- 1/2 tsp. garlic powder
- 1/2 tsp. ground black pepper
- 1 tsp. smoke salt
- 1 tbsp. cornstarch
- 1/2 tsp. olive oil

Directions:

1. Begin by preheating your Instant vortex air fryer oven to 390°F. Place all ingredients in a mixing bowl and let them marinate for at least 1 hour.
2. Pour into the oven rack/basket. Place the Rack on the middle-shelf of the Instant vortex air fryer oven. Set temperature to 390°F, and set time to 25 minutes. Cook the marinated ribs for approximately 25 minutes.
3. Serve hot.

Nutrition:

- Calories: 131
- Fat: 14 g.
- Carbs: 20 g.
- Protein: 21 g.

360. Keto Parmesan Crusted Pork Chops

Preparation time: 10 minutes

Cooking time: 15 minutes

Servings: 8

Ingredients:

- 1 tbsp. grated parmesan cheese
- 1 cup pork rind crumbs
- 2 eggs, beaten
- 1/4 tsp. chili powder
- 1/2 tsp. onion powder
- 1 tsp. smoked paprika
- 1/4 tsp. pepper
- 1/2 tsp. salt
- 4–6 thick pork chops, boneless
- 1 tbsp olive oil

Directions:

1. Ensure your Instant vortex air fryer oven is preheated to 400°F.
2. With pepper and salt, season both sides of pork chops.
3. In a food processor, pulse pork rinds into crumbs. Mix crumbs with other seasonings. Beat eggs and add to another bowl.
4. Dip pork chops into eggs then into pork rind crumb mixture.
5. Spray down the air fryer with olive oil and add pork chops to the basket. Set temperature to 400°F, and set time to 15 minutes.

Nutrition:

- Calories: 422
- Fat: 19 g.
- Protein:38 g.
- Sugar: 2 g.

361. Crispy Fried Pork Chops the Southern Way

Preparation time: 10 minutes

Cooking time: 25 minutes

Servings: 4

Ingredients:

- 1/2 cup all-purpose flour
- 1/2 cup buttermilk, low-fat
- 1/2 tsp. black pepper
- 1/2 tsp. Tabasco® sauce
- 1 tsp. paprika
- 2 bone-in pork chops
- 2 tbsp cooking oil

Directions:

1. Place the buttermilk and hot sauce in a Ziploc® bag and add the pork chops. Allow marinating for at least 1 hour in the fridge.
2. In a bowl, combine the flour, paprika, and black pepper.
3. Remove pork from the Ziploc® bag and dredge in the flour mixture.
4. Preheat the Instant vortex air fryer oven to 390°F.
5. Spray the pork chops with cooking oil.
6. Pour into the oven rack/basket. Place the Rack on the middle-shelf of the Instant vortex air fryer oven. Set temperature to 390°F, and set time to 25 minutes.

Nutrition:

- Calories: 427
- Fat: 21.2 g.
- Protein: 46.4 g.
- Sugar: 2 g.

362. Fried Pork Quesadilla

Preparation time: 10 minutes

Cooking time: 12 minutes

Servings: 2

Ingredients:

- 2 corn or flour tortilla shells (6-inch)
- 1 pork shoulder, medium-sized, approximately 4 oz., sliced
- 1/2 white onion, medium-sized, sliced
- 1/2 red pepper, medium-sized, sliced
- 1/2 green pepper, medium-sized, sliced
- 1/2 yellow pepper, medium-sized, sliced
- 1/4 cup pepper-jack cheese, shredded
- 1/4 cup mozzarella cheese, shredded

Directions:

1. Preheat the Instant vortex air fryer oven to 350°F.
2. In the oven on high heat for 20 minutes, grill the pork, onion, and peppers in foil in the same pan, allowing the moisture from the vegetables and the juice from the pork to mingle together. Remove pork and vegetables in foil from the oven. While they're cooling, sprinkle half the shredded cheese over one of the tortillas, then cover with the pieces of pork, onions, and peppers, and then layer on the rest of the shredded cheese. Top with the second tortilla. Place directly on the hot surface of the air fryer basket.
3. Set the air fryer timer for 6 minutes. After 6 minutes, when the air fryer shuts off, flip the tortillas onto the other side with a spatula; the cheese should be melted enough that it won't fall apart, but be careful anyway not to spill any toppings!
4. Reset the air fryer to 350°F for another 6 minutes.
5. After 6 minutes, when the air fryer

shuts off, the tortillas should be browned and crisp, and the pork, onion, peppers, and cheese will be crispy and hot, and delicious. Remove with tongs and let sit on a serving plate to cool for a few minutes before slicing.

Nutrition:

- Calories: 342
- Fat: 15 g.
- Protein: 38 g.
- Sugar: 2 g.

363. Pork Wonton Wonderful

Preparation time: 10 minutes

Cooking time: 25 minutes

Servings: 3

Ingredients:

- 8 wonton wrappers (Leasa® brand works great, though any will do)
- 2 oz. raw pork, minced
- 1 green apple, medium-sized
- 1 cup water, for wetting the wonton wrappers
- 1 tbsp. vegetable oil
- 1/2 tbsp. oyster sauce
- 1 tbsp. soy sauce
- 1 Large pinch of ground white pepper

Directions:

1. Cover the basket of the Instant vortex air fryer oven with a lining of tin foil, leaving the edges uncovered to allow air to circulate through the basket. Preheat the air fryer to 350°F.

2. In a small mixing bowl, combine the oyster sauce, soy sauce, and white pepper, then add in the minced pork and stir thoroughly. Cover and set in the fridge to marinate for at least 15 minutes. Core the apple, and slice into small cubes— smaller than bite-sized chunks.

3. Add the apples to the marinating meat mixture, and combine thoroughly. Spread

the wonton wrappers, and fill each with a large spoonful of the filling. Wrap the wontons into triangles, so that the wrappers fully cover the filling, and seal with a drop of water.

4. Coat each filled and wrapped wonton thoroughly with the vegetable oil, to help ensure a nice crispy fry. Place the wontons on the foil-lined air-fryer basket.

5. Set the Instant vortex air fryer oven timer to 25 minutes. Halfway through cooking time, shake the handle of the air fryer basket vigorously to jostle the wontons and ensure even frying. After 25 minutes, when the Instant vortex air fryer oven shuts off, the wontons will be crispy golden-brown on the outside and juicy and delicious on the inside. Serve directly from the air fryer basket and enjoy while hot.

Nutrition:

- Calories: 242
- Fat: 12 g.
- Protein: 28 g.
- Sugar: 4 g.

364. Cilantro-Mint Pork BBQ Thai Style

Preparation time: 5 minutes

Cooking time: 15 minutes

Servings: 3

Ingredients:

- 1 hot Chile, minced
- 1 shallot, minced
- 1-lb. pork, ground
- 2 tbsp. fish sauce
- 2 tbsp. lime juice
- 3 tbsp. basil
- 1 tbsp. mint, chopped
- 1 tbsp. cilantro

Directions:

1. In a shallow dish, mix well all ingredients with your hands. Form into 1-inch ovals.
2. Thread ovals in

skewers. Place on skewer rack in the air fryer.

3. For 15 minutes, cook on 360°F. Halfway through cooking time, turnover skewers. If needed, cook in batches.

4. Serve and enjoy.

Nutrition:

- Calories: 455
- Fat: 31.5 g.

Protein: 40.4 g

365. Spicy Pork Tenderloin With Broccoli

Preparation time: 20 minutes

Cooking time: 35 minutes

Servings: 4

Ingredients:

- 1 package (1 1/2 lb.) pork tenderloin, trimmed
- 1 tsp. mustard, ground
- 1/4 tsp. garlic powder
- 2 tbsp. brown sugar
- 1 tbsp. smoked paprika

- 1/4 tsp. cayenne pepper (optional)
- 1 tbsp. olive oil
- 4 cups broccoli, chopped into florets
- 1 tbsp. olive oil
- Salt and black pepper, to taste

Directions:

1. In a bowl, put in the ground mustard, garlic powder, brown sugar, paprika, cayenne pepper, salt, and pepper, stir to mix well. Reserve.

2. Place the pork tenderloin on a clean working surface. Rub the tenderloin with olive oil on both sides, then dredge it in the mustard mixture to coat well. Let it sit for 5 minutes.

3. Gently arrange the tenderloin in the air fryer basket, and

cook in the preheated instant vortex at 400°F for 10 minutes or until cooked through. Flip the tenderloin when the lid indicates "TURN FOOD" halfway through the cooking.

4. In the meantime, in a microwave-safe bowl, put in the broccoli and microwave on high for 3 minutes or until soft, then remove the broccoli from the microwave to a large dish, drizzle with olive oil and sprinkle with salt and pepper, toss to coat well. Reserve.

5. Remove the tenderloin from the basket to a clean working surface. Allow cooling for 10 minutes.

6. Meanwhile, transfer the broccoli to the air fryer basket and cook in the preheated instant vortex at 400°F for 10 minutes. Give the basket a shake when the lid indicates "TURN FOOD" halfway through the cooking.

7. Remove the cooked broccoli from the basket to a large dish. Slice the cooled tenderloin and serve with broccoli.

Nutrition:

- Calories: 270
- Total fat: 11.1 g.
- Cholesterol: 74 mg.
- Sodium: 710 mg.
- Carbs: 14 g.
- Protein: 29.5 g.

366. Mexican Hot Meatloaf

Preparation time: 15 minutes

Cooking time: 35 minutes

Servings: 4

Ingredients:

- 1/2 lb. veal, ground
- 1/2 lb. pork, ground
- 2 tsp. chipotle sauce, gluten-free
- 1/4 cup cilantro, chopped
- 1/4 cup bread crumbs, gluten-free
- 1 large egg, beaten
- 2 spring onions, medium-sized, diced
- Sriracha salt and

ground black pepper, to taste
- 1/2 cup ketchup
- 1 tsp. blackstrap molasses
- 1 tsp. olive oil
- Cooking spray

Directions:

1. In a bowl, mix the chipotle chili sauce, ketchup, molasses, and olive oil. Reserve under room temperature.
2. Combine the veal and pork on a clean working surface.
3. Make a well in the middle of the meat mixture, then put in the cilantro, bread crumbs, beaten egg, spring onion, Sriracha salt, and black pepper. Combine all of them well with your hands.
4. Shape the mixture into a loaf. Grease your hands with cooking spray to avoid a sticky situation. Arrange the meatloaf in a 6×6×2-inch baking pan.
5. Arrange the baking pan in the air fryer basket. Put the air fryer lid on and cook in the preheated instant vortex at 400°F for 25 minutes.
6. Remove the baking pan from the basket and pour the ketchup mixture on top of the meatloaf to cover generously.
7. Arrange the baking pan back to the basket and bake for another 7 minutes or until an instant-read thermometer registers at least 160°F.
8. Let the meatloaf stand in the basket for 5 minutes, then remove the meatloaf from the basket and cool for 5 minutes. Slice to serve.

Nutrition:

- Calories: 272
- Fat: 14.4 g.
- Cholesterol: 123 mg.
- Sodium: 536 mg.
- Carbs: 13.3 g.
- Protein: 22.1 g.

367. Garlicky Pork Belly With New Potatoes

Preparation time: 10 minutes

Cooking time: 30 minutes

Servings: 4

Ingredients:

- 1 1/2 lb. pork belly, cut into 4 pieces, rinsed, and drained
- 1 lb. new potatoes, peeled, scrubbed, and halved
- 1/2 tsp. turmeric powder
- 1 tsp. smoked paprika
- 2 tbsp. oyster sauce
- 2 tbsp. green onions, chopped
- 4 garlic cloves, sliced
- Kosher salt and black pepper, to taste
- Cooking spray

Directions:

1. Lay the pork belly on a cutting board; sprinkle with turmeric powder, smoked paprika, salt, and pepper to season. Let sit for 10 minutes.
2. Generously top the pork belly with oyster sauce. Arrange the belly in the air fryer basket, then spritz the belly with cooking spray on both sides.
3. Put the air fryer lid on and cook in the preheated instant vortex at 380°F for 20 minutes. Flip the belly when it shows "TURN FOOD" on the lid screen halfway through the cooking.
4. Remove the belly from the basket, and reserve. Put the new potatoes, green onions, and sliced garlic in the basket.
5. Put the lid on and cook at 380°F for 15 minutes or until the new potatoes are brown and crispy on the edges and cooked through in the center. Shake the basket periodically.
6. Remove them from the basket and serve with pork belly in a large dish.

Nutrition:

- Calories: 546
- Fat: 30.3 g.

- Carbs: 20.7 g.
- Protein: 45.2 g.
- Sugar: 1.3 g.

368. Spanish Pork Kabobs (*Pinchos Morunos*)

Preparation time: 35 minutes

Cooking time: 2 hours

Servings: 4

Ingredients:

- 2 lb. pork loin chop, center-cut, cut into bite-sized pieces
- 1/4 cup dry red wine
- 1/2 tsp. turmeric, ground
- 1/2 tsp. coriander, ground
- 1 tsp. oregano
- 1 tsp. cumin, ground
- 2 garlic cloves, minced
- 2 tsp. sweet Spanish paprika
- 2 tbsp. extra virgin olive oil
- Sea salt and freshly ground black pepper, to taste
- 1 lemon, 1/2 juiced 1/2 wedges
- 4 skewers, soak for 30 minutes

Directions:

1. Place the pork loin chops in a large bowl, pour the red wine on top, sprinkle with turmeric, coriander, oregano, cumin, minced garlic, Spanish paprika, salt, and pepper, toss to coat evenly, then drizzle with olive oil. Wrap the

bowl with plastic and refrigerate to marinate for 2 hours.

2. To make the kabobs, run the skewers through each marinated loin chop lengthwise, then arrange them in the air fryer basket.

3. Put the air fryer lid on and cook in batches in the preheated instant vortex at 360°F for 15–17 minutes. Shake the basket at least 3 times during the cooking.

4. Remove the kabobs from the basket to a serving dish, top with lemon juice, and garnished with lemon wedges to serve.

Nutrition:

- Calories: 433
- Fat: 24 g.
- Carbs: 3.5 g.
- Protein: 49.5 g.
- Sugar: 0.5 g.

369. Simple Greek Pork Sirloin With Tzatziki

Preparation time: 5 minutes

Cooking time: 20 minutes

Servings: 4

Ingredients:

Greek Pork:

- 2 lb. pork sirloin roast
- 1/2 tsp. celery seeds
- 1/2 tsp. mustard seeds
- 1/2 tsp. ginger, ground
- 1 tsp. fennel seeds
- 1 tsp. smoked

- paprika
- 1 tsp. turmeric powder
- 1 tsp. *Chili ancho* powder
- 2 cloves garlic, finely chopped
- Salt and black pepper, to taste
- 2 tbsp. olive oil

Tzatziki:

- 1/2 cucumber, finely chopped and squeezed
- 1 garlic clove, minced
- 1 cup Greek yogurt, full-fat
- 1 tsp. fresh dill, minced
- 1 tsp. balsamic vinegar
- 1 tbsp. extra-virgin olive oil
- Salt, to taste

Directions:

1. In a large bowl, mix the celery seeds, mustard seeds, ground ginger, fennel seeds, paprika, turmeric powder, chili ancho powder, chopped garlic, salt, and pepper. Toss the sirloin in the mixture to coat well, then drizzle the olive oil on both sides of the sirloin.

2. Arrange the sirloin in the air fryer basket. Place the air fryer lid on and cook in the preheated instant vortex at 360°F for 20 minutes. Flip the sirloin when it shows "TURN FOOD" on the lid screen during the cooking.

3. In the meantime, combine all the *tzatziki i*ngredients in a separate bowl. Leave the *tzatziki* in the fridge to marinate until ready to serve.

4. Remove the sirloin from the basket to a large serving dish. Slice to serve, with *tzatziki* on the side.

Nutrition:

- Calories: 561
- Fat: 30.2 g.
- Carbs: 4.6 g.
- Protein: 64.5 g
- Sugar: 1.8 g.

370. Beef Sausage and Veggie Sandwiches

Preparation time: 5 minutes

Cooking time: 30 minutes

Servings: 4

Ingredients:

- 4 hot dog buns, halved
- 4 beef sausages
- 4 bell peppers, deseeded and cut into 1-inch pieces
- 1 onion, chopped
- 2 tomatoes, medium-sized, cut into slices
- 2 tbsp. canola oil
- 1 tbsp. mustard

Directions:

1. Arrange the bell peppers in the air fryer basket. Brush them with 1 tbsp. of canola oil on both sides.
2. Put the air fryer lid on and cook in the preheated instant vortex at 380°F for 5 minutes.
3. Afterward, give the basket a toss, and put the onion and tomatoes in the basket and cook at 350°F for 5 minutes more or until the onions are translucent and peppers are wilted. Remove them from the basket and set them aside.
4. Place the beef sausages in the basket. Brush the remaining 1 tbsp. of canola oil all over the sausages.
5. Place the lid on and cook at 380°F for 15 minutes. Turn the sausages over when it shows "TURN FOOD" on the lid screen halfway through the cooking.
6. Remove the sausages from the basket to a clean working surface. Assemble each sausage into the hot dog buns. Spread the cooked vegetables and mustard on the top of the buns. Serve warm.

Nutrition:

- Calories: 626
- Fat: 41.8 g.
- Carbs: 41.4 g.
- Protein: 22.3 g.

- Sugar: 9.4 g.

371. Cheese and Sausage Pepper Pocket

Preparation time: 20 minutes

Cooking time: 1 hour

Servings: 12

Ingredients:

- 8 oz. bulk Italian sausage
- 1 (16 oz.) package miniature multi-colored sweet peppers
- 1 (8 oz.) package cream cheese, softened
- 1/2 cup Cheddar cheese, shredded
- 2 tbsp. blue cheese, crumbled (optional)
- 2 tbsp. olive oil, divided
- 1 tbsp. fresh chives, finely chopped
- 1 clove garlic, minced
- 1/4 tsp. black pepper, ground
- 2 tbsp. panko bread crumbs

Directions:

1. Stir fry sausage in the hot pan over medium heat for 5–7 minutes or until browned and golden on the edges. Set aside.
2. Cut a slit on each sweet pepper lengthwise to create a pocket. Brush the pepper's skin with 1 tbsp. olive oil and arrange them in the basket.
3. Put the air fry lid on and cook in the

preheated instant vortex at 356°F for 3 minutes. Flip the batter when it shows "TURN FOOD" on the lid screen halfway through the cooking or until soft and brown for 3 minutes.

4. Remove the peppers to a platter and let them cool down.

5. Meanwhile, in a bowl, stir in sausage, cheddar cheese, cream cheese, blue cheese, garlic, chives, and black pepper, and combine well.

6. In a medium bowl, add the remaining 1 tbsp. olive oil with bread crumbs and mix well.

7. Use a spoon to stuff the cheese mixture into each pepper pocket and top with the bread crumb

mixture. Place the stuffed pepper pockets in the basket and put the air fry lid on. Air fry about 4–5 minutes until filling is cooked and the bread crumbs are crispy.

Nutrition:

- Calories: 101
- Fat: 8.6 g.
- Carbs: 2.6 g.
- Protein: 3.6 g.
- Cholesterol: 20 mg.
- Sodium: 159 mg.

372. Sizzling Beef Steak Fajitas

Preparation time: 5 minutes

Cooking time: 20 minutes

Servings: 4

Ingredients:

- 1 lb. beef steak, cut into strips
- 1 red bell pepper, cut into strips
- 1 green bell pepper, cut into strips
- 2 tbsp. taco or fajita seasoning
- 1/2 red onion, cut into strips
- 2 tbsp. extra-virgin olive oil
- Salt and pepper to

taste

- 2 tbsp parsley
- Cooking spray

Directions:

1. In a large bowl, mix the beefsteak, bell peppers, taco seasoning, onion, olive oil, salt, and pepper. Toss well to coat the beef evenly.

2. Arrange the beef mixture in the air fryer basket and spritz with cooking spray.

3. Put the air fryer lid on and cook the beef in the preheated instant vortex at 380°F for 5 minutes. Flip the beef once when it shows "TURN FOOD" on the air fryer lid screen during cooking time. Cook for an additional 4–5 minutes.

4. Transfer the cooked beef mixture to a platter. Serve with the parsley, if desired.

Nutrition:

- Calories: 491
- Total fat: 16 g.
- Saturated fat: 4 g.
- Cholesterol: 50 mg.
- Sodium: 389 mg.
- Carbs: 52 g.
- Fiber: 4 g.
- Protein: 33 g.

373. Sweet Potato Steak

Preparation time: 10 minutes

Cooking time: 32–35 minutes

Servings: 5

Ingredients:

- 2 tsp. black pepper
- 1 tbsp. maple syrup
- 2 sweet potatoes, large, peeled, and cubed
- 1/2 cup beef broth
- 1 cup water
- 1/2-lb. turkey bacon, sliced
- 2 tbsp. parsley
- 2 tbsp. thyme
- 1 tbsp. olive oil
- 5 carrots make sticks
- 1 large red onion, sliced
- 1 lb. flank steak
- 2 tsp. rock salt
- 2 cloves garlic,

minced

Directions:

1. Pat dry the beef and season it.
2. Arrange your Instant vortex over a dry, clean platform. Plug it into the power socket and turn it on.
3. Now press "Sauté" mode from available options. In the cooking area, add the oil and beef; cook to brown evenly.
4. Add the onion, turkey bacon, and other ingredients.
5. Close the lid and lock. Ensure that you have sealed the valve to avoid leakage.
6. Press "Manual" mode from available cooking settings and set the cooking time to 25 minutes. Instant vortex will start cooking the ingredients after a few minutes.
7. After the timer reads zero, press "Cancel" and quick release pressure.
8. Carefully remove the lid and serve the prepared keto dish warm!

Nutrition:

- Calories: 338
- Fat: 19.5 g.
- Carbs: 17 g.
- Fiber: 1.7 g.
- Protein: 23.5 g.

374. Garlic Roast

Preparation time: 5 minutes

Cooking time: 40–45 minutes

Servings: 8–10

Ingredients:

- 1/2 cup onion, chopped
- 2 cups water
- 1/4 tsp. xanthan gum
- 1 tsp. garlic powder
- 3 lb. chuck roast, boneless
- 1/4 cup balsamic vinegar
- 2 Parsley, chopped to garnish
- 1 tsp. pepper
- 1 tbsp. kosher salt

Directions:

1. Slice your roast in half and season with garlic, pepper, and

salt.

2. Arrange your Instant vortex over a dry, clean platform. Plug it into the power socket and turn it on.

3. Now press "Sauté" mode from available options. In the cooking area, add the meat; cook to brown.

4. Add the onion, water, and vinegar. Stir gently.

5. Close the lid and lock. Ensure that you have sealed the valve to avoid leakage.

6. Press "Manual" mode from available cooking settings and set the cooking time to 35 minutes. Instant vortex will start cooking the ingredients after a few minutes.

7. After the timer reads zero, press "Cancel" and quick release pressure.

8. Carefully remove the lid. Carefully take the meat and make chunks.

9. Set the pot back on sauté; boil the mix for around 10 minutes.

10. Mix the gum and mix the shredded meat. Serve the prepared keto dish warm!

Nutrition:

- Calories: 392
- Fat: 28 g.
- Carbs: 3 g.
- Fiber: 0 g.
- Protein: 29.5 g.

375. Milky Beef Roast

Preparation time: 10 minutes

Cooking time: 30 minutes

Servings: 7–8

Ingredients:

- 1 tbsp. paprika
- 2 lb. beef roast
- 1 cup almond milk
- 1 tsp. salt
- 1 tsp. raw honey

Directions:

1. Combine the almond milk and salt in a mixing bowl. Add the paprika and raw honey. Stir the mixture well; add the beef roast in the almond milk mixture and leave for 15 minutes.

2. Take your Instant vortex; open the top

lid. Plug it and turn it on.

3. In the cooking pot area, add the bowl mix. Using a spatula, stir the ingredients.

4. Close the top lid and seal its valve.

5. Press "MANUAL" setting. Adjust cooking time to 30 minutes.

6. Allow the recipe to cook for the set cooking time.

7. After the set cooking time ends, press "CANCEL" and then press "QPR" (Quick Pressure Release).

8. Instant vortex will quickly release the pressure.

9. Open the top lid, add the cooked recipe mix to serving plates.

10. Serve and enjoy!

Nutrition:

- Calories: 284
- Fat: 14.5 g.
- Carbs: 3 g.
- Fiber: 1 g.
- Protein: 34 g.

376. Beef Avocado Bowl

Preparation time: 10 minutes

Cooking time: 10–12 minutes

Servings: 4

Ingredients:

- 2 tsp. lime juice
- 1 tbsp. olive oil, extra virgin
- 1/2 tsp. cracked pepper
- 1/2 tsp. sea salt
- 1/2 tsp. chili powder
- 2 lb. beef steak strips
- 1 garlic clove, minced
- 1 tbsp. water
- 3 avocados, diced

Directions:

1. Arrange your

Instant vortex over a dry, clean platform. Plug it into the power socket and turn it on.

2. Now press "Sauté" mode from available options. In the cooking area, add the oil and garlic, cook for 1–2 minutes to soften.

3. Add water, lime juice, sea salt, chili powder, and pepper; stir gently.

4. Close the lid and lock. Ensure that you have sealed the valve to avoid leakage.

5. Press "Manual" mode from available cooking settings and set the cooking time to 10 minutes. Instant vortex will start cooking the ingredients after a few minutes.

6. After the timer reads zero, press "Cancel" and quick release pressure. Carefully remove the lid.

7. Press "Sauté" button, add the steak strips, and stir and cook for 2 minutes.

8. Continue sautéing until chili becomes thicker and reduced by half size. Top with diced avocados.

Nutrition:

- Calories: 252
- Fat: 35 g.
- Carbs: 3 g.
- Fiber: 0.5 g.
- Protein: 14.5 g.

377. Broccoli Beef With Garlic Twist

Preparation time: 5–8 minutes

Cooking time: 20 minutes

Servings: 5

Ingredients:

- 1/2 cup poultry broth
- 1/8 tsp. salt
- 1 lb. cooked beef
- 2 tsp. garlic, crushed
- 1 tbsp. animal fat
- 6 cups broccoli, cut to prepare small florets
- 1 onion, chopped
- 1 turnip, chopped

Directions:

1. Arrange your Instant vortex over a dry, clean platform. Plug it into the power

socket and turn it on.

2. Open the lid from the top and put it aside, add the mentioned ingredients and gently stir them.

3. Close the lid and lock. Ensure that you have sealed the valve to avoid leakage.

4. Press "Manual" mode from available cooking settings and set the cooking time to 20 minutes. Instant vortex will start cooking the ingredients after a few minutes.

5. After the timer reads zero, press "Cancel" and quick release pressure.

6. Carefully remove the lid and serve the prepared keto dish warm!

Nutrition:

- Calories: 229
- Fat: 10 g.
- Carbs: 8 g.
- Fiber: 4 g.
- Protein: 19.5 g

378. Beef Broccoli Curry

Preparation time: 8–10 minutes

Cooking time: 45 minutes

Servings: 6

Ingredients:

- 1/2 lb. broccoli florets
- 2 tbsp. curry powder
- 14 oz. coconut milk
- Salt as needed
- 2 1/2 lb. beef stew chunks, small cubes
- 2 zucchinis, medium-sized, chopped
- 1/2 cup water or chicken broth
- 1 tbsp. garlic powder

Directions:

1. Arrange your

Instant vortex over a dry, clean platform. Plug it into the power socket and turn it on.

2. Open the lid from the top and put it aside; add the ingredients and gently stir them.

3. Close the lid and lock. Ensure that you have sealed the valve to avoid leakage.

4. Press "Manual" mode from available cooking settings and set the cooking time to 45 minutes. Instant vortex will start cooking the ingredients after a few minutes.

5. After the timer reads zero, press "Cancel" and quick release pressure.

6. Carefully remove the lid. Add the milk and stir.

7. Add salt as needed and serve the prepared keto dish warm!

Nutrition:

- Calories: 181
- Fat: 25 g.
- Carbs: 6 g.
- Fiber: 0.5 g.
- Protein: 9.5 g.

379. Wine Braised Beef Roast

Preparation time: 10 minutes

Cooking time: 48 minutes

Servings: 5–6

Ingredients:

- 2 celery stalks, chopped
- 1 bell pepper, chopped
- 2 tbsp. olive oil
- 2 tbsp. Italian seasoning
- 2 1/2 lb. beef roast
- 1 onion, sliced
- 2 garlic cloves, sliced
- 1 cup red wine
- 1 cup beef broth

- 2 tbsp. steak sauce, sugar-free

Directions:

1. Take your Instant vortex, open the top lid. Plug it and turn it on.
2. Press the "SAUTÉ" setting and the pot will start heating up.
3. In the cooking pot area, add the meat and half of the oil. Stir and cook for 4–5 minutes until evenly brown from all sides.
4. Set aside on a plate.
5. Heat the remaining olive oil and add the onions, celery, and peppers. Cook for 3 minutes to soften.
6. Stir in the garlic and seasonings and cook for 1 minute. Return the beef to the pot.
7. Add the broth, sauce, and red wine; whisk the mixture.
8. Close the top lid and seal its valve.
9. Press the "MANUAL" setting. Adjust cooking time to 40 minutes.
10. Allow the recipe to cook for the set cooking time.
11. After the set cooking time ends, press "CANCEL" and then press "NPR" (Natural Pressure Release).
12. Instant vortex will slowly and naturally release the pressure.
13. Open the top lid, add the cooked recipe mix to serving plates.
14. Serve and enjoy!

Nutrition:

- Calories: 408
- Fat: 18 g.
- Carbs: 6 g.
- Fiber: 1 g.
- Protein: 41.5 g.

380. Delicious

Beef Roast

Preparation time: 10 minutes

Cooking time: 8 hours

Servings: 2

Ingredients:

- 1 lb. bottom round roast
- 1/2 tsp. oregano, dried
- 1/2 tsp. Rosemary, crushed
- 1/2 tsp. fennel seed
- 1 tsp. garlic, sliced
- 1/4 cup water
- 1/4 cup onions, caramelized
- 1/2 tsp. pepper
- 1/4 tsp. salt

Directions:

1. In a bowl, combine Rosemary, fennel seeds, pepper, oregano, and salt.
2. Rub Rosemary mixture all over meat and place in the refrigerator for 30 minutes.
3. Place marinated roast into the inner pot of instant vortex duo crisp and top with garlic, onions, and water.
4. Seal the pot with a pressure cooking lid and select "Slow" cook mode and cook on low for 8 hours.
5. Remove roast from pot and slice.
6. Serve and enjoy.

Nutrition:

- Calories: 334
- Fat: 12.2 g.
- Carbs: 2.8 g.
- Sugar: 0.6 g.
- Protein: 50.6 g.
- Cholesterol: 151 mg.

381. Spicy Pulled Beef

Preparation time: 10 minutes

Cooking time: 8 hours

Servings: 6

Ingredients:

- 2 lbs. lean beef eye round, trimmed
- 2 tbsp. fresh lime juice
- 1 tbsp. Worcestershire sauce
- 1 cup can tomato, diced
- 1/4 cup beef broth
- 2 jalapeño peppers
- 1 onion, diced
- 1/4 tsp. coriander
- 1/4 tsp. oregano
- 1/2 tsp. cumin
- 1 tsp. garlic, sliced
- 1 red bell pepper, diced

Directions:

1. Season meat with pepper and salt and place into the inner pot of instant vortex duo crisp.
2. Add garlic, red pepper, onion, and jalapeño peppers around the beef.
3. Mix coriander, lime juice, Worcestershire sauce, tomatoes, oregano, cumin, and broth and pour over meat.
4. Seal the pot with a pressure cooking lid and select slow cook mode and cook on low for 8 hours.
5. Remove meat from pot and shred using a fork.
6. Return shredded meat to the pot and stir well.
7. Serve and enjoy.

Nutrition:

- Calories: 278
- Fat: 6.4 g.
- Carbs: 7.6 g.
- Sugar: 4.1 g.
- Protein: 45.5 g.
- Cholesterol: 83 mg.

382. Tasty Beef Tacos

Preparation time: 10 minutes

Cooking time: 8 hours 10 minutes

Servings: 8

Ingredients:

- 3 lbs. lean top round roast
- 4 tbsp. adobo sauce
- 1 onion, diced
- 1 tbsp. garlic, minced
- 2 *ancho* chili peppers, seeded
- 2 cups vegetable broth
- 1/2 tsp. cumin
- 1/2 tsp. coriander
- 1 tsp. oregano
- Pepper
- Salt

Directions:

1. In a bowl, add dried

chilies and broth. Cover and let it sit for 30 minutes.

2. Add broth and dried chilies into the blender along with cumin, coriander, oregano, adobo sauce, onion, and garlic, and blend until smooth.

3. Season beef with pepper and salt and place in the inner pot of instant vortex duo crisp.

4. Pour blended sauce over beef.

5. Seal the pot with a pressure cooking lid and select slow cook mode and cook on low for 8 hours.

6. Remove meat from pot and shred using a fork.

7. Clean the pot. Add shredded meat into the air fryer basket and place the basket into the pot.

8. Seal the pot with an air fryer lid and select broil mode and cook for 10 minutes.

9. Serve and enjoy.

Nutrition:

- Calories: 287
- Fat: 6.2 g.
- Carbs: 5.6 g.
- Sugar: 3.3 g.
- Protein: 49.5 g.
- Cholesterol: 175 mg.

383. Lime Garlic Steak Carnitas

Preparation time: 10 minutes

Cooking time: 6 hours

Servings: 4

Ingredients:

- 1 1/2 lbs. beef chuck, cut into small pieces
- 1 fresh lime juice
- 1 lime zest
- 2 chilies in adobo sauce
- 1 tbsp. garlic, minced
- 1 orange juice
- 1 jalapeño pepper, halved

Directions:

1. Add all ingredients into the inner pot of instant vortex duo crisp and stir well.

2. Seal the pot with a pressure cooking lid and select slow cook mode and cook on low for 6 hours.
3. Serve and enjoy.

Nutrition:

- Calories: 346
- Fat: 11.2 g.
- Carbs: 5.8 g.
- Sugar: 3.2 g.
- Protein: 52 g.

Cholesterol: 152 mg.

384. Smoked Pork Chops

Preparation time: 5 minutes

Cooking time: 25 minutes

Servings: 4

Ingredients:

- 4 pork chops
- 1/2 cup chicken stock
- 2 tbsp. balsamic vinegar
- 1 tbsp. smoked paprika
- 1 tbsp. olive oil
- A pinch of salt and black pepper

Directions:

1. Take a bowl and mix the pork chops with the rest of the ingredients and toss.
2. Put the pork chops in your air fryer's basket and cook at 390°F for 25 minutes
3. Divide between plates and serve.

Nutrition:

- Calories: 276
- Fat: 12 g.
- Fiber: 4 g.
- Carbs: 6 g.
- Protein: 22 g.

385. Roasted Spare Ribs

Preparation time: 5 minutes

Cooking time: 45 minutes

Servings: 4

Ingredients:

- 2 racks of ribs
- 1 tbsp. coriander; chopped
- 2 tbsp. cocoa powder
- 1/2 tsp. chili powder
- 1/2 tsp. cumin, ground
- 1/2 tsp. cinnamon powder
- Cooking spray
- A pinch of salt and black pepper

Directions:

1. Grease the ribs with the cooking spray, mix with the other ingredients, and rub very well.
2. Put the ribs in your air fryer's basket and cook at 390°F for 45 minutes. Divide between plates and serve with a side salad.

Nutrition:

- Calories: 284
- Fat: 14 g.
- Fiber: 5 g.
- Carbs: 7 g.

Protein: 20 g.

386. Lamb Cakes

Preparation time: 20 minutes

Cooking time: 15 minutes

Servings: 8

Ingredients:

- 2 1/2 lb. lamb meat, ground
- 2 spring onions, chopped
- 1/2 cup almond meal
- 3 eggs, whisked
- 1 tbsp. garlic, minced
- 2 tbsp. cilantro, chopped
- Zest of 1 lemon
- Juice of 1 lemon
- Cooking spray
- 2 tbsp. mint. chopped
- A pinch of salt and black pepper

Directions:

1. Take a bowl and mix all the ingredients except the cooking spray, stir well and shape medium cakes out of this mix.
2. Put the cakes in your air fryer, grease them with cooking spray and cook at 390°F for 15 minutes on each side.
3. Divide between plates and serve with a side salad.

Nutrition:

- Calories: 283
- Fat: 13 g.
- Fiber: 4 g.
- Carbs: 6 g.
- Protein: 15 g.

387. Juicy Pork Chops

Preparation time: 5 minutes

Cooking time: 15 minutes

Servings: 2

Ingredients:

- 2 (4 oz.) boneless pork chops
- 2 tbsp. unsalted butter, divided.
- 1/4 tsp. black pepper, ground
- 1/4 tsp. oregano, dried
- 1 tsp. chili powder
- 1/2 tsp. cumin
- 1/2 tsp. garlic powder

Directions:

1. In a small bowl, mix chili powder, garlic powder, cumin, pepper, and oregano. Rub dry rub onto pork chops. Place pork chops into the air fryer basket. Adjust the temperature to 400°F and set the timer for 15 minutes.
2. The internal temperature should be at least 145°F when fully cooked. Serve warm, each topped with 1 tbsp. butter.

Nutrition:

- Calories: 313
- Protein: 24 g.
- Fiber: 7 g.
- Fat: 26 g.

Carbs: 8 g.

388. Lasagna Casserole

Preparation time: 15 minutes

Cooking time: 15 minutes

Servings: 4

Ingredients:

- 3/4 cup pasta sauce, low-carb, no-sugar-added
- 1 lb. 80/20 ground beef; cooked and drained
- 1/2 cup ricotta cheese, full-fat
- 1/4 cup Parmesan cheese, grated
- 1/2 tsp. garlic powder.
- 1 tsp. parsley, dried
- 1/2 tsp. oregano, dried
- 1 cup mozzarella cheese, shredded

Directions:

1. In a 4-cup round baking dish, pour 1/4 cup pasta sauce on the bottom of the dish. Place 1/4 of the ground beef on top of the sauce.
2. In a small bowl, mix ricotta, Parmesan, garlic powder, parsley, and oregano. Place dollops of half the mixture on top of the beef.
3. Sprinkle with 1/3 of the mozzarella. Repeat layers until all beef, ricotta mixture, sauce, and mozzarella are used, ending with the mozzarella on top.
4. Cover the dish with foil and place it into the air fryer basket. Adjust the temperature to 370°F and set the timer for 15 minutes. In the last 2 minutes of cooking, remove the foil to brown the cheese.
5. Serve immediately.

Nutrition:

- Calories: 371
- Protein: 34 g.
- Fiber: 6 g.
- Fat: 24 g.
- Carbs: 8 g.

389. Pub Burger

Preparation time: 5 minutes

Cooking time: 15 minutes

Servings: 4

Ingredients:

- 8 large leaves butter lettuce
- 1 lb. sirloin, ground
- 4 bacon-wrapped onion rings
- 1/2 cup mayonnaise, full-fat
- 8 slices pickle
- 2 tbsp. salted butter; melted
- 2 tsp. sriracha
- 1/4 tsp. garlic powder
- 1/2 tsp. salt
- 1/4 tsp. black pepper, ground

Directions:

1. Take a medium bowl, combine ground sirloin, salt, and pepper. Form 4 patties. Brush each with butter and then place into the air fryer basket. Adjust the temperature to 380°F and set the timer for 10 minutes.
2. Flip the patties halfway through the cooking time for a medium burger. Add 3–5 minutes for well-done.
3. In a small bowl, mix mayonnaise, sriracha, and garlic powder. Set aside.
4. Place each cooked burger on a lettuce leaf and top with an onion ring, 2 pickles, and a dollop of your prepared burger sauce. Wrap another lettuce leaf around tightly to hold. Serve warm.

Nutrition:

- Calories: 442
- Protein: 23 g.
- Fiber: 8 g.
- Fat: 39 g.
- Carbs: 1 g.

390. Herbed Lamb

Preparation time: 25 minutes

Cooking time: 15 minutes

Servings: 4

Ingredients:

- 8 lamb cutlets
- 1/4 cup mustard
- 2 garlic cloves; minced
- 1 tbsp. oregano; chopped
- 1 tbsp. mint chopped.
- 1 tbsp. chives; chopped
- 1 tbsp. basil; chopped
- A drizzle of olive oil
- A pinch of salt and black pepper

Directions:

1. Take a bowl and mix the lamb with the rest of the ingredients and rub well.
2. Put the cutlets in your air fryer's basket and cook at 380°F for 15 minutes on each side.
3. Divide between plates and serve with a side salad.

Nutrition:

- Calories: 284
- Fat: 13 g.
- Fiber: 3 g.
- Carbs: 6 g. Protein: 14 g.

391. Beef and Chorizo Burger

Preparation time: 10 minutes

Cooking time: 15 minutes

Servings: 4

Ingredients:

- 5 slices pickled jalapeños; chopped
- 1/4 lb. Mexican-style ground chorizo
- 3/4lb. 80/20 ground beef.
- 1/4 cup chopped onion
- 1/4 tsp. cumin
- 1 tsp. minced garlic
- 2 tsp. chili powder

Directions:

1. Take a large bowl, mix all ingredients. Divide the mixture into 4 units and form them into

burger patties.

2. Place burger patties into the air fryer basket, working in batches if necessary. Adjust the temperature to 375°F and set the timer for 15 minutes.

3. Flip the patties halfway through the cooking time. Serve warm.

Nutrition:

- Calories: 291
- Protein: 26 g.
- Fiber: 9 g
- Fat: 13 g
- Carbs: 7 g.

392. Lamb Chops and Mint Sauce

Preparation time: 17 minutes

Cooking time: 12 minutes

Servings: 4

Ingredients:

- 8 lamb chops
- 1 cup mint, chopped
- 1 garlic clove, minced
- 2 tbsp. olive oil
- Juice of 1 lemon
- A pinch of salt and black pepper

Directions:

1. In a blender, combine all the ingredients except the lamb and pulse well.

2. Rub lamb chops with the mint sauce put them in your air fryer's basket and cook at 400°F for 12 minutes on each side.

3. Divide everything between plates and serve.

Nutrition:

- Calories: 284
- Fat: 14 g.
- Fiber: 3 g.
- Carbs: 6 g.
- Protein: 16 g.

393. Roasted Rib Eye Steaks

Preparation time: 17 minutes

Cooking time: 12 minutes

Servings: 4

Ingredients:

- 4 rib eye steaks
- 1 tbsp. olive oil
- 1 tsp. Rosemary; chopped
- 1 tsp. sweet paprika
- 1 tsp. cumin, ground
- A pinch of salt and black pepper

Directions:

1. Take a bowl and mix the steaks with the rest of the ingredients, toss and put them in your air fryer's basket and cook at 380°F for 12 minutes on each side.
2. Divide between plates and serve.

Nutrition:

- Calories: 283
- Fat: 12 g.
- Fiber: 3 g.
- Carbs: 6 g.
- Protein: 17 g.

394. Beef and Balsamic Marinade

Preparation time: 5 minutes

Cooking time: 35 minutes

Servings: 4

Ingredients:

- 4 medium beef steaks
- 3 garlic cloves, minced
- 1 cup balsamic vinegar
- 2 tbsp. olive oil
- Salt and black pepper to taste

Directions:

1. Take a bowl and mix steaks with the rest of the ingredients and toss.
2. Transfer the steaks to your air fryer's basket and cook at 390°F for 35

minutes, flipping them halfway.

3. Divide between plates and serve with a side salad.

Nutrition:

- Calories: 27.
- Fat: 14 g.
- Fiber: 4 g.
- Carbs: 6 g.
- Protein: 19 g.

395. Pulled Pork

Preparation time: 10 minutes

Cooking time: 1 hour 50 minutes

Servings: 8

Ingredients:

- 1 (4 lb.) pork shoulder
- 2 tbsp. chili powder
- 1/2 tsp. black pepper, ground
- 1/2 tsp. cumin
- 1/2 tsp. onion powder
- 1 tsp. garlic powder

Directions:

1. In a small bowl, mix chili powder, garlic powder, onion powder, pepper, and cumin. Rub the spice mixture over the pork shoulder, patting it into the skin.

2. Place the pork shoulder into the air fryer basket. Adjust the temperature to 350°F and set the timer for 150 minutes.

3. Pork skin will be crispy and meat easily shredded with 2 forks when done. The internal temperature should be at least 145°F.

Nutrition:

- Calories: 537
- Protein: 46 g.
- Fiber: 8 g.
- Fat: 35 g.

Carbs: 5 g.

396. Beef Meatloaf

Preparation time: 5 minutes

Cooking time: 25 minutes

Servings: 4

Ingredients:

- 1 lb. beef meat, ground
- 1 egg, whisked
- 1 yellow onion, chopped
- 1 tbsp. oregano, chopped
- 3 tbsp. almond meal
- 1 tbsp. parsley; chopped
- Cooking spray
- Salt and black pepper to taste.

Directions:

1. Take a bowl and mix all the ingredients except the cooking spray, stir well, and put in a loaf pan that fits the air fryer.
2. Put the pan in the fryer and cook at 390°F for 25 minutes. Slice and serve hot.

Nutrition:

- Calories: 284
- Fat: 14 g.
- Fiber: 3 g.
- Carbs: 6 g.

Protein: 18 g.

397. Mini Meatloaf

Preparation time: 10 minutes

Cooking time: 25 minutes

Servings: 6

Ingredients:

- 1 lb. 80/20 ground beef
- 1/2 green bell pepper, medium-sized, seeded, and diced
- 1 egg, large
- 1/4 yellow onion, medium-sized, peeled, and diced
- 1/4 cup water
- 2 tbsp. tomato paste
- 1 tbsp. powdered erythritol
- 3 tbsp. almond flour blanched, finely ground
- 1 tbsp. Worcestershire sauce

- 1 tsp. parsley, dried
- 1/2 tsp. garlic powder

Directions:

1. Take a large bowl, combine ground beef, onion, pepper, egg, and almond flour. Pour in the Worcestershire sauce and add the garlic powder and parsley to the bowl. Mix until fully combined.
2. Divide the mixture into 2 and place into 2 (4-inch loaf) baking pans.
3. In a small bowl, mix the tomato paste, water, and erythritol. Spoon half the mixture over each loaf.
4. Working in batches if necessary, place loaf pans into the air fryer basket. Adjust the temperature to 350°F and set the timer for 25 minutes or until internal temperature is 180°F.

Nutrition:

- Calories: 170
- Protein: 19 g.
- Fiber: 9 g.
- Fat: 4 g.
- Carbs: 0 g.

398. Crispy Brats

Preparation time: 5 minutes

Cooking time: 15 minutes

Servings: 4

Ingredients:

- 4 (3-oz). beef bratwursts

Directions:

1. Place brats into the air fryer basket.
2. Adjust the temperature to 375°F and set the timer for 15 minutes.

Nutrition:

- Calories: 286
- Protein: 18 g.
- Fiber: 0 g.
- Fat: 28 g.
- Carbs: 0 g.

399. Dijon Top Chuck With Herbs

Preparation time: 10 minutes

Cooking time: 50 minutes

Servings: 3

Ingredients:

- 1 1/2 lb. top chuck
- 2 tsp. olive oil
- 1 tbsp. Dijon mustard
- Sea salt and ground black pepper, to taste
- 1 tsp. marjoram, dried
- 1 tsp. thyme, dried
- 1/2 tsp. fennel seeds

Directions:

1. Start by preheating your air fryer to 380°F.
2. Add all ingredients in a Ziploc® bag; shake to mix well. Next, spritz the bottom of the air fryer basket with cooking spray.
3. Place the beef in the cooking basket and cook for 50 minutes, turning every 10–15 minutes.
4. Let it rest for 5–7 minutes before slicing and serving. Enjoy!

Nutrition:

- Calories: 406
- Fat: 24.1 g.
- Carbs: 0.3 g.
- Protein: 44.1 g. Sugar: 0 g.

400. Mediterranean-Style Beef Steak and Zucchini

Preparation time: 8 minutes

Cooking time: 12 minutes

Servings: 4

Ingredients:

- 1 1/2 lb. beef steak
- 1 lb. zucchini
- 1 tsp. Rosemary, dried
- 1 tsp. basil, dried
- 1 tsp. oregano, dried
- 2 tbsp. olive oil, extra-virgin
- 2 tbsp. fresh chives, chopped

Directions:

1. Start by preheating your air fryer to 400°F.
2. Toss the steak and zucchini with the

spices and olive oil. Transfer to the cooking basket and cook for 6 minutes.

3. Now, shale the basket and cook for another 6 minutes. Serve immediately garnished with fresh chives. Enjoy!

Nutrition:

- Calories: 396
- Fat: 20.4 g.
- Carbs: 3.5 g.
- Protein: 47.8 g.
- Sugar: 0.1 g.

401. Peperonata With Beef Sausage

Preparation time: 5 minutes

Cooking time: 30 minutes

Servings: 4

Ingredients:

- 2 tsp. canola oil
- 2 bell peppers, sliced
- 1 green bell pepper, sliced
- 1 serrano pepper, sliced
- 1 shallot, sliced
- Sea salt and pepper to taste
- 1/2 thyme, dried
- 1 tsp. Rosemary, dried
- 1/2 tsp. mustard seeds
- 1 tsp. fennel seeds
- 2 lb. thin beef parboiled sausage

Directions:

1. Brush the sides and bottom of the cooking basket with 1 tsp. of canola oil. Add the peppers and shallot to the cooking basket.

2. Toss them with the spices and seeds, and cook at 390°F for 15 minutes; shaking the basket occasionally. Reserve.

3. Turn the temperature to 380°F.

4. Then, add the remaining 1 tsp. of oil. Once hot, add the sausage and cook in the preheated Air Frye for 15 minutes, flipping them halfway through the cooking time.

5. Serve with reserved pepper mixture. Bon appétit!

Nutrition:

- Calories: 563
- Fat: 41.5 g.
- Carbs: 10.6 g.
- Protein: 35.6 g.
- Sugar: 7.9 g.

402. New York Strip With Mustard Butter

Preparation time: 6 minutes

Cooking time: 14 minutes

Servings: 4

Ingredients:

- 1 tbsp. peanut oil
- 2 lb. New York strip
- 1 tsp. cayenne pepper
- Sea salt and freshly cracked black pepper to taste
- 1/2 stick butter, softened
- 1 tsp. whole-grain mustard
- 1/2 tsp. honey

Directions:

1. Rub the peanut oil all over the steak, season with cayenne pepper, salt, and black pepper.
2. Cook in the preheated air fryer at 400°F for 7 minutes, turn over and cook for another 7 minutes.
3. Meanwhile, prepare the mustard butter by whisking the butter, whole-grain mustard, and honey.
4. Serve the roasted New York Strip dolloped with mustard butter. Bon appétit!

Nutrition:

- Calories: 459
- Fat: 27.4 g.
- Carbs: 2.5 g.
- Protein: 48.3 g.
- Sugar: 1.4g

403. Scotch Fillet With Sweet and Sticky Sauce

Preparation time: 10 minutes

Cooking time: 30 minutes

Servings: 4

Ingredients:

- 2 lb. scotch fillet, sliced into strips
- 4 tbsp. tortilla chips, crushed
- 2 green onions, chopped

Sauce:

- 1 tbsp. butter
- 2 garlic cloves, minced
- 1/2 tsp. Rosemary, dried
- 1/2 tsp. dill, dried
- 1/2 cup beef broth
- 1 tbsp. fish sauce
- 2 tbsp. honey

Directions:

2. Start by preheating your air fryer to 390°F.
3. Coat the beef strips with the green onions and crushed tortilla chips on all sides. Spritz with cooking spray on all sides and transfer them to the cooking basket.
4. Cook for 30 minutes, shaking the basket every 10 minutes.
5. Meanwhile, heat the sauce ingredient in a saucepan over medium-high heat. Bring to a boil and reduce the heat; cook until the sauce has thickened slightly.
6. Add the steak to the sauce; let it sit for approximately 8 minutes. Serve over the hot egg noodles if desired.

Nutrition:

- Calories: 556
- Fat: 17.9 g.
- Carbs: 25.8 g.
- Protein: 60 g.
- Sugar: 10.4 g.

404. Roasted Rib Eye With Garlic Mayo

Preparation time: 5 minutes

Cooking time: 15 minutes

Servings: 3

Ingredients:

- 1 1/2 lb. rib eye, bone-in
- 1 tbsp. butter, room temperature
- Salt to taste
- 1/2 tsp. black pepper, crushed
- 1/2 tsp. dill, dried
- 1/2 tsp. cayenne pepper
- 1/2 tsp. garlic powder
- 1/2 tsp. onion powder
- 1 tsp. coriander, ground
- 3 tbsp. mayonnaise
- 1 tsp. garlic, minced

Directions:

1. Start by preheating your air fryer to 400°F.
2. Pat dry the rib eye and rub it with softened butter on all sides. Sprinkle with seasonings and transfer to the cooking basket.
3. Cook in the preheated air fryer for 15 minutes, flipping them halfway through the cooking time.
4. In the meantime, simply mix the mayonnaise with garlic and place it in the refrigerator until ready to serve. Bon appétit!

Nutrition:

- Calories: 437
- Fat: 24.8 g.
- Carbs: 1.8 g.
- Protein: 51 g.
- Sugar: 0.1 g.

405. Crustless Beef and Cheese Tart

Preparation time: 6 minutes

Cooking time: 19 minutes

Servings: 4

Ingredients:

- 1 tbsp. canola oil
- 1 onion, finely chopped
- 2 fresh garlic cloves, minced
- 1/2-lb. ground chuck
- 1/2-lb. chorizo sausage, crumbled
- 1 cup pasta sauce
- Sea salt to taste
- 1/4 tsp. black pepper, ground
- 1/2 tsp. red pepper flakes, crushed
- 1 cup cream cheese, room temperature
- 1/2 cup Swiss cheese, shredded
- 1 egg
- 1/2 cup crackers, crushed

Directions:

1. Start by preheating your air fryer to 370°F.
2. Grease a baking pan with canola oil.
3. Add the onion, garlic, ground chuck, sausage, pasta sauce, salt, black pepper, and red pepper. Cook for 9 minutes.
4. In the meantime, combine cheese with egg. Place the cheese-egg mixture over the beef mixture.
5. Sprinkle with crushed crackers and cook for 10 minutes. Serve warm and enjoy!

Nutrition:

- Calories: 572
- Fat: 44.6 g.
- Carbs: 16.2 g.
- Protein: 28.1 g.
- Sugar: 8.9 g.

406. Beef Taco Roll-Ups With Cotija Cheese

Preparation time: 10 minutes

Cooking time: 15 minutes

Servings: 4

Ingredients:

- 1 tbsp. sesame oil
- 2 tbsp. scallions, chopped
- 1 garlic clove, minced
- 1 bell pepper, chopped
- 1/2-lb. ground beef
- 1/2 tsp. Mexican oregano
- 1/2 tsp. marjoram, dried
- 1 tsp. chili powder
- 1/2 cup refried beans
- Sea salt and ground black pepper, to taste
- 1/2 cup Cotija cheese, shredded
- 8 roll wrappers

Directions:

1. Start by preheating your air fryer to 395°F.
2. Heat the sesame oil in a nonstick skillet over medium-high heat. Cook the scallions, garlic, and peppers until tender and fragrant.
3. Add the ground beef, oregano, marjoram, and chili powder. Continue cooking for 3 minutes longer or until it is browned.
4. Stir in the beans, salt, and pepper. Divide the meat/bean mixture between wrappers that are softened with a little bit of water. Top with cheese.
5. Roll the wrappers and spritz them with cooking oil on all sides.
6. Cook in the preheated air fryer for 11–12 minutes, flipping them halfway through the cooking time. Enjoy!

Nutrition:

- Calories: 417
- Fat: 15.9 g.
- Carbs: 41 g.
- Protein: 26.2 g.
- Sugar: 1.5 g.

407. Barbecue Skirt Steak

Preparation time: 8 minutes

Cooking time: 12 minutes

Servings: 5

Ingredients:

- 2 lb. skirt steak
- 2 tbsp. tomato paste
- 1 tbsp. tomato ketchup
- 1 tbsp. olive oil
- 1 tbsp. soy sauce
- 1/4 cup rice vinegar
- 1 tbsp. fish sauce
- Sea salt to taste
- 1/2 tsp. dill, dried
- 1/2 tsp. Rosemary, dried
- 1/4 tsp. black pepper, freshly cracked
- 1 tbsp. brown sugar

Directions:

1. Place all ingredients in a large ceramic dish, let it marinate for 3 hours in your refrigerator.
2. Coat the sides and bottom of the air fryer with cooking spray.
3. Add your steak to the cooking basket; reserve the marinade. Cook the skirt steak in the preheated air fryer at 400°F for 12 minutes, turning over a couple of times, basting with the reserved marinade.
4. Serve warm with roasted new potatoes, if desired.

Nutrition:

- Calories: 394
- Fat: 19 g.
- Carbs: 4.4 g.
- Protein: 51.3 g.
- Sugar: 3.3 g.

408. Meatballs With Cranberry Sauce

Preparation time: 12 minutes

Cooking time: 28 minutes

Servings: 4

Ingredients:

Meatballs:

- 1 1/2 lb. ground chuck
- 1 egg
- 1 cup rolled oats
- 1/2 cup Romano cheese, grated
- 1/2 tsp. basil, dried
- 1/2 tsp. oregano, dried
- 1 tsp. paprika
- 2 garlic cloves, minced
- 2 tbsp. scallions, chopped
- Sea salt and cracked black pepper, to

taste

Cranberry Sauce:

- 10 oz. BBQ sauce
- 8 oz. cranberry sauce

Directions:

1. In a large bowl, mix all ingredients for the meatballs. Mix until everything is well incorporated, then, shape the meat mixture into 2-inch balls using a cookie scoop.
2. Transfer them to the lightly greased cooking basket and cook at 380°F for 10 minutes. Shake the basket occasionally and work in batches.
3. Add the BBQ sauce and cranberry sauce to a saucepan and cook over moderate heat until you achieve a glaze-like

consistency; it will take about 15 minutes.

4. Gently stir in the air fried meatballs and cook an additional 3 minutes or until heated through. Enjoy!

Nutrition:

- Calories: 520
- Fat: 22.4 g.
- Carbs: 44 g.
- Protein: 45.4 g.
- Sugar: 25.5 g.

409. Kid-Friendly Mini Meatloaves

Preparation time: 5 minutes

Cooking time: 25 minutes

Servings: 4

Ingredients:

- 2 tbsp. bacon, chopped
- 1 small-sized onion, chopped
- 1 bell pepper, chopped
- 1 garlic clove, minced
- 1 lb. ground beef
- 1/2 tsp. basil, dried
- 1/2 tsp. mustard seeds, dried
- 1/2 tsp. marjoram, dried
- Salt and black pepper to taste
- 1/2 cup panko crumbs

- 4 tbsp. tomato puree
- Nonstick spray

Directions:

1. Heat a nonstick skillet over medium-high heat; cook the bacon for 1–2 minutes, add the onion, bell pepper, and garlic. Cook for another 3 minutes or until fragrant.
2. Heat off. Stir in the ground beef, spices, and panko crumbs. Stir until well combined. Shape the mixture into 4 mini meatloaves.
3. Preheat your air fryer to 350°F. Spritz the cooking basket with nonstick spray.
4. Place the mini meatloaves in the cooking basket and cook for 10 minutes, turn them over, top with the tomato puree, and continue to cook for 10 minutes more. Bon appétit!

Nutrition:

- Calories: 451
- Fat: 27.6 g.
- Carbs: 15.3 g.
- Protein: 33.4 .g
- Sugar: 3.7 g.

410. Quick Sausage and Veggie Sandwiches

Preparation time: 5 minutes

Cooking time: 30 minutes

Servings: 4

Ingredients:

- 4 bell peppers
- 2 tbsp. canola oil
- 4 tomatoes, medium-sized, halved
- 4 spring onions
- 4 beef sausages
- 4 hot dog buns
- 1 tbsp. mustard

Directions:

1. Start by preheating your air fryer to 400°F.
2. Add the bell peppers to the cooking basket.

Drizzle 1 tbsp. of canola oil all over the bell peppers.

3. Cook for 5 minutes. Turn the temperature down to 350°F. Add the tomatoes and spring onions to the cooking basket and cook for an additional 10 minutes.

4. Reserve your vegetables.

5. Then, add the sausages to the cooking basket. Drizzle with the remaining 1 tbsp. of canola oil.

6. Cook in the preheated air fryer at 380°F for 15 minutes, flipping them halfway through the cooking time.

7. Add the sausage to a hot dog bun, top with the air-fried vegetables and

mustard, serve.

Nutrition:

- Calories: 627
- Fat: 41.9 g.
- Carbs: 41.3 g.
- Protein: 22.2 g.
- Sugar: 9.3 g.

411. Mayonnaise and Rosemary Grilled Steak

Preparation time: 5 minutes

Cooking time: 15 minutes

Servings: 4

Ingredients:

- 1 cup mayonnaise
- 1 tbsp. fresh Rosemary, finely chopped
- 2 tbsp. Worcestershire sauce
- Sea salt to taste
- 1/2 tsp. black pepper, ground
- 1 tsp. smoked paprika
- 1 tsp. garlic, minced
- 1 1/2 lb. short loin steak

Directions:

1. Combine the mayonnaise, Rosemary, Worcestershire sauce, salt, pepper, paprika, and garlic; mix to combine well.

2. Now, brush the mayonnaise mixture over both sides of the steak. Lower the steak onto the grill pan.

3. Grill in the preheated air fryer at 390°F for 8 minutes. Turn the steaks over and grill an additional 7 minutes.

4. Check for doneness with a meat thermometer. Serve warm and enjoy!

Nutrition:

- Calories: 620
- Fat: 50 g.
- Carbs: 2.8 g.
- Protein: 39.7 g.
- Sugar: 1.3 g.

Chapter 7: Seafood Recipes

412. Coconut Shrimp

Preparation time: 5 minutes

Cooking time: 10 minutes

Servings: 3

Ingredients:

- 1 cup almond flour
- 1 cup panko breadcrumbs
- 1 tbsp. coconut flour
- 1 cup unsweetened, dried coconut
- 1 egg white
- 12 raw large shrimp

Directions:

1. Put shrimp on paper towels to drain.
2. Mix coconut and panko breadcrumbs. Then mix in coconut flour and almond flour in a different bowl. Set to the side.
3. Dip shrimp into the flour mixture, then into egg white, and then into the coconut mixture.
4. Place into air fryer basket. Repeat with remaining shrimp.
5. Cook 10 minutes at 350°F. Turn halfway through the cooking process.

Nutrition:

- Calories: 213
- Fat: 8 g.
- Protein: 15 g.
- Sugar: 3 g

413. Air Fryer Salmon

Preparation time: 5 minutes

Cooking time: 10 minutes

Servings: 2

Ingredients:

- 1/2 tsp. salt
- 1/2 tsp. garlic powder
- 1/2 tsp. smoked paprika
- 2 oz. Salmon

Directions:

1. Mix spices and sprinkle onto salmon.
2. Place seasoned salmon into the air fryer.
3. Cook 8–10 minutes at 400°F.

Nutrition:

- Calories: 185
- Fat: 11 g.
- Protein: 21 g.
- Sugar: 0 g.

414. Healthy Fish and Chips

Preparation time: 15 minutes

Cooking time: 15 minutes

Servings: 3

Ingredients:

- Old Bay seasoning
- 1/2 cup panko breadcrumbs
- 1 egg
- 2 tbsp. almond flour
- 2 (4–6-oz.) tilapia fillets
- Frozen crinkle cut fries

Directions:

1. Add almond flour

to a bowl, beat egg, and in another bowl, and add panko breadcrumbs to the third bowl, mixed with Old Bay® seasoning.

2. Dredge tilapia in flour, then egg, and then breadcrumbs.

3. Place coated fish in the air fryer along with fries.

4. Cook 15 minutes at 390°F.

Nutrition:

- Calories: 219
- Carbs: 18 g.
- Fat: 5 g.
- Protein: 25 g.
- Sugar: 1 g.

415. Ingredient Air Fryer Catfish

Preparation time: 15 minutes

Cooking time: 13 minutes

Servings: 4

Ingredients:

- 1 tbsp. parsley, chopped
- 1 tbsp. olive oil
- 1/4 cup seasoned fish fry
- 4 catfish fillets

Directions:

1. Ensure your air fryer is preheated to 400°F.

2. Rinse off catfish fillets and pat dry.

3. Add fish fry seasoning to Ziploc® baggie, then catfish. Shake the bag and ensure the fish gets well coated.

4. Spray each fillet with olive oil.

5. Add fillets to the air fryer basket. Cook 10 minutes. Then flip and cook for another 2–3 minutes.

Nutrition:

- Calories: 208
- Carbs: 8
- Fat: 5g
- Protein: 17g
- Sugar: 0.5g

416. Bang Panko Breaded Fried Shrimp

Preparation time: 15 minutes

Cooking time: 8 minutes

Servings: 4

Ingredients:

- 1 tsp. paprika
- 2 tbsp Montreal chicken seasoning
- 3/4 cup panko bread crumbs
- 1/2 cup almond flour
- 1 egg white
- 1 lb. raw shrimp, peeled and deveined
- 2 tbsp olive oil

Bang Sauce:

- 1/4 cup sweet chili sauce
- 2 tbsp. sriracha sauce
- 1/3 cup plain Greek yogurt

Directions:

1. Ensure your air fryer is preheated to 400°F.
2. Season all shrimp with seasonings.
3. Add flour to one bowl, egg white in another, and breadcrumbs to a third.
4. Dip seasoned shrimp in flour, then egg whites, and then breadcrumbs.
5. Spray coated shrimp with olive oil and add to the air fryer basket.
6. Cook 4 minutes, flip, and cook an additional 4 minutes.
7. To make the sauce, mix all sauce ingredients until smooth.

Nutrition:

- Calories: 212
- Carbs: 12 g.
- Fat: 1 g.
- Protein: 37 g.
- Sugar: 0.5 g.

417. Louisiana Shrimp Po Boy

Preparation time: 15 minutes

Cooking time: 10 minutes

Servings: 4

Ingredients:

- 1 tsp. creole seasoning
- 8 slices of tomato
- Lettuce leaves
- 1/4 cup buttermilk
- 1/2 cup Louisiana Fish Fry
- 1lb. shrimp, deveined
- 2 tbsp olive oil

Remoulade sauce:

- 1 green onion, chopped
- 1 tsp. hot sauce
- 1 tsp. Dijon mustard
- 1/2 tsp. creole seasoning
- 1 tsp. Worcestershire sauce
- Juice of 1/2 a lemon
- 1/2 cup vegan mayo

Directions:

1. To make the sauce, combine all sauce ingredients until well incorporated. Chill while you cook shrimp.
2. Mix seasonings together and liberally season shrimp.
3. Add buttermilk to a bowl. Dip each shrimp into milk and place in a Ziploc® bag. Chill for 1/2 hour to marinate.
4. Add fish fry to a bowl. Take shrimp from marinating bag and dip into fish fry, then add to the air fryer.
5. Ensure your air fryer is preheated to 400°F.
6. Spray shrimp with olive oil. Cook for 5 minutes, flip and then cook another 5 minutes.
7. Assemble "Keto" Po Boy by adding sauce to lettuce leaves, along with shrimp and tomato.

Nutrition:

- Calories: 337
- Carbs: 55 g.
- Fat: 12 g.
- Protein: 24 g.
- Sugar: 2 g.

418. Panko-Crusted Tilapia

Preparation time: 5 minutes

Cooking time: 11 minutes

Servings: 3

Ingredients:

- 2 tsp. Italian seasoning
- 2 tsp. lemon pepper
- 1/3 cup panko breadcrumbs
- 1/3 cup egg whites
- 1/3 cup almond flour
- 3 tilapia fillets
- Olive oil

Directions:

1. Place panko, egg whites, and flour into separate bowls. Mix lemon pepper and Italian seasoning with breadcrumbs.
2. Pat tilapia fillets dry. Dredge in flour, then egg, breadcrumb mixture. Add to air fryer basket and spray lightly with olive oil.
3. Cook 10–11 minutes at 400°F, making sure to flip halfway through cooking.

Nutrition:

- Calories: 256
- Fat: 9 g.
- Protein: 39 g.
- Sugar: 5 g.

419. Salmon Croquettes

Preparation time: 15 minutes

Cooking time: 10 minutes

Servings: 8

Ingredients:

- 2 Panko breadcrumbs
- 2 oz. Almond flour
- 2 egg whites
- 2 tbsp. chives, chopped
- 2 tbsp. garlic cloves, minced
- 1/2 cup onion, chopped
- 2/3 cup carrots, grated
- 1 lb. salmon fillet, chopped
- 2 tbsp olive oil

Directions:

1. Mix all ingredients minus breadcrumbs, flour, and egg whites.

2. Shape mixture into balls. Then coat them in flour, then egg, and then breadcrumbs. Drizzle with olive oil.

3. Add coated salmon balls to the air fryer and cook for 6 minutes at 350°F. Shake and cook an additional 4 minutes until golden in color.

Nutrition:

- Calories: 503
- Carbs: 61 .g
- Fat: 9 g.
- Protein: 5 g.
- Sugar: 4 g.

420. Air Fryer Fish Tacos

Preparation time: 5 minutes

Cooking time: 15 minutes

Servings: 4

Ingredients:

- 1 lb. cod
- 1 tbsp. cumin
- 1/2 tbsp. chili powder
- 1 1/2 cup almond flour
- 1 1/2 cup coconut flour
- 10 oz. Mexican beer
- 2 eggs

- 1 tsp salt and pepper

Directions:

1. Whisk beer and eggs together.
2. Whisk flours, pepper, salt, cumin, and chili powder together.
3. Slice cod into large pieces and coat in egg mixture then flour mixture.
4. Spray the bottom of your air fryer basket with olive oil and add coated codpieces.
5. Cook 15 minutes at 375°F.
6. Serve on lettuce leaves topped with homemade salsa!

Nutrition:

- Calories: 178
- Fat: 10 g.
- Protein: 19 g.
- Sugar: 1 g.

421. Bacon-Wrapped Scallops

Preparation time: 10 minutes

Cooking time: 6 minutes

Servings: 4

Ingredients:

- 1 tsp. paprika
- 1 tsp. lemon pepper
- 5 slices center-cut bacon
- 20 raw sea scallops
- 2 tbsp olive oil

Directions:

1. Rinse and drain scallops, placing on paper towels to soak up excess moisture.
2. Cut slices of bacon into 4 pieces.
3. Wrap each scallop with a piece of bacon, using toothpicks to secure. Sprinkle the wrapped scallops with paprika and lemon pepper.
4. Spray air fryer basket with olive oil and add scallops.
5. Cook 5–6 minutes at 400°F, making sure to flip halfway through.

Nutrition:

- Calories: 389
- Fat: 17 .g
- Protein: 21 g.
- Sugar: 1 g.

422. Parmesan Shrimp

Preparation time: 10 minutes

Cooking time: 10 minutes

Servings: 6

Ingredients:

- 2 tbsp. olive oil
- 1 tsp. onion powder
- 1 tsp. basil
- 1/2 tsp. oregano
- 1 tsp. pepper
- 2/3 cup Parmesan cheese, grated
- 4 garlic cloves, minced
- 2 lb. shrimp jumbo, cooked, peeled, and deveined
- 3 tbsp lemon juice

Directions:

1. Mix all seasonings and gently toss shrimp with the mixture.
2. Spray olive oil into the air fryer basket and add Parmesan cheese, garlic cloves seasoned shrimp.
3. Cook 8–10 minutes at 350°F.
4. Squeeze lemon juice over shrimp right before devouring!

Nutrition:

- Calories: 351
- Fat: 11 g.
- Protein: 19 g.
- Sugar: 1 g.

423. Honey Glazed Salmon

Preparation time: 5 minutes

Cooking time: 13 minutes

Servings: 2

Ingredients:

- 1 tsp. water
- 3 tsp. rice wine vinegar
- 6 tbsp. soy sauce, low-sodium
- 6 tbsp. raw honey
- 2 salmon fillets

Directions:

1. Combine water, vinegar, honey, and soy sauce together. Pour half of this mixture into a bowl.

2. Place salmon in one bowl of marinade and let chill 2 hours.

3. Ensure your air fryer is preheated to 356°F and add salmon.

4. Cook 8 minutes, flipping halfway through. Baste salmon with some of the remaining marinade mixture and cook another 5 minutes.

5. To make a sauce to serve salmon with, pour remaining marinade mixture into a saucepan, heating till simmering. Let simmer 2 minutes. Serve drizzled over salmon!

Nutrition:

- Calories: 390
- Fat: 8 g.
- Protein: 16 g.
- Sugar: 5 g.

424. Crispy Air Fried Sushi Roll

Preparation time: 15 minutes

Cooking time: 10 minutes

Servings: 12

Ingredients:

Kale Salad:

- 1 tbsp. sesame seeds
- 3/4 tsp. soy sauce
- 1/4 tsp. ginger
- 1/8 tsp. garlic powder
- 3/4 tsp. toasted sesame oil
- 1/2 tsp. rice vinegar
- 1 1/2 cup chopped kale

Sushi Rolls:

- 1/2 avocado, sliced
- 3 sheets sushi nori
- 1 batch cauliflower rice

Sriracha Mayo:

- Sriracha sauce
- 1/4 cup vegan mayo

Coating:

- 1/2 cup panko breadcrumbs

Directions:

1. Combine all of the kale salad ingredients, tossing well. Set to the side.
2. Layout a sheet of nori and spread a handful of rice on it. Then place 2–3 tbsp. of kale salad over rice, followed by avocado. Roll up sushi.
3. To make mayo, whisk mayo ingredients together until smooth.
4. Add breadcrumbs to a bowl. Coat sushi rolls in crumbs till coated and add to the air fryer.
5. Cook rolls 10 minutes at 390°F, shaking gently at 5 minutes.
6. Slice each roll into 6–8 pieces and enjoy!

Nutrition:

- Calories: 267
- Fat: 13 g.
- Protein: 6 g.
- Sugar: 3 g.

425. Crab Legs

Preparation time: 5 minutes

Cooking time: 20 minutes

Servings: 3

Ingredients:

- 3 lb. crab legs
- 1/4 cup salted butter, melted and divided
- 1/2 lemon, juiced
- 1/4 tsp. garlic powder

Directions:

1. In a bowl, toss the crab legs and 2 tbsp. of the melted butter. Place the crab legs in the basket of the fryer.
2. Cook at 400°F for 15 minutes, giving the basket a good shake halfway through.
3. Combine the

remaining butter with lemon juice and garlic powder.

4. Crack open the cooked crab legs and remove the meat. Serve with the butter dip on the side and enjoy!

Nutrition:

- Calories: 392
- Fat: 10 g.
- Protein: 18 g.
- Sugar: 8 g.

426. Crusty Pesto Salmon

Preparation time: 5 minutes

Cooking time: 15 minutes

Servings: 2

Ingredients:

- 1/4 cup spinach, roughly chopped
- 1/4 cup pesto
- 2 (4-oz.) salmon fillets
- 2 tbsp. unsalted butter, melted

Directions:

1. Mix the spinach and pesto.
2. Place the salmon fillets in a round baking dish, roughly 6-inch in diameter.
3. Brush the fillets with butter, followed by the pesto mixture, ensuring to coat both the top and bottom. Put the baking dish inside the fryer.
4. Cook for 12 minutes at 390°F.
5. The salmon is ready when it flakes easily when prodded with a fork. Serve warm.

Nutrition:

- Calories: 290
- Fat: 11 g.
- Protein: 20 g.
- Sugar: 9 g.

427. Buttery Cod

Preparation time: 10 minutes

Cooking time: 12 minutes

Servings: 2

Ingredients:

- 2 (4 oz.) cod fillets
- 2 tbsp. salted butter, melted
- 1 tsp. Old Bay® seasoning
- 1/2 lemon, medium-sized, sliced

Directions:

1. Place the cod fillets in a baking dish.
2. Brush with melted butter, season with Old Bay®, and top with some lemon slices.
3. Wrap the fish in aluminum foil oand put it into your fryer.
4. Cook for 8 minutes at 350°F.
5. The cod is ready when it flakes easily. Serve hot.

Nutrition:

- Calories: 394
- Fat: 5 g.
- Protein: 12 g.
- Sugar: 4 g.

428. Sesame Tuna Steak

Preparation time: 5 minutes

Cooking time: 12 minutes

Servings: 2

Ingredients:

- 1 tbsp. coconut oil, melted
- 2 (6 oz.) tuna steaks
- 1/2 tsp. garlic powder
- 2 tsp. black sesame seeds
- 2 tsp. white sesame seeds

Directions:

1. Apply the coconut oil to the tuna steaks with a brunch, then season with garlic powder.
2. Combine the black and white sesame seeds. Embed them in the tuna steaks,

covering the fish all over. Place the tuna into your air fryer.

3. Cook for 8 minutes at 400°F, turning the fish halfway through.

4. The tuna steaks are ready when they have reached a temperature of 145°F. Serve straight away.

Nutrition:

- Calories: 160
- Fat: 6 g.
- Protein: 26 g.
- Sugar: 7 g.

429. Lemon Garlic Shrimp

Preparation time: 10 minutes

Cooking time: 15 minutes

Servings: 2

Ingredients:

- 1 lemon, medium-sized
- 1/2 lb. shrimp, medium, shelled, and deveined
- 1/2 tsp. Old Bay® seasoning
- 2 tbsp. unsalted butter, melted
- 1/2 tsp. minced garlic

Directions:

1. Grate the rind of the lemon into a bowl. Cut the lemon in half and juice it over the same bowl. Toss in the shrimp, Old Bay®, and

butter, mixing everything to make sure the shrimp is completely covered.

2. Transfer to a round baking dish roughly 6-inch wide, then place this dish in your fryer.

3. Cook at 400°F for 6 minutes. The shrimp is cooked when it turns a bright pink color.

4. Serve hot, drizzling any leftover sauce over the shrimp.

Nutrition:

- Calories: 490
- Fat: 9 g.
- Protein: 12 g.
- Sugar: 11 g.

430. Foil Packet Salmon

Preparation time: 5 minutes

Cooking time: 15 minutes

Servings: 2

Ingredients:

- 2 (4 oz.) salmon fillets, skinless
- 2 tbsp. unsalted butter, melted
- 1/2 tsp. garlic powder
- 1 lemon, medium-sized
- 1/2 tsp. dried dill

Directions:

1. Take a sheet of aluminum foil and cut it into 2 squares measuring roughly 5x5-inch. Lay each of the salmon fillets at the center of each piece. Brush both fillets with 1 tbsp. of bullet and season with 1/4 tsp. of garlic powder.

2. Halve the lemon and grate the skin of one half over the fish. Cut 4 half-slices of lemon, using 2 to top each fillet. Season each fillet with 1/4 tsp. of dill.

3. Fold the tops and sides of the aluminum foil over the fish to create a kind of packet. Place each one in the fryer.

4. Cook for 12 minutes at 400°F.

5. The salmon is ready when it flakes easily. Serve hot.

Nutrition:

- Calories: 240
- Fat: 13 g.
- Protein: 21 g.
- Sugar: 9 g.

431. Foil Packet Lobster Tail

Preparation time: 5 minutes

Cooking time: 15 minutes

Servings: 2

Ingredients:

- 2 (6-oz.) lobster tail halves
- 2 tbsp. salted butter, melted
- 1/2 lemon, medium-sized juiced
- 1/2 tsp. Old Bay® seasoning
- 1 tsp. dried parsley

Directions:

1. Lay each lobster on a sheet of aluminum foil. Pour a drizzle of melted butter and lemon juice over each one, and season with Old Bay®.

2. Fold-down the sides

and ends of the foil to seal the lobster. Place each one in the fryer.

3. Cook at 375°F for 12 minutes.
4. Just before serving, top the lobster with dried parsley.

Nutrition:

- Calories: 510
- Fat: 18 g.
- Protein: 26 g.
- Sugar: 12 g.

432. Avocado Shrimp

Preparation time: 10 minutes

Cooking time: 20 minutes

Servings: 2

Ingredients:

- 1/2 cup onion, chopped
- 2 lb. shrimp
- 1 tbsp. seasoned salt
- 1 avocado
- 1/2 cup pecans, chopped
- Cooking spray

Directions:

1. Preheat the fryer at 400°F.
2. Put the chopped onion in the basket of the fryer and spritz with some cooking spray. Cook for 5 minutes.
3. Add the shrimp and set the timer for a further 5 minutes. Sprinkle with some seasoned salt, then allow to cook for an additional 5 minutes.
4. During these last 5 minutes, halve your avocado and remove the pit. Cube each half, then scoop out the flesh.
5. Take care when removing the shrimp from the fryer. Place it on a dish and top with the avocado and the chopped pecans.

Nutrition:

- Calories: 195
- Fat: 14. g
- Protein: 36 g.

Sugar: 10 g.

433. Lemon Butter Scallops

Preparation time: 15 minutes

Cooking time: 30 minutes

Servings: 1

Ingredients:

- 1 lemon
- 1 lb. scallops
- 1/2 cup butter
- 1/4 cup parsley, chopped

Directions:

1. Juice the lemon into a Ziploc® bag.
2. Wash your scallops, dry them, and season to taste. Put them in the bag with lemon juice. Refrigerate for 1 hour.
3. Remove the bag from the refrigerator and leave for about 20 minutes until it returns to room temperature. Transfer the scallops into a foil pan that is small enough to be placed inside the fryer.
4. Preheat the fryer at 400°F and put the rack inside.
5. Place the foil pan on the rack and cook for 5minutes.
6. In the meantime, melt the butter in a saucepan over medium heat. Zest the lemon over the saucepan, then add in the chopped parsley. Mix well.
7. Take care when removing the pan from the fryer. Transfer the contents to a plate and drizzle with the lemon-butter mixture. Serve hot.

Nutrition:

- Calories: 420
- Fat: 12 g.
- Protein: 23 g.
- Sugar: 13 g.

434. Cheesy Lemon Halibut

Preparation time: 10 minutes

Cooking time: 20 minutes

Servings: 2

Ingredients:

- 1 lb. halibut fillet
- 1/2 cup butter
- 2 1/2 tbsp. mayonnaise
- 2 1/2 tbsp. lemon juice
- 3/4 cup parmesan cheese, grated
- Cooking spray

Directions:

1. Preheat your fryer at 375°F.
2. Spritz the halibut fillets with cooking spray and season as desired.
3. Put the halibut in the fryer and cook for 12 minutes.
4. In the meantime, combine the butter, mayonnaise, and lemon juice in a bowl with a hand mixer. Ensure a creamy texture is achieved.
5. Stir in the grated parmesan.
6. When the halibut is ready, open the drawer and spread the butter over the fish with a butter knife. Allow to cook for a further 2 minutes, then serve hot.

Nutrition:

- Calories: 432
- Fat: 18 .g
- Protein: 14 g.
- Sugar: 12 g.

435. Spicy Mackerel

Preparation time: 10 minutes

Cooking time: 20 minutes

Servings: 2

Ingredients:

- 2 mackerel fillets
- 2 tbsp. red chili flakes
- 2 tsp. garlic, minced
- 1 tsp. lemon juice

Directions:

1. Season the mackerel fillets with red pepper flakes, minced garlic, and a drizzle of lemon juice. Allow sitting for 5 minutes.
2. Preheat your fryer at 350°F.
3. Cook the mackerel for 5 minutes, before opening the drawer, flipping the

fillets, and allowing it to cook on the other side for another 5 minutes.

4. Plate the fillets, making sure to spoon any remaining juice over them before serving.

Nutrition:

- Calories: 240
- Fat: 4 g.
- Protein: 16 g.
- Sugar: 3 g.

436. Thyme Scallops

Preparation time: 5 minutes

Cooking time: 12 minutes

Servings: 1

Ingredients:

- 1 lb. scallops
- Salt and pepper
- 1/2 tbsp. butter
- 1/2 cup thyme, chopped

Directions:

1. Wash the scallops and dry them completely. Season with pepper and salt, then set aside while you prepare the pan.

2. Grease a foil pan in several spots with the butter and cover the bottom with the thyme. Place the scallops on top.

3. Preheat the fryer at 400°F and set the rack inside.

4. Place the foil pan on the rack and allow to cook for 7 minutes.

5. Take care when removing the pan from the fryer and transfer the scallops to a serving dish. Spoon any remaining butter in the pan over the fish and enjoy.

Nutrition:

- Calories: 291
- Fat: 9 g.
- Protein: 17 g.
- Sugar: 5 g.

437. Crispy Calamari

Preparation time: 5 minutes

Cooking time: 15 minutes

Servings: 4

Ingredients:

- 1 lb. fresh squid
- Salt and pepper
- 2 cups flour
- 1 cup water
- 2 garlic cloves, minced
- 1/2 cup mayonnaise

Directions:

1. Remove the skin from the squid and discard any ink. Slice the squid into rings and season with some salt and pepper.
2. Put the flour and water in separate bowls. Dip the squid firstly in the flour, then into the water, then into the flour again, ensuring that it is entirely covered with flour.
3. Preheat the fryer at 400°F. Put the squid inside and cook for 6 minutes.
4. In the meantime, prepare the aioli by combining the garlic with the mayonnaise in a bowl.
5. Once the squid is ready, plate up and serve with the aioli.

Nutrition:

- Calories: 247
- Fat: 3 g.
- Protein: 18 g.
- Sugar: 3 g.

438. Filipino Bistek

Preparation time: 5 minutes

Cooking time: 10 minutes

Servings: 4

Ingredients:

- 2 milkfish bellies, deboned and sliced into 4 portions
- 3/4 tsp. salt
- 1/4 tsp. ground black pepper
- 1/4 tsp. cumin powder
- 2 tbsp. calamansi juice
- 2 lemongrasses, trimmed and cut crosswise into small pieces
- 1/2 cup tamari sauce
- 2 tbsp. fish sauce
- 2 tbsp. sugar
- 1 tsp. garlic powder
- 1/2 cup chicken

broth

- 2 tbsp. olive oil

Directions:

1. Dry the fish using some paper towels.
2. Put the fish in a large bowl and coat with the rest of the ingredients. Allow marinating for 3 hours in the refrigerator.
3. Cook the fish steaks on an air fryer grill basket at 340°F for 5 minutes.
4. Turn the steaks over and allow them to grill for an additional 4 minutes. Cook until medium brown.
5. Serve with steamed white rice.

Nutrition:

- Calories: 259
- Fat: 3 g.
- Protein: 10 g.
- Sugar: 2 g.

439. Saltine Fish Fillets

Preparation time: 10 minutes

Cooking time: 15 minutes

Servings: 4

Ingredients:

- 1 cup crushed saltines
- 1/4 cup extra-virgin olive oil
- 1 tsp. garlic powder
- 1/2 tsp. shallot powder
- 1 egg, well whisked
- 4 white fish fillets
- Salt and ground black pepper to taste
- Fresh Italian parsley to serve

Directions:

1. In a shallow bowl, combine the crushed saltines and olive oil.
2. In a separate bowl, mix the garlic powder, shallot powder, and the beaten egg.
3. Sprinkle a good amount of salt and pepper over the fish, before dipping each fillet into the egg mixture.
4. Coat the fillets with the crumb mixture.
5. Air fry the fish at 370°F for 10–12 minutes.
6. Serve with fresh parsley.

Nutrition:

- Calories: 502
- Fat: 4 g.
- Protein: 11 g.
- Sugar: 9 g.

440. Air Fried Cod With Basil Vinaigrette

Preparation time: 5 minutes

Cooking time: 15 minutes

Servings: 4

Ingredients:

- 1/4 cup olive oil
- 4 cod fillets
- A bunch of basil, torn
- Juice from 1 lemon, freshly squeezed
- Salt and pepper to taste

Directions:

1. Preheat the air fryer for 5 minutes.
2. Season the cod fillets with salt and pepper to taste.
3. Place in the air fryer and cook for 15 minutes at 350°F.
4. Meanwhile, mix the rest of the ingredients in a bowl and toss to combine.
5. Serve the air-fried cod with the basil vinaigrette.

Nutrition:

- Calories: 235
- Carbs: 1.9 g.
- Protein: 14.3 g.
- Fat: 18.9 g.

441. Almond Flour Coated Crispy Shrimps

Preparation time: 5 minutes

Cooking time: 10 minutes

Servings: 4

Ingredients:

- 1/2 cup almond flour
- 1 tbsp. yellow mustard
- 1-lb. raw shrimps, peeled and deveined
- 3 tbsp. olive oil
- Salt and pepper to taste

Directions:

1. Place all ingredients in a Ziploc® bag and give a good shake.
2. Place in the air fryer and cook for 10 minutes at 400°F.

Nutrition:

- Calories: 206
- Carbs: 1.3 g.
- Protein: 23.5 g.
- Fat: 11.9 g.

442. Apple Slaw Topped Alaskan Cod Filet

Preparation time: 5 minutes

Cooking time: 15 minutes

Servings: 3

Ingredients:

- 1/4 cup mayonnaise
- 1/2 red onion, diced
- 2 1/2 lb. Alaskan cod, frozen
- 1 box whole-wheat panko bread crumbs
- 1 Granny Smith® apple, julienned
- 1 tbsp. vegetable oil
- 1 tsp. paprika
- 2 cups Napa cabbage, shredded
- Salt and pepper to taste

Directions:

1. Preheat the air fryer to 390°F.
2. Place the grill pan accessory in the air fryer.
3. Brush the fish with oil and dredge in the breadcrumbs.
4. Place the fish on the grill pan and cook for 15 minutes. Make sure to flip the fish halfway through the cooking time.
5. Meanwhile, prepare the slaw by mixing the remaining ingredients in a bowl.
6. Serve the fish with the slaw.

Nutrition:

- Calories: 316
- Carbs: 13.5 g.
- Protein: 37.8 g.
- Fat: 12.2 g.

443. Baked Cod Fillet Recipe From Thailand

Preparation time: 5 minutes

Cooking time: 20 minutes

Servings: 4

Ingredients:

- 1/4 cup coconut milk, freshly squeezed
- 1 tbsp. lime juice, freshly squeezed
- 1 lb. cod fillet, cut into bite-sized pieces
- Salt and pepper to taste

Directions:

1. Preheat the air fryer for 5 minutes.
2. Place all ingredients in a baking dish that will fit in the air fryer.
3. Place in the air fryer.
4. Cook for 20 minutes at 325°F.

Nutrition:

- Calories: 844
- Carbs: 2.3 g.
- Protein: 21.6 g.
- Fat: 83.1 g.

444. Baked Scallops With Garlic Aioli

Preparation time: 5 minutes

Cooking time: 10 minutes

Servings: 4

Ingredients:

- 1 cup bread crumbs
- 1/4 cup parsley, chopped
- 16 sea scallops, rinsed and drained
- 2 shallots, chopped
- 3 pinches ground nutmeg
- 4 tbsp. olive oil
- 5 garlic cloves, minced
- 5 tbsp. butter, melted
- Salt and pepper to taste
- Cooking spray

Directions:

1. Lightly grease the baking pan of the air fryer with cooking spray.
2. Mix in shallots, garlic, melted butter, and scallops. Season with pepper, salt, and nutmeg.
3. In a small bowl, whisk well olive oil and bread crumbs. Sprinkle over scallops.
4. For 10 minutes, cook on 390°F until tops are lightly browned.
5. Serve and enjoy with a sprinkle of parsley.

Nutrition:

- Calories: 452
- Carbs: 29.8 g.
- Protein: 15.2 g.
- Fat: 30.2 g.

445. Basil 'n Lime-Chili Clams

Preparation time: 5 minutes

Cooking time: 15 minutes

Servings: 3

Ingredients:

- 1/2 cup basil leaves
- 1/2 cup tomatoes, chopped
- 1 tbsp. fresh lime juice
- 25 littleneck clams
- 4 garlic cloves, minced
- 6 tbsp. unsalted butter
- Salt and pepper to taste

Directions:

1. Preheat the air fryer to 390°F.
2. Place the grill pan accessory in the air fryer.
3. On a large foil, place all ingredients. Fold over the foil and close by crimping the edges.
4. Place on the grill pan and cook for 15 minutes.
5. Serve with bread.

Nutrition:

- Calories: 163
- Carbs: 4.1 g.
- Protein: 1.7 g.
  Fat: 15.5 g.

446. Bass Fillet in Coconut Sauce

Preparation time: 5 minutes

Cooking time: 15 minutes

Servings: 4

Ingredients:

- 1/4 cup coconut milk
- 1/2 lb. bass fillet
- 1 tbsp. olive oil
- 2 tbsp. jalapeño, chopped
- 2 tbsp. lime juice, freshly squeezed
- 3 tbsp. parsley, chopped
- Salt and pepper to taste

Directions:

1. Preheat the air fryer for 5 minutes
2. Season the bass with salt and pepper to taste
3. Brush the surface with olive oil.
4. Place in the air fryer and cook for 15 minutes at 350°F.
5. Meanwhile, place in a saucepan, the coconut milk, lime juice, jalapeño, and parsley.
6. Heat over medium flame.
7. Serve the fish with coconut sauce.

Nutrition:

- Calories: 139
- Carbs: 2.7 g.
- Protein: 8.7 g.
- Fat: 10.3 g.

447. Beer Battered Cod Filet

Preparation time: 5 minutes

Cooking time: 15 minutes

Servings: 2

Ingredients:

- 1/2 cup all-purpose flour
- 3/4 tsp. baking powder
- 1 1/4 cup lager beer
- 2 cod fillets
- 2 eggs, beaten
- Salt and pepper to taste

Directions:

1. Preheat the air fryer to 390°F.
2. Pat the fish fillets dry then set them aside.
3. In a bowl, combine the rest of the

ingredients to create a batter.

4. Dip the fillets on the batter and place them on the double layer rack.

5. Cook for 15 minutes.

Nutrition:

- Calories: 229
- Carbs: 33.2 g.
- Protein: 31.1 g.
- Fat: 10.2 g.

448. Buttered Baked Cod With Wine

Preparation time: 5 minutes

Cooking time: 12 minutes

Servings: 2

Ingredients:

- 1 tbsp. butter
- 1 tbsp. butter
- 2 tbsp. dry white wine
- 1/2 lb. thick-cut cod loin
- 1 1/2 tsp. fresh parsley, chopped
- 1 1/2 tsp. green onion, chopped
- 1/2 lemon, cut into wedges
- 1/4 sleeve buttery round crackers (such as Ritz®), crushed
- 1/4 lemon, juiced

Directions:

1. In a small bowl, melt butter in the microwave. Whisk in crackers.

2. Lightly grease the baking pan of the air fryer with the remaining butter. And melt for 2 minutes at 390°F.

3. In a small bowl whisk well lemon juice, white wine, parsley, and green onion.

4. Coat cod filets in melted butter. Pour dressing. Top with butter-cracker mixture.

5. Cook for 10 minutes at 390°F.

6. Serve and enjoy with a slice of lemon.

Nutrition:

- Calories: 266
- Carbs: 9.3 g.
- Protein: 20.9 g.

- Fat: 16.1 g.

449. Buttered Garlic-Oregano on Clams

Preparation time: 5 minutes

Cooking time: 5 minutes

Servings: 4

Ingredients:

- 1/4 cup Parmesan cheese, grated
- 1/4 cup parsley, chopped
- 1 cup breadcrumbs
- 1 tsp. dried oregano
- 2 dozen clams, shucked
- 3 garlic cloves, minced
- 4 tbsp. butter, melted

Directions:

1. In a medium bowl, mix the breadcrumbs, Parmesan cheese, parsley, oregano, and garlic. Stir in the melted butter.
2. Preheat the air fryer to 390°F.
3. Place the baking dish accessory in the air fryer and place the clams.
4. Sprinkle the crumb mixture over the clams.
5. Cook for 5 minutes.

Nutrition:

- Calories: 160
- Carbs: 6.3 g.
- Protein: 2.9 g.

Fat: 13.6 g.

450. Butterflied Prawns With Garlic-Sriracha

Preparation time: 5 minutes

Cooking time: 15 minutes

Servings: 2

Ingredients:

- 1 tbsp. lime juice
- 1 tbsp. sriracha
- 1 lb. large prawns, shells removed and cut lengthwise or butterflied
- 1tsp. fish sauce
- 2 tbsp. melted butter
- 2 tbsp. garlic, minced
- Salt and pepper to taste

Directions:

1. Preheat the air fryer to 390°F.
2. Place the grill pan accessory in the air fryer.
3. Season the prawns with the rest of the ingredients.
4. Place on the grill pan and cook for 15 minutes. Make sure to flip the prawns halfway through the cooking time.

Nutrition:

- Calories: 443
- Carbs :9.7 g.
- Protein: 62.8 g.
- Fat: 16.9 g.

451. Cajun Seasoned Salmon Filet

Preparation time: 5 minutes

Cooking time: 15 minutes

Servings: 1

Ingredients:

- 1 salmon fillet
- 1 tsp. juice from lemon, freshly squeezed
- 3 tbsp. extra virgin olive oil
- A dash of Cajun seasoning mix
- Salt and pepper to taste

Directions:

1. Preheat the air fryer for 5 minutes.
2. Place all ingredients in a bowl and toss to coat.
3. Place the fish fillet in the air fryer

basket.

4. Bake for 15 minutes at 325°F.

5. Once cooked drizzle with olive oil.

Nutrition:

- Calories: 523
- Carbs: 4.6 g.
- Protein: 47.9 g.
- Fat: 34.8 g.

452. Cajun Spiced Lemon-Shrimp Kebabs

Preparation time: 5 minutes

Cooking time: 10 minutes

Servings: 2

Ingredients:

- 1 tsp. cayenne
- 1 tsp. garlic powder
- 1 tsp. kosher salt
- 1 tsp. onion powder
- 1 tsp. oregano
- 1 tsp. paprika
- 12 pcs. XL shrimp
- 2 lemons, sliced thinly crosswise
- 2 tbsp. olive oil

Directions:

1. In a bowl, mix all ingredients except for sliced lemons. Marinate for 10 minutes.

2. Thread 3 shrimps per steel skewer.

3. Place in skewer rack.

4. Cook for 5 minutes at 390°F.

5. Serve and enjoy with freshly squeezed lemon.

Nutrition:

- Calories: 232
- Carbs: 7.9 g.
- Protein: 15.9 g.
- Fat: 15.1 g.

453. Cajun Spiced Veggie-Shrimp Bake

Preparation time: 5 minutes

Cooking time: 20 minutes

Servings: 4

Ingredients:

- 1 bag mixed vegetables, frozen
- 1 tbsp. Cajun seasoning, gluten-free
- Olive oil spray
- Salt and pepper to taste
- 1 regular-sized bag (50–80 small) shrimp, peeled and deveined

Directions:

1. Lightly grease the baking pan of the air fryer with olive oil spray. Add all ingredients and toss well to coat. Season with pepper and salt, generously.
2. For 10 minutes, cook at 330°F. Halfway through cooking time, stir.
3. Cook for 10 minutes at 330°F.
4. Serve and enjoy.

Nutrition:

- Calories: 78
- Carbs: 13.2 g.
- Protein: 2.8 g.
- Fat: 1.5 g.

454. Sweet Cod Fillets

Preparation time: 10 minutes

Cooking time: 15 minutes

Servings: 4

Ingredients:

- 4 cod fillets, boneless
- Salt and black pepper to taste
- 1 cup water
- 4 tbsp. light soy sauce
- 1 tbsp. Sugar:
- 3 tbsp. olive oil + a drizzle
- 4 ginger slices
- 3 spring onions, chopped
- 2 tbsp. coriander, chopped

Directions:

1. Season the fish with salt and pepper, then drizzle some

oil over it and rub well.

2. Put the fish in your air fryer and cook at 360°F for 12 minutes.

3. Put the water in a pot and heat up over medium heat; add the soy sauce and Sugar:, stir, bring to a simmer, and remove from the heat.

4. Heat a pan with the olive oil over medium heat; add the ginger and green onions, stir, cook for 2–3 minutes, and remove from the heat.

5. Divide the fish between plates and top with ginger, coriander, and green onions.

6. Drizzle the soy sauce mixture all over, serve, and enjoy!

Nutrition:

- Calories: 270
- Fat: 12 g.
- Fiber: 8 g.
- Carbs: 16 g.
- Protein: 14 g.

455. Pecan Cod

Preparation time: 10 minutes

Cooking time: 15 minutes

Servings: 2

Ingredients:

- 2 black cod fillets, boneless
- 1 tbsp. olive oil
- Salt and black pepper to taste
- 2 leeks, sliced
- 1/2 cup pecans, chopped

Directions:

1. In a bowl, mix the cod with the oil, salt, pepper, and the leeks; toss and coat well.

2. Transfer the cod to your air fryer and cook at 360°F for 15 minutes.

3. Divide the fish and leeks between

plates, sprinkle the pecans on top, and serve immediately.

Nutrition:

- Calories: 280
- Fat: 4 g.
- Fiber: 2 g.
- Carbs: 12 g.
- Protein: 15 g.

456. Balsamic Cod

Preparation time: 5 minutes

Cooking time: 12 minutes

Servings: 2

Ingredients:

- 2 cod fillets, boneless
- 2 tbsp. lemon juice
- Salt and black pepper to taste
- 1/2 tsp. garlic powder
- 1/3 cup water
- 1/3 cup balsamic vinegar
- 3 shallots, chopped
- 2 tbsp. olive oil

Directions:

1. In a bowl, toss the cod with the salt, pepper, lemon juice, garlic powder, water, vinegar, and oil; coat well.

2. Transfer the fish to your fryer's basket and cook at 360°F for 12 minutes, flipping them halfway.

3. Divide the fish between plates, sprinkle the shallots on top, and serve.

Nutrition:

- Calories: 271
- Fat: 12 g.
- Fiber: 10 g.
- Carbs: 16 g.
- Protein: 20 g.

457. Garlic Salmon Fillets

Preparation time: 5 minutes

Cooking time: 8 minutes

Servings: 2

Ingredients:

- 2 salmon fillets, boneless
- Salt and black pepper to taste
- 3 red chili peppers, chopped
- 2 tbsp. lemon juice
- 2 tbsp. olive oil
- 2 tbsp. garlic, minced

Directions:

1. In a bowl, combine the ingredients, toss, and coat fish well.
2. Transfer everything to your air fryer and cook at 365°F for 8 minutes, flipping the fish halfway.
3. Divide between plates and serve right away.

Nutrition:

- Calories: 280
- Fat: 4 g.
- Fiber: 8 g.
- Carbs: 15 g.
- Protein: 20 g.

458. Shrimp and Veggie Mix

Preparation time: 10 minutes

Cooking time: 20 minutes

Servings: 4

Ingredients:

- 1/2 cup red onion, chopped
- 1 cup red bell pepper, chopped
- 1 cup celery, chopped
- 1-lb. shrimp, peeled and deveined
- 1 tsp. Worcestershire sauce
- Salt and black pepper to taste
- 1 tbsp. butter, melted
- 1 tsp. sweet paprika

Directions:

1. Add all the ingredients to a

bowl and mix well.

2. Transfer everything to your air fryer and cook 320°F for 20 minutes, shaking halfway.

3. Divide between plates and serve.

Nutrition:

- Calories: 220
- Fat: 14 g.
- Fiber: 9 g.
- Carbs: 17 g.

Protein: 20 g.

459. White Fish With Peas and Basil

Preparation time: 10 minutes

Cooking time: 12 minutes

Servings: 4

Ingredients:

- 4 white fish fillets, boneless
- 2 tbsp. cilantro, chopped
- 2 cups peas, cooked and drained
- 4 tbsp. veggie stock
- 1/2 tsp. basil, dried
- 1/2 tsp. sweet paprika
- 2 garlic cloves, minced
- Salt and pepper to taste

Directions:

1. In a bowl, mix the fish with all ingredients except the peas; toss to coat the fish well.

2. Transfer everything to your air fryer and cook at 360°F for 12 minutes.

3. Add the peas, toss, and divide everything between plates.

4. Serve and enjoy.

Nutrition:

- Calories: 241
- Fat: 8 g.
- Fiber: 12 g.
- Carbs: 15 g.

Protein: 18 g.

460. Cod and Chives

Preparation time: 5 minutes

Cooking time: 12 minutes

Servings: 4

Ingredients:

- 4 cod fillets, boneless
- Salt and black pepper to taste
- 3 tsp. lime zest
- 2 tsp. lime juice
- 3 tbsp. chives, chopped
- 6 tbsp. butter, melted
- 2 tbsp. olive oil

Directions:

1. Season the fish with salt and pepper, rub it with the oil, and then put it in your air fryer.
2. Cook at 360°F for 10 minutes, flipping once.
3. Heat a pan with the butter over medium heat, and then add the chives, salt, pepper, lime juice, and zest, whisk; cook for 1–2 minutes.
4. Divide the fish between plates, drizzle the lime sauce all over, and serve immediately.

Nutrition:

- Calories: 280
- Fat: 12 g.
- Fiber: 9 g.
- Carbs: 17 g.
- Protein: 15 g.

461. Paprika Salmon Fillets

Preparation time: 5 minutes

Cooking time: 12 minutes

Servings: 4

Ingredients:

- 4 salmon fillets, boneless
- 1 tbsp. olive oil
- Salt and black pepper to taste
- 1 tsp. cumin, ground
- 1 tsp. sweet paprika
- 1/2 tsp. chili powder
- 1 tsp. garlic powder
- Juice of 1 lime

Directions:

1. In a bowl, mix the salmon with the other ingredients, rub and coat well,

and transfer to your air fryer.

2. Cook at 350°F for 6 minutes on each side.

3. Divide the fish between plates and serve right away with a side salad.

Nutrition:

- Calories: 280
- Fat: 14 g.
- Fiber: 4 g.
- Carbs: 18 g.

Protein: 20 g.

462. Thyme Tuna

Preparation time: 10 minutes

Cooking time: 8 minutes

Servings: 4

Ingredients:

- 1/2 cup cilantro, chopped
- 1/3 cup olive oil
- 1 small red onion, chopped
- 3 tbsp. balsamic vinegar
- 3 tbsp. parsley, chopped
- 2 tbsp. basil, chopped
- 1 jalapeño pepper, chopped
- 4 sushi tuna steaks
- Salt and black pepper to taste
- 1 tsp. red pepper flakes
- 1 tsp. thyme, chopped
- 3 garlic cloves, minced

Directions:

1. Place all ingredients except the fish into a bowl and stir well.
2. Add the fish and toss, coating it well.
3. Transfer everything to your air fryer and cook at 360°F for 4 minutes on each side.
4. Divide the fish between plates and serve.

Nutrition:

- Calories: 306
- Fat: 8 g.
- Fiber: 1 g.
- Carbs: 14 g.
- Protein: 16 g.

463. Buttery Shrimp

Preparation time: 5 minutes

Cooking time: 10 minutes

Servings: 2

Ingredients:

- 1 tbsp. butter, melted
- A drizzle of olive oil
- 1-lb. shrimp, peeled and deveined
- 1/4 cup heavy cream
- 8 oz. mushrooms, roughly sliced
- A pinch of red pepper flakes
- Salt and black pepper to taste
- 2 garlic cloves, minced
- 1/2 cup beef stock
- 1 tbsp. parsley, chopped
- 1 tbsp. chives, chopped

Directions:

1. Season the shrimp with salt and pepper and grease with the oil.
2. Place the shrimp in your air fryer, cook at 360°F for 7 minutes, and divide between plates.
3. Heat a pan with the butter over medium heat, add the mushrooms, stir, and cook for 3–4 minutes.
4. Add all remaining ingredients. Stir and then cook for a few minutes more.
5. Drizzle a butter/garlic mixture over the shrimp and serve.

Nutrition:

- Calories: 305
- Fat: 13 g.
- Fiber: 4 g.
- Carbs: 14 g.
- Protein: 11 g.

464. Maple Salmon

Preparation time: 5 minutes

Cooking time: 10 minutes

Servings: 2

Ingredients:

- 2 salmon fillets, boneless
- Salt and black pepper to taste
- 2 tbsp. mustard
- 1 tbsp. olive oil
- 1 tbsp. maple syrup

Directions:

1. In a bowl, mix the mustard with the oil and the maple syrup; whisk well and brush the salmon with this mix.
2. Place the salmon in your air fryer and cook it at 370°F for 5 minutes on each side.
3. Serve immediately with a side salad.

Nutrition:

- Calories: 290
- Fat: 7 g.
- Fiber: 14 g.
- Carbs: 18 g.
- Protein: 17 g.

465. Balsamic Orange Salmon

Preparation time: 5 minutes

Cooking time: 15 minutes

Servings: 4

Ingredients:

- 4 salmon fillets, boneless and cubed
- 2 lemons, sliced
- 1/4 cup balsamic vinegar
- 1/4 cup orange juice
- A pinch of salt and black pepper

Directions:

1. In a pan that fits your air fryer, mix all ingredients except the fish; whisk.
2. Heat the mixture over medium-high heat for 5 minutes

and add the salmon.

3. Toss gently, and place the pan in the air fryer and cook at 360°F for 10 minutes.

4. Divide between plates and serve right away with a side salad.

Nutrition:

- Calories: 227
- Fat: 9 g.
- Fiber: 12 g.
- Carbs: 14 g.
- Protein: 11 g.

466. Crunchy Pistachio Cod

Preparation time: 10 minutes

Cooking time: 10 minutes

Servings: 4

Ingredients:

- 1 cup pistachios, chopped
- 4 cod fillets, boneless
- 1/4 cup lime juice
- 2 tbsp. honey
- 1 tsp. parsley, chopped
- Salt and black pepper to taste
- 1 tbsp. mustard

Directions:

1. Place all the ingredients except the fish into a bowl and whisk.

2. Spread the mixture over the fish fillets, put them in your air fryer, and cook at 350°F for 10 minutes.

3. Divide the fish between plates and serve immediately with a side salad.

Nutrition:

- Calories: 270
- Fat: 17 g.
- Fiber: 12 g.
- Carbs: 20 g.

Protein: 12 g.

467. Roasted Parsley Cod

Preparation time: 10 minutes

Cooking time: 10 minutes

Servings: 4

Ingredients:

- 3 tbsp. parsley, chopped
- 4 medium cod filets, boneless
- 1/4 cup butter, melted
- 2 garlic cloves, minced
- 2 tbsp. lemon juice
- 1 shallot, chopped
- Salt and black pepper to taste

Directions:

1. In a bowl, mix all ingredients except the fish and whisk well.
2. Spread this mixture over the cod fillets.
3. Put them in your air fryer and cook at 390°F for 10 minutes.
4. Divide the fish between plates and serve.

Nutrition:

- Calories: 280
- Fat: 4 g.
- Fiber: 7 g.
- Carbs: 12, g.
- Protein: 15 g.

468. Salmon With Almonds

Preparation time: 10 minutes

Cooking time: 20 minutes

Servings: 4

Ingredients:

- 2 red onions, chopped
- 2 tbsp. olive oil
- 2 small fennel bulbs, trimmed and sliced
- 1/4 cup almonds, toasted and sliced
- Salt and black pepper to taste
- 4 salmon fillets, boneless
- 5 tsp. fennel seeds, toasted

Directions:

1. Season the fish with salt and pepper, grease it with 1 tbsp. of the oil, and place it in your air fryer's basket.
2. Cook at 350°F for 5–6 minutes on each side and divide between plates.
3. Heat a pan with the remaining oil (1 tbsp.) over medium-high heat; add the onions, stir, and sauté for 2 minutes.
4. Add the fennel bulbs and seeds, almonds, salt, and pepper, and cook for 2–3 minutes more.
5. Spread the mixture over the fish and serve right away; enjoy!

Nutrition:

- Calories: 284 g.
- Fat: 7 g.
- Fiber: 10 g.
- Carbs: 17 g.
- Protein: 16 g.

469. Crispy Paprika Fish Fillets

Preparation time: 5 minutes

Cooking time: 15 minutes

Servings: 4

Ingredients:

- 1/2 cup seasoned breadcrumbs
- 1 tbsp. balsamic vinegar
- 1/2 tsp. seasoned salt
- 1 tsp. paprika
- 1/2 tsp. ground black pepper
- 1 tsp. celery seed
- 1 Fish fillets halved
- 1 egg, beaten

Directions:

1. Add the breadcrumbs, vinegar, salt, paprika, ground

black pepper, and celery seeds to your food processor. Process for about 30 seconds.

2. Coat the fish fillets with the beaten egg; then, coat them with the breadcrumb's mixture.

3. Cook at 350°F for about 15 minutes.

Nutrition:

- Calories: 143
- Fat: 14 g.
- Fiber: 17 g.
- Carbs: 12 g.

Protein: 10 g.

470. Sweet and Savory Breaded Shrimp

Preparation time: 5 minutes

Cooking time: 20 minutes

Servings: 2

Ingredients:

- 1/2 lb. of fresh shrimp, peeled from their shells and rinsed
- 2 Raw eggs
- 1/2 cup of breadcrumbs (we like panko, but any brand or home recipe will do)
- 1/2 white onion, peeled, rinsed, and finely chopped
- 1 tsp. of ginger-garlic paste
- 1/2 tsp. turmeric powder
- 1/2 tsp. red chili powder
- 1/2 tsp. cumin powder
- 1/2 tsp. black pepper powder
- 1/2 tsp. dry mango powder
- A pinch of salt

Directions:

1. Cover the basket of the Cuisinart air fryer oven with a lining of tin foil, leaving the edges uncovered to allow air to circulate through the basket.

2. Preheat the Cuisinart air fryer oven to 350°F.

3. In a large mixing bowl, beat the eggs

until fluffy and until the yolks and whites are fully combined.

4. Dunk all the shrimp in the egg mixture, fully submerging.

5. In a separate mixing bowl, combine the bread crumbs with all the dry ingredients until evenly blended.

6. One by one, coat the egg-covered shrimp in the mixed dry ingredients so that fully covered, and place on the foil-lined air-fryer basket.

7. Set the air fryer timer to 20 minutes.

8. Halfway through the cooking time, shake the handle of the air fryer so that the breaded shrimp jostles inside and fry-coverage is even.

9. After 20 minutes, when the fryer shuts off, the shrimp will be perfectly cooked and their breaded crust golden-brown and delicious! Using tongs, remove from the air fryer oven and set on a serving dish to cool.

Nutrition:

- Calories: 135
- Fat: 14 g.
- Protein:22 g.
- Sugar: 0 g.

471. Quick Paella

Preparation time: 7 minutes

Cooking time: 15 minutes

Servings: 4

Ingredients:

- 1 (10 oz.) package frozen cooked rice, thawed
- 1 (6 oz.) jar artichoke hearts, drained and chopped
- 1/4 cup vegetable broth
- 1/2 tsp. turmeric
- 1/2 tsp. dried thyme
- 1 cup small shrimp, frozen, cooked
- 1/2 cup baby peas, frozen
- 1 tomato, diced

Directions:

1. In a 6x6x2-inch pan, combine the rice,

artichoke hearts, vegetable broth, turmeric, and thyme, and stir gently.

2. Place in the air fryer oven and bake for 8–9 minutes or until the rice is hot. Remove from the air fryer oven and gently stir in the shrimp, peas, and tomato. Cook for 5–8 minutes or until the shrimp and peas are hot and the paella is bubbling.

Nutrition:

- Calories: 345
- Fat: 1 g.
- Protein:18 g.

Fiber:4 g.

472. Cilantro-Lime Fried Shrimp

Preparation time: 10 minutes

Cooking time: 10 minutes

Servings: 4

Ingredients:

- 1 lb. raw shrimp, peeled and deveined with tails on or off
- 1/2 cup chopped fresh cilantro
- Juice of 1 lime
- 1 egg
- 1/2 cup all-purpose flour
- 3/4 cup bread crumbs
- Salt
- Pepper
- Cooking oil
- 1/2 cup cocktail sauce (optional)

Directions:

1. Place the shrimp in a plastic bag and add the cilantro and lime juice. Seal the bag. Shake to combine. Marinate in the refrigerator for 30 minutes.

2. In a small bowl, beat the egg. In another small bowl, place the flour. Place the bread crumbs in a third small bowl, and season with salt and pepper to taste.

3. Spray the air fryer rack/basket with cooking oil.

4. Remove the shrimp from the plastic bag. Dip each in the flour, then the egg, and then the bread crumbs.

5. Place the shrimp in the air fryer oven. It is okay to stack them. Spray the

shrimp with cooking oil. Cook for 4 minutes.

6. Open the air fryer oven and flip the shrimp. I recommend flipping individually instead of shaking to keep the breading intact. Cook for an additional 4 minutes, or until crisp.

7. Cool before serving. Serve with cocktail sauce if desired.

Nutrition:

- Calories: 254
- Fat: 4 g.
- Protein: 29 g.
- Fiber: 1 g.

473. Lemony Tuna

Preparation time: 10 minutes

Cooking time: 10 minutes

Servings: 4

Ingredients:

- (6 oz.) cans water-packed plain tuna
- 1 tsp. Dijon mustard
- 1/2 cup breadcrumbs
- 1 tbsp. fresh lime juice
- 1 tbsp. fresh parsley, chopped
- 1 egg
- 2 Chef man® of hot sauce
- 1 tbsp. canola oil
- 1 tsp Salt and freshly ground black pepper, to taste

Directions:

1. Drain most of the liquid from the canned tuna.

2. In a bowl, add the fish, mustard, crumbs, citrus juice, parsley, and hot sauce and mix till well combined. Add a little canola oil if it seems too dry. Add egg, salt, and stir to combine. Make the patties from the tuna mixture. Refrigerate the tuna patties for about 2 hours.

3. Preheat the air fryer oven to 355°F. Cook for about 10–12 minutes.

Nutrition:

- Calories: 509
- Fat: 12 g.
- Protein: 32 g.
- Fiber: 5 g.

474. Grilled Soy Salmon Fillets

Preparation time: 5 Minutes

Cooking time: 8 Minutes

Servings: 4

Ingredients:

- 2 Salmon fillets
- 1/4 tsp. black pepper, ground
- 1/2 tsp. cayenne pepper
- 1/2 tsp. salt
- 1 tsp. onion powder
- 1 tbsp. fresh lemon juice
- 1/2 cup soy sauce
- 1/2 cup water
- 1 tbsp. honey
- 2 tbsp. extra-virgin olive oil

Directions:

1. Firstly, pat the salmon fillets dry using kitchen towels. Season the salmon with black pepper, cayenne pepper, salt, and onion powder.
2. To make the marinade, combine lemon juice, soy sauce, water, honey, and olive oil. Marinate the salmon for at least 2 hours in your refrigerator.
3. Arrange the fish fillets on a grill basket in your air fryer oven.
4. Air Frying. Bake at 330°F for 8–9 minutes, or until salmon fillets are easily flaked with a fork.
5. Work with batches and serve warm.

Nutrition:

- Calories: 432
- Fat: 15 g.
- Protein: 23 g.
- Fiber: 6 g.

475. Old Bay® Crab Cakes

Preparation time: 10 minutes

Cooking time: 20 minutes

Servings: 4

Ingredients:

- 2 Slices dried bread, crusts removed
- A small amount of milk
- 1 tbsp. mayonnaise
- 1 tbsp. Worcestershire sauce
- 1 tbsp. baking powder
- 1 tbsp. parsley flakes
- 1 tsp. Old Bay® Seasoning
- 1/4 tsp. salt
- 1 egg
- 1 lb. lump crabmeat

Directions:

1. Crush your bread over a large bowl until it is broken down into small pieces. Add milk and stir until bread crumbs are moistened. Mix in mayo and Worcestershire sauce. Add remaining ingredients and mix well. Shape into 4 patties.
2. Cook at 360°F for 20 minutes, flipping halfway through.

Nutrition:

- Calories: 165
- Carbs: 5.8 g.
- Fat: 4.5 g.
- Protein: 24 g.
- Fiber: 0 g.

476. Scallops and Spring Veggies

Preparation time: 10 minutes

Cooking time: 8 minutes

Servings: 4

Ingredients:

- 1/2 lb. asparagus ends trimmed, cut into 2-inch pieces
- 1 cup sugar snap peas
- 1 lb. sea scallops
- 1 tbsp. lemon juice
- 1 tsp. olive oil
- 1/2 tsp. dried thyme
- Pinch salt
- Black pepper, freshly ground

Directions:

1. Place the asparagus and sugar:snap peas in the oven rack/basket. Place

the rack on the air fryer oven.

2. Cook for 2–3 minutes or until the vegetables are just starting to get tender.

3. Meanwhile, check the scallops for a small muscle attached to the side, and pull it off and discard.

4. In a medium bowl, toss the scallops with lemon juice, olive oil, thyme, salt, and pepper. Place into the oven rack/basket on top of the vegetables. Place the rack on the fryer oven.

5. Steam for 5–7 minutes. Until the scallops are just firm, and the vegetables are tender. Serve immediately.

Nutrition:

- Calories: 162
- Carbs: 10 g.
- Fat: 4g.
- Protein: 22g.
- Fiber: 3 g.

477. Scallops and Spring Veggies

Preparation time: 10 minutes

Cooking time: 8 minutes

Servings: 4

Ingredients:

- 1/2 lb. asparagus ends trimmed, cut into 2-inch pieces
- 1 cup sugar snap peas
- 1 lb. sea scallops
- 1 tbsp. lemon juice
- 1 tsp. olive oil
- 1/2 tsp. dried thyme
- Pinch salt
- Black pepper, freshly ground

Directions:

6. Place the asparagus and sugar:snap peas in the oven rack/basket. Place

the rack on the air fryer oven.

7. Cook for 2–3 minutes or until the vegetables are just starting to get tender.

8. Meanwhile, check the scallops for a small muscle attached to the side, and pull it off and discard.

9. In a medium bowl, toss the scallops with lemon juice, olive oil, thyme, salt, and pepper. Place into the oven rack/basket on top of the vegetables. Place the rack on the fryer oven.

10. Steam for 5–7 minutes. Until the scallops are just firm, and the vegetables are tender. Serve immediately.

Nutrition:

- Calories: 162
- Carbs: 10 g.
- Fat: 4g.
- Protein: 22g.
- Fiber: 3 g.

478. Fried Calamari

Preparation time: 8 minutes

Cooking time: 7 minutes

Servings: 6–8

Ingredients:

- 1/2 tsp. salt
- 1/2 tsp. Old Bay® seasoning
- 1/3 cup plain cornmeal
- 1/2 cup semolina flour
- 1/2 cup almond flour
- 5–6 cup olive oil
- 1 1/2 lb. baby squid

Directions:

1. Rinse squid in cold water and slice tentacles, keeping just 1/4-inch of the hood in one piece.
2. Combine 1–2

pinches of pepper, salt, Old Bay® seasoning, cornmeal, and both flours. Dredge squid pieces into flour mixture and place into the air fryer oven.

3. Spray liberally with olive oil. Cook 15 minutes at 345°F till the coating turns a golden brown.

Nutrition:

- Calories: 211
- Carbs: 55 g.
- Fat: 6 g.
- Protein: 21 g.

Sugar: 1 g.

479. Soy and Ginger Shrimp

Preparation time: 8 minutes

Cooking time: 10 minutes

Servings: 4

Ingredients:

- 2 tbsp. olive oil
- 2 tbsp. scallions, finely chopped
- 2 cloves garlic, chopped
- 1 tsp. fresh ginger, grated
- 1 tbsp. dry white wine
- 1 tbsp. balsamic vinegar
- 1/4 cup soy sauce
- 1 tbsp. Sugar:
- 1 lb. shrimp
- Salt and ground black pepper, to taste

Directions:

1. To make the marinade, warm the oil in a saucepan; cook all ingredients, except the shrimp, salt, and black pepper. Now, let it cool.
2. Marinate the shrimp, covered, at least an hour, in the refrigerator.
3. After that, bake the shrimp at 350°F for 8–10 minutes (depending on the size), turning once or twice. Season prepared shrimp with salt and black pepper and serve right away.

Nutrition:

- Calories: 500
- Fat: 3 g.
- Protein: 20 g.
- Fiber: 7 g.

480. Halibut and Sun-Dried Tomatoes Mix

Preparation time: 10 minutes

Cooking time: 10 minutes

Servings: 2

Ingredients:

- 2 medium halibut fillets
- 2 garlic cloves
- 2 tbsp. olive oil
- Salt and black pepper
- 6 sun-dried tomatoes
- 2 small red onions
- 1 fennel bulb
- 9 black olives
- 4 Rosemary springs
- 1/2 tsp. red pepper flakes

Directions:

1. Season fish with pepper, salt, rub with oil and garlic then put in heatproof dish and transfer to the air fryer.
2. Add sun-dried tomatoes, onion slices, fennel, Rosemary, and sprinkle pepper flakes, olives. Add air fryer and cook at 380°F for 10 minutes.
3. Divide veggies and fish on plates then serve.

Nutrition:

- Calories: 400
- Fat: 11 g.
- Protein: 12 g.
- Fiber: 9 g.

481. Black Cod and Plum Sauce

Preparation time: 10 minutes

Cooking time: 15 minutes

Servings: 2

Ingredients:

- 1 egg white
- 1/2 cup red quinoa
- 2 tsp. whole-wheat flour
- 4 tsp. lemon juice
- 1/2 tsp. smoked paprika
- 1 tsp. olive oil
- 2 medium black cod fillets
- 1 red plum
- 2 tsp. raw honey
- 1/4 tsp. black peppercorns
- 2 tsp. parsley
- 1/4 cup water

Directions:

1. Mix 1 tsp. lemon juice, egg white, 1/4 tsp. paprika, flour and whisk well.
2. Place quinoa in a bowl then mixes with 1/3 of egg white mix.
3. Put the fish in a bowl with the rest of the egg white mixture then toss to coat.
4. Put fish into quinoa mix, allow to coat well, and leave it aside for 10 minutes.
5. Heat pan with 1 tsp. oil over medium heat, add honey and plum, peppercorns, stir allow to simmer then cook for 1 minute.
6. Add the remaining lemon juice, paprika, and water. Stir very well and simmer for 5 minutes.
7. Add parsley and stir, take the sauce off the heat.
8. Put fish in the air fryer and cook at 380°F for 10 minutes.
9. Place fish on plates and sprinkle plum sauce on top then serve.

Nutrition:

- Calories: 434
- Fat: 13 g.
- Protein: 22 g.
- Fiber: 17 g.

482. Fish and Couscous

Preparation time: 10 minutes

Cooking time: 15 minutes

Servings: 4

Ingredients:

- 2 red onions
- Cooking spray
- 2 small fennel bulbs
- 1/4 cup almonds
- Salt and black pepper
- 2 1/2 lb. sea bass
- 5 tsp. fennel seeds
- 3/4 cup whole-wheat couscous

Directions:

1. Season fish with salt and pepper, spray with cooking spray, place in your air fryer, and cook at 350°F for 10 minutes.
2. Spray pan with

cooking oil and heat it over medium heat.

3. Put fennel seeds into the pan, stir and toast for 1 minute.

4. Add pepper, salt, onion, fennel bulbs, couscous, and almonds, stir then cook for 2–3 minutes. Divide among plates.

5. Place fish beside couscous mix and serve.

Nutrition:

- Calories: 321
- Fat: 11 g.
- Protein: 23 g.
- Fiber: 12 g.

483. Chinese Cod

Preparation time: 10 minutes

Cooking time: 10 minutes

Servings: 2

Ingredients:

- 2 medium cod fillets
- 1 tsp. peanuts
- 2 tsp. garlic powder
- 1 tbsp. light soy sauce
- 1/2 tsp. ginger

Directions:

1. Place fish fillets in a heat-proof dish, add soy sauce and ginger, garlic powder, toss well, put in the air fryer, and cook at 350°F for 10 minutes.

2. Divide fish and sprinkle peanuts on top then serve.

Nutrition:

- Calories: 209
- Fat: 5 g.
- Protein: 24 g.
- Fiber: 8 g.

484. Cod With Pearl Onions

Preparation time: 10 minutes

Cooking time: 15 minutes

Servings: 2

Ingredients:

- 14 oz. pearl onions
- 2 medium cod fillets
- 1 tbsp. parsley
- 1 tsp. thyme
- Black pepper
- 8 oz. mushrooms

Directions:

1. Place fish in heatproof dish add onions, mushrooms, parsley, black pepper, and thyme, toss well, put in the air fryer, and cook at 350°F and cook for 15 minutes.
2. Divide on plates then serve.

Nutrition:

- Calories: 123
- Fat: 12 g.
- Protein: 28 g.
- Fiber: 14 g.

485. Hawaiian Salmon

Preparation time: 10 minutes

Cooking time: 10 minutes

Servings: 2

Ingredients:

- 20 oz. canned pineapple pieces and juice
- 1/2 tsp. ginger
- 2 tsp. garlic powder
- 1 tsp. onion powder
- 1 tsp. balsamic vinegar
- 2 medium salmon fillets
- Salt and black pepper

Directions:

1. Season salmon with onion powder, salt, and black pepper, garlic powder, rub. Add to heat-proof dish and then add

pineapple chunks and ginger and toss them gently.

2. Drizzle the vinegar all over, put in your air fryer, and cook at 350°F for 10 minutes.

3. Divide everything among plates and serve.

Nutrition:

- Calories: 456
- Fat: 9 g.
- Protein: 30 g.
- Fiber: 27 g.

486. Salmon and Avocado Salad

Preparation time: 10 minutes

Cooking time: 20 minutes

Servings: 4

Ingredients:

- 2 medium salmon fillets
- 1/4 cup butter, melted
- 4 oz. mushrooms
- Sea salt and black pepper
- 12 cherry tomatoes
- 2 tbsp. olive oil
- 8 oz. lettuce leaves
- 1 avocado
- 1 jalapeño pepper
- 5 cilantro springs
- 2 tbsp. white wine vinegar
- 1 oz. feta cheese

Directions:

1. Place salmon on a lined baking sheet, brush using 2 tbsp. melted butter, season with pepper and salt and broil it for 15 minutes over medium heat and keep it warm.

2. Hence, heat the pan with the remaining butter over medium heat. Add mushrooms and stir. Cook for a couple of minutes.

3. Place tomatoes in a bowl. Add salt, 1 tbsp. olive oil and pepper then toss to coat.

4. Mix salmon with mushrooms, avocado, lettuce, jalapeño, tomatoes, and cilantro in a salad bowl.

5. Add remaining oil, pepper, vinegar, salt, and sprinkle cheese

on top then serve.

Nutrition:

- Calories: 545
- Fat: 15 g.
- Protein: 29 g.
- Fiber: 8 g.

487. Salmon and Greek Yogurt Sauce

Preparation time: 10 minutes

Cooking time: 20 minutes

Servings: 2

Ingredients:

- 2 medium salmon fillets
- 1 tbsp. basil
- 6 lemon slices
- Sea salt and black pepper
- 1 cup Greek yogurt
- 2 tsp. curry powder
- A pinch of cayenne pepper
- 1 garlic clove
- 1/2 tsp. cilantro
- 1/2 tsp. mint

Directions:

1. Put salmon fillet on parchment paper make 3 splits each then stuff with basil.
2. Season with pepper and salt. Top every fillets with 3 lemon slices, fold parchment, seal edges, place in the oven at 400°F, and bake for 20 minutes.
3. Mix in a bowl, yogurt with cayenne pepper, salt, curry, garlic, cilantro, and mint and whisk well.
4. Place fish to plates, sprinkle yogurt sauce on top then serve.

Nutrition:

- Calories: 578
- Fat: 17 g.
- Protein: 40 g.
- Fiber: 26 g.

488. Spanish Salmon

Preparation time: 10 minutes

Cooking time: 15 minutes

Servings: 6

Ingredients:

- 2 cups bread croutons
- 3 red onions
- 3/4 cup green olives
- 3 red bell peppers
- 1/2 tsp. smoked paprika
- Salt and black pepper
- 5 tbsp. olive oil
- 6 medium salmon fillets
- 2 tbsp. parsley

Directions:

1. Mix bread croutons with onion wedges, olives, bell pepper ones, salt, paprika, pepper, and 3 tbsp. olive oil in heatproof dish and toss well, place in the air fryer then cook at 356°F for 7 minutes.
2. Polish salmon with the remaining oil, put over veggies, and cook at 360°F for 8 minutes.
3. Divide fish and veggie mix then sprinkle parsley on top and serve.

Nutrition:

- Calories: 300
- Fat: 19 g.
- Protein: 21 g.
- Fiber: 13 g.

489. Marinated Salmon

Preparation time: 10 minutes

Cooking time: 25 minutes

Servings: 6

Ingredients:

- 1 whole salmon
- 1 tbsp. dill
- 1 tbsp. tarragon
- 1 tbsp. garlic
- Juice from 2 lemons
- 1 lemon
- A pinch of salt and black pepper
- Coleslaw for servings

Directions:

1. Mix fish with salt, tarragon, dill, lemon juice, and pepper, toss, and keep in the fridge for 1 hour.
2. Stuff it with lemon slices and garlic, place in the air fryer

and cook at 320°F for 25 minutes.

3. Divide it among plates. Serve with tasty coleslaw on the side.

Nutrition:

- Calories: 200
- Fat: 6 g.
- Protein: 21.3 g.
- Fiber: 7.8 g.

490. Delicious Red Snapper

Preparation time: 10 minutes

Cooking time: 35 minutes

Servings: 4

Ingredients:

- 1 big red snapper
- Salt and black pepper
- 3 garlic cloves
- 1 jalapeño
- 1/4 lb. okra
- 1 tbsp. butter
- 2 tbsp. olive oil
- 1 red bell pepper
- 2 tbsp. white wine
- 2 tbsp. parsley

Directions:

1. Mix jalapeño, garlic with wine and stir it well then rub snapper with it.
2. Season fish with pepper and salt then leave aside for 30 minutes.
3. Heat pan with 1 tbsp. butter over medium heat, add okra and bell pepper, stir then cook for 5 minutes.
4. Stuff red snapper belly with the mix. Add parsley and polish with olive oil.
5. Put in the preheated air fryer. Cook at 400°F for 15 minutes.
6. Divide among plates and serve.

Nutrition:

- Calories: 340
- Fat: 13.7 g.
- Protein: 20.3 g.
- Fiber: 8 g.

491. Snapper Fillets and Veggies

Preparation time: 10 minutes

Cooking time: 14 minutes

Servings: 2

Ingredients:

- 2 red snapper fillets
- 1 tbsp. olive oil
- 1/2 cup red bell pepper
- 1/2 cup green bell pepper
- 1/2 cup leeks
- Salt and black pepper
- 1 tsp. tarragon
- A splash of white wine

Directions:

1. In heatproof dish, mix fish fillets with salt, oil, pepper, green bell pepper, leeks, red bell pepper, tarragon, and wine, toss everything well. Introduce in the preheated air fryer at 350°F and cook for 14 minutes.
2. Divide fish and veggies on plates then serve warm.

Nutrition:

- Calories: 150
- Fat: 3.7 g.
- Protein: 24.7 g.

Fiber :18 g.

492. Air Fried Branzino

Preparation time: 10 minutes

Cooking time: 10 minutes

Servings: 4

Ingredients:

- Zest from 1 lemon
- Zest from 1 orange
- Juice from 1/2 lemon
- Juice from 1/2 orange
- Salt and black pepper
- 4 medium branzino fillets
- 1/2 cup parsley
- 2 tbsp. olive oil
- A pinch of red pepper flakes

Directions:

1. Using a large bowl, mix orange zest, fish fillets with lemon zest, lemon juice,

salt, orange juice, pepper, oil, and pepper flakes, toss it well. Transfer fillets to preheated air fryer at 350°F and bake for 10 minutes.

2. Divide fish on plates. Sprinkle with parsley then serve immediately.

Nutrition:

- Calories: 210
- Fat: 14.7 g.
- Protein: 29.9 g.
- Fiber: 2.7 g.

493. Lemon Sole and Swiss Chard

Preparation time: 10 minutes

Cooking time: 14 minutes

Servings: 4

Ingredients:

- 1 tsp. lemon zest
- 4 white bread slices
- 1/4 cup walnuts
- 1/4 cup Parmesan cheese
- 4 tbsp. olive oil
- 4 sole fillets
- Salt and black pepper
- 4 tbsp. butter
- 1/4 cup lemon juice
- 3 tbsp. capers
- 2 garlic cloves
- 2 bunches Swiss chard

Directions:

1. Mix bread with walnuts, cheese, and lemon zest in a blender and pulse well.

2. Add half olive oil, pulse well again allow for now.

3. Heat pan with butter over medium heat. Add lemon juice, pepper and capers, salt, stir it well. Put fish then toss it.

4. Transfer to your preheated air fryer top with bread mix made earlier and cook at 350°F for 14 minutes.

5. Again, heat different pan with remaining oil, and add garlic, salt, and pepper, Swiss chard, stir it gently. Cook for 2 minutes and take off the heat.

6. Divide fish between plates and serve with sautéed chard on the side.

Nutrition:

- Calories: 455
- Fat: 6.7 g.
- Protein: 23,4 g.
- Fiber: 32 g.

494. Salmon and Blackberry Glaze

Preparation time: 10 minutes

Cooking time: 33 minutes

Servings: 4

Ingredients:

- 1 cup water
- 1-inch ginger piece
- Juice from 1/2 lemon
- 12 oz. blackberries
- 1 tbsp. olive oil
- 1/4 cup sugar
- 4 medium salmon fillets
- Salt and black pepper

Directions:

1. Heat pot with water over high heat. Add ginger, blackberries, and lemon juice and stir. Boil then cook for 4–5 minutes, take off heat, strain and pour into pan mix with sugar.
2. Stir the mix, simmer over low heat then cook for 20 minutes.
3. Allow blackberry sauce to cool. Brush salmon and season with pepper and salt, sprinkle olive oil over then rub fish well.
4. Place fish in the preheated air fryer at 350°F and cook for 10 minutes.
5. Divide between plates, sprinkle some blackberry sauce over and serve.

Nutrition:

- Calories: 156
- Fat: 5.3 g.
- Protein: 33.2 g.
- Fiber: 16.8 g.

Chapter 8:
Snacks Recipes

495. Classic French Fries

Preparation time: 5 minutes

Cooking time: 30 minutes

Servings: 6

Ingredients:

- 3 large russet potatoes
- 1 tbsp. canola oil
- 1 tbsp. extra-virgin olive oil
- Salt
- Pepper
- 1 cup of water

Directions:

1. Peel the potatoes and cut lengthwise to create french fries.

2. Place the potatoes in a large bowl of cold water. Allow the potatoes to soak in the water for at least 30 minutes, preferably 1 hour.

3. Spread the fries onto a baking sheet (optional: lined with parchment paper) and coat them with canola oil, olive oil, and salt and pepper to taste.

4. Transfer half of the fries to the air fryer basket. Cook for 10 minutes.

5. Open the air fryer and shake the basket so that the fries that were at the bottom come up to the top.

6. Cook for an additional 5 minutes.

7. When the first half finished, remove the cooked fries, then repeat steps 4 and 5 for the remaining fries.

8. Cool before serving.

Nutrition:

- Calories: 168
- Total fat: 5 g.
- Saturated fat: 1 g.
- Cholesterol: 0 mg.
- Sodium: 38 mg.
- Carbs: 29 g.
- Fiber: 4 g.
- Protein: 3 g.

496. Olive Oil Sweet Potato Chips

Preparation time: 10 minutes

Cooking time: 20 minutes

Servings: 5

Ingredients:

- 3 sweet potatoes
- 2 tsp. extra-virgin olive oil
- 1 tsp. cinnamon (optional)
- Salt
- Pepper

Directions:

1. Peel the sweet potatoes using a vegetable peeler. Cut the potatoes crosswise into thin slices. You can also use a mandolin to slice the potatoes into chips.
2. Place the sweet potatoes in a large bowl of cold water for 30 minutes. This helps remove the starch from the sweet potatoes, which promotes crisping.
3. Drain the sweet potatoes. Dry the slices thoroughly with paper towels or napkins.
4. Place the sweet potatoes in another large bowl. Drizzle with the olive oil and sprinkle with the cinnamon, if using, and salt and pepper to taste. Toss to fully coat.
5. Place the sweet potato slices in the air fryer. It is okay to stack them, but do not overcrowd them. You may need to cook the chips in 2 batches. Cook the potatoes for 10 minutes.
6. Open the air fryer and shake the basket. Cook the chips for an additional 10 minutes.
7. Cool before serving.

Nutrition:

- Calories: 94
- Total fat: 2 g.
- Saturated fat: 0 g.
- Cholesterol: 0 mg.
- Sodium: 58 mg.
- Carbs: 20 g.
- Fiber: 2 g.
- Protein: 1 g.

497. Parmesan Breaded Zucchini Chips

Preparation time: 15 minutes

Cooking time: 20 minutes

Servings: 5

Ingredients:

For the zucchini chips:

- 2 medium zucchini
- 2 eggs
- 1/3 cup bread crumbs
- 1/3 cup Parmesan cheese, grated
- Salt
- Pepper
- Cooking oil

For the lemon aioli:

- 1/2 cup mayonnaise
- 1/2 tbsp. olive oil
- Juice of 1/2 lemon
- 1 tsp. garlic, minced
- Salt and pepper

Directions:

To make the zucchini chips:

1. Slice the zucchini into thin chips (about 1/8-inch thick) using a knife or mandolin.
2. In a small bowl, beat the eggs. In another small bowl, combine the bread crumbs, Parmesan cheese, and salt and pepper to taste.
3. Spray the air fryer basket with cooking oil.
4. Dip the zucchini slices one at a time in the eggs and then the bread crumb mixture. You can also sprinkle the bread crumbs onto the zucchini slices with a spoon.
5. Place the zucchini chips in the air fryer basket, but do not stack. Cook in batches. Spray the chips with cooking oil from a distance (otherwise, the breading may fly off). Cook for 10 minutes.
6. Remove the cooked zucchini chips from the air fryer, then repeat step 5 with the remaining zucchini.

To make the lemon aioli:

1. While the zucchini is cooking, combine the mayonnaise, olive oil, lemon juice, and garlic in a small bowl, adding salt and pepper to taste. Mix well until fully combined.
2. Cool the zucchini and serve alongside the aioli.

Nutrition:

- Calories: 192
- Total fat: 13 g.
- Saturated fat: 3 g
- Cholesterol: 97 mg.
- Sodium: 254 mg.
- Carbs: 12 g.
- Fiber: 4 g.
- Protein: 6 g.

498. Low-Carb Cheese-Stuffed Jalapeño Poppers

Preparation time: 10 minutes

Cooking time: 5 minutes

Servings: 5

Ingredients:

- 10 jalapeño peppers
- 6 oz. cream cheese
- 1/4 cup cheddar cheese, shredded
- 2 tbsp. panko bread crumbs
- Cooking oil

Directions:

1. Recommend you wear gloves while handling jalapeños. Halve the jalapeños lengthwise. Remove the seeds and the white membrane.
2. Place the cream cheese in a small, microwave-safe bowl. Microwave for 15 seconds to soften.
3. Remove the bowl from the microwave. Add the cheddar cheese. Mix well.
4. Stuff each of the jalapeño halves with the cheese mixture, then sprinkle the panko bread crumbs on top of each popper.
5. Place the poppers in the air fryer. Spray them with cooking oil. Cook for 5 minutes.
6. Cool before serving.

Nutrition:

- Calories: 156
- Total fat: 14 g.
- Saturated fat: 9 g.
- Cholesterol: 43 mg.
- Sodium: 874 mg.

- Carbs: 3 g.
- Fiber: 1 g.
- Protein: 4 g.

499. Vidalia Onion Blossom

Preparation time: 10 minutes

Cooking time: 25 minutes

Servings: 4

Ingredients:

- 1 vidalia onion, large-sized
- 1 1/2 cups all-purpose flour
- 1 tsp. garlic powder
- 1 tsp. paprika
- Salt and pepper to taste
- 2 eggs
- 1 cup milk
- Cooking oil

Directions:

1. Cut off the pointy stem end of the onion. Leave the root end intact. Peel the onion and place it cut-side down. The root end of the onion should be facing up.

2. Starting about 1/2-inch from the root end, cut downward to make 4 evenly spaced cuts. In each piece, make 3 additional cuts. There should be 16 cuts in the onion.

3. Turn the onion over and fluff out the "petals."

4. Place the flour in a large bowl and season it with garlic powder, paprika, and salt and pepper to taste.

5. In another large bowl, whisk the eggs. Add the milk and stir. This will form a batter.

6. Place the onion in the bowl with the flour mixture. Use a large spoon to cover the onion petals in

flour.

7. Transfer the onion to the batter. Use a spoon or basting brush to cover the onion completely.

8. Return the onion to the flour mixture. Cover completely.

9. Wrap the battered onion in foil and place in the freezer for 45 minutes.

10. Spray the air fryer basket with cooking oil. Unwrap the foil covering and place the onion in the air fryer basket. Cook for 10 minutes.

11. Open the air fryer. Spray the onion with cooking oil. If areas of the onion are still white from the flour, focus the spray on these areas.

12. Cook for an additional 10–15 minutes, or until crisp.

Nutrition:

- Calories: 253
- Total fat: 4 g.
- Saturated fat: 2 g.
- Cholesterol: 87 mg.
- Sodium: 101 mg.
- Carbs: 43 g.
- Fiber: 2 g.
- Protein: 10 g.

500. Crispy Fried Pickle Chips

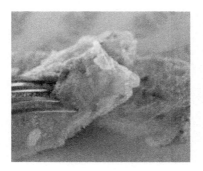

Preparation time: 10 minutes

Cooking time: 10 minutes

Servings: 4

Ingredients:

- 1 lb. whole dill pickles
- 2 eggs
- 1/3 cup all-purpose flour
- 1/3 cup bread crumbs
- Cooking oil

Directions:

1. Cut the pickles crosswise into 1/2-

inch-thick slices.
Dry the slices
completely using a
paper towel.

2. In a small bowl,
beat the eggs. In
another small bowl,
add the flour. Place
the bread crumbs in
a third small bowl.

3. Spray the air fryer
basket with cooking
oil.

4. Dip the pickle slices
in the flour, then
the egg, and then
the bread crumbs.

5. Place the breaded
pickle slices in the
air fryer. It is okay
to stack them. Spray
them with cooking
oil. Cook for 6
minutes.

6. Open the air fryer
and flip the pickles.
Cook for an
additional 2–3
minutes, or until the
pickles are crisp.

Nutrition:

- Calories: 137
- Total fat: 3 g.
- Saturated fat: 1 g.
- Cholesterol: 82 mg.
- Sodium: 2372 mg.
- Carbs: 21 g.
- Fiber: 4 g.
- Protein: 7 g.

501. Spiced Nuts

Preparation time: 5
minutes

Cooking time: 15 minutes

Servings: 4

Ingredients:

- 1/2 tsp. cinnamon
- 1/2 tsp. stevia
- Pepper
- 1 cup nuts (walnuts,
  pecans, and
  almonds work well)
- 1 egg white
- Cooking oil

Directions:

1. In a small bowl,
   combine the
   cinnamon, stevia,
   and pepper to taste.

2. Place the nuts in
   another bowl with
   the egg white. Add
   the spices to the
   nuts.

3. Spray the air fryer
   basket with cooking

oil.

4. Place the nuts in the air fryer. Spray them with cooking oil. Cook for 10 minutes.

5. Open the air fryer and shake the basket. Cook for an additional 3–4 minutes.

6. Serve warm.

Nutrition:

- Calories: 210
- Total fat: 18 g.
- Saturated fat: 2 g.
- Cholesterol: 0 mg.
- Sodium: 237 mg.
- Carbs: 9 g.
- Fiber: 3 g.
- Protein: 7 g.

502. Pigs in a Blanket

Preparation time: 10 minutes

Cooking time: 20 minutes

Servings: 1

Ingredients:

- 1 (8-oz.) can crescent rolls or croissant biscuit rolls
- 16 cocktail franks or mini smoked hot dogs
- Cooking oil

Directions:

1. Separate the crescent roll dough into 8 triangles and place them on a flat work surface. Cut each triangle in half to make 16 triangles.

2. Dry the franks with a paper towel. Place 1 frank on the bottom of a triangle. This should be the widest part of the dough. Roll up the dough. Repeat for the remaining franks and triangles.

3. Spray the air fryer basket with cooking oil.

4. Place 8 pigs in a blanket in the air fryer. It is okay to stack them, but do not overcrowd the basket. Spray them with cooking oil. Cook for 8 minutes.

5. Remove the cooked pigs in a blanket from the air fryer, then repeat step 4 for the remaining 8 pigs in a blanket.

6. Cool before serving.

Nutrition:

- Calories: 75
- Total fat: 5 g.
- Saturated fat: 2 g.
- Cholesterol: 5 mg.

- Sodium: 170 mg.
- Carbs: 6 g.
- Fiber: 0 g.
- Protein: 2 g.

503. Breaded Artichoke Hearts

Preparation time: 15 minutes

Cooking time: 10 minutes

Servings: 1

Ingredients:

- 14 whole artichoke hearts packed in water
- 1 egg
- 1/2 cup all-purpose flour
- 1/3 cup panko bread crumbs
- 1 tsp. Italian seasoning
- Cooking oil

Directions:

1. Squeeze excess water from the artichoke hearts and place them on paper towels to dry.

2. In a small bowl, beat the egg. In another small bowl, place the flour. In a third small bowl, combine the bread crumbs and Italian seasoning, and stir.

3. Spray the air fryer basket with cooking oil.

4. Dip the artichoke hearts in the flour, then the egg, and then the bread crumb mixture.

5. Place the breaded artichoke hearts in the air fryer. It is okay to stack them. Spray them with cooking oil. Cook for 4 minutes.

6. Open the air fryer and flip the artichoke hearts. I recommend flipping instead of shaking because the hearts are small, and this will help keep the breading intact.

Cook for an additional 4 minutes, or until the artichoke hearts have browned and are crisp.

7. Cool before serving.

Nutrition:

- Calories: 54
- Total fat: 1 g.
- Saturated fat: 0 g.
- Cholesterol: 12 mg.
- Sodium: 248 mg.
- Carbs: 9 g.
- Fiber: 1 g.
- Protein: 3 g.

504. Crunchy Pork Egg Rolls

Preparation time: 15 minutes

Cooking time: 15 minutes

Servings: 1

Ingredients:

- Cooking oil
- 2 garlic cloves, minced
- 1 tsp. sesame oil
- 1/4 cup soy sauce
- 2 tsp. fresh ginger, grated
- 12 oz. ground pork
- 1/2 cabbage, shredded (2 cups)
- 4 scallions, green parts (white parts optional), chopped
- 24 egg roll wrappers

Directions:

1. Spray a skillet with cooking oil and place over medium-high heat. Add the garlic. Cook for 1 minute, until fragrant.

2. Add the ground pork to the skillet. Using a spoon, break the pork into smaller chunks.

3. In a small bowl, combine the sesame oil, soy sauce, and ginger. Mix well to combine.

4. Add the sauce to the skillet. Stir to combine. Continue cooking for 5 minutes, until the pork is browned.

5. When the pork has browned, add the cabbage and scallions. Mix well.

6. Transfer the pork mixture to a large bowl.

7. Lay the egg roll wrappers on a flat surface. Dip a basting brush in

water and glaze each of the egg roll wrappers along the edges with the wet brush. This will soften the dough and make it easier to roll.

8. Stack 2 egg roll wrappers (it works best if you double-wrap the egg rolls). Scoop 1–2 tbsp. of the pork mixture onto the center.

9. Roll one long side of the wrappers up over the filling. Press firmly on the area with the filling, tucking it in lightly to secure it in place. Next, fold on the left and right sides.

10. Continue rolling to close. Use the basting brush to wet the seam and seal the egg roll.

11. Place the egg rolls in the basket of the air fryer. It is okay to stack them. Spray them with cooking oil. Cook for 8 minutes.

12. Flip the egg rolls. Cook for an additional 4 minutes.

13. Cool before serving.

Nutrition:

- Calories: 244
- Total fat: 4 g.
- Saturated fat: 1 g.
- Cholesterol: 27 mg.
- Sodium: 683 mg.
- Carbs: 39 g.
- Fiber: 2 g.
- Protein: 12 g.

505. Air Fry Bacon

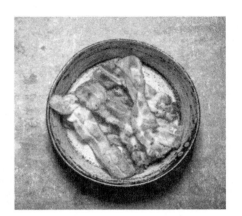

Preparation time: 5 minutes

Cooking time: 10 minutes

Servings: 11

Ingredients:

- 11 bacon slices

Directions:

1. Place half bacon slices in the air fryer basket.
2. Cook at 400°F for 10 minutes.
3. Cook remaining half bacon slices using the same steps.

4. Serve and enjoy.

Nutrition:

- Calories: 103
- Fat: 7.9 g
- Carbs: 0.3 g.
- Sugar: 0 g.
- Protein: 7 g.
- Cholesterol: 21 mg.

506. Crunchy Bacon Bites

Preparation time: 5 minutes

Cooking time: 10 minutes

Servings: 4

Ingredients:

- 4 bacon strips, cut into small pieces
- 1/2 cup pork rinds, crushed
- 1/4 cup hot sauce

Directions:

1. Add bacon pieces to a bowl.
2. Add hot sauce and toss well.
3. Add crushed pork rinds and toss until bacon pieces are well coated.
4. Transfer bacon pieces in the air fryer basket and cook at 350°F for 10 minutes.
5. Serve and enjoy.

Nutrition:

- Calories: 112
- Fat: 9.7 g.
- Carbs: 0.3 g.
- Sugar: 0.2 g.
- Protein: 5.2 g.
- Cholesterol: 3 mg.

507. Easy Jalapeño Poppers

Preparation time: 10 minutes

Cooking time: 13 minutes

Servings: 5

Ingredients:

- 5 jalapeño peppers, slice in half and deseeded
- 2 tbsp. salsa
- 4 oz. goat cheese, crumbled
- 1/4 tsp. chili powder
- 1/2 tsp. garlic, minced
- Pepper
- Salt

Directions:

1. In a small bowl, mix cheese, salsa, chili powder, garlic, pepper, and salt.
2. Spoon cheese mixture into each jalapeño halves and place in the air fryer basket.
3. Cook jalapeño poppers at 350°F for 13 minutes.
4. Serve and enjoy.

Nutrition:

- Calories: 111
- Fat: 8.3 g.
- Carbs: 2.1 g.
- Sugar: 1.2 g.
- Protein: 7.3 g.
- Cholesterol: 24 mg.

508. Perfect Crab Dip

Preparation time: 5 minutes

Cooking time: 7 minutes

Servings: 4

Ingredients:

- 1 cup crabmeat
- 2 tbsp. parsley, chopped
- 2 tbsp. fresh lemon juice
- 2 tbsp. hot sauce
- 1/2 cup green onion, sliced
- 2 cups cheese, grated
- 1/4 cup mayonnaise
- 1/4 tsp. pepper

- 1/2 tsp. salt

Directions:

1. In a 6-inch dish, mix crabmeat, hot sauce, green onion, cheese, mayo, pepper, and salt.
2. Place dish in the air fryer basket and cook dip at 400°F for 7 minutes.
3. Remove dish from air fryer.
4. Drizzle dip with lemon juice and garnish with parsley.
5. Serve and enjoy.

Nutrition:

- Calories: 313
- Fat: 23.9 g.
- Carbs: 8.8 g.
- Sugar: 3.1 g.
- Protein: 16.2 g.
- Cholesterol: 67 mg.

509. Sweet Potato Tots

Preparation time: 10 minutes

Cooking time: 31 minutes

Servings: 24

Ingredients:

- 2 sweet potatoes, peeled
- 1/2 tsp. Cajun seasoning
- Salt
- 1 cup water

Directions:

1. Add water in a large pot and bring to boil. Add sweet potatoes to the pot and boil for 15 minutes. Drain well.
2. Grated boil sweet potatoes into a large bowl using a grated.
3. Add Cajun seasoning and salt in grated sweet potatoes and mix until well combined.
4. Spray air fryer basket with cooking spray.
5. Make small tot of sweet potato mixture and place in the air fryer basket.
6. Cook at 400°F for 8 minutes. Turn tots to another side and cook for 8 minutes more.
7. Serve and enjoy.

Nutrition:

- Calories: 15
- Fat: 0 g.
- Carbs: 3.5 g.
- Sugar: 0.1 g.
- Protein: 0.2 g.
- Cholesterol: 0 mg.

510. Herb Zucchini Slices

Preparation time: 10 minutes

Cooking time: 15 minutes

Servings: 4

Ingredients:

- 2 zucchinis, slice in half lengthwise and cut each half through the middle
- 1 tbsp. olive oil
- 4 tbsp. Parmesan cheese, grated
- 2 tbsp. almond flour
- 1 tbsp. parsley, chopped
- Pepper and salt to taste

Directions:

1. Preheat the air fryer to 350°F.
2. In a bowl, mix cheese, parsley, oil, almond flour, pepper, and salt.
3. Top zucchini pieces with cheese mixture and place in the air fryer basket.
4. Cook zucchini for 15 minutes at 350°F.
5. Serve and enjoy.

Nutrition:

- Calories: 157
- Fat: 11.4 g.
- Carbs: 5.1 g.
- Sugar: 1.7 g.
- Protein: 11 g.
- Cholesterol: 20 mg.

511. Curried Sweet Potato Fries 512.

Preparation time: 10 minutes

Cooking time: 20 minutes

Servings: 3

Ingredients:

- 2 small sweet potatoes, peel and cut into fry's shape
- 1/4 tsp. coriander
- 1/2 tsp. curry powder
- 2 tbsp. olive oil
- 1/4 tsp. sea salt
- Cooking spray

Directions:

1. Add all ingredients into the large mixing bowl and toss well.
2. Spray air fryer basket with cooking spray.
3. Transfer sweet potato fries to the air fryer basket.
4. Cook for 20 minutes at 370°F. Shake halfway through.
5. Serve and enjoy.

Nutrition:

- Calories: 118
- Fat: 9 g.
- Carbs: 9 g.
- Sugar: 2 g.
- Protein: 1 g.
- Cholesterol: 0 mg.

513. Roasted Almonds

Preparation time: 5 minutes

Cooking time: 8 minutes

Servings: 8

Ingredients:

- 2 cups almonds
- 1/4 tsp. pepper
- 1 tsp. paprika
- 1 tbsp. garlic powder
- 1 tbsp. soy sauce
- Cooking spray

Directions:

1. Add pepper, paprika, garlic powder, and soy sauce in a bowl and stir well.
2. Add almonds and stir to coat.
3. Spray air fryer basket with cooking spray.
4. Add almonds in the air fryer basket and cook for 6–8 minutes at 320°F. Shake basket after every 2 minutes.
5. Serve and enjoy.

Nutrition:

- Calories: 143
- Fat: 11.9 g.
- Carbs: 6.2 g.
- Sugar: 1.3 g.
- Protein: 5.4 g.
- Cholesterol: 0 mg.

514. Pepperoni Chips

Preparation time: 2 minutes

Cooking time: 8 minutes

Servings: 6

Ingredients:

- 6 oz. pepperoni slices

Directions:

1. Place one batch of pepperoni slices in the air fryer basket.
2. Cook for 8 minutes at 360°F.
3. Cook remaining pepperoni slices using the same steps.
4. Serve and enjoy.

Nutrition:

- Calories: 51
- Fat: 1 g.
- Carbs: 2 g.
- Sugar: 1.3 g.
- Protein: 0 g.
- Cholesterol: 0 mg.

515. Crispy Eggplant

Preparation time: 5 minutes

Cooking time: 20 minutes

Servings: 4

Ingredients:

- 1 eggplant, cut into 1-inch pieces
- 1/2 tsp. Italian seasoning
- 1 tsp. paprika
- 1/2 tsp. red pepper
- 1 tsp. garlic powder
- 2 tbsp. olive oil

Directions:

1. Add all ingredients into the large mixing bowl and toss well.
2. Transfer eggplant mixture into the air fryer basket.
3. Cook at 375°F for 20 minutes. Shake basket halfway through.
4. Serve and enjoy.

Nutrition:

- Calories: 99
- Fat: 7.5 g.
- Carbs: 8.7 g.
- Sugar: 4.5 g.
- Protein: 1.5 g.
- Cholesterol: 0 mg.

516. Steak Nuggets

Preparation time: 10 minutes

Cooking time: 15 minutes

Servings: 4

Ingredients:

- 1 lb. beef steak, cut into chunks
- 1 egg, large-sized, lightly beaten
- 1/2 cup pork rind, crushed
- 1/2 cup parmesan cheese, grated
- 1/2 tsp. salt

Directions:

1. Add the egg to a small bowl.
2. In a shallow bowl, mix pork rind, cheese, and salt.
3. Dip each steak chunk in egg then coat with pork rind mixture and place on a plate. Place in refrigerator for 30 minutes.
4. Spray air fryer basket with cooking spray.
5. Preheat the air fryer to 400°F.
6. Place steak nuggets in the air fryer basket and cook for 15–18 minutes or until cooked. Shake after every 4 minutes.
7. Serve and enjoy.

Nutrition:

- Calories: 609
- Fat: 38 g.
- Carbs: 2 g.
- Sugar: 0.4 g.
- Protein: 63 g.
- Cholesterol: 195 mg.

517. Cheese Bacon Jalapeño Poppers

Preparation time: 10 minutes

Cooking time: 5 minutes

Servings: 5

Ingredients:

- 10 fresh jalapeño peppers, cut in half, and remove seeds
- 2 bacon slices, cooked and crumbled
- 1/4 cup cheddar cheese, shredded
- 6 oz. cream cheese, softened
- Cooking spray

Directions:

1. In a bowl, combine bacon, cream cheese, and cheddar cheese.
2. Stuff each jalapeño half with bacon cheese mixture.
3. Spray air fryer basket with cooking spray.
4. Place stuffed jalapeño halved in air fryer basket and cook at 370°F for 5 minutes.
5. Serve and enjoy.

Nutrition:

- **Calories:** 195
- **Fat:** 17.3 g.
- **Carbs:** 3.2 g.
- **Sugar:** 1 g.
- **Protein:** 7.2 g.
- **Cholesterol:** 52 mg.

518. Cabbage Chips

Preparation time: 10 minutes

Cooking time: 30 minutes

Servings: 6

Ingredients:

- 1 large cabbage head, tear cabbage leaves into pieces
- 2 tbsp. olive oil
- 1/4 cup parmesan cheese, grated
- Pepper
- Salt

Directions:

1. Preheat the air fryer to 250°F.
2. Add all ingredients

into the large mixing bowl and toss well.

3. Spray air fryer basket with cooking spray.

4. Divide cabbage in batches.

5. Add one cabbage chips batch in the air fryer basket and cook for 25–30 minutes at 250°F or until chips are crispy and lightly golden brown.

6. Serve and enjoy.

Nutrition:

- Calories: 96
- Fat: 5.1 g.
- Carbs: 12.1 g.
- Sugar: 6.7 g.
- Protein: 3 g.
- Cholesterol: 1 mg.

519. Fried Calzones

Preparation time: 10 minutes

Cooking time: 30 minutes

Servings: 2

Ingredients:

- 1 tsp. olive oil
- 1/4 cup red onion, finely chopped
- 3 cups baby spinach leaves
- 1/3 cup rotisserie chicken breast, shredded
- 1/3 cup marinara sauce, low-sodium
- 6 oz. whole-wheat pizza dough, fresh prepared
- 1 1/2 oz. mozzarella cheese, pre-shredded part-skim (about 6 tbsp.)
- Cooking spray

Directions:

1. Get a medium-sized non-stick skillet and in it, heat the oil over medium-high. Toss in the onions, and cook while stirring occasionally. Stop cooking when the onions are tender—this takes about 2 minutes.

2. Now toss in the spinach, and allow to cook until wilted, while covering the skillet. This takes about 1.5 minutes. With-draw the pan from the heat and stir in the chicken and the marinara sauce.

3. Halve the dough into 4 and roll each piece on a lightly floured surface to form a 6-inch circle. Place 1/4-th of the spinach mixture over half of each dough circle, and top with 1/4-th of the cheese. Form half-moons by folding the dough

over the filling, and crimp the edges to seal.

4. Transfer the calzones into the air fryer basket and allow cooking for 12 minutes at 325°F, or until you have the golden-brown dough. Turn the calzones to the other side after the first 8 minutes.

5. Serve.

Nutrition:

- Calories: 200
- Fat: 15 g.
- Protein: 22 g.
- Sugar: 7 g.

520. Reuben Calzones

Preparation time: 10 minutes

Cooking time: 30 minutes

Servings: 6

Ingredients:

- Cooking spray
- 1 tube (13.8 oz.) refrigerated pizza crust
- 4 slices Swiss cheese
- 1 cup sauerkraut, rinsed and well drained
- 1/2 lb. sliced cooked corned beef
- Thousand Island salad dressing

Directions:

1. Ensure that your air fryer is preheated to 400°F.
2. Drizzle some cooking spray over the air fryer basket.
3. Prepare a lightly floured surface, and on it, unroll the pizza crust dough while patting it into a 12-inches square.
4. Cut the dough into 4 squares. Layer a slice of the cheese, 1/4 cup of the sauerkraut, and the corned beef diagonally over half of each square to within 1/2-inch of edges.
5. Form a triangle by folding one corner over filling to the opposite corner. Seal by pressing the edges with your fork.
6. Arrange 2 calzones in a single layer in the sprayed air fryer basket.
7. Allow cooking for about 8–12 minutes or until the calzones are golden brown. Turn the sides after

4–6 minutes of cooking.

8. When fully cooked, withdraw and keep warm while preparing the other calzones.

9. Serve alongside salad dressing.

Nutrition:

- Calories: 176
- Fat: 8 g.
- Protein: 15 g.
- Sugar: 10 g.

521. Popcorn

Preparation time: 10 minutes

Cooking time: 30 minutes

Servings: 6

Ingredients:

- 3 tbsp. corn kernels, dried
- Spray avocado oil (Substitutes: safflower oil; coconut oil; peanut oil)
- Sea salt and ground black pepper to taste

Garnish:

- 2 tbsp. nutritional yeast
- Dried chives

Directions:

1. Ensure that your air fryer is set to 390°F.
2. In the air fryer basket, arrange the ker-nels gently and light-spray some coconut or avocado oil. You may line the tray sides with aluminum foil—this ensures that the popped popcorn does not escape the basket.
3. Return the air fryer basket into the air fryer and allow cooking for 15 minutes. Pay close attention to the cooking kernels to ensure that they do not burn.
4. At the sound of popping sounds, monitor closely until they do not pop anymore—or until the 15 minute's lapses.
5. Withdraw the basket immediately and transfer the contents into a large bowl.
6. Spray the cooked kernels with some avocado or coconut oil.
7. Dust with garnish according to your preference.
8. Serve warm or at room temperature.

Nutrition:

- Calories: 242
- Fat: 13 g.
- Protein: 17 g.
- Sugar: 8 g.

522. Mexican-Style Corn on the Cob

Preparation time: 15 minutes

Cooking time: 25 minutes

Servings: 4

Ingredients:

- 4 ears fresh corn (about 1 1/2 lbs.), shucked
- Cooking spray
- 1 1/2 tbsp. unsalted butter
- 1 tsp. lime zest
- 2 tsp. garlic, chopped
- 1 tbsp. fresh juice (from 1 lime)
- 1/2 tsp. black pepper
- 2 tbsp. fresh cilantro, chopped
- 1/2 tsp. kosher salt

Directions:

1. Coat your corn mildly with some cooking spray before placing it in the air fryer basket following a single layer. Allow cooking at 400°F until the corn is tender or mildly charred—this takes about 14 minutes. Turn the corn over after the first 7 minutes of cooking.
2. While cooking the corn, get a small bowl that is suitable for microwaving, and in it, combine the butter, lime zest, garlic, and lime juice.
3. Set the microwave to "high" and microwave the mixture until the butter is melted and the fragrance of the garlic obvious—this takes about 30 seconds.
4. Transfer the corn to a platter, and pour the butter mixture on it.
5. Add sprinkles of pepper, cilantro, and salt to taste.
6. Serve immediately.

Nutrition:

- Calories: 198
- Fat: 9 g.
- Protein: 22 g.
- Sugar: 2 g.

523. Salt and Vinegar Chickpeas

Preparation time: 25 minutes

Cooking time: 55 minutes

Servings: 2

Ingredients:

- 1 (15 oz.) can chickpeas, drained and rinsed
- 1 cup white vinegar
- 1/2 tsp. sea salt
- 1 tbsp. olive oil

Directions:

1. Get a clean small saucepan, and in it, combine chickpeas and vinegar. Bring to a simmer over high heat. Once simmering, withdraw and allow to stand for 30 minutes.
2. Drain the chickpeas and get rid of all loose skins.
3. Ensure that your air fryer is preheated to 390°F.
4. With the chickpeas spread evenly in the air fryer basket, allow cooking for about 4 minutes or until the chickpeas dry out.
5. Move the dried chickpeas into a heat-proof bowl. Drizzle with sea salt and oil and stir to coat evenly.
6. Place the coated chickpeas into the air fryer again and allow cooking for about 8 minutes. Endeavor to shake the basket at 2–3 minutes intervals. Withdraw once you have lightly browned chickpeas.
7. Serve instantly.

Nutrition:

- Calories: 386
- Fat: 11 g.
- Protein: 22 g.
- Sugar: 7 g.

524. Curry Chickpeas

Preparation time: 15 minutes

Cooking time: 35 minutes

Servings: 4

Ingredients:

- 1 (15-oz) can chickpeas (garbanzo beans), no-salt-added, drained and rinsed (about 1 1/2 cups)
- 2 tbsp. olive oil
- 2 tbsp. red wine vinegar
- 1/4 tsp. coriander, ground
- 1/8 tsp. cinnamon, ground
- 1/4 tsp. cumin, ground
- 2 tsp. curry powder
- 1/2 tsp. turmeric
- Fresh cilantro, thinly sliced
- 1/2 tsp. Aleppo pepper
- 1/4 tsp. kosher salt

Directions:

1. Smash the chickpeas mildly in a medium bowl with your hands. Remove the chickpea skins.
2. Pour over the oil and vinegar into the chickpeas. Stir to coat evenly, and add coriander, cinnamon, cumin, curry powder, and turmeric. Stir the mixture gently to combine.
3. In the air fryer basket, arrange the chickpeas in a single layer and allow cooking at 400°F for about 15 minutes or until the chickpeas are crispy. Ensure that you shake the chickpeas after the first 7–8 minutes of cooking.
4. Move the cooked chickpeas into a bowl, while sprinkling the cilantro, Aleppo pepper, and salt— toss to coat.

Nutrition:

- Calories: 409
- Fat: 16.6 g.
- Protein: 38.6 g.
- Sugar: 17.2 g.

525. Buffalo-Ranch Chickpeas

Preparation time: 15 minutes

Cooking time: 35 minutes

Servings: 2

Ingredients:

- 1 (15 oz.) can chickpeas, drained and rinsed
- 2 tbsp. Buffalo wing sauce
- 1 tbsp. dry ranch dressing mix

Directions:

1. Ensure that your air fryer is preheated to 350°F.
2. After lining your baking sheet with paper towels, spread the chickpeas over the lined paper towels. Cover the chickpeas with another layer of paper towels, and press gently to drain any excess moisture.
3. Place the chickpeas in a bowl and pour in the wing sauce. Stir the mixture to combine.
4. Add ranch dressing powder and mix well to combine.
5. Arrange the air fryer in an even layer in the air fryer basket.
6. Allow cooking for 8 minutes. Stop, shake, and cook for an extra 5 minutes, shake again, and cook for 5 minutes more, and shake again for the last time, before cooking for the final 2 minutes.
7. Set aside the cooked chickpeas for about 5 minutes to allow cooling.
8. Serve immediately.

Nutrition:

- Calories: 106
- Fat: 13 g.
- Protein: 26 g.
- Sugar :19 g.

526. Whole-Wheat Pizzas

Preparation time: 10 minutes

Cooking time: 20 minutes

Servings: 2

Ingredients:

- 2 whole-wheat pita rounds
- 1/4 cup marinara sauce, low-sodium
- 1 cup baby spinach leaves (1 oz.)
- 1 oz. mozzarella cheese, pre-shredded, part-skim (about 1/4 cup)
- 1 garlic clove, small, thinly sliced
- 1 plum tomato, small, cut into 8 slices
- 1/4 oz. Parmigiano-Reggiano cheese, shaved (about 1 tbsp.)

Directions:

1. Layout your pita bread.
2. Spread the marina sauce evenly over the side facing upwards. Add half of the spinach leaves, cheeses, garlic, and tomato slices as toppings.
3. Transfer each pita into the air fryer basket, and allow cooking at 350°F for about 4–5 minutes or until you have melted cheese.
4. Do the same for other pitas.

Nutrition:

- Calories: 300
- Fat: 10 g.
- Protein: 33 g.
- Sugar: 9 g.

527. Basic Hot Dogs

Preparation time: 10 minutes

Cooking time: 15 minutes

Servings: 4

Ingredients:

- 4 hot dog buns
- 4 hot dogs

Directions:

1. Ensure that your air fryer is preheated to 390°F.
2. Move your burns into the air fryer basket and allow cooking for 2 minutes.
3. Withdraw the cooked buns to a plate.
4. Replace the buns with the hot dogs, and allow cooking for 3 minutes.
5. Withdraw and place

on the same plate as the buns.

6. Serve.

Nutrition:

- Calories: 190
- Fat: 7 g.
- Protein: 29 g.
- Sugar: 13 g.

528. Feta Cheese Dough Balls

Preparation time: 10 minutes

Cooking time: 25 minutes

Servings: 8

Ingredients:

- Leftover pizza dough gets the recipe here
- 1 tbsp. Greek yogurt
- 2 oz. soft cheese
- 1 tsp. mustard
- 1 tsp. garlic puree
- 1 tbsp. olive oil
- 2 tsp. Rosemary
- Salt and ground black pepper to taste
- 2 oz. feta cheese

Directions:

1. After removing it from the fridge, allow the pizza dough to acclimatize to room temperature so that working with it is easy.

2. Combine the dough with some flour and knead for a while. This makes the dough soft and gives it the local dough feel. Set aside.

3. In a clean mixing bowl, combine all the ingredients, except the feta and the dough. Mix thoroughly to form a creamy paste.

4. Make 8 equal-sized pieces from the dough and flatten each piece out like a pancake.

5. Top each flat piece with about 1/3 tsp. of the ingredients mix. Now, add a little square of feta and seal it up.

6. Repeat the same process for the

other 7 flatten pieces, so that you have 8 top nice little balls.

7. Now transfer them into the air fryer and allow cooking for 10 minutes at 360°F.

8. Reduce the heat to 320°F and allow cook-ing for an additional 5 minutes.

Nutrition:

- Calories: 245
- Fat: 2 g.
- Protein: 18 g.
- Sugar: 1.3 g.

529. Flourless Crunchy Cheese Straws

Preparation time: 20 minutes

Cooking time: 50 minutes

Servings: 8

Ingredients:

- 4 oz. oats, gluten-free
- 1 large cauliflower
- 1 egg, large sized
- 6 oz. cheddar cheese
- 1 red onion peeled and thinly diced
- 1 tsp. mustard
- 1 tsp. mixed herbs
- Salt and ground black pepper to taste

Directions:

1. Blitz your oats in a food processor until you have the appearance of fine bread-crumbs.

2. Place your cauliflower florets in the steamer and allow to steam for 20 minutes. Immediately after steaming, drain and allow the florets to cool. Get rid of all excess water by squeezing out using a clean pillowcase.

3. Divide the cauliflower into 2, and move the half into a separate bowl, alongside the other ingredients. Mix well to form a dough and if necessary add some more cauliflower to ensure an even combination.

4. Twist the mixture into straw strips and move them into the air fryer baking mat.

5. Allow cooking for 10 minutes at 360°F.

6. Switch sides and allow cooking for an-other 10 minutes at 360°F.
7. Serve.

Nutrition:

- Calories: 109
- Fat: 23 g.
- Protein: 45 g.
- Sugar: 0 g.

530. Veggie Wontons

Preparation time: 10 minutes

Cooking time: 15 minutes

Servings: 10

Ingredients:

- Cooking spray
- 1/2 cup white onion, grated
- 1/2 cup mushrooms, chopped
- 1/2 cup carrot, grated
- 3/4 cup red pepper, chopped
- 3/4 cup cabbage, grated
- 1 tbsp. chili sauce
- 1 tsp. garlic powder
- Salt and pepper to taste
- 30 vegan wonton wrappers
- Water

Directions:

1. Spray oil in a pan.
2. Put the pan over medium heat and cook the onion, mushrooms, carrot, red pepper, and cabbage until tender.
3. Stir in the chili sauce, garlic powder, salt, and pepper.
4. Let it cool for a few minutes.
5. Add a scoop of the mixture on top of the wrappers.
6. Fold and seal the corners using water.
7. Cook in the air fryer at 320°F for 7 minutes or until golden brown.

Nutrition:

- Calories: 290
- Total fat: 1.5 g.
- Saturated fat: 0.3 g.
- Cholesterol: 9 mg.

- Sodium: 593 mg.
- Total Carbohydrate: 58 g.
- Dietary Fiber: 2.3 g.
- Total Sugar: 1.3 g.
- Protein: 9.9 g.
- Potassium: 147 mg.

531. Avocado Rolls

Preparation time: 20 minutes

Cooking time: 25 minutes

Servings: 5

Ingredients:

- 10 rice paper wrappers
- 3 avocados, sliced
- 1 tomato, diced
- Salt and pepper to taste
- 1 tbsp. olive oil
- 4 tbsp. sriracha
- 2 tbsp. sugar
- 1 tbsp. rice vinegar
- 1 tbsp. sesame oil
- 1 cup of water

Directions:

1. Mash avocados in a bowl.
2. Stir in the tomatoes, salt, and pepper.
3. Mix well.
4. Arrange the rice paper wrappers.
5. Scoop mixture on top.
6. Roll and seal the edges with water.
7. Cook in the air fryer at 350°F for 5 minutes.
8. Mix the rest of the ingredients.
9. Serve rolls with the sriracha dipping sauce.

Nutrition:

- Calories: 422
- Saturated fat: 5.8 g.
- Cholesterol: 0 mg.
- Sodium: 180 mg.
- Total Carbohydrate: 38.7 g.
- Dietary Fiber: 8.8 g.
- Total Sugar: 6.5 g.
- Protein: 3.8g
- Potassium: 633 mg.

532. Fried Ravioli

Preparation time: 15 minutes

Cooking time: 8 minutes

Servings: 4

Ingredients:

- 1/2 cup panko breadcrumbs
- Salt and pepper to taste
- 1 tsp. garlic powder
- 1 tsp. oregano, dried
- 1 tsp. basil, dried
- 2 tsp. nutritional yeast flakes
- 1/4 cup Aquafina® liquid
- 8 oz. frozen vegan ravioli
- Cooking spray
- 1/2 cup marinara sauce

Directions:

1. Mix the breadcrumbs, salt, pepper, garlic powder, oregano, basil, and nutritional yeast flakes on a plate.
2. In another bowl, pour the Aquafina® liquid.
3. Dip each ravioli into the liquid and then coat it with the breadcrumb mixture.
4. Put the ravioli in the air fryer.
5. Spray oil on the raviolis.
6. Cook at 390°F for 6 minutes.
7. Flip each one and cook for another 2 minutes.
8. Serve with marinara sauce.

Nutrition:

- Calories: 154
- Total fat: 3.8 g.
- Saturated fat: 0.6g
- Cholesterol: 7 mg.
- Sodium: 169 mg.
- Total Carbohydrate: 18.4 g.
- Dietary Fiber: 1.5 g.
- Total Sugar: 3 g.
- Protein: 4.6 g.
- Potassium: 154 mg .

533. Corn Fritters

Preparation time: 15 minutes

Cooking time: 10 minutes

Servings: 4

Ingredients:

- 1/4 cup cornmeal, ground
- 1/4 cup flour
- Salt and pepper to taste
- 1/2 tsp. baking powder
- 1/4 tsp. garlic powder
- 1/4 tsp. onion powder
- 1/4 tsp. paprika
- 1/4 cup parsley, chopped
- 1 cup corn kernels mixed with 3 tbsp. almond milk
- 2 cups fresh corn kernels
- 4 tbsp. vegan mayonnaise
- 2 tsp. grainy mustard

Directions:

1. Mix the cornmeal, flour, salt, pepper, baking powder, garlic powder, onion powder, paprika, and parsley in a bowl.
2. Put the corn kernels with almond milk in a food processor.
3. Season with salt and pepper.
4. Pulse until well blended.
5. Add the corn kernels.
6. Transfer to a bowl and stir into the cornmeal mixture.
7. Pour a small amount of the batter into the air fryer pan.
8. Pour another a few centimeters away from the first fritter.
9. Cook in the air fryer at 350°F for 10 minutes or until golden.
10. Flip halfway through.
11. Serve with mayo mustard dip.

Nutrition:

- Calories: 135
- Total fat: 4.6 g.
- Saturated fat: 0.2 g.
- Cholesterol: 0 mg.
- Sodium: 136 mg.
- Total Carbohydrate: 22.5 g.
- Dietary Fiber: 2.5 g.
- Total Sugar: 2.7 g.
- Protein: 3.5 g.
- Potassium: 308 mg.

534. Mushroom Pizza

Preparation time: 15 minutes

Cooking time: 10 minutes

Servings: 4

Ingredients:

- 4 large Portobello mushrooms, stems and gills removed
- 1 tsp. balsamic vinegar
- Salt and pepper to taste
- 4 tbsp. vegan pasta sauce
- 1 garlic clove, minced
- 3 oz. zucchini, chopped
- 4 olives, sliced
- 2 tbsp. sweet red pepper, diced
- 1 tsp. basil, dried
- 1/2 cups hummus
- Fresh basil, minced

Directions:

1. Coat the mushrooms with balsamic vinegar and season with salt and pepper.
2. Spread pasta sauce inside each mushroom.
3. Sprinkle with minced garlic.
4. Preheat your air fryer to 330°F.
5. Cook mushrooms for 3 minutes.
6. Take the mushrooms out and top with zucchini, olives, and peppers.
7. Season with salt, pepper, and basil.
8. Put them back to the air fryer and cook for another 3 minutes.
9. Serve mushroom pizza with hummus and fresh basil.

Nutrition:

- Calories: 70
- Total fat: 1.56 g.
- Saturated fat: 0.5 g.
- Cholesterol: 12 mg.
- Sodium: 167 mg.
- Total Carbohydrate: 11 g.
- Dietary Fiber: 3.4 g.
- Total Sugar: 3.8 g.
- Protein: 4.3 g.
- Potassium: 350 mg.

535. Onion Appetizers

Preparation time: 10 minutes

Cooking time: 4 minutes

Servings: 4

Ingredients:

- 2 lb. onions, sliced into rings
- 2 vegan eggs
- 1 cup almond milk
- 2 cups flour
- 1 tbsp. paprika
- Salt and pepper to taste
- 1 tsp. garlic powder
- 1 tsp. cayenne pepper
- Cooking spray
- 1/4 cup vegan mayo
- 1/4 cup vegan sour cream
- 1 tbsp. ketchup

Directions:

1. Combine the eggs and milk on one plate.
2. On another plate, mix the flour, paprika, salt, pepper, garlic powder, and cayenne pepper.
3. Dip each onion into the egg mixture before coating it with the flour mixture.
4. Spray with oil.
5. Air fryer at 350°F for 4 minutes or until golden and crispy.
6. Serve with the dipping sauces.

Nutrition:

- Calories: 364
- Total fat: 14.5 g.
- Saturated fat: 10.3 g.
- Cholesterol: 0 mg.
- Sodium: 143 mg.
- Total Carbohydrate: 52.7 g.
- Dietary Fiber: 7.2 g.
- Total Sugar: 9.3 g.
- Protein: 8.1 g.
- Potassium: 434 mg.

536. Crispy Brussels Sprouts

Preparation time: 5 minutes

Cooking time: 1 minute

Servings: 2

Ingredients:

- 2 cups Brussels sprouts, sliced
- 1 tbsp. olive oil
- 1 tbsp. balsamic vinegar
- Salt to taste

Directions:

1. Toss all the ingredients in a bowl.
2. Cook in the air fryer at 400°F for 10 minutes, shake once or twice during the cooking process.
3. Check to see if crispy enough.
4. If not, cook for another 5 minutes.

Nutrition:

- Calories: 100
- Total fat: 7.3 g.
- Saturated fat: 1.1 g.
- Cholesterol: 0 mg.
- Sodium: 100 mg.
- Total Carbohydrate: 8.1g.
- Dietary Fiber: 3.3 g.
- Total Sugar: 1.9 g.
- Protein: 3 g.
- Potassium: 348 mg.

537. Popcorn Tofu

Preparation time: 15 minutes

Cooking time: 12 minutes

Servings: 4

Ingredients:

- 1/2 cup cornmeal
- 1/2 cup quinoa flour
- 1 tbsp. vegan bouillon
- 2 tbsp. nutritional yeast
- 1 tsp. garlic powder
- 1 tsp. onion powder
- 1 tbsp. mustard
- Salt and pepper to taste
- 3/4 cup almond milk
- 1 1/2 cups breadcrumbs
- 14 oz. tofu, sliced into small pieces
- 1/2 cup vegan mayo
- 2 tbsp. hot sauce

Directions:

1. In the first bowl, mix the first 8 ingredients.
2. In the second bowl, pour the almond milk.
3. In the third bowl, add the breadcrumbs.
4. Dip each tofu slice into each of the bowls starting from the flour mixture, then the almond milk, and finally in the breadcrumbs.
5. Cook in the air fryer at 350°F for 12 minutes, shaking halfway through.
6. Mix the mayo and hot sauce and serve with tofu.

Nutrition:

- Calories: 261
- Total fat: 5.5g
- Saturated fat: 1 g.
- Cholesterol: 12 mg.
- Sodium: 120 mg.
- Total Carbohydrate: 37.5 g.
- Dietary Fiber: 4.8 g.
- Total Sugar: 3 g.
- Protein: 16 g.
- Potassium 430 mg.

538. Black Bean Burger

Preparation time: 10 minutes

Cooking time: 25 minutes

Servings: 6

Ingredients:

- 1 1/4 cup rolled oats
- 16 oz. black beans, rinsed and drained
- 3/4 cup salsa
- 1 tbsp. soy sauce
- 1 1/4 tsp. chili powder
- 1/4 tsp. chipotle chili powder
- 1/2 tsp. garlic powder

Directions:

1. Pulse the oats inside a food processor until powdery.
2. Add all the other ingredients and pulse until well

blended.

3. Transfer to a bowl and refrigerate for 15 minutes.
4. Form into burger patties.
5. Cook in the air fryer at 375°F for 15 minutes.

Nutrition:

- Calories: 158
- Total fat: 2 g.
- Saturated fat: 1 g.
- Cholesterol: 10 mg.
- Sodium: 690 mg.
- Total Carbohydrate: 30 g.
- Dietary Fiber: 9 g.
- Total Sugar: 2.7 g.
- Protein: 8 g.
- Potassium: 351 mg.

539. Crisp Sweet Potato Fries

Preparation time: 5 minutes

Cooking time: 16 minutes

Servings: 2–4

Ingredients:

- 2 sweet potatoes sliced to own preference, peeling is optional
- 1/2 tbsp. chili powder (optional)
- 1/2 tbsp. garlic powder
- 2 tsp. onion powder
- 2 tsp. paprika
- 1 tbsp. olive oil or canola oil
- Salt and pepper to taste
- Vegetable oil to spray

Directions:

1. Thoroughly rinse and dry the sweet potatoes. Slice into circles (1/8-inch), keeping thickness even.
2. Pat the slices dry with paper towels and place them into a large mixing bowl and add the olive oil. Toss the sweet potato slices so that both sides are coated in oil.
3. Add the chili powder, garlic powder, paprika, onion powder, salt, and pepper to the mixing bowl and gently mix to ensure the sweet potato slices are evenly coated in the spices and herbs.
4. Spray the rotisserie basket with cooking oil and place a single layer of sweet potato fries inside the basket.
5. Place the rotisserie basket inside the

Vortex Air Fryer.

6. Press rotate and heat the oven to 360°F and set the cooking time for 22 minutes.

7. The sweet potato fries are ready when the edges have started crisping and golden.

8. Place the fries on a paper towel-lined cooling rack. Please note that the fries crisp during the cooling downtime.

9. Repeat the cooking process with the next batch of fries.

10. Sweet potato chips are best eaten fresh on the day. They can be stored in an airtight container but may lose their crispness.

Nutrition:

- Calories: 187
- Fat: 10 g.
- Protein: 12 g.
- Sugar: 2 g.

540. Snack-Sized Calzones

Preparation time: 25 minutes

Cooking time: 12–15 minutes

Servings: 16

Ingredients:

- 1 lb. pizza dough (at room temperature for 1 hour before use)
- All-purpose flour to roll out the pizza dough
- 8 oz. mozzarella cheese, shredded
- 1 cup pizza sauce of your choice
- Extra pizza sauce as a dip, or dip sauce of own choice
- 6 oz. of pepperoni, sliced thinly

Directions:

1. Lightly flour a

workspace and place pizza dough on it. Roll dough out to a 1/4-inch thickness. Cut out 8 circles with a 3-inch biscuit cutter (or use a large glass). Place the circles on a baking sheet lined with parchment paper.

2. Shape leftover dough into a ball and roll out to a 1/4-inch thickness until you have 16 dough circles altogether.

3. Place 1 tsp. of pepperoni, 1 tbsp. sauce, and 2 tsp. cheese on top of each dough circle.

4. Fold each dough circle over and press edges together. To ensure that the *calzones* are fully sealed, crimp the edges of the dough with a fork.

5. Place the *calzones* on 2 cooking trays, making sure that they do not touch, and place cooking trays into the oven using the middle and bottom positions.

6. Heat your air fryer to 375°F and cook *calzones* for about 8 minutes; they should be golden and crisp.

7. If you have any *calzones* left over, repeat the air frying process.

8. Place *calzones* on a cooling rack to cool down slightly and serve with dipping sauce.

9. *Calzones* can be stored for up to 5 days in an airtight container in the fridge.

Nutrition:

- Calories: 376
- Fat: 11 g.
- Protein: 28 g.
- Sugar: 4 g.

541. Jalapeño and Cheese Balls

Preparation time: 15 minutes

Cooking time: 10 minutes

Servings: 22

Ingredients:

- 1 cup jalapeños, diced (if this is too hot, use 1/2 cup jalapeños and 1/2 bell peppers)
- 1/2 cup all-purpose flour
- 12 bacon slices
- 3 eggs
- 1/2 cup scallions
- 2 cups breadcrumbs panko, or as per your preference
- 8 oz. cream cheese brought to room temperature to soften
- 1/4 tsp. onion powder
- 2 cups cheddar cheese, shredded, sharp flavored
- 1/4 tsp. garlic powder
- 3 tbsp. green pepper sauce (Tabasco® mild green pepper sauce)
- 2 tbsp. milk
- Salt and pepper to taste

Directions:

1. Prepare 2 cooking trays and spray with vegetable oil of your own choice.
2. Line a flat baking sheet with wax paper and set it aside.
3. Cook bacon in a skillet until cooked through and cut into small pieces.
4. Cut jalapeños (and bell pepper if using) and slice scallions thinly.
5. Place the chopped bacon, softened cream cheese, garlic powder, jalapeños, shredded cheddar cheese, green pepper sauce, onion powder, scallions, and salt and pepper into a mixing bowl and mix to combine all the ingredients.
6. Use an ice cream scoop to make balls of roughly 1 1/2 –2 inches and place the balls on the wax paper-lined baking sheet. Place the baking sheet with the balls into the freezer for about 15 minutes. You can omit this step, but freezing the balls for a while makes them much easier to work with when you start dredging them.
7. Preheat the air fryer oven to 400°F on the "Air Fryer" mode.

8. Place 3 mixing bowls on a work surface for dredging.

9. Place the flour into the first bowl, whisk the milk and eggs in a second bowl, and place the breadcrumbs into the third bowl.

10. Roll each ball first in the flour, then in the egg mixture, and lastly in the breadcrumbs. If you prefer a thicker crust, you can repeat the dredging procedure with each ball.

11. Place the balls on the prepared cooking trays, making sure that they don't touch.

12. Cook the balls for 10–12 minutes; they must be golden brown and crisp on the outside.

13. Remove jalapeño balls from the cooking trays with silicone tongs and serve with a dipping sauce.

14. Dip sauce suggestions: marinara sauce, sour cream with smoky paprika chipotle seasoning, or homemade guacamole.

Nutrition:

- Calories: 342
- Fat: 12 g.
- Protein:21 g.
- Sugar: 22 g.

542. Parmesan Chicken Nuggets

Preparation time: 10 minutes

Cooking time: 8 minutes

Servings: 2–4

Ingredients:

- 2 skinned and fileted chicken breasts
- 1 1/2 cups dried breadcrumbs (panko or own preference, can also be substituted with crushed cornflakes)
- Vegetable oil spray
- 1/4 –1/2 cup parmesan cheese
- 1 tsp. Italian seasoning
- 2 tsp. sweet paprika
- 1/3 cup olive oil (more can be added as needed)
- Salt and pepper to

taste

Directions:

1. Set out 2 mixing bowls. Add olive oil to one mixing bowl and add the rest of the ingredients to the other bowl.
2. Cut chicken roughly into 1 1/2-inch cubes (can be slightly smaller if preferred).
3. Lightly spray 2 of the oven's cooking trays and make sure that the drip tray is in place inside the oven.
4. Place chicken cubes one by one into the olive oil and then into the bowl holding the coating ingredients, making sure that each nugget is fully coated.
5. Place the coated chicken cubes onto the cooking trays without the cubes touching each other.
6. Turn the fryer oven to 400°F and cook the chicken cubes for about 8 minutes until crisp (internal temp should be 165°F).
7. Serve with your own choice of dip sauces.

Nutrition:

- Calories: 254
- Fat: 10 g.
- Protein: 16 g.
- Sugar: 2 g.

543. Date Tapas

Preparation time: 5 minutes

Cooking time: 7 minutes

Servings: 2

Ingredients:

- 1 packet pitted dates (variations pitted prunes or maraschino cherries)
- 1 packet bacon (or more, depends on the number of tapas you wish to make)

Directions:

1. Cut all the bacon slices in half.
2. Wrap each pitted prune in a half slice of bacon and place it on the cooking tray. You can pack 2 cooking trays to cook at a time.
3. Heat the air fryer

oven to 500°F and cook them for 7 minutes on the air fryer setting of the oven.

4. It can be served warm or cold.

Nutrition:

- Calories: 398
- Fat: 5 g.
- Protein: 15 g.
- Sugar: 4 g.

544. Hush Puppies

Preparation time: 10 minutes

Cooking time: 10 minutes

Servings: 12

Ingredients:

- 3/4 cup all-purpose flour (can be substituted with gluten-free flour)
- 1 cup cornmeal, yellow
- 1/4 tsp. sugar
- 1/2 tsp. salt
- 1 1/2 tsp. baking powder
- 1 egg
- 1/4 cup onion, finely chopped
- 3/4 milk (whole milk, reduced-fat milk, fat-free, or low-fat milk works equally well)
- Vegetable oil for spraying

Directions:

1. Place flour, baking powder, cornmeal, salt, and sugar into a large mixing bowl and stir to combine. Add in the chopped onion.

2. Add milk and egg to the mixture and whisk until all ingredients are combined.

3. Set batter aside to rest and for the dough to firm up for about 5 minutes.

4. Spray 2 cooking trays with non-stick spray.

5. Divide the dough into 12 balls and form small balls with your hands.

6. Set temperature to 390°F for the air fryer function.

7. Place dough balls well-spaced on the cooking trays and insert them into the

oven using the center and bottom positions.

8. Cook for 5 minutes, then use silicone tongs to turn hush puppies over, spray them with oil spray, and continue cooking for another 5 minutes.

9. When they are crisp, check to make sure they are cooked through and return to the oven for a few minutes if necessary.

10. Remove from cooking trays and place them on a wire cooling rack.

11. It can be served hot or cold with a dipping sauce of your preference.

Nutrition:

- Calories: 173
- Fat: 2 g.
- Protein: 40 g.

- Sugar: 2 g.

545. Flavorful Salsa

Preparation time: 10 minutes

Cooking time: 30 minutes

Servings: 8

Ingredients:

- 12 cups fresh tomatoes, peeled, seeded, and diced
- 3 tbsp. cayenne pepper
- 2 tbsp. garlic powder
- 3 tbsp. sugar
- 1/2 cup vinegar
- 12 oz. can tomato paste
- 1 cup jalapeño pepper, chopped
- 3 onions, chopped
- 2 green peppers, chopped
- 1 tbsp. salt

Directions:

1. Add all ingredients into the instant vortex and stir well.
2. Seal pot with lid and cook on manual high pressure for 30 minutes.
3. Once done then allow to release pressure naturally then open the lid.
4. Allow cooling completely then serve or store.

Nutrition:

- Calories: 145
- Fat: 1.1 g.
- Carbs: 32.5 g.
- Sugar: 20.3 g.
- Protein: 5.1 g.
- Cholesterol: 0 mg.

546. Cheddar Cheese Dip

Preparation time: 10 minutes

Cooking time: 9 minutes

Servings: 16

Ingredients:

- 1 lb. bacon slices, cooked and crumbled
- 1 green onion, sliced
- 1/4 cup heavy cream
- 2 cups cheddar cheese, shredded
- 1 cup non-alcoholic beer
- 1 tsp. garlic powder
- 1 1/2 tbsp. Dijon mustard
- 1/4 cup sour cream
- 18 oz. cream cheese, softened

Directions:

1. Add cream cheese, bacon, beer, garlic powder, mustard, and sour cream into the instant vortex and stir well.
2. Seal pot with lid and cook on manual high pressure for 5 minutes.
3. Once done then release pressure using the quick-release method then open the lid.
4. Stir in heavy cream and cheese and cook on "Sauté" mode for 3–4 minutes.
5. Garnish with green onion and serve.

Nutrition:

- Calories: 195
- Fat: 17.4 g.
- Carbs: 2 g.
- Sugar: 0.2 g.
- Protein: 6.3 g.
- Cholesterol: 54 mg.

547. Creamy Eggplant Dip

Preparation time: 10 minutes

Cooking time: 20 minutes

Servings: 4

Ingredients:

- 1 eggplant
- 1/8 tsp. paprika
- 1/2 tbsp. olive oil
- 1/2 lemon juice
- 2 tbsp. tahini
- 1 garlic clove
- 1 cup of water
- 1/8 tsp. salt

Directions:

1. Pour water into the instant vortex then place eggplant into the pot.
2. Seal pot with lid and cook on manual mode for 20 minutes.
3. Once done then release pressure using the quick-release method then open the lid.
4. Remove eggplant from the pot and let it cool.
5. Remove the skin of the eggplant and place eggplant flesh into the food processor.
6. Add remaining ingredients into the food processor and process until smooth.
7. Serve and enjoy.

Nutrition:

- Calories: 91
- Fat: 6.1 g.
- Carbs: 8.7 g.
- Sugar: 3.6 g.
- Protein: 2.5 g.
- Cholesterol: 0 mg.

548. Delicious Nacho Dip

Preparation time: 10 minutes

Cooking time: 20 minutes

Servings: 10

Ingredients:

- 1 lb. ground beef
- 1 cup Mexican cheese
- 4 oz. cream cheese
- 14 oz. salsa
- 15 oz. can black beans, drained
- 1/4 cup water
- 2 tsp. cayenne pepper
- 1 1/2 tsp. ground cumin
- 1 1/2 tsp. chili powder
- 3 garlic cloves, chopped
- 1 jalapeño pepper, chopped
- 1 small onion, chopped

- 1 tbsp. olive oil
- 1 tsp. salt

Directions:

1. Add oil into the instant vortex and set the pot on "sauté" mode.
2. Add jalapeño peppers and onion and sauté for 5 minutes.
3. Add garlic and sauté for 1 minute.
4. Add ground beef, cayenne, cumin, chili powder, and salt and sauté until browned.
5. Add water and stir well.
6. Add salsa and beans and stir well.
7. Seal pot with lid and cook on manual high pressure for 10 minutes.
8. Once done then allow to release pressure naturally then open the lid.
9. Stir in cream cheese.
10. Serve and enjoy.

Nutrition:

- Calories: 214
- Fat: 10.4 g.
- Carbs: 12.1 g.
- Sugar: 2 g.
- Protein: 19 g.
- Cholesterol: 58 mg.

549. Spinach Dip

Preparation time: 10 minutes

Cooking time: 4 minutes

Servings: 10

Ingredients:

- 1 lb. fresh spinach
- 1 tsp. onion powder
- 1 cup mozzarella cheese, shredded
- 7.5 oz. cream cheese, cubed
- 1/2 cup mayonnaise
- 1/2 cup sour cream
- 1/2 cup chicken broth
- 1 tbsp. olive oil
- 2 garlic cloves, minced
- 1/4 tsp. pepper
- 1/2 tsp. salt

Directions:

1. Add oil into the instant vortex and

set the pot on "Sauté" mode.

2. Add spinach and garlic and sauté until spinach is wilted. Drain excess liquid.

3. Add remaining ingredients and stir well.

4. Seal pot with lid and cook on manual high pressure for 4 minutes.

5. Once done then release pressure using the quick-release method then open the lid.

6. Stir well and serve.

Nutrition:

- Calories: 179
- Fat: 15.9 g.
- Carbs: 6.1 g.
- Sugar: 1.1 g.
- Protein: 4.5 g.
- Cholesterol: 33 mg.

550. *Chipotle* Bean Dip

Preparation time: 10 minutes

Cooking time: 43 minutes

Servings: 6

Ingredients:

- 1 cup dry *pinto* beans, rinsed
- 1/2 tsp. cumin
- 1 tsp. liquid smoke
- 1/2 cup salsa
- 2 garlic cloves, peeled
- 2 chipotle peppers in adobo sauce
- 5 cups water
- 1/4 tsp. pepper
- 1 tsp. salt

Directions:

1. Add water, beans, chipotle peppers, and garlic into the instant vortex.

2. Seal pot with lid and cook on manual high pressure for 43 minutes.

3. Once done then allow to release pressure naturally then open the lid.

4. Transfer beans to the blender and blend until smooth.

5. Add remaining ingredients and blend until just mixed.

6. Serve and enjoy.

Nutrition:

- Calories: 124
- Fat: 0.8 g.
- Carbs: 22.3 g.
- Sugar: 1.4 g.
- Protein: 7.7 g.
- Cholesterol: 2 mg.

551. Asian Boiled Peanuts

Preparation time: 10 minutes

Cooking time: 60 minutes

Servings: 4

Ingredients:

- 1 lb. raw peanuts
- 3 red chili peppers, dried
- 3 garlic cloves
- 2 cinnamon stick
- 3 whole star anise
- 3 tbsp. kosher salt

Directions:

1. Add all ingredients into the instant vortex and stir well.
2. Pour enough water into the pot to cover peanuts.
3. Seal pot with lid and cook on manual high pressure for 60 minutes.
4. Once done then allow to release pressure naturally then open the lid.
5. Serve and enjoy.

Nutrition:

- Calories: 672
- Fat: 55.9 g.
- Carbs: 24.3 g.
- Sugar: 4.8 g.
- Protein: 30.3 g.
- Cholesterol: 0 mg.

552. Mexican *Pinto* Bean Dip

Preparation time: 10 minutes

Cooking time: 45 minutes

Servings: 6

Ingredients:

- 1 cup dry *pinto* beans
- 1 1/2 tsp. chili powder
- 4 chilies
- 4 cups water
- 1 tsp. salt

Directions:

1. Add water, chilies, and beans into the instant vortex.
2. Seal pot with lid and cook on manual high pressure for 45 minutes.
3. Once done then allow to release pressure naturally

for 10 minutes then release using the quick-release method. Open the lid.

4. Transfer beans into the blender along with chili powder and salt and blend until smooth.

5. Serve and enjoy.

Nutrition:

- Calories: 115
- Fat: 0.5 g.
- Carbs: 20.7 g.
- Sugar: 0.9 g.
- Protein: 7 g.

Cholesterol: 0 mg.

553. Perfect Cinnamon Toast

Preparation time: 10 minutes

Cooking time: 5 minutes

Servings: 6

Ingredients:

- 2 tsp. pepper
- 1 1/2 tsp. vanilla extract
- 1 1/2 tsp. cinnamon
- 1/2 cup sweetener of choice
- 1 cup coconut oil
- 12 slices whole-wheat bread

Directions:

1. Melt coconut oil and mix with sweetener until dissolved. Mix in remaining ingredients minus bread till incorporated.

2. Spread mixture onto bread, covering all area.

3. Place coated pieces of bread in your instant vortex air fryer oven. Close the air fryer lid and cook 5 minutes at 400°F.

4. Remove and cut diagonally. Enjoy!

Nutrition:

- Calories: 124
- Fat: 2 g.
- Protein: 0 g.
- Sugar: 4 g.

554. Easy Baked Chocolate Mug Cake

Preparation time: 5 minutes

Cooking time: 15 minutes

Servings: 3

Ingredients:

- 1/2 cup cocoa powder
- 1/2 cup stevia powder
- 1 cup coconut cream
- 1 package cream cheese, room temperature
- 1 tbsp. vanilla extract
- 1 tbsp. butter

Directions:

1. Preheat the instant vortex air fryer ovenfor 5 minutes.
2. In a mixing bowl, combine all ingredients.
3. Use a hand mixer to mix everything until fluffy.
4. Pour into greased mugs.
5. Place the mugs in the fryer basket.
6. Close the air fryer lid and bake for 15 minutes at 350°F.
7. Place in the fridge to chill before serving.

Nutrition:

- Calories: 744
- Fat: 69.7 g.
- Protein: 13.9 g.
- Sugar: 4 g.

555. Perfect Cinnamon Toast

Preparation time: 10 minutes

Cooking time: 5 minutes

Servings: 6

Ingredients:

- 2 tsp. pepper
- 1 1/2 tsp. vanilla extract
- 1 1/2 tsp. cinnamon
- 1/2 cup sweetener of choice
- 1 cup coconut oil
- 12 slices whole-wheat bread

Directions:

5. Melt coconut oil and mix with sweetener until dissolved. Mix in remaining ingredients minus

bread till incorporated.

6. Spread mixture onto bread, covering all area.
7. Place coated pieces of bread in your instant vortex air fryer oven. Close the air fryer lid and cook 5 minutes at 400°F.
8. Remove and cut diagonally. Enjoy!

Nutrition:

- Calories: 124
- Fat: 2 g.
- Protein: 0 g.
- Sugar: 4 g.

556. Angel Food Cake

Preparation time: 5 minutes

Cooking time: 30 minutes

Servings: 12

Ingredients:

- 1/4 cup butter, melted
- 1 cup powdered erythritol
- 1 tsp. strawberry extract
- 12 egg whites
- 2 tsp. cream of tartar
- A pinch of salt

Directions:

1. Preheat the instant vortex air fryer ovenfor 5 minutes.
2. Mix the egg whites and cream of tartar.
3. Use a hand mixer and whisk until white and fluffy.
4. Add the rest of the ingredients except for the butter and whisk for another minute.
5. Pour into a baking dish.
6. Place in the instant vortex air fryer ovenbasket, close the air fryer lid, and cook for 30 minutes at 400°F, or if a toothpick inserted in the middle comes out clean.
7. Drizzle with melted butter once cooled.

Nutrition:

- Calories: 65
- Fat: 5 g.
- Protein: 3.1 g.

Fiber: 1 g.

557. Fried Peaches

Preparation time: 2 hours 10 minutes

Cooking time: 15 minutes

Servings: 4

Ingredients:

- 4 ripe peaches (1/2 a peach = 1 serving)
- 1 1/2 cups flour
- Salt
- 2 egg yolks
- 3/4 cups cold water
- 1 1/2 tbsp. olive oil
- 2 tbsp. brandy
- 4 egg whites
- Cinnamon/sugar mix

Directions:

1. Mix flour, egg yolks, and salt in a mixing bowl.
2. Slowly mix in water, then add brandy.
3. Set the mixture aside for 2 hours and go do something for 1 hour 45 minutes.
4. Boil a large pot of water and cut and x at the bottom of each peach.
5. While the water boils fill another large bowl with water and ice.
6. Boil each peach for about a minute, then plunge it into the ice bath.
7. Now the peels should fall off the peach.
8. Beat the egg whites and mix them into the batter mix.
9. Dip each peach in the mix to coat.
10. Transfer the peaches to the air fryer. Close the air fryer lid and cook at 360°F for 10 minutes.
11. Prepare a plate with cinnamon/sugar mix, roll peaches in the mix and serve.

Nutrition:

- Calories: 306
- Fat: 3 g.
- Protein: 10 g.
- Fiber: 2.7 g.

558. Easy Donuts

Preparation time: 5 minutes

Cooking time: 10 minutes

Servings: 8

Ingredients:

- Pinch of allspice
- 4 tbsp. dark brown sugar
- 1/2–1 tsp. cinnamon
- 1/3 cup granulated sweetener
- 3 tbsp. coconut oil, melted
- 1 can of biscuits

Directions:

1. Preparing the ingredients. Preheat the unit by selecting "Bake/Roast," setting the temperature to 300°F, and setting the time to 5 minutes.
2. Press "Start/Stop" to begin.
3. Mix allspice, sugar, sweetener, and cinnamon.
4. Take out biscuits from the can and with a circle cookie cutter, cut holes from centers, and place into the instant crisp air fryer.
5. Air frying the dish. Close the air fryer lid.
6. Select "Bake," set the temperature to 350°F, and set the time to 5 minutes.
7. Select start to begin. As batches are cooked, use a brush to coat with melted coconut oil and dip each into sugar mixture.
8. Serve warm!

Nutrition:

- Calories: 242
- Fat: 6 g.
- Protein: 28 g.
- Sugar: 18 g.

559. Apple Pie in Air Fryer

Preparation time: 5 minutes

Cooking time: 35 minutes

Servings: 4

Ingredients:

- 1/2 tsp. vanilla extract
- 1 beaten egg
- 1 apple, large-sized, chopped
- 1 Pillsbury™ refrigerated pie crust
- 1 tbsp. butter
- 1 tbsp. cinnamon, ground
- 1 tbsp. raw sugar
- 2 tbsp. sugar
- 2 tsp. lemon juice
- Cooking spray

Directions:

1. Preparing the ingredients. Lightly grease baking pan of the instant vortex air fryer oven with cooking spray. Spread pie crust on the bottom of the pan up to the sides.
2. In a bowl, mix vanilla, sugar, cinnamon, lemon juice, and apple. Pour on top of pie crust. Top apple with butter slices.
3. Cover apple with the other pie crust. Pierce with the knife the tops of the pie.
4. Spread beaten egg on top of crust and sprinkle sugar.
5. Cover with foil.
6. Close air fryer lid. Cook for 25 minutes at 390°F.
7. Remove foil cook for 10 minutes at 330°F until tops are browned.
8. Serve and enjoy.

Nutrition:

- Calories: 372
- Fat: 19 g.
- Protein: 4.2 g.
- Sugar: 5 g.

560. Raspberry Cream Roll-Ups

Preparation time: 10 minutes

Cooking time: 25 minutes

Servings: 4

Ingredients:

- 1 cup fresh raspberries, rinsed and patted dry
- 1/2 cup cream cheese, softened to room temperature
- 1/4 cup brown sugar
- 1/4 cup sweetened condensed milk
- 1 egg
- 1 tsp. corn starch
- 6 spring roll wrappers (any brand will do, we like blue dragon or tasty joy, both available through target or Walmart, or any large grocery chain
- 1/4 cup of water

Directions:

1. Cover the basket of the instant vortex air fryer ovenwith a lining of tin foil, leaving the edges uncovered to allow air to circulate through the basket.
2. Preheat the air fryer to 350°F.
3. In a mixing bowl, combine the cream cheese, brown sugar, condensed milk, cornstarch, and egg.
4. Beat or whip thoroughly, until all ingredients are completely mixed and fluffy, thick, and stiff.
5. Spoon even amounts of the creamy filling into each spring roll wrapper, then top each dollop of filling with several raspberries.
6. Roll up the wraps around the creamy raspberry filling, and seal the seams with a few dabs of water.
7. Place each roll on the foil-lined instant vortex air fryer ovenbasket, seams facing down.
8. Close air fryer lid. Set the air fryer timer to 10 minutes.
9. During cooking, shake the handle of the fryer basket to ensure a nice even surface crisp.
10. After 10 minutes, when the air fryer shuts off, the spring rolls should be golden brown and perfect on the outside, while the raspberries and cream filling will have cooked together in a

glorious fusion.

11. Remove with tongs
    and serve hot or
    cold.

Nutrition:

- Calories: 142
- Fat: 2 g.
- Protein: 18 g.
- Sugar: 3 g.

Chapter 9: Dessert Recipes

561. Lemon-Zucchini Muffins

Preparation time: 10 minutes

Cooking time: 20 minutes

Servings: 6

Ingredients:

- 1 cup wheat flour
- 4 tbsp. brown sugar
- 1 tbsp. baking powder
- 1/4 tsp. sea salt
- 2 tbsp. olive oil
- 1/4 tsp. cinnamon, ground
- 1/4 tsp. nutmeg
- 1 cup zucchini, shredded
- 3/4 cup milk, non-fat
- 1 egg
- 2 tbsp. fresh lemon juice
- Nonstick cooking spray

Directions:

1. Prepare a 6-muffin tin by spraying with cooking spray or lining with muffin liners.
2. In a large mixing bowl, add flour, baking powder, sugar, salt, nutmeg, and cinnamon. Mix well.
3. In another mixing bowl, combine milk, zucchini lemon juice, eggs, and oil. Mix well.
4. Add zucchini mixture to flour mixture. Stir till just combined. Do not over-stir.
5. Pour muffin cups. Place pan on a 1-inch rack and bake for 20 minutes at 350°F (High) or until light golden brown.

Nutrition:

- Calories: 371
- Total fat: 17.5 g.
- Total carbs: 47.6 g.
- Protein: 8 g.

562. Baked Stuffed Apples

Preparation time: 4 minutes

Cooking time: 6 minutes

Servings: 4

Ingredients:

- 4 apples, large-sized
- 1/4 cup coconut flakes
- 1/4 cup cranberries or apricots, dried
- 2 tbsp. orange zest, grated
- 1/2 cup orange juice
- 2 tbsp. brown sugar

Directions:

1. Cut top off the apples and hollow out center with knife or apple corer. Arrange in non-stick baking pan.
2. In a large mixing bowl, combine coconut, cranberries, and orange zest. Divide evenly and fill centers of apples.
3. In a bowl, mix orange juice and brown sugar. Pour over apples.
4. Place pan on a 1-inch rack and cook for 5–6 minutes until apples are tender.
5. Serve warm.

Nutrition:

- Calories: 156
- Total fat: 6.7 g.
- Total carbs: 26.1 g.
- Protein: 2 g.

563. Carrot Cake Cookies

Preparation time: 3 minutes

Cooking time: 14 minutes

Servings: 24

Ingredients:

- 1/4 cup brown sugar
- 1/4 cup vegetable oil
- 1/2 tsp. baking soda
- 1/4 cup applesauce or fruit puree
- 1/4 tsp. nutmeg
- 1 egg
- 1/2 tsp. vanilla
- 1/2 cup flour
- 1/2 cup wheat flour

- 1/2 tsp. baking powder
- A dash of salt
- 1/2 tsp. cinnamon, ground
- 1/4 tsp. ginger, ground
- 1 cup old-fashioned rolled oats
- 3/4 cup carrots, grated
- 1/2 cup raisins or golden raisins

Directions:

1. In a large mixing bowl combine sugar, oil, applesauce, egg, and vanilla.
2. In another bowl, mix all dry ingredients. Then, add dry ingredients to wet ingredients. Mix till blended. Toss in carrots and raisins.
3. Drop by teaspoon. full onto silicone baking ring or parchment-lined cookie sheet.
4. Place on 1-inch rack and cook at 300°F (Level 8) for 12–14 minutes or until golden brown.

Nutrition:

- Calories: 252
- Carbs: 20 g.
- Total fat: 7 g.
- Protein: 3 g.

564. Broiled Peaches With Honey

Preparation time: 9 minutes

Cooking time: 6 minutes

Servings: 4

Ingredients:

- 2 peaches, large-sized
- 1 tbsp. extra-virgin olive oil
- 1 tbsp. honey

Directions:

1. Divide peaches in half and eliminate pits.
2. Brush cut side of

peaches with olive oil.

3. Put on parchment-lined pan and place on 4-inch rack. Cook in the air fryer oven on high power (350°C) for 5–6 minutes or until peaches are golden brown and caramelized.

4. Drizzle with honey and serve.

Nutrition:

- Calories: 161
- Fat: 3 g.
- Protein: 1 g.
- Carbs: 10 g.

565. Dehydrated Cinnamon Apple Chips

Preparation time: 25 minutes

Cooking time: 4 hours

Servings: 4

Ingredients:

- 4 large apples
- 1 tbsp. sugar
- 1 tbsp. cinnamon

Directions:

1. Slice off top side (stem) of apples and then slice apples into rounds around 1/8-inch–1/4-inch thick. This is easiest with a mandolin slicer but can also be done with a sharp knife.

2. Place apple slices in a medium bowl and dash with cinnamon and sugar. Mix gently to coat.

3. Spray 4-inch rack with cooking spray. Arrange apple slices on rack.

4. Cook on 150°F for 4 hours.

5. Remove from oven immediately. Allow cooling before serving.

Nutrition:

- Calories: 90
- Total fat: 0 g.
- Carbs: 26 g.
- Protein: 1 g.

566. Gourmet Honey Cornbread

Preparation time: 5 minutes

Cooking time: 20 minutes

Servings: 8

Ingredients:

- 1 cup whole wheat flour
- 1/4 cup sugar
- 1 cup heavy cream
- 2 tbsp. vegetable oil
- 1 cup cornmeal
- 1/4 cup honey
- 2 eggs, large-sized
- 1 tbsp. baking powder

Directions:

1. Grease baking pan lightly.
2. In a large mixing bowl, combine flour, sugar, cornmeal, and baking powder. Add in cream, oil, eggs, and honey. Stir to combine.
3. Pour into baking pan. Bake on 1-inch rack at 350°F for 20 minutes. Let rest for 1–2 minutes before removing from oven.

Nutrition:

- Calories: 270
- Total fat: 7 g.
- Carbs: 26 g.
- Protein: 3 g.

567. Marvelous Chocolate Zucchini Bread

Preparation time: 10 minutes

Cooking time: 45 minutes

Servings: 2

Ingredients:

- 3 eggs, medium-sized
- 1 cup sugar
- 1 cup vegetable oil
- 2 cups zucchini, grated
- 1 tsp. vanilla extract
- 3/4 cup chocolate chips, semisweet
- 1/3 cup cocoa powder

- 2 cups wheat flour
- 1 tsp. baking soda
- A pinch of salt
- 1 tsp. ground cinnamon
- Cooking spray

Directions:

1. Spray 2 baking pans with cooking spray.
2. In a medium mixing bowl, add cocoa powder, eggs, oil, grated zucchini, vanilla, and sugar. Stir to combine. Fold in flour, baking soda, salt, and cinnamon. Then, add chocolate chips.
3. Pour the batter into baking pans. Bake on 1-inch rack at 350°C for 40–45 minutes until a knife inserted in center comes out clean. Allow bread to rest inside the dome for 1–2 minutes before removing it from the oven. Allow cooling before slicing.

Nutrition:

- Calories: 217.0
- Total fat: 8.0 g.
- Total carbs: 37.0 g.
- Protein: 3.0 g.

568. Pineapple Banana Nut Bread

Preparation time: 20 minutes

Cooking time: 50 minutes

Servings: 2

Ingredients:

- 3 cup wheat flour
- Cooking spray
- 3/4 tsp. sea salt
- 1 tsp. baking soda
- 8 oz. crushed pineapple
- 2 cup sugar
- 1 tsp. cinnamon
- 1 cup walnuts
- 3 medium eggs
- 4 ripe bananas

- 2 tsp. vanilla extract

Directions:

1. Spray baking pans with cooking spray.
2. In a large mixing bowl, add sugar, flour, baking soda, salt, and cinnamon.
3. Stir in walnuts, oil, banana, pineapple, eggs, and vanilla. Mix till blended. Pour batter into the pans.
4. Place pans on a 1-inch rack and bakes at 350ºC) for 45–50 minutes or until a toothpick inserted in the center comes out clean. Allow rest under the dome for 1–2 minutes before removing from oven. Cool before slicing.

Nutrition:

- Calories: 216
- Fat: 10 g.
- Carbs: 30 g.
- Protein: 3 g.

569. Appetizer Blueberry Lemon Cake

Preparation time: 25 minutes

Cooking time: 50 minutes

Servings: 1

Ingredients:

- 1 tsp. baking powder
- 2 butter sticks
- 1 cup sugar
- 1/4 cup fresh lemon juice
- 2 tbsp. lemon zest
- 1 tsp. vanilla extract
- 1/8 tsp. salt
- 4 eggs, large-sized
- 2 cup wheat flour
- 1 1/2 cup fresh

blueberries

- Cooking spray

Directions:

1. Spray the pan with cooking spray.
2. Whisk together butter, sugar, and baking powder until smooth and fluffy. Add lemon juice, lemon zest, vanilla, and salt. Stir to combine.
3. Add eggs, one at a time, beating until smooth after each. Add flour and mix until just combined. Fold in blueberries.
4. Spread the batter into the pan. Shake pan to even out the batter.
5. Place Extender Ring on base. Place pan on a 1-inch rack and cook at 325°F for 45–50 minutes or until knife inserted in center comes out clean.
6. Remove from oven and allow cooling before slicing.

Nutrition:

1. Calories: 265
2. Total fat: 4.1 g.
3. Total carbs: 52.2 g.

570. Useful Cranberry Bars

Preparation time: 20 minutes

Cooking time: 45 minutes

Servings: 12

Ingredients:

- 1 1/2 cup whole cranberries
- 3/4 cup white sugar
- 3/4 cup water
- 1 package yellow cake mix
- 6 tbsp. butter, melted
- 2 eggs
- 3/4 cup rolled oats
- 1 tsp. ginger, ground
- 1 tsp. cinnamon,

ground

- 1/2 cup brown sugar
- Cooking spray

Directions:

1. Spray baking pan with cooking spray.
2. Add cranberries, sugar, and water to a saucepan. Cook over medium heat, stirring continuously, until all cranberries pop and the mixture thickened for 10–15 minutes. Remove from heat and allow cooling.
3. In a large mixing bowl, add cake mix, butter, brown sugar, oats, ginger, eggs, and cinnamon. Spread 2/3 of the mixture into the baking pan. Use the back of a spoon to press down evenly to form a crust.

Spread cranberry mixture evenly over crust. Top with the remaining mixture.

4. Place on 1-inch rack and bake at 350°C for 30–35 minutes, until the top is lightly browned. Allow cooling before cutting.

Nutrition:

- Calories: 280
- Total fat: 14 g.
- Carbs: 38 g.
- Protein: 3 g.

571. Tasty Banana Cake

Preparation time: 10 minutes

Cooking time: 30 minutes

Servings: 4

Ingredients:

- 1 tbsp. butter, soft
- 1 egg
- 1/3 cup brown sugar
- 2 tbsp. honey
- 1 banana
- 1 cup white flour
- 1 tbsp. baking powder
- 1/2 tbsp. cinnamon powder
- Cooking spray

Directions:

1. Spurt cake pan with cooking spray.
2. Mix in butter with honey, sugar, banana, cinnamon, egg, flour and

baking powder in a bowl then beat.

3. Empty mix in a cake pan with cooking spray put into the air fryer, and cook at 350°F for 30 minutes.
4. Allow the cooling, slice.
5. Serve.

Nutrition:

- Calories: 435
- Total fat: 7 g.
- Total carbs: 15 g.

572. Simple Cheesecake

Preparation time: 10 minutes

Cooking time: 15 minutes

Servings: 15

Ingredients:

- 1 lb. cream cheese
- 1/2 tbsp. vanilla extract
- 2 eggs
- 4 tbsp. sugar
- 1 cup Graham® crackers
- 2 tbsp. butter

Directions:

1. Mix in butter with crackers in a bowl.
2. Compress crackers blend to the bottom cake pan, put into the air fryer, and cook at 350°F for 4 minutes.
3. Mix cream cheese with sugar, vanilla, egg in a bowl and beat properly.
4. Sprinkle filling on crackers crust and cook the cheesecake in the air fryer at 310°F for 15 minutes.
5. Keep cake in the fridge for 3 hours, slice.
6. Serve.

Nutrition:

- Calories: 257
- Total fat: 18 g.

Total carbs: 22 g.

573. Bread Pudding

Preparation time: 10 minutes

Cooking time: 10 minutes

Servings: 4

Ingredients:

- 6 glazed doughnuts
- 1 cup cherries
- 4 egg yolks
- 1 1/2 cups whipping cream
- 1/2 cup raisins
- 1/4 cup sugar
- 1/2 cup chocolate chips.

Directions:

1. Mix in cherries with whipping cream and egg in a bowl then turn properly.
2. Mix in raisins with chocolate chips, sugar and doughnuts in a bowl then stir.
3. Mix the 2 mixtures, pour into the oiled pan then into the air fryer and cook at 310°F for 1 hour.
4. Cool pudding before cutting.
5. Serve.

Nutrition:

- Calories: 456
- Total fat: 11 g.
- Total carbs: 6 g.

574. Bread Dough and Amaretto Dessert

Preparation time: 15 minutes

Cooking time: 8 minutes

Servings: 12

Ingredients:

- 1 lb. bread dough
- 1 cup sugar
- 1/2 cup butter
- 1 cup heavy cream
- 12 oz. chocolate chips
- 2 tbsp. amaretto liqueur

Directions:

1. Turn dough, cut into 20 slices and cut each piece in halves.
2. Sweep dough pieces with spray sugar, butter, put into air

fryer's basket, and cook them at 350°F for 5 minutes. Turn them, cook for 3 minutes still. Move to a platter.

3. Melt the heavy cream in a pan over medium heat, put chocolate chips and turn until they melt.
4. Put in liqueur, turn and move to a bowl.
5. Serve bread dippers with the sauce.

Nutrition:

- Calories: 179
- Total fat: 18 g.
- Total carbs: 17 g.

575. Wrapped Pears

Preparation time: 10 minutes

Cooking time: 10 minutes

Servings: 4

Ingredients:

- 4 puff pastry sheets
- 14 oz. vanilla custard
- 2 pears
- 1 egg
- 1/2 tbsp. cinnamon powder
- 2 tbsp. sugar

Directions:

1. Put wisp pastry slices on a flat surface, add a spoonful of vanilla custard at the center of each, add pear halves and wrap.
2. Sweep pears with egg, cinnamon, and spray sugar, put into air fryer's basket and cook at 320°F for 15 minutes.
3. Split parcels on plates.
4. Serve.

Nutrition:

- Calories: 285
- Total fat: 14 g.
- Total carbs: 30 g.

576. Air Fried Bananas

Preparation time: 5 minutes

Cooking time: 10 minutes

Servings: 4

Ingredients:

- 3 tbsp. butter
- 2 eggs
- 8 bananas
- 1/2 cup cornflour
- 3 tbsp. cinnamon sugar
- 1 cup panko

Directions:

1. Warm-up a pan with the butter over medium heat, put panko, turn and cook for 4 minutes then move to a bowl.
2. Spin each in flour, panko, egg blend, assemble them in the air fryer's basket, grime with cinnamon sugar, and cook at 280°F for 10 minutes.
3. Serve immediately.

Nutrition:

- Calories: 337
- Total fat: 3 g.
- Total carbs: 23 g.

577. Cocoa Cake

Preparation time: 5 minutes

Cooking time: 17 Minutes

Servings: 6

Ingredients:

- 3.5 oz. butter
- 3 eggs
- 3 oz. sugar
- 1 tbsp. cocoa powder
- 3 oz. flour
- 1/2 tbsp. lemon juice

Directions:

1. Mix in 1 tbsp. butter with cocoa powder in a bowl and beat.
2. Mix in the rest of the butter with eggs, flour, sugar and lemon juice in another bowl, blend properly, and move half into a cake pan
3. Put half of the

cocoa blend, spread, add the rest of the butter layer, and crest with remaining cocoa.

4. Put into air fryer and cook at 360°F for 17 minutes.
5. Allow cooling before slicing.
6. Serve.

Nutrition:

- Calories: 221
- Total fat: 5 g.

Total carbs: 12 g.

578. Apple Bread

Preparation time: 5 minutes

Cooking time: 40 minutes

Servings: 6

Ingredients:

- 3 cups apples
- 1 cup sugar
- 1 tbsp. vanilla
- 2 eggs
- 1 tbsp. apple pie spice
- 2 cups white flour
- 1 tbsp. baking powder
- 1 butter stick
- 1 cup water

Directions:

1. Mix in egg with 1 butter stick, sugar, apple pie spice and turn using a mixer.
2. Put apples and turn properly.
3. Mix baking powder with flour in another bowl and turn.
4. Blend the 2 mixtures, turn and move it to a springform pan.
5. Get springform pan into the air fryer and cook at 320°F for 40 minutes
6. Slice.
7. Serve.

Nutrition:

- Calories: 401
- Total fat: 9 g.
- Total carbs: 29 g.

579. Banana Bread

Preparation time: 5 minutes

Cooking time: 40 minutes

Servings: 6

Ingredients:

- 3/4 cup sugar
- 1/3 cup butter
- 1 tbsp. vanilla extract
- 1 egg
- 2 bananas
- 1 tbsp. baking powder
- 1 1/2 cups flour
- 1/2 tbsp. baking soda
- 1/3 cup milk
- 1 1/2 tbsp. cream of tartar
- Cooking spray

Directions:

1. Mix in milk with cream of tartar, vanilla, egg, sugar, bananas and butter in a bowl and turn whole.
2. Mix in flour with baking soda and baking powder.
3. Blend the 2 mixtures, turn properly, move into a oiled pan with cooking spray, put into the air fryer, and cook at 320°F for 40 minutes.
4. Remove bread, allow to cool, slice.
5. Serve.

Nutrition:

- Calories: 540
- Total fat: 16 g.
- Total carbs: 28 g.

580. Mini Lava Cakes

Preparation time: 5 minutes

Cooking time: 20 minutes

Servings: 3

Ingredients:

- 1 egg
- 4 tbsp. sugar
- 2 tbsp. olive oil
- 4 tbsp. milk
- 4 tbsp. flour
- 1 tbsp. cocoa powder
- 1/2 tbsp. baking powder
- 1/2 tbsp. orange zest

Directions:

1. Mix in egg with sugar, flour, salt, oil, milk, orange zest, baking powder, and cocoa powder, turn properly. Move it to oiled ramekins.

2. Put ramekins in the air fryer and cook at 320°F for 20 minutes.
3. Serve warm.

Nutrition:

- Calories: 329
- Total fat: 8.5 g.
- Total carbs: 12.4 g.

581. Crispy Apples

Preparation time: 10 minutes

Cooking time: 10 minutes

Servings: 4

Ingredients:

- 2 tbsp. cinnamon powder
- 5 apples
- 1/2 tbsp. nutmeg powder
- 1 tbsp. maple syrup
- 1/2 cup water
- 4 tbsp. butter
- 1/4 cup flour
- 3/4 cup oats
- 1/4 cup brown sugar
- 1 tsp salt

Directions:

1. Get the apples in a pan, put in nutmeg, maple syrup, cinnamon, and water.
2. Mix in butter with flour, sugar, salt, and oat, turn, put a spoonful of the blend over apples, get into the air fryer and cook at 350°F for 10 minutes.
3. Serve while warm.

Nutrition:

- Calories: 387
- Total fat: 5.6 g.

Total carbs: 12.4 g.

582. Ginger Cheesecake

Preparation time: 20 minutes

Cooking time: 20 minutes

Servings: 6

Ingredients:

- 2 tbsp. butter
- 1/2 cup ginger cookies
- 16 oz. cream cheese
- 2 eggs
- 1/2 cup sugar
- 1 tbsp. rum
- 1/2 tbsp. vanilla extract
- 1/2 tbsp. nutmeg

Directions:

1. Spread pan with the butter and sprinkle cookie crumbs on the bottom.
2. Whisk cream cheese with rum, vanilla, nutmeg, and eggs. Beat properly and sprinkle the cookie crumbs.
3. Put in air fryer and cook at 340°F for 20 minutes.
4. Allow cheesecake to cool in the fridge for 2 hours before slicing.
5. Serve.

Nutrition:

- Calories: 312
- Total fat: 9.8 g.
- Total carbs: 18 g.

583. Cocoa Cookies

Preparation time: 10 minutes

Cooking time: 14 minutes

Servings: 12

Ingredients:

- 6 oz. coconut oil
- 6 eggs
- 3 oz. cocoa powder
- 2 tbsp. vanilla
- 1/2 tbsp. baking powder
- 4 oz. cream cheese
- 5 tbsp. sugar

Directions:

1. Mix in eggs with coconut oil, baking powder, cocoa powder, cream cheese, vanilla in a blender and sway and turn using a mixer.
2. Get it into a lined baking dish and the

fryer at 320°F and bake for 14 minutes.

3. Split cookie sheet into rectangles.
4. Serve.

Nutrition:

- Calories: 149
- Total fat: 2.4 g.
- Total carbs: 27.2 g.

584. Special Brownies

Preparation time: 10 minutes

Cooking time: 22 minutes

Servings: 4

Ingredients:

- 1 egg
- 1/3 cup cocoa powder
- 1/3 cup sugar
- 7 tbsp. butter
- 1/2 tbsp. vanilla extract
- 1/4 cup white flour
- 1/4 cup walnuts
- 1/2 tbsp. baking powder
- 1 tbsp. peanut butter

Directions:

1. Warm pan with 6 tbsp. butter and the sugar over medium heat, turn, cook for 5 minutes, move to a bowl, put salt, egg, cocoa powder, vanilla extract, walnuts, baking powder, and flour, turn mix properly and into a pan.
2. Mix peanut butter with one tbsp. butter in a bowl, heat in a microwave for some seconds, turn properly, and sprinkle brownies blend over.
3. Put in the air fryer and bake at 320°F and bake for 17 minutes.
4. Allow brownies to cool, cut.
5. Serve.

Nutrition:

- Calories: 438
- Total fat: 18 g.
- Total carbs: 16.5 g.

585. Blueberry Scones

Preparation time: 10 minutes

Cooking time: 10 minutes

Servings: 10

Ingredients:

- 1 cup white flour
- 1 cup blueberries
- 2 eggs
- 1/2 cup heavy cream
- 1/2 cup butter
- 5 tbsp. sugar
- 2 tbsp. vanilla extract
- 2 tbsp. baking powder

Directions:

1. Mix in flour, baking powder, salt, and blueberries in a bowl and turn.
2. Mix heavy cream with vanilla extract, sugar, butter and eggs and turn properly.
3. Blend the 2 mixtures, squeeze till the dough is ready, obtain 10 triangles from the mix, put on the baking sheet into the air fryer, and cook them at 320°F for 10 minutes.
4. Serve cold.

Nutrition:

- Calories: 525
- Total fat: 21 g.
- Total carbs: 37 g.

586. Mango Cupcakes

Preparation time: 5 minutes

Cooking time: 20 minutes

Servings: 4

Ingredients:

- 1/2 cup almond flour
- 1/2 cup cocoa powder
- 4 tbsp. sugar
- 1/2 cup mango, peeled and cubed
- 1 tsp. baking powder
- 4 eggs, whisked
- 1 tsp. almond extract
- 4 tbsp. avocado oil
- 1/4 cup almond milk
- Cooking spray

Directions:

1. In a bowl, mix the

flour with the cocoa powder and the other ingredients except for the cooking spray and whisk well.

2. Grease a cupcake tin that fits the air fryer with the cooking spray, pour the mix inside, put the pan in your air fryer, cook at 350°F for 20 minutes and serve cold.

Nutrition:

- Calories: 103
- Fat: 4 g.
- Fiber: 2 g.
- Carbs: 6 g.
- Protein: 3 g.

587. Avocado Cookies

Preparation time: 5 minutes

Cooking time: 20 minutes

Servings: 6

Ingredients:

- 1 cup almond flour
- 1 cup avocado, peeled, pitted, and cubed
- 3 tbsp. sugar
- 1/2 tsp. baking powder
- 1/4 tsp. vanilla extract
- 2 eggs, whisked

Directions:

1. In a bowl, mix the avocado with the flour and the other ingredients and toss.
2. Scoop 6 servings of this mix on a baking sheet that fits the air fryer lined with parchment paper, put the baking sheet in your air fryer, and cook at 350°F for 20 minutes.
3. Serve the cookies cold.

Nutrition:

- Calories: 125
- Fat: 7 g.
- Fiber: 1 g.
- Carbs: 5 g.
- Protein: 4 g.

588. Walnut Bars

Preparation time: 5 minutes

Cooking time: 35 minutes

Servings: 8

Ingredients:

- 2 cups coconut flour
- 3 tbsp. sugar
- 1/2 cup walnuts, chopped
- 1 cup ghee, melted
- 1/2 cup heavy cream
- 2 eggs, whisked
- 1/2 tsp. almond extract
- 1/2 tsp. vanilla extract

Directions:

1. In a bowl, mix the flour with the sugar, walnuts, and the other ingredients and toss.
2. Press this on the bottom of a baking sheet that fits the air fryer lined with parchment paper.
3. Introduce this in the air fryer and cook at 350°F for 35 minutes.
4. Cool down, cut into bars, and serve.

Nutrition:

- **Calories:** 182
- **Fat:** 12 g.
- **Fiber:** 2 g.
- **Carbs:** 4 g.
- **Protein:** 4 g.

589. Pineapple Bars

Preparation time: 10 minutes

Cooking time: 35 minutes

Servings: 6

Ingredients:

- 1/2 cup ghee, melted
- 1 cup pineapple, peeled and chopped
- 3 tbsp. sugar
- 2 cups almond flour
- 2 eggs, whisked
- 1 tbsp. lime juice

Directions:

1. In a bowl, mix the ghee with the pineapple and the other ingredients, stir well and press into a baking dish that fits the air fryer lined with parchment paper.
2. Put the dish in your

air fryer and cook at 350°F for 35 minutes.

3. Cool down, cut into bars, and serve.

Nutrition:

- Calories: 210
- Fat: 12 g.
- Fiber: 1 g.
- Carbs: 4 g.
- Protein: 8 g.

590. Squash Bread

Preparation time: 10 minutes

Cooking time: 40 minutes

Servings: 12

Ingredients:

- 2 cups coconut flour
- 1 cup butternut squash, peeled and cubed
- 1 tsp. baking soda
- 4 tbsp. sugar
- 1/2 cup butter, melted
- 1 tsp. almond extract
- 3 eggs, whisked
- Cooking spray

Directions:

1. In a bowl, mix the flour with the squash and the other ingredients except for the cooking spray and stir well.

2. Grease a loaf pan that fits the air fryer with the cooking spray, line with parchment paper, and pour the squash mix inside.

3. Put the pan in the air fryer and cook at 370°F for 40 minutes.

4. Cool down, slice, and serve.

Nutrition:

- Calories: 143
- Fat: 11 g.
- Fiber: 1 g.
- Carbs: 3 g.
- Protein: 3 g.

591. Lemon Cream

Preparation time: 10 minutes

Cooking time: 25 minutes

Servings: 4

Ingredients:

- 2 eggs, whisked
- 3 tbsp. sugar
- 2 cups heavy cream
- Juice and zest of 1 lemon
- 2 tbsp. butter, melted
- 1 tsp. vanilla extract
- 1/2 tsp. lemon extract
- Cooking spray

Directions:

1. In a bowl, combine the eggs with the sugar and the other ingredients except for the cooking spray and stir well.
2. Grease a ramekin that fits the air fryer with the cooking spray, pour the mixture inside, put the pan in the air fryer, and cook at 360°F for 25 minutes.
3. Divide into bowls and serve.

Nutrition:

- Calories: 212
- Fat: 15 g.
- Fiber: 2 g.
- Carbs: 6 g.
- Protein: 4 g.

592. Strawberry Cake

Preparation time: 5 minutes

Cooking time: 30 minutes

Servings: 4

Ingredients:

- 3 eggs, whisked
- 4 tbsp. sugar
- 1 cup strawberries, sliced
- 1 and 1/2 cups almond flour
- 1 tsp. almond extract
- 1 tsp. baking powder
- 1/2 cup butter, melted
- Cooking spray

Directions:

1. In a bowl, mix the eggs with the sugar and the other ingredients except for the cooking

spray and whisk everything.

2. Grease a cake with the cooking spray, and pour the strawberries mix inside.

3. Put the pan in the air fryer and cook at 370°F for 30 minutes.

4. Cool down, slice, and serve.

Nutrition:

- Calories: 182
- Fat: 12 g.
- Fiber: g.
- Carbs: 6 g.
- Protein: 5 g.

593. Carrot Donuts

Preparation time: 5 minutes

Cooking time: 20 minutes

Servings: 4

Ingredients:

- 2 cups almond flour
- 3 tbsp. sugar
- 1 egg, whisked
- 3 tbsp. butter, melted
- 1 1/2 cups almond milk
- 1/2 cup carrots, peeled and grated
- 1 tsp. baking powder

Directions:

1. In a bowl, mix the flour with the sugar and the other ingredients and whisk well.

2. Shape donuts from this mix, place them in your air fryer's basket, and cook at 370°F for 15 minutes.

3. Serve them right away.

Nutrition:

- Calories: 190,
- Fat: 12 g.
- Fiber: 1 g.
- Carbs: 4 g.

Protein: 6 g.

594. Almond Cookies

Preparation time: 10 minutes

Cooking time: 20 minutes

Servings: 8

Ingredients:

- 2 eggs, whisked
- 1 tbsp. coconut cream
- 1/2 cup almonds, chopped
- 3 tbsp. sugar
- 1/2 cup butter, melted
- 1 tsp. vanilla extract
- 2 cups coconut flour
- Cooking spray

Directions:

1. In a bowl, mix the eggs with the almonds, cream, and the other ingredients except

595. Apple Jam

Preparation time: 10 minutes

Cooking time: 30 minutes

Servings: 6

Ingredients:

- 1/4 cup sugar
- 1 lb. apples, peeled, cored, and chopped
- 1 tbsp. lemon juice
- 1/2 cup water

Directions:

1. In a pan that fits the air fryer, mix the sugar with the apples and the other ingredients, put the pan in the machine, and cook at 380°F for 30 minutes.
2. Divide the mix into cups, cool down, and serve.

Nutrition:

- Calories: 100
- Fat: 1 g.
- Fiber: 0 g.
- Carbs: 1 g.
- Protein: 1 g.

596. Ginger Cream

Preparation time: 10 minutes

Cooking time: 15 minutes

Servings: 6

Ingredients:

- 2 cups almond milk
- 1/2 cup heavy cream
- 1 tbsp. ginger, grated
- 2 tbsp. sugar
- 1 egg, whisked
- 1 tsp. vanilla extract
- 1/4 tsp. nutmeg, ground

Directions:

1. In a bowl, mix the almond milk with the cream and the other ingredients and whisk well.
2. Transfer this to 6 ramekins, put them in the air fryer's basket, and cook at 360ºF for 15 minutes.
3. Cool down and serve.

Nutrition:

- Calories: 220
- Fat: 13 g.
- Fiber: 2 g.
- Carbs: 4 g.

Protein: 3 g.

597. Blueberry Muffins

Preparation time: 10 minutes

Cooking time: 20 minutes

Servings: 4

Ingredients:

- 1 cup blueberries
- 1/4 cup butter, melted
- 3 tbsp. sugar
- 2 eggs, whisked
- 1/4 cup almond flour
- 1/2 tsp. baking soda
- 1/2 tsp. baking powder
- Cooking spray

Directions:

1. In a bowl, mix the berries with the melted butter and the other ingredients except for the cooking spray and whisk

well.

2. Grease a muffin pan that fits the air fryer with the cooking spray, pour the muffin mix, put the pan in the machine, and cook at 350°F for 20 minutes.

3. Serve the muffins cold.

Nutrition:

- Calories: 223
- Fat: 7 g.
- Fiber: 2 g.
- Carbs: 4 g.
- Protein: 5 g.

598. Strawberry Cream

Preparation time: 4 minutes

Cooking time: 20 minutes

Servings: 4

Ingredients:

- 2 cups strawberries, sliced
- 1 cup heavy cream
- 2 tbsp. sugar
- 1 tsp. vanilla extract
- 1 tsp. nutmeg, ground

Directions:

1. In a bowl, mix all the berries with the cream and the other ingredients and whisk well.

2. Divide this into 4 ramekins, put them in the air fryer, and cook at 340°F for 20 minutes.

3. Cool the cream down and serve.

Nutrition:

- Calories: 123
- Fat: 2 g.
- Fiber: 2 g.
- Carbs: 4 g.
- Protein: 3 g.

599. Cocoa Cream

Preparation time: 5 minutes

Cooking time: 20 minutes

Servings: 4

Ingredients:

- 2 eggs, whisked
- 3 tbsp. sugar
- 3 tbsp. butter, melted
- 1 cup heavy cream
- 1 tsp. vanilla extract

Directions:

1. In a bowl, mix the eggs with the sugar and the other ingredients and stir well.
2. Pour this into 4 ramekins, put them in the machine, and cook at 340°F for 20 minutes.
3. Cool down and serve.

Nutrition:

- Calories: 191
- Fat: 12 g.
- Fiber: 2 g.
- Carbs: 4 g.
- Protein: 6 g.

600. Blackberry Jam

Preparation time: 10 minutes

Cooking time: 30 minutes

Servings: 10

Ingredients:

- 2 cups blackberries
- 1 cup water
- 1/4 cup sugar
- 3 tbsp. lemon juice

Directions:

1. In a pan that fits the air fryer, combine the berries with the water and the other ingredients and toss.
2. Put the pan in the machine and cook at 340°F for 30 minutes.
3. Divide into bowls and serve cold.

Nutrition:

- Calories: 100

- Fat: 2 g.
- Fiber: 1 g.
- Carbs: 3 g.
- Protein: 1 g.

601. Air Fryer Oreo Cookies

Preparation time: 5 minutes

Cooking time: 5 minutes

Servings: 9

Ingredients:

- 1/2 cup pancake mix
- 1/2 cup water
- Cooking spray
- 9 chocolate sandwich cookies (e.g. Oreo®)
- 1 tbsp. confectioner's sugar, or to taste

Directions:

1. Blend the pancake mixture with the water until well mixed.
2. Line the parchment paper on the basket of an air fryer. Spray nonstick cooking spray on parchment paper. Dip each cookie into the mixture of the pancake and place it in the basket. Make sure they do not touch; if possible, cook in batches.
3. The air fryer is preheated to 400°F (200°C). Add basket and cook for 4–5 minutes; flip until golden brown, 2–3 more minutes. Sprinkle the sugar over the cookies and serve.

Nutrition:

- Calories: 77
- Fat: 2.1 g.
- Sodium 156 mg.
- Carbs: 13.7 g.
- Protein: 1.2 g.

602. Air Fried Butter Cake

Preparation time: 10 minutes

Cooking time: 15 minutes

Servings: 4

Ingredients:

- Cooking spray
- 7 tbsp. butter, at ambient temperature
- 1/4 cup plus 2 tbsp. white sugar
- 1 egg
- 1 2/3 cups all-purpose flour
- 1 pinch of salt or to taste
- 6 tbsp. milk

Directions:

1. Preheat an air fryer to 350°F (180°C). Spray the cooking spray on a tiny fluted tube pan.
2. Take a large bowl and add 1/4 cup butter and 2 tbsp. of sugar in it.
3. Take an electric mixer to beat the sugar and butter until smooth and fluffy. Stir in salt and flour. Stir in the egg, milk and thoroughly combine the batter. Move the batter to the prepared saucepan; use a spoon back to level the surface.
4. Place the pan inside the basket of the air fryer. Set the timer within 15 minutes. Bake the batter until a toothpick comes out clean when inserted into the cake.
5. Turn the cake out of the saucepan and allow it to cool for about 5 minutes.

Nutrition:

- Calories: 470
- Fat: 22.4 g.
- Cholesterol: 102 mg.
- Sodium: 210 mg.
- Carbs: 59.7 g.
- Protein: 7.9 g.

603. Chocolate Chip Cookies

Preparation time: 15 minutes

Cooking time: 5 minutes

Servings: 18

Ingredients:

- 2 sticks (1 cup) unsalted butter:
- 3/4 cup dark brown sugar
- 3/4 tbsp. of dark brown sugar
- 2 tbsp. vanilla extract
- 2 large eggs
- 1 tsp. kosher salt
- 1 tsp. baking soda
- 2 1/3 cups All-purpose flour
- 2 cups chocolate chips
- 3/4 cups chopped walnuts
- Cooking spray
- Flaky sea salt, for garnish (optional)

Directions:

1. Take a large bowl and add unsalted butter in it. Beat the butter with an electric hand mixer. Add 3/4 cup of granulated sugar with 3/4 cup of dark brown sugar and beat at normal speed for 2–3 minutes.
2. Add 1 spoonful of vanilla extract, 2 large eggs and 1 tbsp. of kosher salt, and beat until mixed. Add in increments 1 tbsp. baking soda and 2 1/3 cups all-purpose flour, stirring until it is just mixed.
3. Add 2 cups chocolate chip chunks and 3/4 cup of chopped walnuts and stir until well combined with a rubber spatula.
4. Preheat the air fryer to bake at 350°F and set aside for 5 minutes. Line the air fryer racks with parchment paper, making sure to leave space for air to circulate on all sides.
5. Drop the dough's 2 tbsp. scoops onto the racks, spacing them 1-inch apart. Gently flatten each scoop to form a cookie. If you like, sprinkle with flaky sea salt. Bake for about 5 minutes, until golden brown. Remove the air fryer's racks and set it to cool for 3–5 minutes. Repeat with leftover dough. Serve warm.

Nutrition:

- Calories: 330
- Fat: 17.5 g.

- Saturated: 8.5 g.
- Carbs: 42.9 g.
- Fiber: 1.9 g.
- Sugar: 28.0 g.
- Protein: 4.0 g.
- Sodium: 172.1 mg.

604. Air Fryer S'mores

Preparation time: 5 minutes

Cooking time: 1 minute

Servings: 4

Ingredients:

- 4 Graham® crackers, each half split to make 2 squares, for a total of 8 squares
- 8 Squares of Hershey's® chocolate bar, broken into squares
- 4 Marshmallows

Directions:

Take deliberate steps. Air-fryers use hot air for cooking food. Marshmallows are light and fluffy, and this should keep the marshmallows from flying around the basket if you follow these steps.

1. Put 4 squares of Graham® crackers on a basket of the air fryer.
2. Place 2 squares of chocolate bars on each cracker.
3. Place back the basket in the air fryer and fry on air at 390°F for 1 minute. It is barely long enough for the chocolate to melt. Remove basket from air fryer.
4. Top with a marshmallow over each cracker. Throw the marshmallow down a little bit into

the melted chocolate. This will help to make the marshmallow stay over the chocolate.

5. Put back the basket in the air fryer and fry at 390°F for 2 minutes. (The marshmallows should be puffed up and browned at the tops.)

6. Using tongs to carefully remove each cracker from the basket of the air fryer and place it on a platter. Top each marshmallow with another square of Graham® crackers.

7. Enjoy it right away!

Nutrition:

-   Calories: 412
-   Fat: 5 g.
-   Protein: 18 g.
-   Sugar: 6 g.

605. Double-Glazed Cinnamon Biscuit Bites

Preparation time: 25 minutes

Cooking time: 12 minutes

Servings: 8

Ingredients:

-   2/3 cup (approx. 2 7/8 oz.) all-purpose flour
-   1/4 tsp. cinnamon
-   2 tbsp. granulated sugar
-   4 tsp. baking powder
-   1/4 tsp. kosher salt
-   2/3 cup (approx. 2 2/3 oz.) whole-wheat flour
-   4 tbsp. salted butter, cold, cut into small pieces,
-   1/3 cup whole milk
-   Cooking spray
-   2 cups (approx. 8 oz.) powdered sugar
-   3 tbsp. water

Directions:

1. Take a medium-sized bowl, whisk the flours together, granulated sugar, baking powder, cinnamon, and salt.

2. Add butter; use 2 knives or a pastry cutter to cut into mixture until butter is well mixed with flour and mixture resembles coarse cornmeal. Add milk, then stir until dough forms a ball.

3. Place the dough on a floured surface and knead for about 30 seconds until it is smooth, forming a cohesive disk. Cut the dough into 16 pieces equal to each other. Wrap each piece gently into a

smooth ball.

4. Coat air fryer basket with spray to cook well. Place 8 balls in a basket, leave room between each; spray the donut balls with the spray for cooking. Cook for 10–12 minutes, at 350 °F until browned and puffed.

5. Remove the donut balls gently from the basket, and place over foil on a wire rack. Keep it cool for 5 minutes. Repeat the same process with the remaining donut balls.

6. Whisk the powdered sugar and water together until smooth in a medium cup. Spoon half of the glaze gently over donut sticks. Let cool for 5 minutes; glaze again,

allowing excess to drip away.

Nutrition:

- Calories: 325
- Fat: 7 g.
- Sat Fat: 4 g.
- Unsaturated Fat: 3 g.
- Protein: 8 g.
- Carbs: 60 g.
- Fiber: 5 g.
- Added Sugar: 18 g.
- Calcium: 17 g.
- Sodium: 67 mg.
- Calcium: 10 mg.
- Potassium: 4 mg.

606. Apple Cider Donuts

Preparation time: 25 minutes

Cooking time: 45 minutes

Servings: 14

Ingredients:

For the donuts:

- 2 cups apple cider
- 3 cups all-purpose flour
- 1/2 cup medium brown sugar
- 2 tsp. baking powder:
- 1 tsp. cinnamon, ground
- 1 tsp. ginger, ground
- 1/2 tsp. baking soda
- 1/2 tsp. kosher salt
- 8 tbsp. unsalted butter, cold (1 stick)
- 1/2 cup frozen milk

For finishing and

shaping:

- 1/4 cup all-purpose flour
- 8 tbsp. unsalted butter
- 1 cup granulated sugar
- 1 tsp. cinnamon

Directions:

Dough preparation time:

1. Pour 2 cups apple cider into a small saucepan over medium-high heat and bring to a boil. Boil until half (to 1 cup) is reduced, for 10–12 minutes. Error on the over-reducing side (you can always add a bit of extra apple cider to the reduced amount). Move the cider reduction to a measuring cup that is heatproof and cool fully, about 30 minutes.

2. In a wide bowl, put 3 cups all-purpose flour, 1/2 cup of light brown powdered sugar, 1 tsp. of crushed cinnamon, 1 tsp. of ground ginger, 2 tsp. of baking powder, 1/2 tsp. of kosher salt, and 1/2 tsp. of baking soda to mix.

3. Grate 8 tbsp. of cold unsalted butter on a grater's large holes. Add the grated butter to the flour mixture and melt the butter with your fingers until it is about the size of tiny pebbles. Create a well in the center of the mixture. Add the 1 cup reduced cider and 1/2 cup cold milk to the well and mix the dough using a large spatula.

Shaping the dough:

1. Sprinkle a few spoonsful of flour on a work surface. Put the batter on the floor. Pat the dough with a rolling pin into an even layer about 1-inch-thick, then add more flour with it. Fold on the dough and pat it down until 1-inch thick. Again, fold and pat, repeat the process 6 times, until the dough is slightly springy. Pat the dough into a 9x13-inch rough rectangle about 1/2-inch thick.

2. Cut donuts with a floured donut cutter (or 3-inch and 1-inch round cutter) out of the dough. From the first round of cutting, you will be getting

around 8 donuts. Place the doughnuts onto butter paper. Collect the scraps, pat the dough down again and repeat cutting until approximately 18 donuts are in place. Refrigerate the donuts for about 10 minutes, while preheating the air fryer to 375°F.

Prepare the coating:

1. Melt and put the remaining 8 tbsp. of butter in a medium dish. In a small bowl, place 1 cup of granulated sugar and 1 tsp. of ground cinnamon, and whisk with a fork.

Cooking:

1. Air fry in groups of 3–4 at a time, flipping them halfway through, 12 minutes per group, depending on the size of your air fryer; switch the donuts to a wire rack and load the next batch onto the air fryer. In the meantime, first, dip the fried doughnuts in the butter and then cinnamon sugar. Place the wire rack back in. For dipping, serve the donuts warm or at room temperature with the dipping of hot cider.

Nutrition:

- Calories: 318
- Fat: 12.4 g.
- Saturated fat: 7.7 g.
- Carbs: 49.1 g.
- Fiber: 1.1 g.
- Sugar: 25.8 g.
- Protein: 3.5 g.
- Sodium: 173.8 mg.

607. Mini Apple Pies

Preparation time: 30 minutes

Cooking time: 15 minutes

Servings: 4

Ingredients:

- 4 tbsp. butter
- 6 tbsp. brown sugar
- 1 tsp. cinnamon, ground
- 2 Granny Smith® apples, medium-sized and diced
- 1 tsp. cornstarch
- 2 tsp. cold water
- 1/2 (14 oz.) 9-inch double-crust pastry pack
- Cooking spray
- 1/2 tbsp. grapeseed oil
- 1/4 cup powdered sugar:
- 1 tsp. milk, or more if required

Directions:

1. In a nonstick skillet, combine the apples, butter, brown sugar, and cinnamon. Cook over normal heat for about 6 minutes, until apples have softened.

2. Take cold water and dissolves cornstarch in it. Stir in apple mixture and cook for about 1 minute, until sauce thickens. Remove from heat the apple pie filling and set aside to cool while the crust is being prepared.

3. Put the pie crust on a lightly floured surface and slightly roll out to smooth the dough surface. Cut the dough into small enough rectangles to allow 2 to fit in your air fryer at once. Repeat with the remainder of the crust until you have 8 equal rectangles, re-rolling some of the dough scraps if necessary.

4. Wet the outer corners of 4 rectangles with water, and place some apple filling around 1/2-inch from the edges in the center. Roll the remaining 4 rectangles out, so they're slightly larger than the ones filled. Place those rectangles on top of the fill; crimp the edges with a fork. Cut 4 tiny slits into the heads of the pies.

5. Grease an air fryer basket with cooking spray. Use a spatula to brush the tops of 2 pies with grapeseed oil and transfer pastries to the air fryer basket.

6. Insert a basket and set the temperature to 385°F (195°C). Bake for about 8 minutes, until golden brown. Remove the pies from the basket and repeat with the 2 pies that are remaining.

7. Take a small bowl and add the powdered sugar and milk to it. Brush the glaze and allow it to dry on warm pies. Serve the pies warm.

Nutrition:

- Calories: 498
- Fat: 28.6 g.
- Cholesterol: 31 mg.
- Sodium: 328 mg.
- Carbs: 59.8 g.
- Protein: 3.3 g.

608. Air Fryer Glazed Cake Doughnut Holes

Preparation time: 25 Minutes

Cooking time: 35 Minutes

Servings: 14

Ingredients:

- 1 1/4 cups all-purpose flour (approx. 5 3/8 oz.), plus more for working surfaces
- 1 tbsp. granulated sugar
- 1 tsp. baking powder
- 1/4 tsp. table salt
- 4 tbsp. salted butter, cold, cut into small cubes
- 1/3 cup whole milk
- Cooking spray
- 1 cup powdered sugar (approx. 8 oz.)
- 3 tbsp. water

Directions:

1. In a medium bowl, whisk the flour, sugar, baking powder, and salt together. Add butter; use 2 knives or a pastry cutter to cut into flour until the butter is well mixed and looks like coarse cornmeal. Add milk, and stir until the ball forms a dough.

2. Place the dough on a floured surface and knead for about 30 seconds until the dough is smooth, forming a cohesive disk. Cut the dough into 14 identical balls. Gently roll each to form even smooth balls.

3. Coat the air fryer basket bottom thoroughly with a cooking spray. Place 7 dough balls in the air fryer tray, spaced uniformly so as not to hit. Spray cooking spray on dough balls. Cook for about 10 minutes, at 350°F until browned and puffed. Remove gently from the basket, and put on a rack of wire.

4. Whisk the caster sugar and water together until smooth in a medium cup. Place the cooked dough balls in glaze, one at a time; roll to coat. Put to dry on a wire rack or baking sheet lined with parchment paper.

5. Repeat the procedure with dough and glaze remaining.

6. Serve warm.

Nutrition:

- Calories: 176
- Fat: 7 g.
- Protein: 23 g.
- Sugar: 6 g.

609. Air Fryer Cinnamon Sugar Churros

Preparation time: 60 minutes

Cooking time: 10 minutes

Servings: 26

Ingredients:

For the churros:

- 1 cup water
- 1/2 cup butter
- 1 tbsp. granulated sugar
- 1 cup all-purpose flour
- 3 eggs
- 1/2 tsp. vanilla extract
- 1/2 cup granulated sucrose
- 2 tsp. cinnamon

For the chocolate sauce:

- 3/4 cup chocolate chips
- 1 tbsp. coconut oil

Directions:

1. Boil water in a saucepan on the burner and add in 1 tbsp. of sugar and butter.
2. Reduce heat to medium/low once melted, and fold in the flour. Take off fire.
3. Whisk the eggs and the vanilla extract together in a separate bowl.
4. Little by little, insert some eggs into the dough. Continue to repeat until eggs are well mixed into the dough. Let's let it

5. Place dough with a star-shaped tip inside a pastry bag. Pipe 6-inch long churros on a baking pan or silicone mat lined with parchment paper.

6. Place the tray in the fridge for 35 minutes to chill. (This makes the dough stickier and simpler to deal with.)

7. Place a single layer of churros in the air fryer, and do not touch each other— Air-fry at 380°F for 10 minutes.

8. Mix 1/2 cup of sugar and the cinnamon on a small plate.

9. Once the churros have been cooked, roll them in the mixture of cinnamon sugar and place them on a cookie cooling rack. Repeat this until all of the churros are fried.

10. Melt chocolate chips and coconut oil in a glass bowl for about 20–30 seconds, using the microwave to make the chocolate sauce. Mix well, then dip warm churros in the serving sauce!

Nutrition:

- Calories: 289
- Protein: 32 g.
- Carbs: 17 g.
- Fat: 8 g.

610. Air Fryer Brownies

Preparation time: 5 minutes

Cooking time: 30 minutes

Servings: 2

Ingredients:

- 1/2 cup granulated sugar
- 1/3 cup cocoa powder
- 1/4 cup all-purpose flour
- 1/4 tsp. baking powder
- A pinch of kosher salt
- 1/4 cup butter, melted and gently cooled
- 1 egg, large-sized

Directions:

1. Grease a 7-inch round cake pan with cooking spray. Mix sugar, cocoa

powder, flour, baking powder, and salt in a medium bowl.

2. Whisk butter and egg until combined in a small bowl. Mix dry ingredients to wet ingredients and stir until combined.

3. Transfer brownie batter to the greasy cake pan and smooth top. Cook for 16–18 minutes in the air fryer at 350°F. Let it cool for 10 minutes before slicing.

Nutrition:

- Calories: 389
- Protein: 22 g.
- Carbs: 16 g.
  Fat: 9 g.

611. Strawberry Cheesecake Chimichanga

Preparation time: 20 minutes

Cooking time: 10 minutes

Servings: 6

Ingredients:

- 1 package cream cheese, kept at room temperature
- 1/4 cup sour cream
- 1/4 cup plus 1 tbsp. sugar
- 1 tsp. vanilla extract
- 1/2 tsp. lemon zest

- 6 (8-inch) soft flour tortillas
- 1 3/4 cups sliced strawberries
- 1 tbsp. cinnamon

Directions:

1. Beat the sour cream with the cream cheese, 1 tbsp. of sugar, vanilla extract, and lemon zest in the container of an electric mixer fitted with the paddle attachment, scraping down the sides of the bowl as desired.

2. Fold up the sliced strawberries in 3/4 cup.

3. If you warm them up a little bit in the microwave, the tortillas can bend easier. Leave them in the kit and spend 30–45 seconds in.

4. Divide the mixture evenly between the

tortillas, slathering each portion of each tortilla in the bottom third.

5. Then turn the 2 sides of each tortilla towards the middle and roll up the tortilla like a burrito, and protect it with a toothpick.

6. The remaining tortillas replicate the rolling process.

7. Take a deep bowl, and add the remaining 1/4 cup sugar with the cinnamon and set them aside.

8. Set the air fryer at 400°F.

9. Place the chimichangas in the basket of an air fryer.

10. Spray some cooking spray over the chimichanga.

11. Set the timer within 6 minutes.

12. Take out chimichangas from the basket after 6 minutes.

13. Roll them out into the mixture of cinnamon sugar.

14. Remove the chimichangas from all the toothpicks and place them on the serving plates.

15. Cover each slice of strawberries with chimichanga and serve immediately.

Nutrition:

- Calories: 249
- Protein: 12 g.
- Carbs: 37 g.
- Fat: 3 g.

612. Peanut Butter Cookies

Preparation time: 2 minutes

Cooking time: 5 minutes

Servings: 1

Ingredients:

- 1 cup peanut butter
- 1 cup sugar
- 1 egg
- 2 tbsp canola oil
- 3 tbsp milk for serving

Directions:

1. Mix all the ingredients with a hand mixer.

2. Spray trays of the air fryer with canola oil. (Alternatively, parchment paper can also be used, but it will take longer to cook your cookies)

3. Set the air fryer temperature to 350°F and preheat it.

4. Place rounded dough balls onto air fryer trays. Press gently down with the back of a fork.

5. Place air fryer tray in your air fryer in the middle place.

Cook for 5 minutes.

6. Use milk to serve with cookies.

Nutrition:

- Calories: 236
- Fat: 13 g.
- Saturated fat: 3 g.
- Cholesterol: 19 mg.
- Sodium: 130 mg.
- Carbs: 26 g.
- Fiber: 1 g.
- Sugar: 22 g.
- Protein: 6 g.

Conclusion

Hopefully, after going through this cookbook and trying out a couple of recipes, you will get to understand the flexibility and utility of the air fryers. The use of this kitchen appliance ensures that the making of some of your favorite snacks and meals will be carried out in a stress-free manner without hassling around, which invariably legitimizes its worth and gives you value for your money.

We are so glad you leaped this healthier cooking format with us!

This is just the start. There are no restrictions to working with the air fryer, and we will explore some more recipes as well. In addition to all the great options that we talked about before, you will find that there are tasty desserts that can make those sweet teeth in no time, and some great sauces and dressing to always be in control over the foods you eat. There are just so many options to choose from that it won't take long before you find a whole bunch of recipes to use, and before you start to wonder why you didn't get the air fryer so much sooner. There are so numerous things to admire about the air fryer, and it becomes an even better tool to use when you have the right recipes in place and can use them. And there are so many fantastic recipes that work well in the air fryer and can get supper on the table in no time.

We are pleased that you pursue this air fryer cookbook.

Printed in Great Britain
by Amazon

75305732R00303